own below.

Cognition and Categorization

Sponsored by the Social Science Research Council

EDITED BY

Eleanor Rosch
University of California
Berkeley

Barbara B. Lloyd
University of Sussex
England

LAWRENCE ERLBAUM ASSOCIATES, PUBLISHERS
1978   Hillsdale, New Jersey

DISTRIBUTED BY THE HALSTED PRESS DIVISION OF
JOHN WILEY & SONS
New York   Toronto   London   Sydney

SOCIAL SCIENCE RESEARCH COUNCIL
COMMITTEE ON COGNITIVE RESEARCH

Members, 1972 through 1976

Lawrence Erlbaum Associates, Inc., Publishers
62 Maria Drive
Hillsdale, New Jersey 07642

Distributed solely by Halsted Press Division
John Wiley & Sons, Inc., New York

Library of Congress Cataloging in Publication Data

Main entry under title:

Cognition and categorization.

    1. Cognition.   I. Rosch, Eleanor.   II. Lloyd,
Barbara Bloom.   III. Social Science Research Council.
BF311.C5473   153.4   78-6570
ISBN 0-470-26377-6

Printed in the United States of America

Contents

Preface

In the spring of 1976, a small group of psychologists, linguists, and anthropologists met at Lake Arrowhead, California, in a conference sponsored by the Social Science Research Council to discuss the nature and principles of category formation. Participants coming from the East Coast talked about Roger Brown's memorial lecture for Eric Lenneberg given a few days earlier.[1] In considering "the new paradigm of reference," Brown had described the conceptual revolution that had overtaken the study of language and cognition. We were rather bemused and somewhat self-conscious at the thought that our conference might be taken as evidence of the success of that revolution.

Roger Brown had chosen to speak about the new paradigm of reference using research in the domain of color. But research in fields such as ethnoscience, perception, and developmental psychology was beginning to appear and might also have been cited to support the claim that categorization, rather than being arbitrary, may be predicted and explained. Indeed, some of this research was the theme of our conference. Our aim was to bring together people whose work in a variety of disciplines bore relevance to principles of categorization. The initial intention had been to focus on the categorization of concrete objects. The discussion widened to include knowledge of the world and deepened to consider the processes through which categories were formed and their representation.

The conference and the book reflect the aims of the Social Science Research Council, which sponsored the conference. The Council seeks to promote new developments at the cutting edge of the social sciences by identifying major issues at the point of growth. The new approach to problems of classification

---

[1] Brown, R. In memorial tribute to Eric Lenneberg. *Cognition*, 1976, *4*, 125–153.

and reference was one of those issues. The Council provides support through the formation of committees that sponsor workshops and conferences. The Council's Committee on Cognitive Processes sponsored two workshops on the nature and principles of categorization, the first in the spring of 1974.

Neither the fruitful interaction at the conference nor the existence of this book in its present form could have occurred without the participation of the other members of the conference: Camille Hanlon, William Labov, Jay Rosenberg, and committee members Michael Cole, Roy D'Andrade, Frank Palmer, and Herbert Pick. Nor could the conference itself have been organized in its present format without the exciting groundwork and precedent set by participants in the first workshop on categorization: John Bransford, Peter Dodwell, Werner Honig, William Labov, Wolfgang Metzger, Stephen Reed, Donald Riley, Timothy Teyler, David Thomas, and members of the committee. Perhaps our greatest single debt of thanks is owed to David Jenness, of the staff of the Social Science Research Council, who for 4 years astonished us with his ability to combine abstract substantive issues with those details that enable conferences to take place other than in the heads of their organizers. We are also indebted to Carolyn Mervis, who took notes on the first workshop, and to Joan Reagan, who noted and transcribed much of the second workshop.

ELEANOR ROSCH
BARBARA B. LLOYD

Introduction

There is an old story about a man found searching under a street light in the middle of the night. A would-be-samaritan stops and asks, "What are you looking for?" The man replies, "My house-key." "And where did you lose it?" "In the bushes over there." "Then why are you looking here?" queries the puzzled samaritan. The man replies, "Because there's light here."

Answers depend on the questions asked. Unasked questions will remain unanswered. And the nature of a question constrains the kinds of answers that can be derived.

Categorization is important. The world consists of an infinite number of potentially different stimuli. Thus a basic task of all organisms (indeed, one mark of living things) is a segmentation of the environment into classifications by means of which nonidentical stimuli can be treated as equivalent. As originally stated by Bruner, Goodnow, and Austin (1956): "categorizing serves to cut down the diversity of objects and events that must be dealt with uniquely by an organism of limited capacities [p. 235]." For lower organisms, specific responses may be biologically hard-wired to relatively broad classes of stimulus conditions (Lettvin et al., 1959). But with the development of the cortex, there is far greater plasticity of behavior. For humans, categorizations are clearly far more flexibly connected to environmental constraints than for the frog; yet humans come with the propensity to pay attention to certain features of the perceptual environment and to form complex connections between perceptual events, their own needs, and functions.

Why do human cultures categorize the world in the way they do? Why do we in English label "green" and "blue," thus marking particular segments of the spectrum as two different colors? Why do we label "sheep" and "goats" as two different animals? Until quite recently such questions received virtually no attention in the social sciences. In so far as it was widely accepted that the segmentation of the world was essentially arbitrary, the question was not raised. Instead, researchers focused on the formation and function of these arbitrary segmentations.

We may wonder why such an approach seemed reasonable for so long. In the stimulus–response learning paradigm that dominated American psychology in the first half of the twentieth century, both the stimulus and the response were dealth with as arbitrary systems; the focus was primarily on the connection between them. In developmental psychology, children were considered beings born into a culture in which categories and stimuli were already determined by the adult world. Anthropology, which might have sought universal principles of human experience, under the influence of Boazian cultural relativism, concentrated on cultural diversity and the arbitrary nature of the definition of categories.

As the chapters in this volume amply demonstrate, psychologists and other social scientists now realize the incompleteness of this approach. But it is only recently that investigators have become aware of the need to look at the stimuli and categories of the real world rather than assuming that they could be completely arbitrarily imposed. For example, Berlin, Rosch, and Garner (Chapters 1, 2, and 5, respectively) show the viability of looking to the world for informational factors in the stimulus.

This new approach is not a complete about-face, however. None of our authors suggests that categories exist a priori in the real world waiting to be discovered. Rather, a more complex argument is presented; categories are considered to arise out of an interaction between stimuli and process. The contribution of the processor who brings a variety of capacities and strategies to the task of making sense out of the stimuli, objects, and events of the world is not overlooked.

In trying to understand the processor, the nature of the questions asked again constrains the answers we may derive. As with questions about real-world stimuli and categories that were not examined because attention was directed elsewhere, questions about the nature of the processor have been bypassed. The processor was assumed to be rational, and attention was directed to the logical nature of problem-solving strategies. The "mature western mind" was presumed to be one that, in abstracting knowledge from the idiosyncrasies of particular everyday experiences, employed Aristologian laws of logic. When applied to categories, this meant that to know a category was to have abstracted clear-cut, necessary, and sufficient criteria for category membership. If other thought processes such as imagery, ostensive definition, reasoning by analogy to particular instances, or the use of metaphors were considered at all, they were usually relegated to lesser beings such as women, children, primitive people, or even to nonhumans. Within this tradition, developmental psychology, particularly under the influence of Piaget, has been the study of the acquisition of rationality. Learning theory has been the study of the acquisition of Aristotelian structures (as in the concept identification paradigm). And the psychological investigation of group differences, whether cultural or social, has focused on the issue of why "they" are not as able to abstract as "we."

The papers in the present volume take us beyond this traditional dichotomy. For example, Berlin describes elegantly the logic of Aguaruna plant taxonomies, and Brooks demonstrates that mature adults do sometimes use particular instances to help them understand the world. The role of traditional and nontraditional logics in cognitive processing is a theme that runs through many of the chapters.

This volume is organized in three sections: real-world categories, the cognitive processes underlying categorization, and the nature of representation. Part I examines different structural aspects of real-world categories: folk biological taxonomies, within and between category structures for material objects, and some categories in a language that codes the world in a visual—gestural mode. All three chapters in Part I assume category processors who are able to perform at least three cognitive functions: They can judge similarity between stimuli; they can perceive and process the attributes of a stimulus; and they can learn. Part II presents analyses of these three cognitive functions. All discussion of psychological structures and processes lead eventually to the issue of representation, and Part III examines representational assumptions underlying the earlier discussions.

To psychologists accustomed to studying categorization in terms of precise, easily manipulated dimensions, the discussion of natural categories, particularly in Part I, may appear to be an effort to lead them away from the streetlight of our opening parable and into the dark and thorny bushes. Rather than asking our readers to share our belief that there is a key to be found by searching the bushes, we offer the ten chapters in this volume as material and invite the reader to draw his or her own conclusions.

REFERENCES

Bruner, J. S., Goodnow, J. J., & Austin, G. A. *A study of thinking.* New York: Wiley, 1956.
Lettvin, J. Y., Maturana, H. R., McCulloch, W. S., & Pitts, W. H. What the frog's eye tells the frog's brain. *Proceedings of the Institute of Radio Engineering,* 1959, *47,* 1940—1951.

Part **▌** STRUCTURE

The chapters in Part I are concerned in different ways with the structure of real-world categories. Brent Berlin, an anthropologist, describes biological taxonomies and speculates about the psychological processes that give rise to these organizations. Eleanor Rosch, a cognitive psychologist, presents her theory about within and between category structures and uses evidence from performance on a variety of cognitive tasks to support her structural hypotheses. Ursula Bellugi and Elissa Newport, psycholinguists, describe American Sign Language (ASL) and show that despite the change in modality that communication in ASL imposes, the everyday world that the deaf share with the hearing is categorized similarly, although it is encoded differently.

Two of the themes that we have identified in the general introduction, the need to ask fruitful questions and concern with a dimension that may be labeled logicality or abstraction, are intertwined in the work of Brent Berlin. The force of this assertion was brought out in the comments of Roy D'Andrade in his discussion following Berlin's paper. His comments are summarized here insofar as they illumine Berlin's chapter.

The study of natural systems of classification has an obvious reality that the manipulation of investigator-selected symbols or even the examination of a small segment of a natural system appears to lack. But the shift of research interest to material that is meaningful to one's subjects cannot guarantee that fruitful questions will be asked. Recounting the history of the antropological study of classification, D'Andrade noted two approaches, each of which provided only partial answers. In the first, the ethnographer seemed to be examining folk taxonomies with an eye to establishing his people as exemplary biological taxonomists. In the other, the pursuit of folk understanding was overshadowed by the ethnographer's desire to present his people's natural system of classification in a formally elegant manner, most often in a set theoretical model. By avoiding each of these excesses, Berlin has provided a more plausible account of folk biological taxonomies.

Unencumbered by a desire to find a completely logical, fully explicated system, Berlin was able to focus on the taxonomies with which his peoples, the Tzeltal and the Aguaruna, understood the biological world around them. Crucial to his understanding of their taxonomies was recognition of the importance of the group of taxa that he labeled the generic rank — that level at which plants or animals are morphologically and behaviorally most distinct — which appear to "cry out to be named." The ranks below this level, the specific and the varietal, appear culturally arbitrary, both in the sense that fewer are formed and that the recognition and labeling are correlated with function. The ranks above the generic also have an arbitrary nature in that not all generic ranks are included in the restricted array. Often, there are cross-classifications; usually three or four taxa of the immediately superordinate life form rank, and the same generic, depending on its habitat (e.g., a juniper growing as a bush or tree), may belong to one or another life-form taxon. The level that defines the domain (i.e., plants or animals), though cognitively recognized, often remains unnamed. From the description thus far, a second major conclusion can be adduced. Not only are folk biological systems organized around the level at which the taxa appear to have a basis in reality, but the entire system is relatively restricted. Here we have identified five ranks: the domain or unique beginner, the life form, the generic; then, below the generic, specific and varietal taxa. Occasionally natural systems of classification include six levels, but much more common are systems of three or four levels.

At the point at which we wish to consider the psychological reality of the ranks that Berlin has identified, it becomes difficult to separate his work from the contribution by Rosch. In talking about the reality of the generic rank and our ability to image a cat but not an animal per se, we are into the area of Rosch's work on category levels and prototypes. In her discussion of the importance of the basic level in classification, Rosch provides a formalization of these intuitions in terms of cue validity. The basic level, or in Berlin's system, the generic rank, is that level at which objects share, with other members of the class or taxa, the most attributes. At lower levels, attributes of members of a particular class or taxa overlap with attributes of members of other classes or taxa, whereas at the superordinate level, there is less total similarity within a given class because there are fewer features common to the variety of members. The validity of this analysis was established by Rosch in a series of studies in which common attributes, motor movements, shape similarity, and identifiability of average shapes was investigated at three levels of category structure: the superordinate, basic, and subordinate using both natural objects and man-made artifacts.

Thus far we have examined only one aspect of Rosch's chapter — that concerned with the vertical structure of categories. The complementary horizontal organization also receives considerable attention. This part of the presentation focuses on the internal structure of a category but considers this structure in relation to other categories at the same level. Evidence for the reality of internal category structure is provided by results from an array of tasks in which "good examples" or prototypic class members facilitate performance. Furthermore, prototypical members of superordinate categories were shown to provide apt substitutes for superordinates in model sentences and to function in the formation of superordinates in the sign language of the deaf.

For those readers unfamiliar with American Sign Language, Ursula Bellugi and Elissa Newport provide a convincing argument that ASL is indeed a language, but one articulated in a new modality. The existence of a community of language users who share the same biological world and material culture as hearing Americans but who communicate in a visual—gestural language provides a unique opportunity to study the impact of the environment and of presumably shared perceptual and functional aspects of categorization pried loose from our usual linguistic encoding conventions. The authors establish the validity of Rosch's basic level and note that there are more commonly agreed upon signs at this level than at either the superordinate or subordinate. As already mentioned, data for ASL also comments on the usefulness of the concept of prototypicality. In forming superordinate levels signs in ASL, single lexical signs are rare, and most super- and subordinates are compound signs. It is important to note both that (1) the coordinate signs labeling a superordinate category are not simply lists of signs but have particular grammatical features indicating their status, and (2) the choice of basic-level objects to include is also fixed (i.e., "best instances" or prototypical class members are employed).

The three chapters included in Part I are similar in that they use empirical methods to explore the structure of some real-world categories. None offers a theory of the mental representation of those categories, and none offers a model for the mental processing of those structures. We advise the reader eager for such models to hold eagerness in abeyance until later sections of this volume and to read the chapters of Part I simply for content.

1

Ethnobiological Classification

Brent Berlin
University of California, Berkeley

In this chapter I consider the nature of man's folk classification of plants and animals with the hope of sharing with the reader some notions that have been developed about the properties of non Western conceptual systems for describing the biological world. I suggest as well that some of the features of ethnobiological classification appear to be generally applicable for an understanding of other natural categories such as those discussed by Rosch (1973), Nelson (1974), and most recently, Anglin (1977).

It is important to consider at the outset why ethnobiological classification might provide a useful starting point for possible generalizations about semantic structure. First, although not an aspect of human experience as ubiquitous as the domains of color or kinship, all human societies must deal in some fashion with major aspects of their biological world. The biological diversity of the plant and animal kingdoms make these domains exceptionally rich. Any principles that might be discovered about how this diversity is conceptually organized may have implications for human cognitive abilities.

Second, the substantive area is rather precisely defined. There are fairly well agreed upon procedures for recognizing an instance of some particular plant or animal type that are less ambiguous than recognizing instances of demons, mythical beings, binary oppositions, or, for that matter, even making judgments of grammaticality.

Third, plants and animals are particularly important from an ethno-semantic point of view in that these domains are of central concern for the societies with which anthropologists usually work. In the two preliterate societies in which I have carried out field research, knowledge of the biological world constitutes — I would claim — a greater chunk than all other types of knowledge combined. I base this judgment on long hours of informal observations of people living their daily lives and estimating, intuitively, how much of the daily routine is tied up with issues dealing, in some way or other, with their biological environment. Thus an understanding of folk biological classification can contribute in a significant way to ethnographic description.

Unfortunately, very few studies have been carried out on full systems of plant and animal classification. At least two reasons account for this scarcity of information: (1) historically, interest has been focused on the use of plants and animals rather than on their conceptual organization; and (2) the nature of the task makes the description of a full system a formidable undertaking. The domains are large (e.g., an average plant and animal vocabulary of some preliterate society may easily comprise 1000—1200 "basic-level" names), and numerous difficulties exist in determining the referents of each name. Unlike other areas of lexicographic research, the only way to determine precisely the meaning of a particular plant or animal name is to collect large numbers of examples (specimens) with numerous informants at different times of the year. Collecting the basic data can account for more than two-thirds of the ethnographer's time over several field seasons.

On the other hand, the few studies that have been carried out on full systems are remarkably similar in many respects — so similar as to suggest that a relatively small number of organizing principles are at work in all of them. These observations allow me to propose several general hypotheses about the structure of folk biological classification on the basis of about a dozen full-scale descriptions from such varied geographic areas as the American southwest (Wyman & Bailey, 1964; Wyman & Harris, 1941), Mexico (Berlin, Breedlove, & Raven, 1974; Hunn, 1977), New Guinea (Hays, 1974; Bulmer & Tyler, 1968; Bulmer & Menzies, 1972, 1973; Bulmer, Menzies, & Parker, 1975), Highland and Amazonian Peru (Berlin, n.d.; Brunel, 1974), China (Anderson, 1967), and the Philippines (Conklin, 1954). Most of my examples, however, are drawn from the two systems that I know best — the Tzeltal Maya of Southern Mexico (Berlin, Breedlove, & Raven, 1966, 1968, 1973, 1974; Berlin, 1972, 1973) and the Aguaruna Jívaro of North Central Peru (Berlin, 1976a, n.d.). Although I believe that many of the features discussed apply equally to plants and animals, I focus more on plants than animals because this is where my knowledge is greatest.

Two fundamental patterns emerge from each of these full-scale studies concerning the nature of folk biological knowledge. The first and most obvious (to biologists) but somewhat surprising (to cultural anthropologists) is that the basic principles of classification of biological diversity appear to arise directly out of the recognition by man of groupings of plants and animals formed on the basis of such visible similarities and differences as can be inferred from gross features of morphology and behavior. This is simply to say that organisms are grouped into named classes primarily on the basis of overall perceptual similarities. This finding would seem to controvert the view that preliterate man names and classifies only those organisms in the environment that have some immediate functional significance for survival. More than one-third of the named plants in both Tzeltal and Aguaruna, for example, lack any cultural utility, and these are not pestiferous plants that must be avoided due to poisonous properties or the like. I develop this point later, but for the moment it is important to note that most of the recognized plant and animal groupings in folk systems of classification represent perceptually distinct discontinuities in the biological world that appear to "cry out to be named" (Berlin, 1972). This is not to say that cross-cutting folk classifications based on the function of the organisms (say, in food, medicine, house builidng, etc.) are not present or relevant — they are simply not as basic or as fundamental as classification based on the appearance of the organisms.

The second fundamental pattern that has emerged from the work on ethnobiological classifiation — and the one that receives attention in this chapter — is that recognized classes of plants and animals (hereafter referred to as *taxa*) are organized into a taxonomic hierarchy whereby taxa of greater and lesser inclusiveness are related by the logical relation of class inclusion. A major substantive generalization about the nature of this organization, which is borne out by all the full-scale studies undertaken thus far, is that there exist a small number of folk biological ranks that contain mutually exclusive taxa that exhibit essentially comparable degrees of biological differentiation one from another. I believe that it can be shown that taxa of the same rank exhibit similar *taxonomic, linguistic, biological,* and *psychological* characteristics. The number of ranks involved in any complete system is probably not more than six and not less than three. The names that one might use to refer to these ranks in the discussion that follows is clearly arbitrary, but I have borrowed terminology from Western biosystematics as a useful starting point. Each rank, with some suggested examples of plant and animal taxa, derived from English folk biology, can be seen in Table 1.1. In the sections that follow, I discuss each of these ranks before presenting more general conclusions.

THE DOMAIN OF PLANTS AND ANIMALS
IN FOLK BIOLOGICAL CLASSIFICATION

Inspection of Table 1.1 indicates that I have used the term "kingdom" to refer to the most inclusive taxon in the domain, indeed that which identifies the domain. This taxon is that single, most general class that strictly includes every other taxon in the semantic domain in question. It occurs at Level 0, taxonomically, and is sometimes called the "unique beginner" (Berlin, Breedlove, & Raven, 1973; Kay, 1971).

Ethnobiologists have focused on the biological kingdom (or those aspects of the biological kingdom that are readily visible to humans without the aid of microscopes) as the most inclusive category for the productive study of folk biological knowledge — in ethnobotany, the world of *plants,* in ethnozoology,

TABLE 1.1
Proposed Hierarchy of Folk Biological Ranks

Folk Biological Ranks	Examples from English Ethnobiology
Kingdom	Plant, animal
Life form	Tree, fish
(Intermediate)	Evergreen, fresh water fish
Generic	Pine, bass
Specific	Whitepine, black bass
Varietal	Western white pine, large mouthed (black) bass

the world of *animals*. The reasonableness of this practice is obvious to all but the most recalcitrant cultural relativist, although I am not prepared to make the supporting argument here. On strictly operational considerations, the boundaries of "plant" and "animal" (again, I am speaking of organisms easily visible to the naked eye) are defined in terms of well-understood biological (and folk biological) criteria. As such, each domain serves as a biologically universal realm of experience in terms of which comparative hypotheses about the nature of man's organization of biological diversity can be formulated and tested in a cross-cultural fashion.

Many ethnographers are apparently willing to accept the domain of "plant" or "animal" as the starting point for ethnobiological investigation only if these domains can be shown to consitute a conceptual category by virtue of some habitually applied label (see Brown, 1974; Conklin, 1954, 1962). I believe such a stricture is overly restrictive. I have argued elsewhere that although a name may be an unambiguous indicator of a category, absence of a label does not necessarily imply absence of a category. If one observes that "plant" or "animal" is named in some language but not in others, the empirical question immediately arises, "Are there sufficient data to indicate the cognitive recognition of the category in those languages where [these categories] are not named?" (Berlin, 1974, p. 328). The answer, of course, will depend on the ethnobiological facts in any particular case.

A finding that has emerged from the few studies thus far available suggests that it is commonly the case that the taxon of the most inclusive rank is not named with a separate word. The domain of plants is usually referred to in Hanunóo as "those elements that germinate and grow in place." In Tzeltal, it is possible to elicit the descriptive phrase "those things that don't move, don't walk, possess roots, and are planted in the earth." In Aguaruna, the domain may be referred to as "all trees" or "all leaves."

In spite of the lack of a single linguistic designation for the kingdom as a whole, considerable behavioral evidence can be amassed in these situations to show that the domain of plants is nonetheless conceptually recognized. In Tzeltal, for example, all names that later proved to refer to plants occur with the numeral classifier *tehk,* whereas all animal names occur with the contrasting classifier *koht*. In Aguaruna, although no such unambiguous grammatical evidence is present, a rich vocabulary of terms can be elicited that refer exclusively to plant morphology and growth which, in turn, occur with names that, on independent botanical grounds, can be shown to refer only to plants. In the languages with which I have worked that lack a word for "plant," there is a large amount of evidence that shows that the domain is nonetheless cognitively salient.

A puzzling question is raised by the fact that the most inclusive taxon, a perceptually distinctive and cognitively recognized category, is provided with a separate label in some languages but not in others. I have speculated that the kingdom is the last rank to acquire a distinctive label in the growth of ethnobiological nomenclature (Berlin, 1972). Anglin (1977) has noted a comparable progression in the growth of children's vocabulary in English. However, I have no good ideas at the moment as to the sociocultural factors that might account for these facts.

TAXA OF LIFE-FORM RANK

The next most inclusive taxa in folk biological taxonomies have been called *life-form taxa*. In Table 1.1, this rank includes (as examples) the taxa labeled as *tree* and *fish*. In the discussion of this rank and of those below it, I consider the taxa that comprise each rank in terms of four analytic features — taxonomic, linguistic, biological, and psychological — which, in combination, allow for their recognition in most cases.

1. *Taxonomically,* life-form categories occur at Level 1 of the folk taxonomy, are few in number, are invariably polytypic, and among them include the majority of all taxa of lesser rank.

2. *Linguistically,* life-form taxa are labeled by primary lexemes and immediately precede taxa (e.g., *pine* and *bass*) most of which are also labeled by primary lexemes.

3. *Biologically,* life-form taxa are diverse in extension as can be objectively measured by an enumeration of the number of distinct biological species included within each.

4. *Psychologically,* life-form taxa can be defined by a small number of perceptual characters that are biological in nature. In folk botany, stem habit is often a defining characteristic, whereas in folk zoology, skin covering and mode of locomotion are often important.

Data from Aguaruna ethnobotany can be discussed as illustrating these four characteristics. There are but four Level 1 taxa that exhibit all of these features. Among them they include 75% of all taxa of lesser rank. Each is labeled by a primary lexeme. All are biologically diverse in range, and each can be defined by a small number of biological characters. These taxa and their respective glosses are:

númi   "trees and shrubs exhibiting woody (nonpithy) stems with erect habit"

dáek   "plants exhibiting twining stem habit, including woody lianas and herbaceous vines"

dúpa   "net-leaved plants and small shrubs exhibiting herbaceous or pithy stems"

šíŋki   "palms, excluding the small reed-like (e.g., *yáún Chamaedorea* spp.) and trunkless (e.g., *takának Taenianthera* sp.) forms"

Any plant that, in its adult form, consistently exhibits all of the characteristics of one of the major life-form taxa will be assigned to that taxon, although there exist a substantial number of taxa of lesser rank that are excluded from these four major groupings due to distinctive morphological characteristics (see below). Thus, although life-form taxa in Aguaruna are broad ranging, they do not totally exhaust the plant kingdom. In this respect, the Aguaruna system of plant classification is identical to that of the Tzeltal (Berlin, Breedlove, & Raven, 1974), the Ndumba (Hays, 1974), Quechua (Brunel, 1974), several languages of the American northwest (Turner, 1972), Hanunóo (Conklin, 1954), and K'ekchi (Wilson, 1972). Except for the conceptual recognition of a subset of palms, these broad taxa are reminiscent of classical Greek and Latin plant classification (tree, vine, herb). These three major groupings, it might be speculated, represent such distinct perceptual discontinuities that their recognition may constitute a substantive near-universal in prescientific man's view of the plant world.

TAXA OF GENERIC RANK

The generic rank is comprised of a large number of highly salient taxa and are thought by investigators of ethnobiological systems to represent the core of any folk biological taxonomy. In Table 1.1, this rank includes (as examples) the taxa labeled as *pine* and *bass*.

Several terms have been used to refer to categories of this rank. The ethno-zoologist, Ralph Bulmer, in his detailed zoological research among the Kalam of New Guinea, has referred to taxa of this type as "speciemes" (borrowing from the analogous concept of phoneme in linguistics), because they constitute the smallest biological discontinuities in nature that are readily perceived on the basis of numerous characters of form and behavior (Bulmer, 1968, 1970; Bulmer & Tyler, 1968). Conklin (1954), in his early study of Hanunóo ethnobotany, refers to these fundamental taxa as "basic plant categories [p. 163]." My colleagues and I, following what appears to be a long historical precedent, have chosen to refer to these basic classes as *generic taxa,* as did Bartlett (1940) in his early description of the generic concept in botany. The appelation "generic" for this fundamental set has apparently been useful to Hays (1974), Brunel (1974), Hunn (1976, 1977), and Turner (1973) in their recent full-scale ethnobiological descriptions.

The generic level consists of biological categories whose discontinuities are readily and easily perceived. In a sense this is the level at which groupings seem to require, as Bartlett (1940) noted, a "distinctive name." Let us consider the nature of generic taxa in terms of the diagnostic features already introduced in the discussion of the higher-level life-form taxa.

1. *Taxonomically*, the majority of generic taxa will be included in one of the recognized life-form taxa. Of Aguaruna generic taxa, for example, a full 85% are taxonomically encompassed in one of the four life forms, and in Tzeltal, about 80% are so included. Yet in all systems there is a residue of generic forms not easily subsumed in any of the major life-form classes.

The Arguaruna residue includes approximately 98 generic taxa that are un-affiliated or are ambiguously affiliated with one or more life forms. An *un-affiliated generic* is one that encompasses organisms that, in all contexts of actual plant identification, are consistently said not to be included in one of the major life forms. Thus far, one-half, or 49, taxa have been isolated that show this characteristic.

An *ambiguously affiliated generic* is one that encompasses a group of or-ganisms, most of which exhibit a good deal of polymorphism. In some contexts of identification, a specimen said to be a member of a particular generic may be classified as a member of one life form; on another occasion, a different specimen of the same generic class may be seen to be a member of another life form, or placed in no life form at all. The other half of the residual taxa in Aguaruna plant classification are of this type.

Because generic categories mark the smallest classes of plants and animals that can be recognized without close study, one might expect generic taxa to include no further named subdivisions (i.e., to be *monotypic*). Indeed, those generic taxa that are *polytypic* exhibit some special linguistic, biological, and psycho-logical characteristics not found for monotypic genera. The ratio of monotypic to polytypic generic taxa as found in several full-scale studies of folk biological classification is shown in Table 1.2. With the exception of Conklin's study of Hanunóo botany, the results are curiously close. In the five other systems, the range of polytypic forms is from 11–18%, with an average of 15–16% polytypic forms. I am not presently able to suggest an explanation for this apparent "con-stant" in the organization of folk biological taxonomies but suspect that an adequate account will include the subtle interplay of biological and cultural constraints.

2. *Linguistically*, generic taxa are labeled by primary lexemes that include the three main types shown in Table 1.3. Simple primary lexemes, such as *pine, oak*, or *bass*, are linguistically unanalyzable. Complex primary lexemes of type 1,

TABLE 1.2
Ratios of Monotypic and Polytypic Generic Taxa
in Six Systems of Folk Biological Classification

	Monotypic (%)	Polytypic (%)
Tzeltal botany	84	16
Tzeltal zoology	83	17
Augaruna botany	82	18
Ndambu botany	86	14
Quechua botany	89	11
Hanunóo botany	57	43

such as *poison oak,* are polymorphemic, but no constituent of the term labels a taxon superordinate to the class in question. Thus, *poison oak* is not a kind of *oak,* and similarly the Tzeltal *ȼaʔ tuluk'* or "turkey excrement" has nothing to do with excrement.

Complex lexemes of type 2 are polymorphemic, and one constituent labels a superordinate taxon, such as *tree* in *tulip tree.* However, such lexemes contrast directly with taxa labeled with simple primary lexemes or complex primary

TABLE 1.3
Generic Names for Plants and Animals
in Three Languages Exhibiting Three Lexical Types

Simple	
tree, pine, oak, bass, flicker	(English)
númi "tree," ipák "achiote," máma "manioc," takaš "frog," datém *"Banisteriopsis"*	(Aguaruna)
teʔ "tree," ʔon "avocado," čenek' "bean," č'aben *"Crotolaria,"* ʔak' "vine"	(Tzeltal)

Complex 1 (Unproductive)	
poison oak, hens-and-chickens, baby's tears	(English)
hémpe umpuánbau "hummingbird's garden," iwánči papahį "devil's papaya," antáš bukéa "chicken's comb"	(Aguaruna)
ȼaʔ tuluk' "turkey excrement," pányo ʔat "handkerchief penis," ȼis čauk "thunder fart"	(Tzeltal)

Complex 2 (Productive)	
tulip tree, creosote bush, pipe vine	(English)
númi ménte "kapok tree," takašú dupáhį "frog's herb," páipaiš dáek "papaya vine"	(Aguaruna)
ʔaȼ 'am teʔ "salt tree," kuliš wamal "cabbage herb," ȼ 'unun ʔak' "hummingbird vine"	(Tzeltal)

lexemes of type 1. Thus, *tulip tree* is a kind of *tree* that occurs in a contrast set with *pine* or *oak* (i.e., other generic taxa). (For a more detailed discussion of lexical characteristics of generic names, see Berlin, Breedlove, & Raven, 1973).

3. *Biologically,* generic taxa appear to correspond rather closely with the species in modern biology as the fundamental taxonomic unit. That this should be so is not surprising in that the species in any one restricted geographic region, especially the species of vertebrates and major flowering plants, tend to represent highly perceptually distinct discontinuities in nature.

In my data for the Tzeltal plant and animal kingdoms, more than 60% of the known folk generic taxa correspond in a one-to-one fashion with scientific species. Although my data from Aguaruna have not been exhaustively compared at the generic level with scientific species, I believe that the overall pattern is similar.

4. *Psychologically,* generic taxa are highly salient and are the first terms encountered in ethnobiological inquiry, presumably because they refer to the most commonly used, every-day categories of folk biological knowledge. There is one study of the acquisition of folk botanical vocabulary (Stross, 1974) that shows that generic names are among the first acquired by children as they learn to name the plant kingdom.

Hunn (1977), who has provided us with a monographic study of Tzeltal folk zoology, argues that a particular instance (exemplar) of a generic taxon is recognized by a process analogous to the strategy of inductive category formation described by Bruner, Goodnow, and Austin (1956). One learns to recognize a particular instance of a generic category not so much by acquiring a deductive rule as by being exposed to multiple instances of the category numerous times. By contrast, he argues that the life-form taxon, *bird,* might be learned deductively in terms of some such rule that states: feathered creature, most of which fly. Generic categories are formed, or so it now appears, as gestalten or prototypical images such as those described by Rosch. Practicing taxonomists work with such images all of the time. Thus, the influential plant taxonomist Cronquist (1968) has stated: "if the circumstances permit, we try to define genera in such a way that one can recognize a genus from its aspect, without recourse to technical characters not readily visible to the naked eye [p. 30]."

A balanced consideration of each of the above criteria should, in an actual field situation, allow for the recognition of most generic taxa in an unambiguous fashion.

TAXA OF SPECIFIC AND VARIETAL RANK

Subgeneric taxa in folk biological taxonomies are described as being of specific or varietal rank. Taxa that occur as members of these ranks differ from those of the higher ranks along the dimensions we have already considered, taxonomically, linguistically, biologically, and psychologically. Before examining these features, it is important to discuss the relationship of subgeneric taxa to factors of cultural importance.

It is worth noting again that one significant feature of generic taxa was that they represented perceptually distinct discontinuities in the biological world that could be easily recognized, as the botanist Cain (1956) has stated, "without close study [p. 97]." Although generic taxa are the smallest discontinuities that stand out as easily perceptual and thus nameable chunks, specific and varietal taxa are different in just this respect. It appears likely that subgeneric taxa are cognitively recognized primarily because of the close attention they receive due to their cultural significance.

Evidence to support this claim comes from an analysis of the cultural significance of the plants included in generic taxa. A gross scale that my colleagues and I have used in our work on Tzeltal plants defines four categories of cultural importance (Berlin, Breedlove, Laughlin, & Raven, 1974). From the greatest to least important, these categories rank plants into *cultivated forms* (consciously planted), *protected plants* (not planted but not consciously destroyed), *significant plants* (recognized as producing useful products but not systematically protected), and *unimportant plants* (no known cultural utility). A comparable scale has been developed for Aguaruna ethnobotany (Berlin, 1976a).

Table 1.4 shows the distribution of monotypic and polytypic generic taxa over these four categories of cultural significance for Tzeltal and Aguaruna. It is necessary in considering Table 1.4 to bear in mind that polytypic generic taxa include, by definition, specific taxa. Table 1.4 provides evidence not only for the claim that subgeneric level taxa are recognized primarily because of their cultural significance but also allows us to assess the validity of this claim when applied to the generic level.

By the loosest of definitions of cultural significance (i.e., combining the categories of cultivated, protected, and significant plants), we can see that well over one-half of all Aguaruna generics have some cultural significance. However, a full one-third of all known plants (189) are conceptually recognized but lack any cultural importance. The same proportion holds true for the distribution of unimportant plants in Tzeltal. Thus it would be false to suggest that the Aguaruna or Tzeltal classify only those plants in their environment that have some cultural utility.

An analysis of polytypic generics alone reveals greater cultural significance of these cognitively recognized taxa. Of all Aguaruna *polytypic* generics (hence specific taxa), 81% are members of one of the three categories of cultural importance — *a mere 11% of those generics that have been classified as unimportant are polytypic.* For Tzeltal, 86% of the polytypic generics are useful to man in some fashion, and only 6% of the unimportant generics are polytypic.

Furthermore, the likelihood that a generic will be further subdivided is a direct function of its cultural importance. Thus, for Aguaruna, 40% of all cultivated plants include folk species, 31% of the protected plants are polytypic, and 19% of the significant plants include named subdivisions. Generic plants

TABLE 1.4
Aguaruna and Tzeltal Monotypic and Polytypic Generic Plant Taxa
and Their Relative Cultural Significance

		Cultivated	*Protected*	*Significant*	*Unimportant*
Tzeltal	monotypic	32	32	167	167
	polytypic	31	9	28	5
Aguaruna	monotypic	37	31	215	177
	polytypic	24	14	53	12

that are considered to be unimportant culturally, however, are overwhelmingly monotypic — a small handful of 12 generics (of the 189 unimportant plants), or 6%, are further subdivided into specific classes. The same general pattern holds true for the Tzeltal data.

A possible explanation for this apparent lack of subgeneric taxa in plants with no cultural importance — or, for that matter, for those plants with marginal cultural significant — might be that such folk generic groupings exhibit much less internal polymorphism (biological differentiation) than those with cultural importance. All the evidence available to me now, however, indicates that such is not the case. In fact, the actual numbers of biological species included in generic taxa of little or no cultural importance is often many times greater than those included in taxa of major cultural significance. Thus unimportant generics exhibit more *biological potential* for further subdivisions than do culturally important forms.

A more likely explanation of these data from Aguaruna and Tzeltal (as well as other languages) is that the conceptual recognition of specific taxa is not so much a function of the "close scrutiny" given polymorphic groupings of plants as they exist in nature as it is a result of special attention due to their presumed functional importance for cultural reasons. In rather imprécise terms, the native folk biologist apparently recognizes *generic* taxa "because they are there" and recognizes *specific* (and *varietal*) taxa "because it is culturally important to do so."

Having considered the cultural significance of specific and varietal taxa, let us return to their analysis in terms of taxonomic, linguistic, biological, and psychological features.

Taxonomically, most specific taxa occur in sets of two or three members. When the set of folk species rises to six, the members are always items of major cultural importance. Varietal taxa rarely occur in folk taxonomies.

The data for the 103 polytypic Aguaruna generic taxa conform closely to the foregoing general characterization. More than one-half of the specific taxa occur in sets of two members, and more than two-thirds the total members are in sets of either two or three members. All of the larger sets of specific taxa refer to organisms of major cultural importance [e.g., manioc (30 folk species), banana

(21 folk species), ginger (9), etc.]. Varietal taxa are infrequent in Aguaruna and have been found only with two important cultigens: yams and bananas.

Linguistically, specific and varietal classes are labeled, with predictable exceptions, by binominal secondary lexemes. This contrasts with generic and life-form names that are marked by primary lexemes. Examples of several specific contrast sets whose members illustrate lexemes of this type are seen in Table 1.5.

Although it is the case that binomial nomenclature is the rule for taxa of specific rank, some are labeled by primary lexemes and, as a consequence, constitute an exception to the binomiality principle. However, the majority of such monomial specifics in Aguaruna can be shown to be what I have called elsewhere "type specifics" (Berlin, 1972; Berlin, Breedlove, & Raven, 1973). Some of these forms refer to the central or focal members of the polytypic generic category. Reasons for focality include such factors as the cultural importance of the members of the class, widespread distribution, or prominence due to one or more morphological features. On the other hand, monomial specifics may also mark the residue of some folk generic that are not members of any of the contrasting specific taxa in the set. Hunn, who was the first to my knowledge to note this phenomenon in folk biological classification (Hunn, 1977, pp. 57–58), calls such taxa "residual categories." Nomenclaturally, all type-specific taxa (those that indicate focal members or those that indicate residual categories) are marked with expressions that are polysemous with the label of the superordinate generic. Examples of both types of specific taxa labeled by monomial expressions can be found in Table 1.6.

Type-specific monomials, however, do not exhaust the inventory of monomial-specific names in Aguaruna. In several important cultivated plants, specific taxa

TABLE 1.5
Binomial Specific Nomenclature
in Aguaruna Folk Botany

Generic Name	Specific Names	
ipák 'achiote' (*Bixa orellana*))	beéŋ ipák	"kidney-achiote"
	čamíŋ ipák	"yellow achiote"
	hémpe ipák	"hummingbird achiote"
	šíŋ ipák	"genuine achiote"
namúk (*Sicana odorifera*)	mún namúk	"large secana"
	ɟénɟak namúk	"dart-like secana"
	ikám namúk	"forest secana"
	kapántu namúk	"red secana"
aháŋke (*Uncaria* spp.)	mun aháŋke	"large Uncaria" (*U. guianeusis*)
	učí aháŋke	"small *Uncaria*" (no determinations)

TABLE 1.6
Examples of Specific Taxa in Aguaruna Folk Botany
Labeled by Expressions Polysemous with the
Superordinate Generic Name

Monomials marking type specifics	ȼapátaƞ (*Siolmatra* ssp.)	ȼapátaƞ	(*Siolmatra mexiae*)
		mun ȼapátaƞ	(No determinations as yet)
	datém (*Banisteropsis* spp.)	datém	(*Banisteriopsis* sp.)
		tehés datém	(No determinations)
Monomials marking residual categories	saunák (several species of the Cyclanthaceae	saunák	(Residual category of cyclanthaceous plants)
		mun saunák	(Exceptionally large cyclanth)
	suƞkíp (several aroid spp.)	suƞkíp	(Residual category of this group of aroids)
		yawá̱ suƞkíp ⎫	Both distinctive unidentified
		mehén suƞkíp ⎭	species or aroids

labeled by primary lexemes have been elicited that cannot be analyzed as examples of type species. This nomenclatural feature is especially common for the critical cultigens banana, manioc, yam, and cocoyam (*Xanthosoma*).

Data from Terrence Hays on the Ndambu of New Guinea (1974) and Nancy Turner's materials from the Pacific Northwest (1973) also indicate cases of monomial-specific names that are not analyzable as labels for type species. However, such expressions occur in a predictable fashion, and it now appears that where a generic taxon is further partitioned into specific classes, and one or more of the included species are monomially designated (type specifics excluded), *the monomials will invariably refer to a taxon of major cultural importance.* One will not find, in light of this hypothesis, monomial, non-type-specific names for organisms that lack major cultural significance.

Biologically, contrasting specific taxa differ on the basis of very few morphological characters, many of which are readily visible and sometimes verbalizable. Table 1.5 provides botanical examples of members of specific contrast sets that are quite similar except for a few distinctive features. The four classes of *ipák* are readily distinguished by the shape of the seed capsule as well as relative

TABLE 1.7
Examples of Covert Groupings of "Trees" in Aguaruna Botany

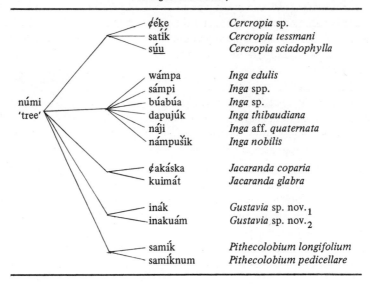

	¢éke	*Cercropia* sp.
	satík	*Cercropia tessmani*
	súu	*Cercropia sciadophylla*
	wámpa	*Inga edulis*
	sámpi	*Inga* spp.
	búabúa	*Inga* sp.
númi 'tree'	dapujúk	*Inga thibaudiana*
	náji	*Inga* aff. *quaternata*
	námpušik	*Inga nobilis*
	¢akáska	*Jacaranda coparia*
	kuimát	*Jacaranda glabra*
	inák	*Gustavia* sp. nov.$_1$
	inakuám	*Gustavia* sp. nov.$_2$
	samík	*Pithecolobium longifolium*
	samíknum	*Pithecolobium pedicellare*

TABLE 1.8
Examples of Covert Groupings of "Trees" in Tzeltal

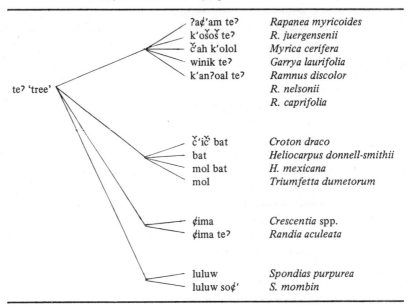

	?a¢'am te?	*Rapanea myricoides*
	k'ošoš te?	*R. juergensenii*
	čah k'olol	*Myrica cerifera*
	winik te?	*Garrya laurifolia*
	k'an?oal te?	*Ramnus discolor*
		R. nelsonii
		R. caprifolia
te? 'tree'	č'ič bat	*Croton draco*
	bat	*Heliocarpus donnell-smithii*
	mol bat	*H. mexicana*
	mol	*Triumfetta dumetorum*
	¢ima	*Crescentia* spp.
	¢ima te?	*Randia aculeata*
	luluw	*Spondias purpurea*
	luluw so¢'	*S. mombin*

abundance and surface distribution of the flexible spine-like protuberances that cover the surface of all but one folk species. The secana types (*Sicana odorifera*) differ in rind color and size and shape of fruit. The two specific types of *čánke* (*mun ahánke* and *učí ahánke*) apparently differ on one character — the presence or absence of axillary spines on the young growing stem of the vine. Differences between specific taxa of the same contrast are often verbalizable, as well, and I have observed informants avidly discussing the assignment of some specimen to some specific class with enthusiasm.

Psychologically, specific and varietal taxa differ from classes at the generic level in that their recognition is in part, as noted previously, a function of their cultural importance. In a sense, they represent differences that members of a society have consciously learned to attend to and are not always readily perceivable.

The psychological processes involved in the identification of these taxa are distinct in that a deductive rule can be learned and applied. Thus, in American English folk botany, a pinyon pine can be identified as a pine with two very short needles with edible seeds. A Pondersosa and Jeffrey pine can only be distinguished by learning to recognize the pineapple-like odor of the Jeffrey pine, a feature lacking in the Ponderosa. In each case, one can formulate easily a rule that captures the essence of the criterial attributes of the categories involved.

TAXA OF INTERMEDIATE RANK:
COVERT CATEGORIES

In 1968, and later in 1974, my colleagues and I presented evidence from Tzeltal that indicated the presence of groupings of plants of greater generality than those we identified as taxa of generic rank but of greater specificity than those identified as taxa of life-form rank. These were much like the taxon labeled by the English expression *evergreen,* a category that includes taxa labeled by the terms *pine, spruce,* and *fir,* yet which itself is included in the higher-level taxon, *tree.* In Tzeltal, a distinctive characteristic of these midlevel groupings was that they were rarely labeled. As a consequence, we referred to them as *covert categories.* Subsequent work by Hunn (1977), Hays (1974, 1976), Bulmer (1974), and others have indicated the occurrence of such covert taxa in other systems of botanical and zoological folk classification as well.

Although the data on such covert groupings from Aguaruna folk botany are not yet all analyzed, it is clear that as many as 40 such taxa are commonly recognized. The basis of these groupings appears to be in the recognition of gross, visually recognized, morphological similarities of the organisms involved and do not — in the main — represent groupings formed on the basis of functional considerations (for a discussion of this point, see Brown, 1974, and Berlin, 1974). Examples of covert categories of groups of trees in Tzeltal and Aguaruna seen in Tables 1.7 and 1.8.

CONCLUSIONS

I have presented evidence that suggests that folk biological classification is based on a recognition of natural discontinuities in the biological world that are considered to be similar or different because of gross, readily perceivable characteristics of form and behavior. These recognized classes of plants and animals are organized into a taxonomic hierarchy that consists of a small number of folk biological ranks. These ranks include taxa that exhibit essentially the same degree of internal diversity one from another. Taxa of each rank are mutually exclusive and share formal and substantive features in common. The similarities noted in the overall structure of folk biological systematics suggest that man — at least prescientific man — brings order to his biological world in essentially the same ways, and no doubt the most interesting conclusions for psychologists to ponder and for ethnobiologists to establish are the bases of this classification.

I have said at a number of points that I believe the generic rank to provide the core of the entire folk biological taxonomy. At this rank, both plants and animals appear perceptually most distinct to the human classifier, and these differences in morphology and behavior virtually "cry out to be named." At subgeneric ranks, specific and varietal taxa appear to gain their distinctiveness in terms of cultural utility. Suprageneric categories are not always named; the entire kingdom may lack a linguistic designation though its cognitive distinctiveness is difficult to question. Between the generic and life-form ranks, limited and clearly distinct categories may be found that represent covert intermediate categories. That we organize the system around the generic level suggests that it may well be basic to the process of classification. It seems reasonable to assume that we may learn more about the psychological dimensions of these category systems by considering Rosch's work on basic-level objects. Should the general principles underlying ethnobiological classification be supported by further research, the study of man's conceptual organization of biological diversity might ultimately contribute to a more general understanding of human classificatory abilities.

ACKNOWLEDGMENTS

I would like to thank both Eleanor Rosch and Barbara Lloyd for their concerted efforts in editing an earlier version of this chapter. I have also benefited from the comments of the participants at the Lake Arrowhead conference, especially from those of Roy G. D'Andrade. Financial support of the research on which this chapter is based has come from the National Science Foundation (Grant No. 76-17985), the National Institute of Mental Health (Grants MH22012 and MH 25703), the Center for Latin American Studies, and the Faculty Research Committee of the University of California, Berkeley.

REFERENCES

Anderson, E. N. *The ethnoichthyology of the Hong Kong boat people.* Unpublished doctoral dissertation, University of California, Berkeley, 1967.

Anglin, J. M. *Word, object, and conceptual development.* New York: Norton & Company, 1977.

Bartlett, H. H. History of the generic concept in botany. *Bulletin of the Torrey Botanical Club,* 1940, *67,* 349–362.

Berlin, B. Speculations on the growth of ethnobotanical nomenclature. *Journal of Language and Society,* 1972, *1,* 63–98.

Berlin, B. The relation of folk systematics to biological classification and nomenclature. *Annual Review of Systematics and Ecology,* 1973, *4,* 259–271.

Berlin, B. Further notes on covert categories and folk taxonomies: A reply to Brown. *American Anthropologist,* 1974, *76,* 327–329.

Berlin, B. The concept of rank in ethnobiological classification: Some evidence from Aguaruna folk botany. *American Ethnologist,* 1976, *3,* 381–399. (a)

Berlin, B. *Folk biology.* Unpublished manuscript, University of California, Berkeley, 1976. (b)

Berlin, B., Breedlove, D. E., Laughlin, R. M., & Raven, P. H. Cultural significance and lexical retention in Tzeltal-Tzotzil ethnobotany. In Munro Edmonson (Ed.), *Meaning in Mayan languages.* The Hague: Mouton, 1974.

Berlin, B., Breedlove, D. E., & Raven, P. H. Folk taxonomies and biological classification. *Science,* 1966, *154,* 273–275.

Berlin, B., Breedlove, D. E., & Raven, P. H. Covert categories and folk taxonomies. *American Anthropologist,* 1968, *70,* 290–299.

Berlin, B., Breedlove, D. E., & Raven, P. H. General principles of classification and nomenclature in folk biology. *American Anthropologist,* 1973, *75,* 214–242.

Berlin, B., Breedlove, D. E., & Raven, P. H. *Principles of Tzeltal plant classification: An introduction to the botanical ethnography of a Mayan-speaking community in highland Chiapas.* New York: Academic Press, 1974.

Brown, C. Unique beginners and covert categories in folk biological taxonomies. *American Anthropologist,* 1974, *76,* 325–327.

Brunel, G. *Variation in Quechua folk biology.* Unpublished doctoral dissertation, University of California, Berkeley, 1974.

Bruner, J., Goodnow, J. J., & Austin, G. A. *A study of thinking.* New York: Wiley, 1956.

Bulmer, R. Worms that croak and other mysteries of Karam natural science. *Mankind,* 1968, *6,* 621–639.

Bulmer, R. Which came first the chicken or the egghead? In J. Pouillion & P. Maranda (Eds.), *Echanges et communication, mélanges offerts à Claude Lévi-Strauss a l'occasion de son 60éme aniversaire.* The Hague-Mouton, 1970.

Bulmer, R. Folk biology in the New Guinea highlands. *Social Science Information,* 1974, *13,* 9–28.

Bulmer, R., & Menzies, J. I. Karam classification of marsupials and rodents (Part II). *Journal of the Polynesian Society,* 1972, *81,* 472–499.

Bulmer, R., & Menzies, J. I. Karam classification of marsupials and rodents (Part II). *Journal of the Polynesian Society,* 1973, *82,* 86–107.

Bulmer, R., Menzies, J. I., & Parker, F. Karam classification of reptiles and fishes. *The Journal of the Polynesian Society,* 1975, *84,* 267–307.

Bulmer, R., & Tyler, M. J. Karam classification of frogs. *Journal of the Polynesian Society,* 1968, *77,* 333–385.

Cain, A. J. The genus in evolutionary taxonomy. *Systematic Zoology,* 1956, *5,* 97–109.

Conklin, H. *The relation of Hanunóo culture to the plant world.* Unpublished doctoral dissertation, Yale University, 1954.

Conklin, H. Lexicographical treatment of folk taxonomies. In F. W. Householder & S. Saporta (Eds.), *Indiana University Research Center in anthropology folklore, and linguistics publication 21: Problems in lexicography.* Bloomington: University of Indiana, 1962.

Cronquist, A. *The evolution and classification of flowering plants.* New York: Houghton Mifflin, 1968.

Hays, T. *Mauna: Explorations in Ndumba ethnobotany.* Unpublished doctoral dissertation, University of Washington, 1974.

Hays, T. An empirical method for the identification of covert categories. *American Ethnologist,* 1976, *3,* 489–507.

Hunn, E. Toward a perceptual model of folk biological classification. *American Ethnologist,* 1976, *3,* 508–524.

Hunn, E. *Tzeltal folk zoology: The classification of discontinuities in nature.* New York: Academic Press, 1977.

Kay, P. Taxonomy and semantic contrast. *Language,* 1971, *41,* 866–887.

Nelson, K. Concept, word, and sentence. *Psychological Review,* 1974, *77,* 267–285.

Rosch, E. H. On the internal structure of perceptual and semantic categories. In T.E. Moore (Ed.), *Cognitive development and the acquisition of language.* New York: Academic Press, 1973.

Stross, B. How Tzeltal children learn botanical terminology. In M. S. Edmonson (Ed.), *Meaning in Mayan languages.* The Hague-Mouton, 1974.

Turner, N. J. *Squamish plant names.* Unpublished manuscript, University of British Columbia, 1972.

Turner, N. J. *Palnt taxonomic systems and the ethnobotany of three contemporary Indian groups of the Pacific Northwest.* Unpublished doctoral dissertation, University of British Columbia, 1973.

Wilson, M. *A highland Maya people and their habitat: Tha natural history, demography, and economy of the K'ekchi'.* Unpublished doctoral dissertation, University of Oregon, 1972.

Wyman, L. C., & Bailey, F. L. Navaho Indian ethnoentomology. *Publications in Anthropology,* 1974(No. 12).

Wyman, L. C., & Bailey, F. L. Navaho Indian medical ethnobotany. *University of New Mexico Bulletin 366,* Anthropological Series 3.5, 1941.

2 Principles of Categorization

Eleanor Rosch
University of California, Berkeley

The following is a taxonomy of the animal kingdom. It has been attributed to an ancient Chinese encyclopedia entitled the *Celestial Emporium of Benevolent Knowledge:*

> On those remote pages it is written that animals are divided into (a) those that belong to the Emperor, (b) embalmed ones, (c) those that are trained, (d) suckling pigs, (e) mermaids, (f) fabulous ones, (g) stray dogs, (h) those that are included in this classification, (i) those that tremble as if they were mad, (j) innumerable ones, (k) those drawn with a very fine camel's hair brush, (l) others, (m) those that have just broken a flower vase, (n) those that resemble flies from a distance   (Borges, 1966, p. 108).

Conceptually, the most interesting aspect of this classification system is that it does not exist. Certain types of categorizations may appear in the imagination of poets, but they are never found in the practical or linguistic classes of organisms or of man-made objects used by any of the cultures of the world. For some years, I have argued that human categorization should not be considered the arbitrary product of historical accident or of whimsy but rather the result of psychological principles of categorization, which are subject to investigation. This chapter is a summary and discussion of those principles.

The chapter is divided into five parts. The first part presents the two general principles that are proposed to underlie categorization systems. The second part shows the way in which these principles appear to result in a basic and primary level of categorization in the levels of abstraction in a taxonomy. It is essentially a summary of the research already reported on basic level objects (Rosch et al., 1976). Thus the second section may be omitted by the reader already sufficiently

27

familiar with that material. The third part relates the principles of categorization to the formation of prototypes in those categories that are at the same level of abstraction in a taxonomy. In particular, this section attempts to clarify the operational concept of prototypicality and to separate that concept from claims concerning the role of prototypes in cognitive processing, representation, and learning for which there is little evidence. The fourth part presents two issues that are problematical for the abstract principles of categorization stated in Part I: (1) the relation of context to basic level objects and prototypes; and (2) assumptions about the nature of the attributes of real-world objects that underlie the claim that there is structure in the world. The fifth part is a report of initial attempts to base an analysis of the attributes, functions, and contexts of objects on a consideration of objects as props in culturally defined events.

It should be noted that the issues in categorization with which we are primarily concerned have to do with explaining the categories found in a culture and coded by the language of that culture at a particular point in time. When we speak of the formation of categories, we mean their formation in the culture. This point is often misunderstood. The principles of categorization proposed are not as such intended to constitute a theory of the development of categories in children born into a culture nor to constitute a model of how categories are processed (how categorizations are made) in the minds of adult speakers of a language.

THE PRINCIPLES

Two general and basic principles are proposed for the formation of categories: The first has to do with the function of category systems and asserts that the task of category systems is to provide maximum information with the least cognitive effort; the second has to do with the structure of the information so provided and asserts that the perceived world comes as structured information rather than as arbitrary or unpredictable attributes. Thus maximum information with least cognitive effort is achieved if categories map the perceived world struc- tructure as closely as possible. This condition can be achieved either by the mapping of categories to given attribute structures or by the definition or redefinition of attributes to render a given set of categories appropriately struc- tured. These principles are elaborated in the following.

Cognitive Economy.   The first principle contains the almost common-sense notion that, as an organism, what one wishes to gain from one's categories is a great deal of information about the environment while conserving finite resources as much as possible. To categorize a stimulus means to consider it, for purposes of that categorization, not only equivalent to other stimuli in the same category but also different from stimuli not in that category. On the one hand, it would appear to the organism's advantage to have as many properties as possible predictable from knowing any one property, a principle that would lead to formation of large numbers of categories with as fine discriminations between categories as possible. On the other hand, one purpose of categorization is to reduce the infinite differences among stimuli to behaviorally and cognitively usable proportions. It is to the organism's advantage not to differentiate one stimulus from others when that differentiation is irrelevant to the purposes at hand.

Perceived World Structure.   The second principle of categorization asserts that unlike the sets of stimuli used in traditional laboratory-concept attainment tasks, the perceived world is not an unstructured total set of equiprobable co-occurring attributes. Rather, the material objects of the world are perceived to possess (in Garner's, 1974, sense) high correlational structure. That is, given a knower who perceives the complex attributes of feathers, fur, and wings, it is an empirical fact provided by the perceived world that wings co-occur with feathers more than with fur. And given an actor with the motor programs for sitting, it is a fact of the perceived world that objects with the perceptual attributes of chairs are more likely to have functional sit-on-able-ness than objects with the appearance of cats. In short, combinations of what we perceive as the attributes of real objects do not occur uniformly. Some pairs, triples, etc., are quite probable, appearing in combination sometimes with one, sometimes another attribute; others are rare; others logically cannot or empirically do not occur.

It should be emphasized that we are talking about the perceived world and not a metaphysical world without a knower. What kinds of attributes *can* be perceived are, of course, species-specific. A dog's sense of smell is more highly differentiated than a human's, and the structure of the world for a dog must surely include attributes of smell that we, as a species, are incapable of perceiving. Furthermore, because a dog's body is constructed differently from a human's, its motor interactions with objects are necessarily differently structured. The "out there" of a bat, a frog, or a bee is surely more different still from that of a human. What attributes *will* be perceived given the ability to perceive them is undoubtedly determined by many factors having to do with the functional needs of the knower interacting with the physical and social environment. One influence on how attributes will be defined by humans is clearly the category system already existent in the culture at a given time. Thus, our segmentation of a bird's body such that there is an attribute called "wings" may be influenced not only by perceptual factors such as the gestalt laws of form that would lead us to consider the wings as a separate part (Palmer, in press) but also by the fact that at present we already have a cultural and linguistic category called "birds." Viewing attributes as, at least in part, constructs of the perceiver does not negate the higher-order structural fact about attributes at issue, namely that the attributes of wings and that of feathers do co-occur in the perceived world.

These two basic principles of categorization, a drive toward cognitive economy combined with structure in the perceived world, have implications both for the level of abstraction of categories formed in a culture and for the internal structure of those categories once formed.

For purposes of explication, we may conceive of category systems as having both a vertical and horizontal dimension. The vertical dimension concerns the level of inclusiveness of the category — the dimension along which the terms collie, dog, mammal, animal, and living thing vary. The horizontal dimension concerns the segmentation of categories at the same level of inclusiveness — the dimension on which dog, cat, car, bus, chair, and sofa vary. The implication of the two principles of categorization for the vertical dimension is that not all possible levels of categorization are equally good or useful; rather, the most basic level of categorization will be the most inclusive (abstract) level at which the categories can mirror the structure of attributes perceived in the world. The implication of the principles of categorization for the horizontal dimension is that to increase the distinctiveness and flexibility of categories, categories tend to become defined in terms of prototypes or prototypical instances that contain the attributes most representative of items inside and least representative of items outside the category.

THE VERTICAL DIMENSION OF CATEGORIES: BASIC-LEVEL OBJECTS

In a programmatic series of experiments, we have attempted to argue that categories within taxonomies of concrete objects are structured such that there is generally one level of abstraction at which the most basic category cuts can be made (Rosch et al., 1976a). By *category* is meant a number of objects that are considered equivalent. Categories are generally designated by names (e.g., *dog, animal*). A *taxonomy* is a system by which categories are related to one another by means of class inclusion. The greater the inclusiveness of a category within a taxonomy, the higher the level of abstraction. Each category within a taxonomy is entirely included within one other category (unless it is the highest level category) but is not exhaustive of that more inclusive category (see Kay, 1971). Thus the term *level of abstraction* within a taxonomy refers to a particular level of inclusiveness. A familiar taxonomy is the Linnean system for the classification of animals.

Our claims concerning a basic level of abstraction can be formalized in terms of cue validity (Rosch et al., 1976a) or in terms of the set theoretic representation of similarity provided by Tversky (1977, and Chapter 4 in this volume). Cue validity is a probabilistic concept; the validity of a given cue x as a predictor of a given category y (the conditional probability of y/x) increases as the frequency with which cue x is associated with category y increases and decreases as the frequency with which cue x is associated with categories other than y increases (Beach, 1964a, 1964b; Reed, 1972). The cue validity of an entire category may be defined as the summation of the cue validities for that category of each of the attributes of the category. A category with high cue validity is, by definition, more differentiated from other categories than one of lower cue validity. The elegant formulization that Tversky provides in Chapter 4 is in terms of the variable "category resemblance," which is defined as the weighted sum of the measures of all of the common features within a category minus the sum of the measures of all of the distinctive features. Distinctive features include those that belong to only some members of a given category as well as those belonging to contrasting categories. Thus Tversky's formalization does not weight the effect of contrast categories as much as does the cue validity formulation. Tversky suggests that two disjoint classes tend to be combined whenever the weight of the added common features exceeds the weight of the distinctive features.

A working assumption of the research on basic objects is that (1) in the perceived world, information-rich bundles of perceptual and functional attributes occur that form natural discontinuities, and that (2) basic cuts in categorization are made at these discontinuities. Suppose that basic objects (e.g., chair, car) are at the most inclusive level at which there are attributes common to all or most members of the category. Then both total cue validities and category resemblance are maximized at that level of abstraction at which basic objects are categorized. This is, categories one level more abstract will be superordinate categories (e.g., furniture, vehicle) whose members share only a few attributes among each other. Categories below the basic level will be bundles of common and, thus, predictable attributes and functions but contain many attributes that overlap with other categories (for example, kitchen chair shares most of its attributes with other kinds of chairs).

Superordinate categories have lower total cue validity and lower category resemblance than do basic-level categories, because they have fewer common attributes; in fact, the category resemblance measure of items within the superordinate can even be negative due to the high ratio of distinctive to common features. Subordinate categories have lower total cue validity than do basic categories, because they also share most attributes with contrasting subordinate categories; in Tversky's terms, they tend to be combined because the weight of the added common features tend to exceed the weight of the distinctive features. That basic objects are categories at the level of abstraction that maximizes cue validity and maximizes category resemblance is another way of asserting that basic objects are the categories that best mirror the correlational structure of the environment.

We chose to look at concrete objects because they appeared to be a domain that was at once an indisputable aspect of complex natural language classifications yet at the same time were amenable to methods of empirical analysis. In our investigations of basic categories, the correlational structure of concrete objects was considered to consist of a number of inseparable aspects of form and function, any one of which could serve as the starting point for analysis. Four investigations provided converging operational definitions of the basic level of abstraction: attributes in common, motor movements in common, objective similarity in shape, and identifiability of averaged shapes.

Common Attributes.   Ethnobiologists had suggested on the basis of linguistic criteria and field observation that the folk genus was the level of classification at which organisms had bundles of attributes in common and maximum discontinuity between classes (see Chapter 1). The purpose of our research was to provide a systematic empirical study of the co-occurrence of attributes in the most common taxonomies of biological and man-made objects in our own culture.

The hypothesis that basic level objects are the most inclusive level of classification at which objects have numbers of attributes in common was tested for categories at three levels of abstraction for nine taxonomies: tree, bird, fish, fruit, musical instruments, tool, clothing, furniture, and vehicle. Examples of the three levels for one biological and one nonbiological taxonomy are shown in Table 2.1. Criteria for choice of these specific items were that the taxonomies contain the most common (defined by word frequency) categories of concrete nouns in English, that the levels of abstraction bear simple class-inclusion relations to each other, and that those class-inclusion relations be generally known to our subjects (be agreed upon by a sample of native English speakers). The middle level of abstraction was the hypothesized basic level: For nonbiological taxonomies, this corresponded to the intuition of the experimenters (which also turned out to be consistent with Berlin's linguistic criteria); for biological categories, we assumed that the basic level would be the level of the folk generic.

Subjects received sets of words taken from these nine taxonomies; the subject's task was to list all of the attributes he could think of that were true of the items included in the class of things designated by each object name. Thus, for purposes of this study, attributes were defined operationally as whatever subjects agreed them to be with no implications for whether such analysis of an object could or could not be perceptually considered prior to knowledge of the object itself. Results of the study were as predicted: Very few attributes were listed for the superordinate categories, a significantly greater number listed for the supposed

TABLE 2.1
Examples of Taxonomies Used in Basic Object Research

Superordinate	Basic Level	Subordinate
Furniture	Chair	Kitchen chair
		Living-room chair
	Table	Kitchen table
		Dining-room table
	Lamp	Floor lamp
		Desk lamp
tree	Oak	White oak
		Red oak
	Maple	Silver maple
		Sugar maple
	Birch	River birch
		White birch

basic-level objects, and not significantly more attributes listed for subordinate-level objects than for basic-level. An additional study showed essentially the same attributes listed for visually present objects as for the object names. The single unpredicted result was that for the three biological taxonomies, the basic level, as defined by numbers of attributes in common, did not occur at the level of the folk generic but appeared at the level we had originally expected to be superordinate (e.g., *tree* rather than *oak*).

Motor Movements.   Inseparable from the perceived attributes of objects are the ways in which humans habitually use or interact with those objects. For concrete objects, such interactions take the form of motor movements. For example, when performing the action of sitting down on a chair, a sequence of body and muscle movements are typically made that are inseparable from the nature of the attributes of chairs — legs, seat, back, etc. This aspect of objects is particularly important in light of the role that sensory—motor interaction with the world appears to play in the development of thought (Bruner, Olver, & Greenfield, 1966; Nelson, 1974; Piaget, 1952).

In our study of motor movements, each of the sets of words used in the previous experiment was administered to new subjects. A subject was asked to describe, in as much finely analyzed detail as possible, the sequences of motor movements he made when using or interacting with the object. Tallies of agreed upon listings of the same movements of the same body part in the same part of the movement sequence formed the unit of analysis. Results were identical to those of the attribute listings; basic objects were the most general classes to have motor sequences in common. For example, there are few motor programs we carry out to items of furniture in general and several specific motor programs carried out in regard to sitting down on chairs, but we sit on kitchen and living-room chairs using essentially the same motor programs.

Similarity in Shapes.   Another aspect of the meaning of a class of objects is the appearance of the objects in the class. In order to be able to analyze correlational structures by different but converging methods, it was necessary to find a method of analyzing similarity in the visual aspects of the objects that was not dependent on subjects' descriptions, that was free from effects of the object's name (which would not have been the case for subjects' ratings of similarity), and that went beyond similarity of analyzable, listable attributes that had already been used in the first study described. For this purpose, outlines of the shape of two-dimensional representations of objects were used, an integral aspect of natural forms. Similarity in shape was measured by the amount of overlap of the two outlines when the outlines (normalized for size and orientation) were juxtaposed.

Results showed that the ratio of overlapped to nonoverlapped area when two objects from the same basic-level category (e.g., two cars) were superimposed was far greater than when two objects from the same superordinate category were superimposed (e.g., a car and a motorcycle). Although some gain in ratio of overlap to nonoverlap also occurred for subordinate category objects (e.g., two sports cars), the gain obtained by shifting from basic-level to subordinate objects was significantly less than the gain obtained by shifting from superordinate to basic-level objects.

Identifiability of Averaged Shapes.   If the basic level is the most inclusive level at which shapes of objects of a class are similar, a possible result of such similarity may be that the basic level is also the most inclusive level at which an averaged shape of an object can be recognized. To test this hypothesis, the same normalized superimposed shapes used in the previous experiment were used to draw an average outline of the overlapped figures. Subjects were then asked to identify both the superordinate category and the specific object depicted. Results showed that basic objects were the most general and inclusive categories at which the objects depicted could be identified. Furthermore, overlaps of subordinate objects were no more identifiable than objects at the basic level.

In summary, our four converging operational definitions of basic objects all indicated the same level of abstraction to be basic in our taxonómies. Admittedly, the basic level for biological objects was not that predicted by the folk genus; however, this fact appeared to be simply accounted for by our subjects' lack of knowledge of the additional depth of real-world attribute structure available at the level of the folk generic (see Rosch et al., 1976a).

Implications for Other Fields

The foregoing theory of categorization and basic objects has implications for several traditional areas of study in psychology; some of these have been tested.

Imagery.   The fact that basic-level objects were the most inclusive categories at which an averaged member of the category could be identified suggested that basic objects might be the most inclusive categories for which it was possible to form a mental image isomorphic to the appearance of members of the class as a whole. Experiments using a signal-detection paradigm and a priming paradigm, both of which have been previously argued to be measures of imagery (Peterson & Graham, 1974; Rosch, 1975c), verified that, in so far as it was meaningful to use the term *imagery,* basic objects appeared to-be the most abstract categories for which an image could be reasonably representative of the class as a whole.

Perception.   From all that has been said of the nature of basic classifications, it would hardly be reasonable to suppose that in perception of the world, objects were first categorized either at the most abstract or at the most concrete level possible. Two separate studies of picture verification (Rosch et al., 1976a; Smith, Balzano, & Walker, 1978) indicate that, in fact, objects may be first seen or recognized as members of their basic category, and that only with the aid of additional processing can they be identified as members of their super-ordinate or subordinate category.

Development.   We have argued that classification into categories at the basic level is overdetermined because perception, motor movements, functions, and iconic images would all lead to the same level of categorization. Thus basic objects should be the first categorizations of concrete objects made by children. In fact, for our nine taxonomies, the basic level was the first named. And even when naming was controlled, pictures of several basic-level objects were sorted into groups "because they were the same type of thing" long before such a technique of sorting has become general in children.

Language.   From all that has been said, we would expect the most useful and, thus, most used name for an item to be the basic-level name. In fact, we found that adults almost invariably named pictures of the subordinate items of the nine taxonomies at the basic level, although they knew the correct super-ordinate and subordinate names for the objects. On a more speculative level, in the evolution of languages, one would expect names to evolve first for basic-level objects, spreading both upward and downward as taxonomies increased in depth. Of great relevance for this hypothesis are Berlin's (1972) claims for such a pattern for the evolution of plant names, and our own (Rosch et al., 1976a) and Newport and Bellugi's (Chapter 3, this volume) finding for American Sign Language of the Deaf, that it was the basic-level categories that were most often coded by single signs and super- and subordinate categories that were likely to be missing. Thus a wide range of converging operations verify as basic the same levels of abstraction.

THE HORIZONTAL DIMENSION:
INTERNAL STRUCTURE OF CATEGORIES: PROTOTYPES

Most, if not all, categories do not have clear-cut boundaries. To argue that basic object categories follow clusters of perceived attributes is not to say that such attribute clusters are necessarily discontinuous.

In terms of the principles of categorization proposed earlier, cognitive econ-omy dictates that categories tend to be viewed as being as separate from each other and as clear-cut as possible. One way to achieve this is by means of formal, necessary and sufficient criteria for category membership. The attempt to impose such criteria on categories marks virtually all definitions in the tradition of Western reason. The psychological treatment of categories in the standard concept-identification paradigm lies within this tradition. Another way to achieve separateness and clarity of actually continuous categories is by conceiving of each category in terms of its clear cases rather than its boundaries. As Wittgenstein (1953) has pointed out, categorical judgments become a problem only if one is concerned with boundaries — in the normal course of life, two neighbors know on whose property they are standing without exact demarcation of the boundary line. Categories can be viewed in terms of their clear cases if the perceiver places emphasis on the correlational structure of perceived attributes such that the categories are represented by their most structured portions.

By prototypes of categories we have generally meant the clearest cases of category membership defined operationally by people's judgments of goodness of membership in the category. A great deal of confusion in the discussion of prototypes has arisen from two sources. First, the notion of prototypes has tended to become reified as though it meant a specific category member or mental structure. Questions are then asked in an either—or fashion about whether something is or is not the prototype or part of the prototype in exactly the same way in which the question would previously have been asked about the category boundary. Such thinking precisely violates the Wittgensteinian insight that we can judge how clear a case something is and deal with categories on the basis of clear cases in the total absence of information about boundaries. Second, the empirical findings about prototypicality have been confused with theories of processing — that is, there has been a failure to distinguish the structure of categories from theories concerning the use of that structure in processing. Therefore, let us first attempt to look at prototypes in as purely structural a fashion as possible. We will focus on what may be said about prototypes based on operational definitions and empirical findings alone without the addition of processing assumptions.

Perception of typicality differences is, in the first place, an empirical fact of people's judgments about category membership. It is by now a well-documented finding that subjects overwhelmingly agree in their judgments of how good an example or clear a case members are of a category, even for categories about whose boundaries they disagree (Rosch, 1974, 1975b). Such judgments are reliable even under changes of instructions and items (Rips, Shoben, & Smith, 1973; Rosch, 1975b, 1975c; Rosch & Mervis, 1975). Were such agreement and reliability in judgment not to have been obtained, there would be no further point in discussion or investigation of the issue. However, given the empirical verification of degree of prototypicality, we can proceed to ask what principles determine which items will be judged the more prototypical and what other variables might be affected by prototypicality.

In terms of the basic principles of category formation, the formation of category prototypes should, like basic levels of abstraction, be determinate and be closely related to the initial formation of categories. For categories of concrete objects (which do not have a physiological basis, as categories such as colors and forms apparently do — Rosch, 1974), a reasonable hypothesis is that prototypes develop through the same principles such as maximization of cue validity and maximization of category resemblance[1] as those principles governing the formation of the categories themselves.

In support of such a hypothesis, Rosch and Mervis (1975) have shown that the more prototypical of a category a member is rated, the more attributes it has in common with other members of the category and the fewer attributes in common with members of the contrasting categories. This finding was demonstrated for natural language superordinate categories, for natural language basic-level categories, and for artificial categories in which the definition of attributes and the amount of experience with items was completely specified and controlled. The same basic principles can be represented in ways other than through attributes in common. Because the present theory is a structural theory, one aspect of it is that centrality shares the mathematical notions inherent in measures like the mean and mode. Prototypical category members have been found to represent the means of attributes that have a metric, such as size (Reed, 1972; Rosch, Simpson, & Miller, 1976).

In short, prototypes appear to be just those members of a category that most reflect the redundancy structure of the category as a whole. That is, if categories form to maximize the information-rich cluster of attributes in the environment and, thus, the cue validity or category resemblance of the attributes of categories, prototypes of categories appear to form in such a manner as to maximize such clusters and such cue validity still further within categories.

It is important to note that for natural language categories both at the superordinate and basic levels, the extent to which items have attributes common to the category was highly negatively correlated with the extent to which they have attributes belonging to members of contrast categories. This appears to be part of the structure of real-world categories. It may be that such structure is given by the correlated clusters of attributes of the real world. Or such structure, may be a result of the human tendency once a contrast exists to define attributes for contrasting categories so that the categories will be maximally distinctive. In either case, it is a fact that both representativeness within a category and distinctiveness from contrast categories are correlated with prototypicality in real categories. For artificial categories, either principle alone will produce prototype effects (Rosch et al., 1976b; Smith & Balzano, personal communication) depending on the structure of the stimulus set. Thus to perform experiments to try to distinguish which principle is the *one* that determines prototype formation and category processing appears to be an artificial exercise.

---

[1]Tversky formalizes prototypicality as the member or members of the category with the highest summed similarity to all members of the category. This measure, although formally more tractable than that of cue validity, does not take account, as cue validity does, of an item's dissimilarity to contrast categories. This issue is discussed further later.

Effects of Prototypicality on
Psychological Dependent Variables

The fact that prototypicality is reliably rated and is correlated with category structure does not have clear implications for particular processing models nor for a theory of cognitive representations of categories (see the introduction to Part III and Chapter 9). What is very clear from the extant research is that the prototypicality of items within a category can be shown to affect virtually all of the major dependent variables used as measures in psychological research.

Speed of Processing: Reaction Time.   The speed with which subjects can judge statements about category membership is one of the most widely used measures of processing in semantic memory research within the human information-processing framework. Subjects typically are required to respond true or false to statements of the form: X item is a member of Y category, where the dependent variable of interest is reaction time. In such tasks, for natural language categories, responses of true are invariably faster for the items that have been rated more prototypical. Furthermore, Rosch et al. (1976b) had subjects learn artificial categories where prototypicality was defined structurally for some subjects in terms of distance of a gestalt configuration from a prototype, for others in terms of means of attributes, and for still others in terms of family resemblance between attributes. Factors other than the structure of the category, such as frequency, were controlled. After learning was completed, reaction time in a category membership verification task proved to be a function of structural prototypicality.

Speed of Learning of Artificial Categories (Errors) and Order of Development in Children.   Rate of learning of new material and the naturally obtainable measure of learning (combined with maturation) reflected in developmental order are two of the most pervasive dependent variables in psychological research. In the artificial categories used by Rosch et al. (1976b), prototypicality for all three types of stimulus material predicted speed of learning of the categories. Developmentally, Anglin (1976) obtained evidence that young children learn category membership of good examples of categories before that of poor examples. Using a category-membership verification technique, Rosch (1973) found that the differences in reaction time to verify good and poor members were far more extreme for 10-year-old children than for adults, indicating that the children had learned the category membership of the prototypical members earlier than that of other members.

Order and Probability of Item Output.   Item output is normally taken to reflect some aspect of storage, retrieval, or category search. Battig and Montague (1969) provided a normative study of the probability with which college students listed instances of superordinate semantic categories. The order is correlated with prototypicality ratings (Rosch, 1975b). Furthermore, using the artificial categories in which frequency of experience with all items was controlled, Rosch et al. (1976b) demonstrated that the most prototypical items were the first and most frequently produced items when subjects were asked to list the members of the category.

Effects of Advance Information on Performance: Set, Priming.   For colors (Rosch, 1975c), for natural superordinate semantic categories (Rosch, 1975b), and for artificial categories (Rosch et al., 1976b), it has been shown that degree of prototypicality determines whether advance information about the category name facilitates or inhibits responses in a matching task.

The Logic of Natural Language Use of Category Terms: Hedges, Substitutability into Sentences, Superordination in ASL.   Although logic may treat categories as though membership is all or none, natural languages themselves possess linguistic mechanisms for coding and coping with gradients of category membership.

1. *Hedges.* In English there are qualifying terms such as "almost" and "virtually," which Lakoff (1972) calls "hedges." Even those who insist that statements such as "A robin is a bird" and "A penguin is a bird" are equally true, have to admit different hedges applicable to statements of category membership. Thus it is correct to say that a penguin is technically a bird but not that a robin is technically a bird, because a robin is more than just technically a bird; it is a real bird, a bird par excellence. Rosch (1975a) showed that when subjects were given sentence frames such as *"X is virutally Y,"* they reliably placed the more prototypical member of a pair of items into the referent slot, a finding which is isomorphic to Tversky's work on asymmetry of similarity relations (Chapter 4).

2. *Substitutability into sentences.* The meaning of words is initimately tied to their use in sentences. Rosch (1977) has shown that prototypicality ratings for members of superordinate categories predicts the extent to which the member term is substitutable for the superordinate word in sentences. Thus, in the sentence "Twenty or so birds often perch on the telephone wires outside my window and twitter in the morining," the term "sparrow" may readily be substituted for "bird" but the result turns ludicrous by substitution of "turkey," an effect which is not simply a matter of frequency (Rosch, 1975d).

3. *Productive superordinates in ASL.* Newport and Bellugi (Chapter 3) demonstrate that when superordinates in ASL are generated by means of a partial fixed list of category members, those members are the more prototypical items in the category.

In summary, evidence has been presented that prototypes of categories are related to the major dependent variables with which psychological processes are typically measured. What the work summarized does not tell us, however, is considerably more than it tells us. The pervasiveness of prototypes in real-world categories and of prototypicality as a variable indicates that prototypes must have some place in psychological theories of representation, processing, and learning. However, prototypes themselves do not constitute any particular model of processes, representations, or learning. This point is so often misunderstood that it requires discussion:

1. To speak of *a prototype* at all is simply a convenient grammatical fiction; what is really referred to are judgments of degree of prototypicality. Only in some artificial categories is there by definition a literal single prototype (for example, Posner, Goldsmith, & Welton, 1967; Reed, 1972; Rosch et al., 1976b). For natural-language categories, to speak of a single entity that is the prototype is either a gross misunderstanding of the empirical data or a covert theory of mental representation.

2. Prototypes do not constitute any particular processing model for categories. For example, in pattern recognition, as Palmer (Chapter 9) points out, a prototype can be described as well by feature lists or structural descriptions as by templates. And many different types of matching operations can be conceived for matching to a prototype given any of these three modes of representation of the prototype. Other cognitive processes performed on categories such as verifying the membership of an instance in a category, searching the exemplars of a category for the member with a particular attribute, or understanding the meaning of a paragraph containing the category name are not bound to any single process model by the fact that we may acknowledge prototypes. What the facts about prototypicality do contribute to processing notions is a constraint — process models should not be inconsistent with the known facts about prototypes. For example, a model should not be such as to predict equal verification times for good and bad examples of categories nor predict completely random search through a category.

3. Prototypes do not constitute a theory of representation of categories. Although we have suggested elsewhere that it would be reasonable in light of the basic principles of categorization, if categories were represented by prototypes that were most representative of the items in the category and least representative of items outside the category (Rosch & Mervis, 1975; Rosch, 1977), such a statement remains an unspecified formula until it is made concrete by inclusion in some specific theory of representation. For example, different theories of semantic memory can contain the notion of prototypes in different fashions (Smith, 1978). Prototypes can be represented either by propositional or image systems (see Chapters 8 and 9). As with processing models, the facts about prototypes can only constrain, but do not determine, models of representation. A representation of categories in terms of conjoined necessary and sufficient attributes alone would probably be incapable of handling all of the presently

known facts, but there are many representations other than necessary and sufficient attributes that are possible.

4. Although prototypes must be learned, they do not constitute any particular theory of category learning. For example, learning of prototypicality in the types of categories examined in Rosch and Mervis (1975) could be represented in terms of counting attribute frequency (as in Neuman, 1974), in terms of storage of a set of exemplars to which one later matched the input (see Chapter 6 and the introduction to Part II), or in terms of explicit teaching of the prototypes once prototypicality within a category is established in a culture (e.g., "Now that's a *real* coat.")

In short, prototypes only constrain but do not specify representation and process models. In addition, such models further constrain each other. For example, one could not argue for a frequency count of attributes in children's learning of prototypes of categories if one had reason to believe that children's representation of attributes did not allow for separability and selective attention to each attribute (see Chapter 5 and the introduction to Part II).

TWO PROBLEMATICAL ISSUES

The Nature of Perceived Attributes.   The derivations of basic objects and of prototypes from the basic principles of categorization have depended on the notion of a structure in the perceived world — bundles of perceived world attributes that formed natural discontinuities. When the research on basic objects and their prototypes was initially conceived (Rosch et al., 1976a), I thought of such attributes as inherent in the real world. Thus, given an organism that had sensory equipment capable of perceiving attributes such as wings and feathers, it was a fact in the real world that wings and feathers co-occurred. The state of knowledge of a person might be ignorant of (or indifferent or inattentive to) the attributes or might know of the attributes but be ignorant concerning their correlation. Conversely, a person might know of the attributes and their correlational structure but exaggerate that structure, turning partial into complete correlations (as when attributes true only of many members of a category are thought of as true of all members). However, the environment was thought to constrain categorizations in that human knowledge could not provide correlational structure where there was none at all. For purposes of the basic object experiments, perceived attributes were operationally defined as those attributes listed by our subjects. Shape was defined as measured by our computer programs. We thus seemed to have our system grounded comfortably in the real world.

On contemplation of the nature of many of the attributes listed by our subjects, however, it appeared that three types of attributes presented a problem for such a realistic view: (1) some attributes, such as "seat" for the object "chair," appeared to have names that showed them not to be meaningful prior to knowledge of the object as chair; (2) some attributes such as "large" for the object "piano" seemed to have meaning only in relation to categorization of the object in terms of a superordinate category — piano is large for furniture but small for other kinds of objects such as buildings; (3) some attributes such as "you eat on it" for the object "table" were functional attributes that seemed to require knowledge about humans, their activities, and the real world in order to be understood (see Chapter 10). That is, it appeared that the analysis of objects into attributes was a rather sophisticated activitiy that our subjects (and indeed a system of cultural knowledge) might well be considered to be able to impose only *after* the development of the category system.

In fact, the same laws of cognitive economy leading to the push toward basic-level categories and prototypes might also lead to the definition of attributes of categories such that the categories once given would appear maximally distinctive from one another and such that the more prototypical items would appear even more representative of their own and less representative of contrastive categories. Actually, in the evolution of the meaning of terms in languages, probably both the constraint of real-world factors and the construction and reconstruction of attributes are continually present. Thus, given a particular category system, attributes are defined such as to make the system appear as logical and economical as possible. However, if such a system becomes markedly out of phase with real-world constraints, it will probably tend to evolve to be more in line with those constraints — with redefinition of attributes ensuing if necessary. Unfortunately, to state the matter in such a way is to provide no clear place at which we can enter the system as analytical scientists. What is the unit with which to start our analysis? Partly in order to find a more basic real-world unit for analysis than attributes, we have turned our attention to the contexts in which objects occur — that is, to the culturally defined events in which objects serve as props.

The Role of Context in Basic-Level Objects and Prototypes.   It is obvious, even in the absence of controlled experimentation, that a man about to buy a chair who is standing in a furniture store surrounded by different chairs among which he must choose will think and speak about chairs at other than the basic level of "chair." Similarly, in regard to prototypes, it is obvious that if asked for the most typical African animal, people of any age will not name the same animal as when asked for the most typical American pet animal. Because interest in context is only beginning, it is not yet clear just what experimentally defined contexts will affect what dependent variables for what categories. But it is predetermined that there will be context effects for both the level of abstraction at which an object is considered and for which items are named, learned, listed, or expected in a category. Does this mean that our findings in regard to basic levels and prototypes are relevant only to the artificial situation of the laboratory in which a context is not specified?

Actually, both basic levels and prototypes are, in a sense, theories about context itself. The basic level of abstraction is that level of abstraction that is appropriate for using, thinking about, or naming an object in most situations in which the object occurs (Rosch et al., 1976a). And when a context is not specified in an experiment, people must contribute their own context. Presumably, they do not do so randomly. Indeed, it seems likely that, in the absence of a specified context, subjects assume what they consider the normal context or situation for occurrence of that object. To make such claims about categories appears to demand an analysis of the actual events in daily life in which objects occur.

THE ROLE OF OBJECTS IN EVENTS

The attempt we have made to answer the issues of the origin of attributes and the role of context has been in terms of the use of objects in the events of daily human life. The study of events grew out of an interest in categorizations of the flow of experience. That is, our initial interest was in the question of whether any of the principles of categorization we had found useful for understanding concrete objects appeared to apply to the cutting up of the continuity of experience into the discrete bounded temporal units that we call *events*.

Previously, events have been studied primarily from two perspectives in psychology. Within ecological and social psychology, an observer records and attempts to segment the stream of another person's behavior into event sequences (for example, Barker & Wright, 1955; Newtson, 1976). And within the artificial intelligence tradition, Story Understanders are being constructed that can "comprehend," by means of event scripts, statements about simple, culturally predictable sequences such as going to a restaurant (Shank, 1975).

The unit of the event would appear to be a particularly important unit for analysis. Events stand at the interface between an analysis of social structure and culture and an analysis of individual psychology. It may be useful to think of scripts for events as the level of theory at which we can specify how culture and social structure enter the individual mind. Could we use events as the basic unit from which to derive an understanding of objects? Could we view objects as props for the carrying out of events and have the functions, perceptual attributes, and levels of abstraction of objects fall out of their role in such events?

Our research to date has been a study rather than an experiment and more like a pilot study at that. Events were defined neither by observation of others nor by a priori units for scripts but introspectively in the following fashion. Students in a seminar on events were asked to choose a particular evening on which to list the events that they remembered of that day — e.g., to answer the question what did I do? (or what happened to me?) that day by means of a list of the names of the events. They were to begin in the morning. The students were aware of the nature of the inquiry and that the focus of interest was on the units that they would perceive as the appropriate units into which to chunk the days' happenings. After completing the list for that day, they were to do the same sort of lists for events remembered from the previous day, and thus to continue backwards to preceding days until they could remember no more day's events. They also listed events for units smaller and larger than a day: for example, the hour immediately preceding writing and the previous school quarter.

The results were somewhat encouraging concerning the tractability of such a means of study. There was considerable agreement on the kinds of units into which a day should be broken — units such as making coffee, taking a shower, and going to statistics class. No one used much smaller units: That is, units such as picking up the toothpaste tube, squeezing toothpaste onto the brush, etc., never occurred. Nor did people use larger units such as "got myself out of the house in the morning" or "went to all my afternoon classes." Furthermore, the units that were listed did not change in size or type with their recency or remoteness in time to the writing. Thus, for the time unit of the hour preceding writing, components of events were not listed. Nor were larger units of time given for a day a week past than for the day on which the list was composed. Indeed, it was dramatic how, as days further and further in the past appeared, fewer and fewer events were remembered although the type of unit for those that were remembered remained the same. That is, for a day a week past, a student would not say that he now only remembered getting himself out of the house in the morning (though such "summarizing" events could be inferred); rather he either did or did not remember feeding the cat that day (an occurrence that could also be inferred but for which inference and memory were introspectively clearly distinguishable). Indeed, it appeared that events such as "all the morning chores" as a whole do not have a memory representation separate from memory of doing the individual chores — perhaps in the way that superordinate categories, such as furniture, do not appear to be imageable per se apart from imaging individual items in the category. It should be noted that event boundaries appeared to be marked in a reasonable way by factors such as changes of the actors participating with ego, changes in the objects ego interacts with, changes in place, and changes in the type or rate of activity with an object, and by notable gaps in time between two reported events.

A good candidate for the basic level of abstraction for events is the type of unit into which the students broke their days. The events they listed were just those kinds of events for which Shank (1975) has provided scripts. Scripts of events analyze the event into individual units of action; these typically occur in a predictable order. For example, the script for going to a restaurant contains script elements such as entering, going to a table, ordering, eating, and paying. Some recent research has provided evidence for the psychological reality of scripts and their elements (Bower, 1976).

Our present concern is with the role of concrete objects in events. What categories of objects are required to serve as props for events at the level of abstraction of those listed by the students? In general, we found that the event name itself combined most readily with superordinate noun categories; thus, one gets dressed with clothes and needs various kitchen utensils to make breakfast. When such activities were analyzed into their script elements, the basic level appeared as the level of abstraction of objects necessary to script the events; e.g., in getting dressed, one puts on pants, sweater, and shoes, and in making breakfast, one cooks eggs in a frying pan.

With respect to prototypes, it appears to be those category members judged the more prototypical that have attributes that enable them to fit into the typical and agreed upon script elements. We are presently collecting normative data on the intersection of common events, the objects associated with those events and the other sets of events associated with those objects.[2] In addition, object names for eliciting events are varied in level of abstraction and in known prototypicality in given categories. Initial results show a similar pattern to that obtained in the earlier research in which it was found that the more typical members of superordinate categories could replace the superordinate in sentence frames generated by subjects told to "make up a sentence" that used the superordinate (Rosch, 1977). That is, the task of using a given concrete noun in a sentence appears to be an indirect method of eliciting a statement about the events in which objects play a part; that indirect method showed clearly that prototypical category members are those that can play the role in events expected of members of that category.

The use of deviant forms of object names in narratives accounts for several recently explored effects in the psychological literature. Substituting object names at other than the basic level within scripts results in obviously deviant descriptions. Substitution of superordinates produces just those types of narrative that Bransford and Johnson (1973) have claimed are not comprehended; for example, "The procedure is actually quite simple. First you arrange things into different groups. Of course, one pile may be sufficient [p. 400]." It should be noted in the present context that what Bransford and Johnson call context cues are actually names of basic-level events (e.g., washing clothes) and that one function of hearing the event name is to enable the reader to translate the superordinate terms into basic-level objects and actions. Such a translation appears to be a necessary aspect of our ability to match linguistic descriptions to world knowledge in a way that produces the "click of comprehension."

On the other hand, substitution of subordinate terms for basic-level object names in scripts gives the effect of satire or snobbery. For example, a review (Garis, 1975) of a pretentious novel accused of actually being about nothing more than brand-name snobbery concludes, "And so, after putting away my 10-

---

[2]This work is being done by Elizabeth Kreusi.

year-old Royal 470 manual and lining up my Mongol number 3 pencils on my Goldsmith Brothers Formica imitation-wood desk, I slide into my oversize squirrel-skin L. L. Bean slippers and shuffle off to the kitchen. There, holding *Decades* in my trembling right hand, I drop it, *plunk,* into my new Sears 20-gallon, celadon-green Permanex trash can [p. 48] ."

Analysis of events is still in its initial stages. It is hoped that further understanding of the functions and attributes of objects can be derived from such an analysis.

SUMMARY

The first part of this chapter showed how the same principles of categorization could account for the taxonomic structure of a category system organized around a basic level and also for the formation of the categories that occur within this basic level. Thus the principles described accounted for both the vertical and horizontal structure of category systems. Four converging operations were employed to establish the claim that the basic level provides the cornerstone of a taxonomy. The section on prototypes distinguished the empirical evidence for prototypes as structural facts about categories from the possible role of prototypes in cognitive processing, representation, and learning. Then we considered assumptions about the nature of the attributes of real-world objects and assumptions about context — insofar as attributes and contexts underlie the claim that there is structure in the world. Finally, a highly tentative pilot study of attributes and functions of objects as props in culturally defined events was presented.

REFERENCES

Anglin, J. Les premiers termes de référence de l'enfant. In S. Ehrlich & E. Tulving (Eds.), *La memoire sémantique*. Paris: Bulletin de Psychologie, 1976.

Barker, R., & Wright, H. *Midwest and its children*. Evanston, Ill.: Row-Peterson, 1955.

Battig, W. F., & Montague, W. E. Category norms for verbal items in 56 categories: A replication and extension of the Connecticut category norms. *Journal of Experimental Psychology Monograph,* 1969, *80*(3, Pt. 2).

Beach, L. R. Cue probabilism and inference behavior. *Psychological Monographs.* 1964, *78*, (Whole No. 582). (a)

Beach, L. R. Recognition, assimilation, and identification of objects. *Psychological Monographs,* 1964, *78*(Whole No. 583). (b)

Berlin, B. Speculations on the growth of ethnobotanical nomenclature. *Language in Society,* 1972, *1,* 51–86.

Borges, J. L. *Other inquisitions 1937–1952.* New York: Washington Square Press, 1966.

Bower, G. *Comprehending and recalling stories.* Paper presented as Division 3 presidential address to the American Psychological Association, Washington, D.C., September 1976.

Bransford, J. D., & Johnson, M. K. Considerations of some problems of comprehension. In W. Chase (Ed.), *Visual information processing.* New York: Academic Press, 1973.

Bruner, J. S., Olver, R. R., & Greenfield, P. M. *Studies in cognitive growth.* New York: Wiley, 1966.

Garis, L. The Margaret Mead of Madison Avenue. *Ms.,* March 1975, pp. 47–48.

Garner, W. R. *The processing of information and structure.* New York: Wiley, 1974.

Kay, P. Taxonomy and semantic contrast. *Language,* 1971, *47,* 866–887.

Lakoff, G. Hedges: A study in meaning criteria and the logic of fuzzy concepts. *Papers from the eighth regional meeting, Chicago Linguistics Society.* Chicago: University of Chicago Linguistics Department, 1972.

Nelson, K. Concept, word and sentence: Interrelations in acquisition and development. *Psychological Review,* 1974, *81,* 267–285.

Neuman, P. G. An attribute frequency model for the abstraction of prototypes. *Memory and Cognition,* 1974, *2,* 241–248.

Newtson, D. Foundations of attribution: The perception of ongoing behavior. In J. Harvey, W. Ickes, & R. Kidd (Eds.), *New directions in attribution research.* Hillsdale, N.J.: Lawrence Erlbaum Associates, 1976.

Palmer, S. Hierarchical structure in perceputal representation. *Cognitive Psychology,* in press.

Peterson, M. J., & Graham, S. E. Visual detection and visual imagery. *Journal of Experimental Psychology,* 1974, *103,* 509–514.

Piaget, J. *The origins of intelligence in children.* New York: International Universities Press, 1952.

Posner, M. I., Goldsmith, R., & Welton, K. E. Perceived distance and the classification of distorted patterns. *Journal of Experimental Psychology,* 1967, *73,* 28–38.

Reed, S. K. Pattern recognition and categorization. *Cognitive Psychology,* 1972, *3,* 382–407.

Rips, L. J., Shoben, E. J., & Smith, E. E. Semantic distance and the verification of semantic relations. *Journal of Verbal Learning and Verbal Behavior,* 1973, *12,* 1–20.

Rosch, E. On the internal structure of perceptual and semantic categories. In T. E. Moore (Ed.), *Cognitive development and the acquisition of language.* New York: Academic Press, 1973.

Rosch, E. Linguistic relativity. In A. Silverstein (Ed.), *Human communication: Theoretical perspectives.* New York: Halsted Press, 1974.

Rosch, E. Cognitive reference points. *Cognitive Psychology,* 1975, *7,* 532–547. (a)

Rosch, E. Cognitive representations of semantic categories. *Journal of Experimental Psychology: General.,* 1975, *104,* 192–233. (b)

Rosch, E. The nature of mental codes for color categories. *Journal of Experimental Psychology: Human Perception and Performance,* 1975, *1,* 303–322. (c)

Rosch, E. Universals and cultural specifics in human categorization. In R. Brislin, S. Bochner, & W. Lonner (Eds.), *Cross-cultural perspectives on learning.* New York: Halsted Press, 1975. (d)

Rosch, E. Human categorization. In N. Warren (Ed.), *Advances in cross-cultural psychology* (Vol. 1). London: Academic Press, 1977.

Rosch, E., & Mervis, C. B. Family resemblances: Studies in the internal structure of categories. *Cognitive Psychology,* 1975, *7,* 573–605.

Rosch, E., Mervis, C. B., Gray, W. D., Johnson, D. M., & Boyes-Braem, P. Basic objects in natural categories. *Cognitive Psychology,* 1976, *8,* 382–439. (a)

Rosch, E., Simpson, C., & Miller, R. S. Structural bases of typicality effects. *Journal of Experimental Psychology: Human Perception and Performance.* 1976, *2,* 491–502. (b)

Shank, R. C. The structure of episodes in memory. In D. G. Bobrow & A. Collins (Eds.), *Representation and understanding: Studies in cognitive science.* New York: Academic Press, 1975.

Smith, E. E. Theories of semantic memory. In W. K. Estes (Ed.), *Handbook of learning and cognitive processes* (Vol. 5). Hillsdale, N.J.: Lawrence Erlbaum Associates, 1978.

Smith, E. E., & Balzano, G. J. Personal communication, April 1977.

Smith, E. E., Balzano, G. J., & Walker, J. H. Nominal, perceptual, and semantic codes in picture categorization. In J. Cotton & R. Klatzky (Eds.), *Semantic factors in cognition.* Hillsdale, N.J.: Lawrence Erlbaum Associates, 1978.

Tversky, S. Features of similarity. *Psychological Review,* 1977, *84,* 327–352.

Wittgenstein, L. *Philosophical investigations.* New York: Macmillan, 1953.

3

Linguistic Expression of Category Levels in a Visual-Gestural Language: A Flower Is a Flower Is a Flower

Elissa L. Newport
University of California, San Diego
Ursula Bellugi
The Salk Institute for Biological Studies

On the basis of several insightful studies of categorization, Eleanor Rosch (1976) has hypothesized that certain ways of categorizing concrete objects are cognitively efficient. Rosch, Mervis, Gray, Johnson, and Boyes-Braem (1976) have examined in detail the structure of nine taxonomies[1] of concrete objects. Subjects were asked to list attributes and motor programs and to identify averaged shapes of category members at each level of the taxonomies. On the basis of these converging measures, Rosch et al. have argued that categories at various levels of the taxonomy are organized in distinct ways. Across taxonomies, there is a *basic level* of categorization (e.g., chair) at which perceptual and functional attributes are shared by all or most members of the category but are different from those attributes of contrast categories (e.g., table). At the *subordinate level* (e.g., kitchen chair), attributes are likewise shared by all or most members of the category; but these attributes are also shared with members of contrast categories (e.g., living-room chair). At the *superordinate level* of categorization (e.g., furniture), few, if any, attributes are common to all members of the category. Instead, the superordinate categories are internally organized around a few prototypical members (e.g., chair, table), which alone share significant numbers of attributes with other members of the category. In short, the

---

[1]Rosch et al. (1976) define *taxonomy* as a

system by which categories are related to one another by means of class inclusion. ... Each category within a taxonomy is entirely included within one other category (unless it is the highest level category) but is not exhaustive of that more inclusive category. Thus the term *level of abstraction* within a taxonomy refers to a particular level of inclusiveness [p. 383].

basic level is the level at which attributes common to members within a category are distinct from attributes of other categories; it is thus claimed to be the level at which objects are most usefully and naturally categorized. Other levels of categorization either lack significant numbers of shared attributes within the category or lack significant numbers of distinctive attributes across categories.

In this chapter, we describe the devices used in American Sign Language (ASL) for representing these three levels of categorization. As we show, these levels are formally (syntactically) distinguished in ASL, supporting the view that the category levels studied by Rosch are psychologically salient; further, we show that Rosch's "basic" level is in fact the basic level of lexical representation in ASL.

A BRIEF INTRODUCTION TO AMERICAN SIGN LANGUAGE

American Sign Language is the language used by the community of deaf people in the United States for everyday conversation among themselves. It is a language in its own right, differing from other sign languages as well as from spoken languages. It is neither a borrowed system based on English nor a universally understood pantomime. Studies of historical change in ASL (Frishberg, 1975, 1976) reveal that, although many of its lexical items (signs) were derived originally from pantomimic attempts to represent visually something in experience, the current signs have become more arbitrary and formally constrained. In further detail, the general direction of historical change in ASL has included an increasing concentration of lexical content in the hands rather than in facial or bodily movement, and a concentration of the hand-movements in a limited, centered "signing space." The result of these changes in the form of signs is a suppression of their iconic[2] character, so that their meanings are only very rarely derivable by nonsigners out of context (Bellugi & Klima, 1976). Further, at least for deaf offspring of deaf parents who have learned ASL as a primary language, the signs are encoded and stored not in terms of iconic properties but rather in terms of a sublexical level of simultaneous formational parameters: Hand Configuration (shape of the hand in making the sign), Place of Articulation (location of the hand in making the sign), and Movement (movement of the hand in making the sign).[3]

---

[2]"Iconic" here is not used in the sense of "iconic" storage; rather, the term refers to symbols that are representational.

[3]In studies of short-term memory errors (Bellugi & Siple, 1974; Bellugi, Klima, & Siple, 1975) and "slips of the hand" (Newkirk & Pedersen, 1976), errors in memory and production of individual signs are frequently substitutions of one or more configurational parameters. Thus, for example, the sign BIRD, which (insofar as it seems iconic) appears to represent the opening beak of a bird, is misrememberd or misproduced not as, e.g., WING (which is an iconic associate), but as NEWSPAPER, a sign that shares Hand Configuration and Movement with BIRD and differs from it only in Location (that is, a formational associate).

Despite this general diminution of iconicity in ASL, in signs for concrete objects[4] there is often some post hoc discernable relationship between the form of the sign and the object to which it refers; although, as we stated above, non-signers cannot guess its meaning in the absence of further information, the informed signer can often state some nonarbitrary relationship between form and referent. For example, given the sign CAR[5] (see Fig. 3.1), signers note that it represents the movement of the driver's hands on a steering wheel. In view of this "sometimes" relationship between sign and referent, and Rosch et al.'s claims about the conceptual structure of categories of concrete objects, study of the form of signs in ASL for concrete objects at various taxonomic levels seemed particularly promising.

SIGNS FOR SUPERORDINATE-, BASIC-, AND SUBORDINATE-LEVEL CATEGORIES

ASL has developed side-by-side with spoken English, and it is used in the same geographic communities with common cultural settings. It therefore affords a unique basis for comparison between two languages, in terms of the way in which categories of objects are coded, uncontaminated by vast differences in artifacts, social values, and the like. At least with respect to simple basic objects such as those in the categories of furniture, tools, fruit, and vehicles, the culture in America is the same for hearing and deaf people; it is their languages that differ.

An experiment by Rosch and Boyes-Braem (Rosch et al., 1976) first sparked our interest in investigating the linguistic means in ASL for expressing various levels of taxonomies for concrete objects. Their informants were three deaf individuals whose native language was ASL and one hearing linguist fluent in ASL. They used as stimuli exemplars from the nine taxonomies that Rosch et al. (1976) have studied extensively (see Table 3.1). Informants were asked about the existence of signs for items at each of the three levels of abstraction — super-

---

[4]The vocabulary of American Sign Language is not concentrated on signs for concrete objects. There are common primary signs at all levels of abstraction; for example, signs for IDEA, THOUGHT, REASON, GOVERNMENT, SCIENCE, GOD, RESPONSIBILITY, FAITH, EXAMINATION, RULE, MATHEMATICS, WAR, CATEGORY, CHARACTER, LIFE, and INSTITUTION.

[5]On notational conventions: The English translation-equivalents of ASL signs are represented here in capital letters, as in IDEA. (Naturally the form of the ASL sign need have no relation to the form of the English word.) If more than one English word is required to translate a single sign, we hyphenate the two words (e.g., LOOK-AT). If two or more consecutive signs form a compound sign in ASL, we connect them with a symbol: ⌢. In this chapter, we are referring to signs with special status in the language and even to nonsigns. We represent special bound signs which we call size-and-shape specifiers with capital letters enclosed in quotation marks (e.g., "PIPE-SHAPED"). Finally, we represent mimetic descriptions using lower-case type enclosed in quotation marks (e.g., "piano-top shaped").

ordinates (e.g., vehicle); basic-level objects (e.g., car, bus, truck); and subordinates (e.g., sports car, four-door sedan). Rosch and Boyes-Braem hypothesized that basic-level categories are the most necessary in a language. Further, they claimed that ASL has fewer fixed signs for concrete objects than does English. In such situations, where the lexicon is limited, it should be basic-level categories that will be coded and names for superordinate and/or subordinate categories that may be lacking. As they predicted, basic-level terms in ASL were almost as many as in English, although there were significantly fewer superordinate and subordinate terms.

Rosch and Boyes-Braem claimed that English has designations for superordinate and subordinate levels that ASL does not. We have reexamined the taxonomies studied by Rosch, concentrating on the nonbiological taxonomies of Table 3.1. As we will show, there *are* regular designations for superordinate and subordinate as well as basic-level categories in ASL. In fact, in accord with Rosch's notions of categorization, the forms for signs at these three levels are consistent and linguistically distinct across taxonomies.[6] Our results confirm Rosch and Boyes-Braem's finding that simple lexical items tend to cohere at the basic level of categorization. This finding does not, however, mean that superordinate and subordinate terms are absent from the language. As in other natural languages (including English), where simple lexemes (signs) are lacking, ASL instead supplies syntactic means: rule-governed arrangements of signs. Whereas terms at the basic level are elemental single-unit forms, terms at the superordinate level are primarily coordinate compounds of basic-level signs; and terms at the subordinate level are primarily conjuncts of single signs and visual descriptive devices. These formal properties of the terms for the three category levels suggest that superordinate and subordinate signs are usually derived from signs at the basic level: They contain basic-level signs as their components. In short, Rosch's basic level is formally basic in American Sign Language. Let us begin by considering signs for basic-level categories.

Signs for Basic-Level Categories

The basic level is the level of categorization at which perceptual and functional attributes are said to be held in common by members of the category but not by members of contrast categories. In fact, the basic level is the level at which simple lexicalization occurs in ASL. There are common single-lexeme signs for most of the items in the list of basic-level objects in Table 3.1: GUITAR, PIANO, DRUM, APPLE, PEACH, GRAPES, HAMMER, SAW SCREWDRIVER,

---

[6]In this investigation we have confined ourselves to the taxonomies studied by Rosch et al. Outside of these taxonomies, in the absence of further experimentation, ascertaining the basic level (by intuition) is sometimes problematic. Insofar as we have examined signs outside of these taxonomies, the same general patterns (simple lexemes at the basic level, particular kinds of compounds at the superordinate and subordinate levels), although not absolute, tend to predominate.

TABLE 3.1
The Six Nonbiological Taxonomies Used as Stimuli[a]

Superordinate	Basic Level	Subordinates	
Musical	Guitar	Folk guitar	Classical guitar
instrument	Piano	Grand piano	Upright piano
	Drum	Kettle drum	Bass drum
Fruit	Apple	Delicious apple	Mackintosh apple
	Peach	Freestone peach	Cling peach
	Grapes	Concord grapes	Green seedless grapes
Tool	Hammer	Ball-peen hammer	Claw hammer
	Saw	Hacksaw	Cross-cutting hand saw
	Screwdriver	Phillips screwdriver	Regular screwdriver
Clothing	Pants	Levis	Double-knit pants
	Socks	Knee socks	Ankle socks
	Shirt	Dress shirt	Knit shirt
Furniture	Table	Kitchen table	Dining-room table
	Lamp	Floor lamp	Desk lamp
	Chair	Kitchen chair	Living-room chair
Vehicle	Car	Sports car	Four-door sedan
	Bus	City bus	Cross-country bus
	Truck	Pickup truck	Tractor-trailer truck

[a]Adapted from Rosch et al. (1976).

PANTS, SOCKS, TABLE, LAMP, CHAIR, CAR, and TRUCK. (See Fig. 3.1 for examples of basic-level signs.)

What are the properties of these signs and of single-unit signs in general? We have already indicated the basic organization of signs in terms of three major formational parameters: (1) a unique Hand Configuration at (2) a unique Place of Articulation, with (3) a unique Movement. Changing any one of these major simultaneous parameters can produce a different sign: the signs HOME and YESTERDAY differ only in Hand Configuration; the signs HOME and FLOWER differ only in the Place of Articulation; and the signs HOME and PEACH differ only in Movement.

For some signs, even signs for concrete objects, these sublexical formational parameters may be the only organization; the meanings of such signs are related arbitrarily to their forms. The forms of the signs APPLE and SOCKS, for example, seem unrelated to their meanings (see Fig. 3.2). But for many signs for concrete objects, *global* aspects of form are visually related to meaning. (For further discussion of the dual aspect of signs — iconic and at the same time abstract — see Bellugi and Klima, 1976.)

In particular, signs at the basic level, when looked at globally, often represent one of the shared distinctive attributes of the category members, one that is maximally characteristic of members of the category and uncharacteristic of members of other categories. For example, the sign PIANO represents the hand and finger movements made on a piano, while the sign GUITAR represents those made on a guitar. One could presumably not represent "piano" by showing that it makes sounds (e.g., by pointing to the ear), because such a sign would not distinctively represent "piano" in contrast to "guitar." When asked to invent a new sign for piano, our informants considered a point to the ear a "bad" sign for piano. Likewise, a sign that represents sitting in a bouncy, moving seat is a "bad" sign for airplane, because it does not distinguish "airplane" from "train" or "car."

Other basic-level signs in Table 3.1 that are considered iconic signs include: DRUM, tapping with drumsticks; GRAPES, cluster of grapes; HAMMER, motion of hammering a nail; SAW, sawing motion; SCREWDRIVER, movement of driving a screw; PANTS, indication of pant legs; SHIRT, outlining part of body covered; TABLE, horizontal surface; LAMP, radiation of light; and CHAIR, sitting motion.

In sum, signs at the basic level of categorization are, appropriately, single-lexeme signs that often represent a characteristic perceptual or functional attribute of the category members. In contrast, at the superordinate level of categorization, category members are claimed not to share significant numbers of attributes. What is the form of signs for superordinate categories?

FIG. 3.1. Basic-level signs in American Sign Language.

CAR   PLANE   TRAIN

CLARINET   PIANO   GUITAR

APPLE   SOCKS

FIG. 3.2. The basic-level signs APPLE and SOCKS, which are not highly iconic.

Signs for Superordinate Categories

There are few commonly accepted single signs in ASL for the superordinate categories of Table 3.1.[7] For example, although some signers have a sign FUR-NITURE, its use is not widespread. There is a sign DRESS, which can be used as a superordinate term for clothing. For the other taxonomies of Table 3.1, there are no single superordinate lexical terms in common use. Our informants indicated that they can, if necessary, borrow from English to fingerspell these terms; but, in general, there seems to be a lexical gap in ASL for superordinate categories of concrete objects. There are, however, productive syntactic means by which superordinates can be created in ASL: Superordinates can be formed by compounding basic-level signs. We digress now to describe the general process of compounding in ASL; we then describe the special means by which superordinate compounds are formed.

Compound Constructions in American Sign Language. In a study of compounding in ASL (Bellugi & Klima, in press), we describe the process of forming compound signs with particular reference to compounds that are well-established lexicalized units. The lexicalized comounds are composed of fixed signs in a fixed order. In addition, these lexicalized compounds conform to the general characterizations of compound signs: The components are independent lexical items within the language;[8] the compounds function as single lexical units in sentences of ASL; and the compounds have specialized meaning. For ex-

---

[7]There are, of course, single signs for some superordinate categories in ASL (e.g., FAM-ILY, SWEETS, ANIMAL, COUNTRY, NATIONALITY, GAME).

[8]Note, however, that there are some special compounds whose components are bound forms (e.g., the size-and-shape specifiers referred to in our discussion of subordinate categories).

ample, the signs BLUE and SPOT in a noun-phrase mean "a spot that is colored blue." As a compound, the composite BLUE⁀SPOT means "a bruise." (See Fig. 3.3.)

In English, compound words are differentiated from syntactic phrases by a difference in stress: A compound has primary stress on its first element, and a phrase has primary stress on its last element. The compound *lady* killers ("men with the reputation of fascinating women") is thus differentiated from the phrase lady *killers* ("killers who are female") (Bloomfield, 1933; Gleitman & Gleitman, 1970; Jespersen, 1961; and Lees, 1960).

The distinguishing characteristic of compounds in ASL, contrasted with the same signs in a syntactic phrase, is also rhythmic. However, in ASL the first element of a compound has *reduction* in movement and duration; i.e., it is temporally compressed. Thus the phrase BLUE SPOT is differentiated from the compound BLUE⁀SPOT by the radical compression of the first sign element. In the phrase, the sign BLUE has a repeated twisting movement of the wrist; in the compound BLUE⁀SPOT the same sign has lost the twisting movement and is made with a single brief half-turn only.

The characteristic temporal property of compounds underscores the independence of English and ASL. Although there are general processes of compound formation in both languages, the compounds that occur in the two

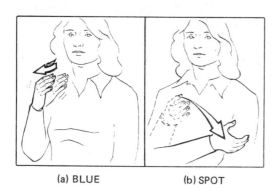

(a) BLUE   (b) SPOT

(c) BLUE⁀SPOT

FIG. 3.3. The signs BLUE and SPOT [(a) and (b)] and the compound BLUE⁀SPOT (c) meaning a bruise.

languages differ, and the distinguishing characteristics of compounds differ: heavy stress on the first element in English and reduction of the first element in ASL.

One type of compound that occurs rarely in English[9] is rather more common in ASL: copulative or coordinate compounds. For example:

Component Signs	Meaning in English
MOTHER⌢FATHER	Parents
COOK⌢BAKE	Oven
KNIFE⌢FORK	Silverware
SIGN⌢SPELL	Total communication
BROTHER⌢SISTER	Siblings

To sign "parents," one uses the compound sign MOTHER⌢FATHER. This indicates the class of all parents, not just one's own. Compounds that are more clearly superordinate terms are KNIFE⌢FORK ("silverware") and SIGN⌢SPELL ("total communication" or communicating by signing, spelling, speaking, lip-reading, etc.), because here the component signs do not enumerate all possible members of the class (i.e., mothers and fathers exhaust the class of parents, but knives and forks do not exhaust the class of all silverware). These compounds are lexicalized forms (as is "silverware" in English); that is, the two component signs are fixed and occur in a fixed order.

In addition to such lexicalized coordinate compounds in ASL, there is a productive process by which an indefinitely large class of compounds can be *created*.[10] Further, this productive process of coordinate compounding is apparently the means by which terms for superordinates (tool, fruit, etc.) are created.

Coordinate Compounds as Signs for Superordinate Categories.   The coordinate compounds just described are representative of an indefinitely large class of compounds that can be formed of lower-level signs and used to express superordinate concepts. For this purpose, basic-level signs are strung together — two, three, or four of them — followed optionally by a sign glossed as ETC. Thus the sequence APPLE⌢ORANGE⌢BANANA ETC. means "fruit." The sequence BEANS⌢CARROTS⌢CORN ETC. means "vegetable." RING⌢BRACELET⌢ NECKLACE ETC. means "jewelry," and so forth. Table 3.2 lists additional examples.

---

[9]But see Cooper and Ross (1975), who present an analysis of coordinates ("freezes") very common in English: "horse and buggy," "now and then," "meat and vegetables." Although freezes bear some formal resemblance to coordinate compounds in ASL (e.g., fixed component order), they are not used in English with superordinate meaning.

[10]Our research has uncovered other syntactically based processes of compounding in ASL as well (Newport & Bellugi, in preparation).

TABLE 3.2
Superordinate Terms in ASL

Component Signs of Coordinate Compound	Meaning of Superordinate in English
Superordinates from Table 3.1	
CLARINET⁀PIANO⁀GUITAR ETC.	Musical instrument
APPLE⁀ORANGE⁀BANANA ETC.	Fruit
HAMMER⁀SAW⁀SCREWDRIVER ETC.	Tool
DRESS⁀BLOUSE⁀PANTS ETC.	Clothing[a]
CHAIR⁀TABLE⁀LAMP ETC.	Furniture[a]
CAR⁀PLANE⁀TRAIN ETC.	Transportation vehicle
Other Superordinate Terms Created by Coordinate Compounding	
KILL⁀STAB⁀RAPE ETC.	Crime
BEANS⁀CARROTS⁀PEAS ETC.	Vegetable
CAT⁀DOG⁀BIRD ETC.	Pet[a]
BEATER⁀CAN-OPENER⁀BOTTLE-OPENER ETC.	Kitchen utensil
RING⁀BRACELET⁀NECKLACE ETC.	Jewelry
LAWNMOVER⁀RAKE⁀SHOVEL ETC.	Garden tool
PANTIES⁀BRA⁀SLIP ETC.	Lingerie
CHICKEN⁀DUCK⁀TURKEY ETC.	Fowl
GUN⁀KNIFE⁀BOMB ETC.	Weapon
MOTHER⁀FATHER⁀BROTHER⁀SISTER ETC.	Family[a]
COW⁀CHICKEN⁀PIG ETC.	Farm animal
SWEATER⁀COAT⁀VEST ETC.	Outer clothing
FOOTBALL⁀BASKETBALL⁀TRACK ETC.	Sport[a]
CANDY⁀ICE-CREAM⁀CHOCOLATE ETC.	Sweets[a]
ARMY⁀NAVY⁀AIRFORCE ETC.	Military service
CAR⁀MOTORCYCLE⁀BICYCLE ETC.	Vehicle

[a]For these categories there are single-unit signs as well as coordinate compounds.

Unlike the lexicalized coordinate compounds, the superordinate compounds do not have fixed sign order, nor are the particular signs chosen for coordination necessarily the same each time the superordinate meaning is expressed. However, ASL superordinates are not merely ad hoc listings of basic-level terms, because their formation is regular and limited in a number of ways: (1) they have special rhythmic properties; (2) they have a special superordinate class meaning, not the composite meaning of the list members; (3) their components are selected "best examples" or prototypes for a superordinate category; and (4) they are subject to a preferred limit on length and particular ordering of elements. We describe these characteristics in detail in the following:

1. *Rhythmic properties of coordinate compounds.* Each sign in a super-ordinate compound is rendered in a physically reduced form: The *movement*

of each sign is reduced, pauses between signs are minimal or eliminated, and the transitions between signs are minimal. The temporal compression in superordinate compounds differs from the compression in ordinary compounds, such as BLUE⁀SPOT, where it is primarily the *first* sign that is reduced in time. In making the superordinate compounds, there is an equal and dramatic reduction in the movement of *each* of the component signs.

Two such superordinate compounds are represented in the illustrations in Fig. 3.4. We first show the full citation form of the component signs as they would be made in a list (e.g., the signs CAR, PLANE, and TRAIN). Below each group is a representation of the temporally compressed superordinate term made up of these signs (e.g., in this case, "vehicle," or, more specifically, "transportation vehicle"). Note that in the superordinate term, the handshapes, locations, and types of movements for each component remain the same, but the movement of each is reduced in two ways: in *extent* and *number of repetitions*. For example, the full form of the sign CAR is made with the hands alternating up and down several times. As a member of a superordinate term, the movement of the sign CAR is much smaller, and the number of repetitions is greatly reduced; but the direction of movement and its alternating aspect are retained. The temporal compression is shown by the time line which appears underneath each picture.[11] For example, CAR signed as part of a list was 49 fields. As part of a superordinate term, the same sign CAR was only 8 fields. (There is also a reduction in the transitions between signs, which is not represented here.) It is as though the sequence is being squeezed temporally into a single lexical-item duration, just as it is conceptually a single (superordinate) term, a claim to which we now turn.

2. *The meaning of the coordinate compound.* How do we know that coordinate compounds refer to a *superordinate* category and not just to a list of items? The first line of evidence comes from the intuitions of deaf signers about their use and their appropriate translations into English. For example:

(a) DOCTOR SAY-NO-ME EAT CARROTS⁀BEANS⁀PEAS ETC., THAT.
"The doctor forbade me to eat vegetables."
(b) MY WEAKNESS RING⁀BRACELET⁀NECKLACE ETC., FOR-SURE BUY.
"I have a weakness for jewelry; I buy it all the time."
(c) KEN EXPERT ANY FOOTBALL⁀BASKETBALL⁀TRACK ETC. REGULAR BORN.
"Ken is expert at any sport; he's a born sportsman."

As further evidence, consider how odd the following (sensible) ASL sentence would be if the compound were interpreted as a mere list (p. 62):

---

[11]There are 60 fields, or images, for each second of videotape. Each time line represents an average of four performances.

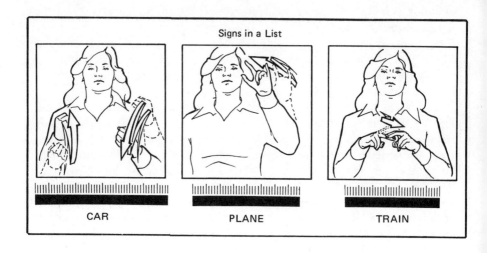

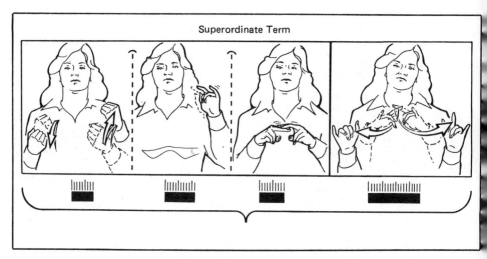

(a) CAR‾PLANE‾TRAIN ETC. meaning "vehicle"

Legend: ||||| = 5 fields or .083 seconds.

FIG. 3.4. Superordinate terms in ASL: coordinate compounds of basic level signs. (a) CAR‾ PLANE‾TRAIN, ETC. meaning "vehicle." (b) *opposite page:* CLARINET‾PIANO‾GUITAR ETC. meaning "musical instrument." Top rows depict individual signs as they would appear in a list; bottom rows depict the compression of movements when the same signs appear in a coordinate compound. Time lines indicate the temporal reduction in compounds.

(continued)

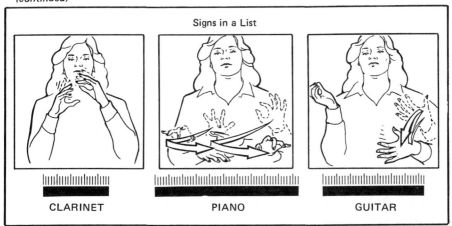

Signs in a List

CLARINET   PIANO   GUITAR

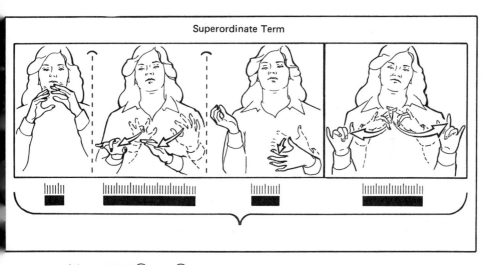

Superordinate Term

(b) CLARINET PIANO GUITAR ETC. meaning "musical instrument"

(d) ME BUY NEW HAMMER⁀SCREWDRIVER⁀WRENCH ETC., BUT NO
SCREWDRIVER.
"I bought a new set of tools, but no screwdriver."

Here, HAMMER⁀SCREWDRIVER⁀WRENCH ETC. clearly refers to tools
and not to the individual items listed. On a list interpretation, the sentence
would be bizarre: "I bought a new hammer, screwdriver, and wrench, etc., but
no screwdriver." Further examples we have elicited include:

(e) HOUSE FIRE, LOSE ALL CHAIR⁀TABLE⁀BED ETC., BUT ONE
LEFT, BED.
"I lost all my furniture in the house fire, but one thing was left: the bed."
(f) MY WEAKNESS RING⁀BRACELET⁀NECKLACE ETC., BUT DISLIKE
BRACELET.
"I have a weakness for jewelry, but I dislike bracelets."
(g) TODAY ME NEED CAR⁀PLANE⁀TRAIN ETC. GO L.A., BUT AFRAID,
DON'T-WANT PLANE.
"I need transportation to L.A. today, but I'm afraid of riding in planes."
(h) SUPPOSE CAN BUY ANY DRUM⁀FLUTE⁀VIOLIN ETC., BEST PIANO.
"If you could buy any musical instrument, the best would be a piano."

Such examples provide supporting evidence for these coordinate compounds
as superordinate terms.

3. *The restriction to "best instances" of a category.* It seems that there are
"best" instances of basic-level items that fit and are judged appropriate in creating
a superordinate compound. Not just any member of a superordinate category
can form part of the compound. For example, in the category "clothing," there
are the following primary signs in ASL: DRESS, SKIRT, PANTS, BLOUSE,
SWEATER, COAT, JACKET, HAT, CAP, BRA, PANTIES, SHORTS, SLIP,
SOCKS, SCARF, RIBBON, SHOES, EAR-MUFFS, PURSE, GLOVES, PAJA-
MAS, SLIPPERS, UMBRELLA, HANDKERCHIEF, STOCKINGS, and BATH-
ING SUIT. Yet deaf informants will not accept most of these as components of
a superordinate term meaning "clothing." In fact, our informant would allow only
DRESS, SKIRT, PANTS, and BLOUSE among all the apparent possibilities. The
informant's intuition was that only a limited number of "best instances" would
function as components of the superordinate "clothing." As further examples,
the items that were acceptable for "fruit" were APPLE, ORANGE, BANANA,
GRAPE, PEACH, and PEAR. For "tool" they were HAMMER, SAW, DRILL,
SCREWDRIVER, PLIERS, and WRENCH; for "musical instrument" they were
PIANO, FLUTE, GUITAR, VIOLIN, and DRUM; for "furniture" they were
CHAIR, TABLE, BED, LAMP, and DRESSER; and for "vehicle" they were
CAR, TRAIN, PLANE, MOTORCYCLE, BICYCLE, TRUCK, and BUS.

Most importantly, for each of these superordinate categories there were many
signs that would *not* be used to form a superordinate compound, evidently
because they were not considered as among the best examples of that category.

For instance, for the category "fruit," the signs LEMON, PINEAPPLE, or MELON would not be included; for the category "musical instruments," HARP, ACCORDION, or HARMONICA would not be included.

4. *Ordering of items within a coordinate compound.* Although there is no fixed order of elements within the coordinate compounds, there are preferred orders. It seems that the preference primarily has to do with how easily the signs join to one another in terms of transitional movements. Recall the temporal properties of compounds. The elements of a compound are so compressed in time that the resultant compound is signed almost as fast as a single-unit sign. To accomplish this, each component sign is greatly reduced in movement, and transitional movements between the components are minimized as well. The preferred order for the compound is the one that allows maximum compression at the sign junctures (i.e., that requires minimal transitional movement.

Consider, as an example, the signs that make up the superordinate "jewelry." Rendering this as RING⌒NECKLACE⌒BRACELET⌒EARRINGS ETC. would require the hand to move from finger to throat to wrist to ears, and this ordering is unacceptable to our informants. Either of the two orders — RING⌒BRACELET⌒NECKLACE⌒EARRINGS ETC. or EARRINGS⌒NECKLACE⌒BRACELET⌒RING ETC. — was acceptable, because both minimized the transitions (one moves up the body from hand to ear, the other moves downward from ear to hand). Thus the requirement of rapid, compressed movement leads to some order preferences. The same requirement for speed also leads to item length preferences in superordinate terms. Our informants preferred a limit of three signs, but occasionally — with highly practiced coordinate compounds — allowed four.

In sum, a few coordinate compounds referring to superordinate terms seem to have become a part of the commonly accepted vocabulary of ASL. The compound KNIFE⌒FORK refers to silverware; this is a commonly accepted compound, a lexicalized form like the compound "silver-ware" in English. When a compound like this is commonly accepted and used regularly, it takes on the ordinary characteristics of compounds in ASL: Two signs are sufficient, and they occur in a fixed order. Other superordinate terms — for which there are no commonly accepted signs or compounds — can be created by this special syntactic device: Select three to four signs that are best instances of a superordinate category, order them in the way(s) that yield maximum temporal compression, and optionally add the sign ETC.

Thus, at the superordinate level, as at the basic level, the form of signs in ASL is appropriate for the category structure of concrete objects. Unlike basic-level categories, superordinate categories are claimed to lack significant numbers of attributes shared by all members of the category. Instead, superordinate categories are structured around a few prototypical members. Appropriately, signs at this level can be formed by conjoining basic-level signs for three or four prototypical members.

Signs for Subordinate Categories

We have shown that many basic-level objects have regular single-item signs in American Sign Language and that there is a particular linguistic device (coordinate compounding) for creating superordinate terms from these. We now turn to the level of subordinate categories, where ASL again uses syntactic means, rather than primary lexemes, for providing category names.

We describe three ASL devices for forming subordinates: conventional non-coordinate compounds (as in English and many other spoken languages), compounds of basic signs with size-and-shape specifiers (similar in function to inflectional processes in a spoken language like Navajo), and conjuncts of basic signs with mimetic shape elaboration (the latter is perhaps unique to sign languages). Rosch et al. claim that, at the subordinate level, category members share most attributes not only with each other but also with members of contrast categories. Only a few attributes are shared only by members of a single subordinate category. Appropriately, then, subordinates in ASL are often represented either by a relatively *detailed* specification of the subordinate's distinctive shape or by a specification of *both* size and shape; in conjunction with the sign for the relevant basic-level category, such size and/or shape depictions refer uniquely to the subordinate.

Conventional Compounds. A glance at Table 3.1 reveals that in English, subordinates in the taxonomies we are considering do not have simple lexical names. In fact, the single exception is "Levis"; the other terms are for the most part expressed by compound words. The same is true of ASL. For example:

PURPLE⁀GRAPES	(Concord grapes)
GREEN⁀APPLE	(pippin apple)
COOK⁀CHAIR	(kitchen chair)
FOOD⁀CHAIR	(dining-room chair)
COOK⁀TABLE	(kitchen table)
FOOD⁀TABLE	(dining-room table)
FORMAL⁀PANTS	(dress pants)
STRETCH⁀PANTS	(double-knit pants)
SLEEP⁀SHOES	(slippers)
EVERYDAY⁀CAR	(second car)
SCHOOL⁀TRUCK	(school bus)

These compounds have the rhythmic pattern typical for noncoordinate compounds in ASL.

Compounds of Basic Signs with Size-and-Shape Specifiers. A second class of compounds expressing subordinate terms is linguistically quite different. Here, one element of the compound is a primary ASL sign; but the other is a "size-

and-shape specifier" (SASS). A few SASSes are illustrated in Fig. 3.5. Figure 3.5(a), for example, shows a SASS referring to a relatively flat rectangular shape. This SASS, which we will gloss as "RETANGULAR," enters into such compounds as:

Component Signs	English Gloss
RED⌒"RECTANGULAR"	Brick
GLASS⌒"RECTANGULAR"	Tile
LETTER⌒"RECTANGULAR"	Envelope, or post card
PICTURE⌒"RECTANGULAR"	Photograph
STAMP⌒"RECTANGULAR"	Book of stamps
SIGNATURE⌒"RECTANGULAR"	Credit card
WIRE⌒"RECTANGULAR"	Telegram
PAPER⌒"RECTANGULAR"	Small pad

There are size limitations on the SASS "RECTANGULAR": If the object is as small as a postage stamp, another specifier sign would be used; and if it is as large as a normal sheet of typing paper, still a different specifier sign would be used. But note that once a SASS is chosen for a particular referent, the size and shape of the SASS does not change depending on the particular details of the form of the objects that it specifies. Although a brick, a post card, a telegram, a credit card, an envelope, and a book of stamps differ among themselves in size and shape, all are roughly rectangular. They are expressed with the same SASS in construction with a differentiating basic-level sign regardless of further differences in spatial details.

As another illustration, consider the SASS "DOTS", which is used in compounds that refer to *small objects,* including circles, spheres, cubes, slices, etc., even little rectangles. It is used, for instance, for the following: small cookies, pennies, watermelon seeds, pepperoni slices, chopped nuts, croutons, plums, grapes, peas, meat chunks, cheese twists, and bite-sized shredded wheat. [The original shredded wheat size, a two-inch rectangle, would require the rectangular SASS shown in Fig. 3.5(a) instead.] Although these objects differ in shape or size, the standard SASS shown in Fig. 3.5(e) refers to any of them.

Individual SASSes do vary in shape but not as a consequence of differences in the shapes of objects in the real world: They are deformed when they undergo morphological processes like pluralization. For example, to pluralize the sign for brick ("many bricks"), the SASS shown in Fig. 3.5(a) would be repeated several times in different places in the signing space, as in Fig. 3.5(f). Under the pressure of multiple repetitions and their temporal constraints, the SASS shown in Fig. 3.5(a) loses its rectangular appearance; despite the loss of straight lines in the movement of the sign, it still refers to rectangular dimensions.

Several SASSes occur as components of the sign sequences used for the subordinate terms in Table 3.1; we describe only one of these. Consider the sign for "upright piano" (a subordinate of "piano"). In ASL, "upright piano" is a com-

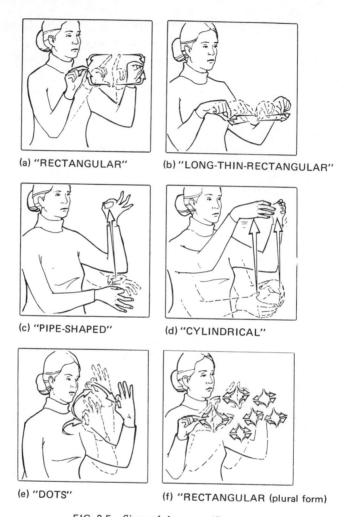

(a) "RECTANGULAR"   (b) "LONG-THIN-RECTANGULAR"

(c) "PIPE-SHAPED"   (d) "CYLINDRICAL"

(e) "DOTS"   (f) "RECTANGULAR (plural form)

FIG. 3.5.   Size-and-shape specifiers.

pound consisting of the basic sign PIANO, followed by two SASSes indicating the shape of the top and sides of the piano [see Fig. 3.6(a)]. In the first of these, the two hands in a "C" shape begin in contact and move apart, palms facing downward. The same SASS occurs as a bound element following the sign CHAIR to indicate long chairs, e.g., "park bench" [see Fig. 3.6(b)].

This same SASS occurs with a number of other signs as a bound element. When it follows the sign TABLE, the compound refers to a relatively long table, like a coffee table; when it follows the sign BREAD, it refers to a loaf of bread; when it follows the sign SEWING and precedes the sign CARRY, the compound refers to a case for a portable sewing machine, and so forth. Again, the SASS is

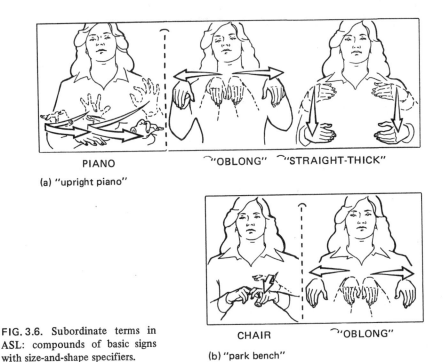

PIANO

(a) "upright piano"

⌒"OBLONG"   ⌒"STRAIGHT-THICK"

CHAIR   ⌒"OBLONG"

FIG. 3.6. Subordinate terms in ASL: compounds of basic signs with size-and-shape specifiers.

(b) "park bench"

a conventionalized gesture used as a bound part of compounds to refer to a generally elongated shape. It does not describe the precise dimensions of that shape but, rather, stands for a general class of shapes.

Conjuncts of Basic Signs with Mimetic Description.   There is a third class of subordinate terms in ASL that are quite special and that may prove to be one of the hallmarks of this language in a different mode. We comment on them rather tentatively here, because our investigation of this class is not yet complete. There are ways of signing subordinate terms even when no conventionalized signs and no appropriate SASSes exist. In such cases, signers produce expressions consisting of a basic-level sign followed by a *mimetic depiction,* which follows fairly carefully the shape of the particular subordinate.[12] It is important to note

---

[12]In ASL there are several kinds of processes that may be called "mimetic depiction" lying somewhere between conventionalized signs and pure pantomime. The discussion here focuses only on mimetic *shape* depictions, which appear quite commonly in representations of concrete objects. There are, however, mimetic depictions of *action* (e.g., water shooting out of a faucet) or *perceptual phenomena* (e.g., the stroboscopic effect of trees passing as one drives down a road), which do not arise in the discussion of signs for concrete objects. For an attempt to sort out these various kinds of depiction and their formal regularities, see Newport and Supalla (in preparation).

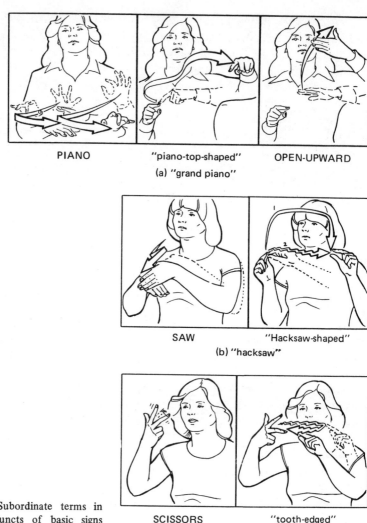

PIANO   "piano-top-shaped"   OPEN-UPWARD

(a) "grand piano"

SAW   "Hacksaw-shaped"

(b) "hacksaw"

FIG. 3.7. Subordinate terms in
ASL: conjuncts of basic signs
with mimetic description.

SCISSORS   "tooth-edged"

(c) "pinking shears"

the distinction between these mimetic shape depictions and the foregoing SASSes:
While SASSes are conventional and standardized across signers, the mimetic
shape depictions are not. Although there may be some conventional aspects
to these depictions (i.e., there seem to be certain handshapes used for surfaces
and other handshapes used for edges; see Coulter, 1975), the depictions as a
whole differ considerably from one signer to another, depending on the aspect
of the referent he or she chooses to represent. Signers often follow mimetic
depictions with the sign YOU-KNOW (i.e., "you know what I mean"), as though
checking to be sure the listener has understood the nonstandardized form.

Consider as an example the way of signing "grand piano"; there is no generally accepted sign or compound "grand piano" and no appropriate SASS that could be called into service. Our informants signed PIANO, then invented a kind of pictorial description of the outer perimeter of a grand piano, and finally followed that by a conventializied sign for "open upward" [see Fig. 3.7(a)] .

Each signer indicated the outer shape of a grand piano, using either a flat hand for the side surface or an index finger for the top edge, and mirroring as well as they could the precise bean-like shape of its top. (Note that there is likewise no word in English for this shape. We use "bean-like" advisedly.)

Figure 3.7 gives two further examples. "Hacksaw" was made by signing SAW, then depicting the outline of a hacksaw with the index finger. "Pinking shears" was made by signing SCISSORS, then depicting the saw-tooth edge. Other items from Table 3.1 that were produced with at least one part mimetic depiction were: "Phillips screwdriver," "floor lamp," "pickup truck," and "tractor-trailer truck."

Although depiction is not standardized within ASL, it is a common way of dealing with lexical gaps. One simply acts out some spatial delineation. While similar gestural depiction may occur during the process of oral speech, it seems to us that it plays a special role in sign language. The novel gestures are more tightly incorporated into the discourse (the "sign stream"): The mimetic depiction often takes the place of a lexical item in a sentence and thus itself obeys the sign-order constraints of the language. In contrast, a gesture accompanying spoken discourse is external to the sound-stream; i.e., it has no fixed appearance in terms of word-order and cannot grammatically replace a word: Instead, in English one uses a noun place-holder (e.g., "Whatchamacallit") while gesturing in the air.

This aspect of ASL is obviously closely related to gestural description or pantomime. It occurs rather freely in ASL as a way of indicating subordinate-level objects (and other objects as well) for which there are no commonly accepted signs. Reiterating, mimetic depiction is rather like drawing the shape of an object in the air and is quite different from regular signs.

SUMMARY

We have presented a brief analysis of the linguistic means in ASL for representing three different levels of categorization of concrete objects described by Rosch:

1. the level of basic objects, for which there are primary ASL signs;

2. the level of superordinate terms, for which basic object signs prototypical of the superordinate category are seriated as a coordinate compound, which then represents the superordinate category; and

3. the level of subordinate terms, which are made with a variety of linguistic devices: (a) compound signs composed of regular ASL signs; (b) compound signs

composed of regular signs in conjunction with size-and-shape specifiers; and (c) conjuncts of signs and mimetic depiction of the shape of objects. We suspect that this latter device is unique to a visual—gestural language.

Across the taxonomies we have examined, the linguistic devices for expressing the three levels of categorization are consistently distinct from one another, confirming the psychological salience of Rosch's three category levels. In addition, this sketch supports the notion that the level of basic categories is linguistically central: First, there are single primary signs for this level; and second, these primary basic-level signs are most often the components from which signs at other levels are constructed. Thus lexical and syntactic evidence from ASL supports Rosch's notions of a basic conceptual level of categorization for concrete objects.

ACKNOWLEDGMENTS

This work was supported in part by National Institutes of Health Grant #NS-09811 and by National Science Foundation Grant #BNS-76-12866 to The Salk Institute for Biological Studies, and by National Institute of Mental Health Grant #MH-15828 to the Center for Human Information Processing.

Our thanks to Carlene Canady Pedersen and Bonnie Gough for serving as our informants; to Claudia Cohen, Geoff Coulter, Henry Gleitman, Ed Klima, and Patricia Worden for helpful discussion; and to Ted Supalla, for serving simultaneously as informant, linguist, and discussant, thereby directing us to the construction we sought. Our special thanks to Lila Gleitman, who was both ghostwriter and ghostthinker.

Illustrations were made by Frank A. Paul.

REFERENCES

Bellugi, U., & Klima, E. S. Two faces of sign: Iconic and abstract. In S. Harnad (Ed.), *The origins of evolution of language and speech.* New York: New York Academy of Sciences, (1976).

Bellugi, U., & Klima, E. S. On the creation of new lexical items by compounding in American Sign Language. In E. S. Klima & U. Bellugi, *The signs of language.* Cambridge, Mass.: Harvard University Press, in press.

Bellugi, U., Klima, E. S., & Siple, P. Remembering in sign *Cognition: International Journal of Cognitive Psychology,* 1975, *3*(2), 93–125.

Bellugi, U., & Siple, P. Remembering with and without words. In F. Bresson (Ed.), *Current problems in psycholinguistics.* Paris: Centre National de la Recherche Scientifique, 1974.

Bloomfield, L. *Language.* New York: Henry Holt & Co., 1933.

Cooper, W. E., & Ross, J. R. World order. In R. E. Grossman, L. J. San, P. J. Vance (Eds.), *Papers from the parasession on functionalism.* Chicago: Chicago Linguistic Society, 1975.

Coulter, G. *American Sign Language pantomime.* Unpublished manuscript, The Salk Institute, San Diego, 1975.

Frishberg, N. Arbitrariness and iconicity: Historical change in American Sign Language. *Language,* 1975, *51,* 696–719.

Frishberg, N. *Some aspects of the historical development of signs in American Sign Language.* Unpublished doctoral dissertation, University of California, San Diego, 1976.

Gleitman, L. R., & Gleitman, H. *Phrase and paraphrase.* New York: W. W. Norton & Co., Inc., 1970.

Jespersen, O. *A modern English grammar.* London, England: Allen & Unwin, 1961.

Lees, R. B. *The grammar of English nominalizations.* The Hague: Mouton, 1960.

Newkirk, D., & Pedersen, C. C. *Interferences between sequentially produced signs in American Sign Language.* Unpublished manuscript, The Salk Institute, San Diego, 1976.

Newport, E. L., & Bellugi, U. Productive processes of compounding in American Sign Language. Manuscript in preparation, 1978.

Newport, E. L., & Supalla, T. Manuscript in preparation, 1978.

Rosch, E. Classifications of real-world objects: Origins and representations in cognition. *Bulletin de Psychologie,* 1976, Special Annual, 242–250.

Rosch, E., Mervis, C. B., Gray, W., Johnson, D., & Boyes-Braem, P. Basic objects in natural categories. *Cognitive Psychology,* 1976, *8,* 382–439.

Part II PROCESS

The focus of the chapters in Part I is on structural facts about category systems. All three chapters assume a category processor who is able to perform at least three primitive functions: He can judge similarity between stimuli, he can perceive and process the attributes of a stimulus, and he can learn. The chapters in Part II present analyses of these three cognitive processes.

SIMILARITY

Both Berlin and Rosch argue that the basic level of abstraction in taxonomies can be derived from considerations of the perceived similarity between objects. Neither, however, offers a theory of the nature of similarity judgments. Similarity has traditionally been treated in psychological theory as distance between stimuli in Euclidean space. Tversky's chapter presents a new set-theoretical approach to similarity in which objects are represented as collections of features, and similarity is described as a feature-matching process. These contrasting treatments of similarity offer a clear example of how the assumptions of a theory can constrain empirical research. If similarity is defined by distance in Euclidean space, the distance from A to B and from B to A within that space is necessarily symmetrical.

It would scarcely occur to an investigator to look for asymmetries. In Tversky's formulation of similarity, directionality and asymmetry are predicted, a prediction amply justified by Tversky's numerous experimental demonstrations.

Of what relevance is the nature of a formal model of similarity to the issues of categorization raised in Part I? First, Tversky's theory predicts basic or generic levels of abstraction; basic categories are those for which the ratio of common to distinctive features is maximized. No such prediction can be derived from a distance model. Second, Tversky's theory predicts salient reference items within the cognitive space in relation to which other stimuli are judged. Category prototypes may play just such a role (Rosch, 1975).

STIMULUS ATTRIBUTES

Garner (1970, 1974) has reintroduced into psychology a focus on the stimulus in information processing. Garner's concept of structure (in the sense of predictable redundancy among attributes within a set of stimuli) underlies Berlin's concept of the folk genus and Rosch's concept of basic-level categories. Two examples of Garner's analysis of the nature of attributes serve to demonstrate the ways in which such an analysis can be relevant to issues in categorization. The examples are attribute separability—integrality and the distinction between dimensions and features.

SEPARABLE AND INTEGRAL ATTRIBUTES

Phenomenologically, integral dimensions (e.g., hue and brightness) are perceived as unitary wholes; a change in one dimension appears to produce a stimulus that is qualitatively different (e.g., a different color). On the other hand, separable dimensions (e.g., a dot above versus below a form) are seen as perceptually distinct components. Converging operations support this distinction.

Whether stimulus dimensions are separable or integral places constraints on the type of category structure model that can be entertained. For example, if stimulus dimensions are integral and selective attention to a single dimension is not possible, then the extreme form of a criterial attribute model (see Chapter 9), which specifies the category in terms of a list of necessary and sufficient features conjoined by *and*s, is not tenable. To illustrate: Let us say that hue x is a relevant criterial attribute that exists at n levels of saturation. Level of saturation is irrelevant. If selective attention can be paid to hue, the processor can simply check the stimulus for the presence of a single attribute, and the feature may be represented in the category by some means such as +hue x. If, however, hue and saturation are integral and the processor actually sees N qualitatively different colors, the feature must be represented in a more complex manner such as color 1 (hue x at saturation 1) *or* color 2 (hue x at saturation 2) *or* color n.

Shepp (Chapter 6) shows that such constraints on category structure are not simply hypothetical. Young children appear unable to attend selectively to attribute dimensions that for adults are separable. Any model of category development must take such evidence into account.

DIMENSIONS VERSUS FEATURES

Stimulus dimensions are variables for which mutually exclusive levels exist; e.g., red, blue, and green are levels of the dimension *color*. Features are variables that exist or do not exist; e.g. an object either has or does not have legs. Unlike levels of a dimension, when a feature is missing in a particular stimulus, the stimulus provides no information about what alternative stimuli there are in a meaningful set. In Chapter 5, Garner shows that the distinction between dimensions and features has empirical implications for many basic processing tasks: concept learning, decision making, and speed and accuracy of stimulus identification.

The distinction between dimensions and features provides a fine example of the interaction of constraints on perception provided by the world and by the active processor. The perceiver may choose to process levels of a dimension as though they were features for any given task. Furthermore, features may be defined as pseudodimensions. Such definition occurs precisely when categories are created. Thus, an automatic transmission can be treated as a feature that an object may or may not have; however, once we have decided that our set of objects are cars and that a car must have a transmission, "automatic" and "standard" become two levels on the pseudodimension "transmission." When the perceiver determines whether he will treat an attribute as a dimension or as a feature, however, he is constrained in his processing of the stimulus by the information properties of those modes.

LEARNING

Brooks' discussion of learning provides another vivid example of how the nature of the question asked determines the possible answers. The stimuli and tasks in concept-identification studies are structured so that abstraction of criterial attributes according to logical rules must occur. Brooks demonstrates that when task or stimulus materials are changed, subjects give every evidence of storing particular instances and of using those instances to classify new cases by analogy (or some other similiarity match) to the old.

Brooks' chapter is of crucial importance for understanding how the structure of categories described by the chapters in Part I could be acquired. If Aristotelian categorization is built into one's model of the learner and the process of learning, it is difficult to account for the development of a prototype structure for categories. Storage of particular instances provides a more suitable mechanism for the development of prototypes.

One may ask what leads people to store prototypical particular instances rather than examples that are atypical. First, the more instances of a single category that are stored and the stronger the family resemblance structure of the category (Rosch & Mervis, 1975), the more a similarity match to several randomly chosen members of the category will be like matching to a single highly prototypical instance. (Note that one would not expect such a result for artificial categories, which do not have the necessary internal and external family resemblances.) And most real-world categories are such that one would expect early experience with more than a single instance — e.g., shoes, chairs, or apples.

Even in the case where only a single member of the category is stored, people are more likely to store prototypical instances if: (1) prototypical instances are highly salient (Rosch, 1977); (2) prototypical instances are frequent or are frequently experiences in conjunction with the revelant categorization; (3) adult members of the culture explicitly teach that some instances are more prototypical than others; or (4) the category is one likely to be taught by example, and adult members of the culture are likely to provide prototypical examples — perhaps a more frequent occurrence than we admit, even in highly abstract disciplines (Kuhn, 1970).

Given storage of particular examples as a learning strategy, there are cases of important categories for which one would not predict the development of culturally shared prototypes. The most striking instance is the category of people (and to a lesser extent, pets). Unlike experience of apples, a child in our society is likely to encounter, over a long and crucial period, only a single instance of the category of mothers — an instance that is quite different from many other members of the category. One would thus expect people to differ considerably in their conceptions of and expectations concerning other humans. Many of Brooks' examples are of this type of category. One great value of the learning mechanism of stored instances is that it can be used to predict cases in which a culturally shared structure of categories will not develop, as well as cases in which it will.

Brooks' learning principle requires that the learner store particular instances in memory in an unanalyzed form. But one does not literally store objects in one's head nor even represent them by means of a first-order isomorphism (the representation of green is not green). Thus the instance must be analyzed and transformed in some fashion in order to be stored at all. What is required is a model of representation that allows for differing levels of analysis; at the minimum, we must allow for a type of representation that is sufficiently analyzed to be stored but not coded into criterial features. The important issue of the nature of representation is discussed in Part III.

REFERENCES

Garner, W. R. The stimulus in information processing. *American Psychologist,* 1970, *25,* 350–358.

Garner, W. R. *The processing of information and structure.* New York: Halsted Press, 1974.

Kuhn, T. S. *The structure of scientific revolutions* (2nd ed.). Chicago: University of Chicago Press, 1970.

Rosch, E. Cognitive reference points. *Cognitive Psychology,* 1975, *7,* 532–547.

Rosch, E. Human categorization. In N. Warren (Ed.), *Advances in cross cultural psychology* (Vol. 1). London: Academic Press, 1977.

Rosch, E., & Mervis, C. B. Family resemblances: Studies in the internal structure of categories. *Cognitive Psychology,* 1975, *7,* 573–605.

4
Studies of Similarity

Amos Tversky
Itamar Gati
Hebrew University, Jerusalem

Any event in the history of the organism is, in a sense, unique. Consequently, recognition, learning, and judgment presuppose an ability to categorize stimuli and classify situations by similarity. As Quine (1969) puts it: "There is nothing more basic to thought and language than our sense of similarity; our sorting of things into kinds [p. 116]." Indeed, the notion of similarity — that appears under such different names as proximity, resemblance, communality, representativeness, and psychological distance — is fundamental to theories of perception, learning, and judgment. This chapter outlines a new theoretical analysis of similarity and investigates some of its empirical consequences.

The theoretical analysis of similarity relations has been dominated by geometric models. Such models represent each object as a point in some coordinate space so that the metric distances between the points reflect the observed similarities between the respective objects. In general, the space is assumed to be Euclidean, and the purpose of the analysis is to embed the objects in a space of minimum dimensionality on the basis of the observed similarities, see Shepard (1974).

In a recent paper (Tversky, 1977), the first author challenged the dimensional-metric assumptions that underlie the geometric approach to similarity and developed an alternative feature-theoretical approach to the analysis of similarity relations. In this approach, each object a is characterized by a set of features, denoted A, and the observed similarity of a to b, denoted $s(a, b)$, is expressed as a function of their common and distinctive features (see Fig. 4.1). That is, the observed similarity $s(a, b)$ is expressed as a function of three arguments: $A \cap B$, the features shared by a and b; $A - B$, the features of a that are not shared by b; $B - A$, the features of b that are not shared by a. Thus the similarity between

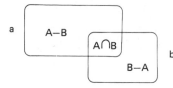

FIG. 4.1. A graphical illustration of the relation between two feature sets.

objects is expressed as a feature-matching function (i.e., a function that measures the degree to which two sets of features match each other) rather than as the metric distance between points in a coordinate space.

The theory is based on a set of qualitative assumptions about the observed similarity ordering. They yield an interval similarity scale S, which preserves the observed similarity order [i.e., $S(a, b) > S(c, d)$ iff $s(a, b) > s(c, d)$], and a scale f, defined on the relevant feature space such that

$$S(a, b) = \theta f(A \cap B) - af(A - B) - \beta f(B - A) \quad \text{where } \theta, a, \beta \geqslant 0. \quad (1)$$

According to this form, called the *contrast model*, the similarity of a to b is described as a linear combination (or a contrast) of the measures of their common and distinctive features. Naturally, similarity increases with the measure of the common features and decreases with the measure of the distinctive features.

The contrast model does not define a unique index of similarity but rather a family of similarity indices defined by the values of the parameters θ, a, and β. For Example, if $\theta = 1$, and $a = \beta = 0$, then $S(a, b) = f(A \cap B)$; that is, similarity equals the measure of the common features. On the other hand, if $\theta = 0$, and $a = \beta = 1$, then $-S(a, b) = f(A - B) + f(B - A)$; that is, the dissimilarity of a to b equals the measure of the symmetric difference of the respective feature sets, see Restle (1961). Note that in the former case ($\theta = 1, a = \beta = 0$), the similarity between objects is determined only by their common features, whereas in the latter case ($\theta = 0, a = \beta = 1$), it is determined by their distinctive features only. The contrast model expresses similarity between objects as the weighted difference of the measures of their common and distinctive features, thereby allowing for a variety of similarity relations over the same set of objects.

The contrast model is formulated in terms of the parameters (θ, a, β) that characterize the task, and the scale f, which reflects the salience or prominence of the various features. Thus f measures the contribution of any particular (common or distinctive) feature to the similarity between objects. The scale value $f(A)$ associated with stimulus a is regarded, therefore, as a measure of the overall salience of that stimulus. The factors that contribute to the salience of a stimulus include: intensity, frequency, familiarity, good form, and informational content. The manner in which the scale f and the parameters (θ, a, β) depend on the context and the task are discussed in the following sections.

This chapter employs the contrast model to analyze the following three problems: the relation between judgments of similarity and difference; the nature of asymmetric similarities; and the effects of context on similarity. All three problems concern changes in similarity induced, respectively, by the formulation of the *task* (as judgment of similarity or as judgment of difference), the *direction* of comparison, and the effective *context* (i.e., the set of objects under consideration).

To account for the effects of these manipulations within the present theoretical framework, we introduce several hypotheses that relate focus of attention to the experimental task. In particular, it is assumed that people attend more to common features in judgments of similarity than in judgments of difference, that people attend more to the subject than to the referent of the comparison, and that people attend primarily to features that have classificatory significance.

These hypotheses are formulated in terms of the contrast model and are tested in several experimental studies of similarity. For a more comprehensive treatment of the contrast model and a review of relevant data (including the present studies), see Tversky (1977).

SIMILARITY VERSUS DIFFERENCE

What is the relation between judgments of similarity and judgements of difference? Some authors emphasized that the two judgments are conceptually independent; others have treated them as perfectly correlated. The data appear to support the latter view. For example, Hosman and Kuennapas (1972) obtained independent judgments of similarity and difference for all pairs of lower-case letters on a scale from 0 to 100. The product-moment correlation between the judgments was $-.98$, and the slope of the regression line was $-.91$. We also collected judgments of similarity and difference for 21 pairs of countries using a 20-point rating scale. The product moment correlation between the ratings was again $-.98$. The near-perfect negative correlation between similarity and difference, however, does not always hold.

In applying the contrast model to judgments of similarity and of difference, it is reasonable to assume that enlarging the measure of the common features increases similarity and decreases difference, whereas enlarging the measure of the distinctive features decreases similarity and increases difference. More formally, let $s(a, b)$ and $d(a, b)$ denote ordinal measures of similarity and difference, respectively. Thus $s(a, b)$ is expected to increase with $f(A \cap B)$ and to decrease with $f(A - B)$ and with $f(B - A)$, whereas $d(a, b)$ is expected to decrease with $f(A \cap B)$ and to increase with $f(A - B)$ and with $f(B - A)$.

The relative weight assigned to the common and the distinctive features may differ in the two judgments because of a change in focus. In the assessment of similarity between stimuli, the subject may attend more to their common features, whereas in the assessment of difference between stimuli, the subject may attend more to their distinctive features. Stated differently, the instruction to consider similarity may lead the subject to focus primarily on the features that contribute to the similarity of the stimuli, whereas the instruction to consider difference may lead the subject to focus primarily on the features that contribute to the difference between the stimuli. Consequently, the relative weight of the common features is expected to be greater in the assessment of similarity than in the assessment of difference.

To investigate the consequences of this focusing hypothesis, suppose that both similarity and difference measures satisfy the contrast model with opposite signs but with different weights. Furthermore, suppose for simplicity that both measures are symmetric. Hence, under the contrast model, there exist non-negative constants θ and λ such that

$$s(a, b) > s(c, e) \quad \text{iff} \quad \theta f(A \cap B) - f(A - B) - f(B - A) \\ > \theta f(C \cap E) - f(C - E) - f(E - C), \quad (2)$$

and

$$d(a, b) > d(c, e) \quad \text{iff} \quad f(A - B) + f(B - A) - \lambda f(A \cap B) \\ > f(C - E) + F(E - C) - \lambda f(C \cap E) \quad (3)$$

The weights associated with the distinctive features can be set equal to 1 in the symmetric case with no loss of generality. Hence, θ and λ reflect the *relative* weight of the common features in the assessment of similarity and difference, respectively.

Note that if θ is very large, then the similarity ordering is essentially determined by the common features. On the other hand, if λ is very small, then the difference ordering is determined primarily by the distinctive features. Consequently, both $s(a, b) > s(c, e)$ and $d(a, b) > d(c, e)$ may be obtained whenever

$$f(A \cap B) > f(C \cap E) \quad \text{and} \quad f(A - B) + f(B - A) > f(C - E) + f(E - C). \quad (4)$$

That is, if the common features are weighed more heavily in judgments of similarity than in judgments of difference, then a pair of objects with many common and many distinctive features may be perceived as both more similar and more different than another pair of objects with fewer common and fewer distinctive features.

Study 1: Similarity Versus Difference

All subjects that took part in the experiments reported in this chapter were undergraduate students majoring in the social sciences from the Hebrew University in Jerusalem and the Ben-Gurion University in Beer-Sheba. They participated in the studies as part of the requirements for a psychology course. The material was presented in booklets and administered in the classroom. The instructions were printed in the booklet and also read aloud by the experimenter. The different forms of each booklet were assigned randomly to different subjects.

Twenty sets of four countries were constructed. Each set included two pairs of countries: a prominent pair and a nonprominent pair. The prominent pairs consisted of countries that were well known to the subjects (e.g., U.S.A.–U.S.S.R.). The nonprominent pairs consisted of countries that were known to our subjects but not as well as the prominent pairs (e.g., Paraguay–Ecuador). This assumption was verified in a pilot study in which 50 subjects were presented with all 20 quadruples of countries and asked to indicate which of the two pairs include countries that are more prominent, or better known. For each quadruple, over 85% of the subjects ordered the pairs in accord with our a priori ordering. All 20 sets of countries are displayed in Table 4.1.

Two groups of 30 subjects each participated in the main study. All subjects were presented with the same 20 sets in the same order. The pairs within each set were arranged so that the prominent pairs appeared an equal number of times on the left and on the right. One group of subjects – the similarity group – selected between the two pairs of each set the pair of countries that are more

TABLE 4.1

Percentage of Subjects That Selected the Prominent Pair in the Similarity Group (Π_s) and in the Difference Group (Π_d)

	Prominent Pairs	Nonprominent Pairs	Π_s	Π_d	$\Pi_s + \Pi_d$
1	W. Germany–E. Germany	Ceylon–Nepal	66.7	70.0	136.7
2	Lebanon–Jordan	Upper Volta–Tanzania	69.0	43.3	112.3
3	Canada–U.S.A.	Bulgaria–Albania	80.0	16.7	96.7
4	Belgium–Holland	Peru–Costa Rica	78.6	21.4	100.0
5	Switzerland–Denmark	Pakistan–Mongolia	55.2	28.6	83.8
6	Syria–Iraq	Liberia–Kenya	63.3	28.6	91.9
7	U.S.S.R.–U.S.A.	Paraguay–Ecuador	20.0	100.0	120.0
8	Sweden–Norway	Thailand–Burma	69.0	40.7	109.7
9	Turkey–Greece	Bolivia–Honduras	51.7	86.7	138.4
10	Austria–Switzerland	Zaire–Madagascar	79.3	24.1	103.4
11	Italy–France	Bahrain–Yemen	44.8	70.0	114.8
12	China–Japan	Guatemala–Costa Rica	40.0	93.1	133.1
13	S. Korea–N. Korea	Nigeria–Zaire	63.3	60.0	123.3
14	Uganda–Libya	Paraguay–Ecuador	23.3	65.5	88.8
15	Australia–S. Africa	Iceland–New Zealand	57.1	60.0	117.1
16	Poland–Czechoslovakia	Colombia–Honduras	82.8	37.0	119.8
17	Portugal–Spain	Tunis–Morocco	55.2	73.3	128.5
18	Vatican–Luxembourg	Andorra–San Marino	50.0	85.7	135.7
19	England–Ireland	Pakistan–Mongolia	80.0	58.6	138.6
20	Norway–Denmark	Indonesia–Philippines	51.7	25.0	76.7
	Average		59.1	54.4	113.5

similar. The second group of subjects — the difference group — selected between the two pairs in each set the pair of countries that are more different.

Let Π_s and Π_d denote, respectively, the percentage of subjects who selected the prominent pair in the similarity task and in the difference task. (Throughout this chapter, percentages were computed relative to the number of subjects who responded to each problem, which was occasionally smaller than the total number of subjects.) These values are presented in Table 4.1 for all sets. If similarity and difference are complementary (i.e., $\theta = \lambda$), then the sum $\Pi_s + \Pi_d$ should equal 100 for all pairs. On the other hand, if $\theta > \lambda$, then this sum should exceed 100. The average value of $\Pi_s + \Pi_d$ across all subjects and sets is 113.5, which is significantly greater than 100 ($t = 3.27$, $df = 59$, $p < .01$). Moreover, Table 4.1 shows that, on the average, the prominent pairs were selected more frequently than the nonprominent pairs both under similarity instructions (59.1%) and under difference instructions (54.4%), contrary to complementarity. These results demonstrate that the relative weight of the common and the distinctive features vary with the nature of the task and support the focusing hypothesis that people attend more to the common features in judgments of similarity than in judgments of difference.

DIRECTIONALITY AND ASYMMETRY

Symmetry has been regarded as an essential property of similarity relations. This view underlies the geometric approach to the analysis of similarity, in which dissimilarity between objects is represented as a metric distance function. Although many types of proximity data, such as word associations or confusion probabilities, are often nonsymmetric, these asymmetries have been attributed to response biases. In this section, we demonstrate the presence of systematic asymmetries in direct judgments of similarity and argue that similarity should not be viewed as a symmetric relation. The observed asymmetries are explained in the contrast model by the relative salience of the stimuli and the directionality of the comparison.

Similarity judgments can be regarded as extensions of similarity statements (i.e., statements of the form "a is like b"). Such a statement is directional; it has a subject, a, and a referent, b, and it is not equivalent in general to the converse similarity statement "b is like a." In fact, the choice of a subject and a referent depends, in part at least, on the relative salience of the objects. We tend to select the more salient stimulus, or the prototype, as a referent and the less salient stimulus, or the variant, as a subject. Thus we say "the portrait resembles the person" rather than "the person resembles the portrait." We say "the son resembles the father" rather than "the father resembles the son," and we say "North Korea is like Red China" rather than "Red China is like North Korea."

As is demonstrated later, this asymmetry in the *choice* of similarity statements is associated with asymmetry in *judgments* of similarity. Thus the judged similarity of North Korea to Red China exceeds the judged similarity of Red China to North Korea. In general, the direction of asymmetry is determined by the relative salience of the stimuli: The variant is more similar to the prototype than vice versa.

If $s(a, b)$ is interpreted as the degree to which a is similar to b, then a is the subject of the comparison and b is the referent. In such a task, one naturally focuses on the subject of the comparison. Hence, the features of the subject are weighted more heavily than the features of the referent (i.e., $a > \beta$). Thus similarity is reduced more by the distinctive features of the subject than by the distinctive features of the referent. For example, a toy train is quite similar to a real train, because most features of the toy train are included in the real train. On the other hand, a real train is not as similar to a toy train, because many of the features of a real train are not included in the toy train.

It follows readily from the contrast model, with $a > \beta$, that

$$s(a, b) \; > \; s(b, a) \qquad \text{iff}$$
$$\theta f(A \cap B) - af(A - B) - \beta f(B - A) \; > \; \theta f(A \cap B) - af(B - A) - \beta f(A - B)$$
$$\text{iff} \; f(B - A) \; > \; f(A - B). \tag{5}$$

Thus $s(a, b) > s(b, a)$ whenever the distinctive features of b are more salient than the distinctive features of a, or whenever b is more prominent than a. Hence, the conjunction of the contrast model and the focusing hypothesis ($a > \beta$) implies that the direction of asymmetry is determined by the relative salience of the stimuli so that the less salient stimulus is more similar to the salient stimulus than vice versa.

In the contrast model, $s(a, b) = s(b, a)$ if either $f(A - B) = f(B - A)$ or $a = \beta$. That is, symmetry holds whenever the objects are equally salient, or whenever the comparison is nondirectional. To interpret the latter condition, compare the following two forms:

1. Assess the degree to which a and b are similar to each other.
2. Assess the degree to which a is similar to b.

In (1), the task is formulated in a nondirectional fashion, and there is no reason to emphasize one argument more than the other. Hence, it is expected that $a = \beta$ and $s(a, b) = s(b, a)$. In (2), on the other hand, the task is directional, and hence the subject is likely to be the focus of attention rather than the referent. In this case, asymmetry is expected, provided the two stimuli are not equally salient. The directionality of the task and the differential salience of the stimuli, therefore, are necessary and sufficient for asymmetry.

In the following two studies, the directional asymmetry prediction, derived from the contrast model, is tested using semantic (i.e., countries) and perceptual (i.e., figures) stimuli. Both studies employ essentially the same design. Pairs of stimuli that differ in salience are used to test for the presence of asymmetry in the choice of similarity statements and in direct assessments of similarity.

Study 2: Similarity of Countries

In order to test the asymmetry prediction, we constructed 21 pairs of countries so that one element of the pair is considerably more prominent than the other (e.g., U.S.A.–Mexico, Belgium–Luxembourg). To validate this assumption, we presented all pairs to a group of 68 subjects and asked them to indicate in each pair the country they regard as more prominent. In all cases except one, more than two-thirds of the subjects agreed with our initial judgment. All 21 pairs of countries are displayed in Table 4.2, where the more prominent element of each pair is denoted by p and the less prominent by q.

Next, we tested the hypothesis that the more prominent element is generally chosen as the referent rather than as the subject of similarity statements. A group of 69 subjects was asked to choose which of the following two phrases they prefer to use: "p is similar to q," or "q is similar to p." The percentage of subjects that selected the latter form, in accord with our hypothesis, is displayed in Table 4.2 under the label Π. It is evident from the table that in all cases the great majority of subjects selected the form in which the more prominent country serves as a referent.

TABLE 4.2
Average Similarities and Differences for 21 Pairs of Countries

	p	q	Π	$s(p, q)$	$s(q, p)$	$d(p, q)$	$d(q, p)$
1	U.S.A.	Mexico	91.1	6.46	7.65	11.78	10.58
2	U.S.S.R.	Poland	98.6	15.12	15.18	6.37	7.30
3	China	Albania	94.1	8.69	9.16	14.56	12.16
4	U.S.A.	Israel	95.6	9.70	10.65	13.78	12.53
5	Japan	Philippines	94.2	12.37	11.95	7.74	5.50
6	U.S.A.	Canada	97.1	16.96	17.33	4.40	3.82
7	U.S.S.R.	Israel	91.1	3.41	3.69	18.41	17.25
8	England	Ireland	97.1	13.32	13.49	7.50	5.04
9	W. Germany	Austria	87.0	15.60	15.20	6.95	6.67
10	U.S.S.R.	France	82.4	5.21	5.03	15.70	15.00
11	Belgium	Luxembourg	95.6	15.54	16.14	4.80	3.93
12	U.S.A.	U.S.S.R.	65.7	5.84	6.20	16.65	16.11
13	China	N. Korea	95.6	13.13	14.22	8.20	7.48
14	India	Ceylon	97.1	13.91	13.88	5.51	7.32
15	U.S.A.	France	86.8	10.42	11.09	10.58	10.15
16	U.S.S.R.	Cuba	91.1	11.46	12.32	11.50	10.50
17	England	Jordan	98.5	4.97	6.52	15.81	14.95
18	France	Israel	86.8	7.48	7.34	12.20	11.88
19	U.S.A.	W. Germany	94.1	11.30	10.70	10.25	11.96
20	U.S.S.R.	Syria	98.5	6.61	8.51	12.92	11.60
21	France	Algeria	95.6	7.86	7.94	10.58	10.15

To test the hypothesis that $s(q, p) > s(p, q)$, we instructed two groups of 77 subjects each to assess the similarity of each pair on a scale from 1 (no similarity) to 20 (maximal similarity). The two groups were presented with the same list of 21 pairs, and the only difference between the two groups was the order of the countries within each pair. For example, one group was asked to assess "the degree to which Red China is similar to North Korea," whereas the second group was asked to assess "the degree to which North Korea is similar to Red China." The lists were balanced so that the more prominent countries appeared about an equal number of times in the first and second position. The average ratings for each ordered pair, denoted $s(p, q)$ and $s(q, p)$ are displayed in Table 4.2. The average $s(q, p)$ was significantly higher than the average $s(p, q)$ across all subjects and pairs. A t-test for correlated samples yielded $t = 2.92, df = 20$, and $p < .01$. To obtain a statistical test based on individual data, we computed for each subject a directional asymmetry score, defined as the average similarity for comparisons with a prominent referent [i.e., $s(q, p)$ minus the average similarity for comparison with a prominent subject, i.e., $s(p, q)$]. The average difference (.42) was significantly positive: $t = 2.99, df = 153, p < .01$.

The foregoing study was repeated with judgments of difference instead of judgments of similarity. Two groups of 23 subjects each received the same list of 21 pairs, and the only difference between the groups, again, was the order of the countries within each pair. For example, one group was asked to assess "the degree to which the U.S.S.R. is different from Poland," whereas the second group was asked to assess "the degree to which Poland is different from the U.S.S.R." All subjects were asked to rate the difference on a scale from 1 (minimal difference) to 20 (maximal difference).

If judgments of difference follow the contrast model (with opposite signs) and the focusing hypothesis ($a > \beta$) holds, then the prominent stimulus p is expected to differ from the less prominent stimulus q more than q differs from p [i.e., $d(p, q) > d(q, p)$]. The average judgments of difference for all ordered pairs are displayed in Table 4.2. The average $d(p, q)$ across all subjects and pairs was significantly higher than the average $d(q, p)$. A t-test for correlated samples yielded $t = 2.72, df = 20, p < .01$. Furthermore, the average difference between $d(p, q)$ and $d(q, p)$, computed as previously for each subject (.63), was significantly positive: $t = 2.24, df = 45, p < .05$. Hence, the predicted asymmetry was confirmed in direct judgments of both similarity and difference.

Study 3: Similarity of Figures

Two sets of eight pairs of geometric figures served as stimuli in the present study. In the first set, one figure in each pair, denoted p, had better form than the other, denoted q. In the second set, the two figures in each pair were roughly equivalent with respect to goodness of form, but one figure, denoted p, was richer or more complex than the other, denoted q. Examples of pairs of figures from each set are presented in Fig. 4.2.

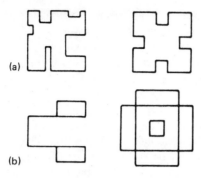

FIG. 4.2.   Examples of pairs of figures used to test the prediction of asymmetry. (a) Example of a pair of figures (from Set 1) that differ in goodness of form. (b) Example of a pair of figures (from Set 2) that differ in complexity.

We hypothesized that both goodness of form and complexity contribute to the salience of geometric figures. Moreover, we expected a "good figure" to be more salient than a "bad figure," although the latter is generally more complex. For pairs of figures that do not vary much with respect to goodness of form, however, the more complex figure is expected to be more salient.

A group of 69 subjects received the entire list of 16 pairs of figures. The two elements of each pair were displayed side by side. For each pair, the subjects were asked to choose which of the following two statements they preferred to use: "the left figure is similar to the right figure," or "the right figure is similar to the left figure." The positions of the figures were randomized so that p and q appeared an equal number of times on the left and on the right. The proportion of subjects that selected the form "q is similar to p" exceeded 2/3 in all pairs except one. Evidently, the more salient figure (defined as previously) was generally chosen as the referent rather than as the standard.

To test for asymmetry in judgments of similarity, we presented two groups of 66 subjects each with the same 16 pairs of figures and asked the subjects to rate (on a 20-point scale) the degree to which the figure on the left is similar to the figure on the right. The two groups received identical booklets, except that the left and right positions of the figures in each pair were reversed. The data shows that the average $s(q, p)$ across all subjects and pairs was significantly higher than the average $s(p, q)$. A t-test for correlated samples yielded $t = 2.94$, $df = 15$, $p < .01$. Furthermore, in both sets the average difference between $s(q, p)$ and $s(p, q)$ computed as previously for each individual subject (.56) were significantly positive. In Set 1, $t = 2.96$, $df = 131$, $p < .01$, and in Set 2, $t = 2.79$, $df = 131$, $p < .01$.

The preceding two studies revealed the presence of systematic and significant asymmetries in judgments of similarity between countries and geometric figures. The results support the theoretical analysis based on the contrast model and the focusing hypothesis, according to which the features of the subject are weighted more heavily than the features of the referent. Essentially the same results were obtained by Rosch (1975) using a somewhat different design. In her studies, one stimulus (the standard) was placed at the origin of a semicircular board, and the subject was instructed to place the second (variable) stimulus on the board so as "to represent his feeling of the distance between that stimulus and the one fixed at the origin." Rosch used three stimulus domains: color, line orientation, and number. In each domain, she paired prominent, or focal, stimuli with nonfocal stimuli. For example, a pure red was paired with an off-red, a vertical line was paired with a diagonal line, and a round number (e.g., 100) was paired with a nonround number (e.g., 103).

In all three domains, Rosch found that the measured distance between stimuli was smaller when the more prominent stimulus was fixed at the origin. That is, the similarity of the variant to the prototype was greater than the similarity of the prototype to the variant. Rosch also showed that when presented with sentence frames containing hedges such as "____ is virtually ____," subjects generally placed the prototype in the second blank and the variant in the first. For example, subjects preferred the sentence "103 is virtually 100" to the sentence "100 is virtually 103."

In contrast to direct judgments of similarity, which have traditionally been viewed as symmetric, other measures of similarity such as confusion probability or association were known to be asymmetric. The observed asymmetries, however, were commonly attributed to a response bias. Without denying the important role of response biases, asymmetries in identification tasks occur even in situations to which a response bias interpretation does not apply (e.g., in studies where the subject indicates whether two presented stimuli are identical or not). Several experiments employing this paradigm obtained asymmetric confusion probabilities of the type predicted by the present analysis. For a discussion of these data and their implications, see Tversky (1977).

CONTEXT EFFECTS

The preceding two sections deal with the effects of the formulation of the task (as judgment of similarity or of difference) and of the direction of comparison (induced by the choice of subject and referent) on similarity. These manipulations were related to the parameters (θ, a, β) of the contrast model through the focusing hypothesis. The present section extends this hypothesis to describe the manner in which the measure of the feature space f varies with a change in context.

The scale f is generally not invariant with respect to changes in context or frame of reference. That is, the salience of features may vary widely depending on implicit or explicit instructions and on the object set under consideration. East Germany and West Germany, for example, may be viewed as highly similar from a geographical or cultural viewpoint and as quite dissimilar from a political viewpoint. Moreover, the two Germanys are likely to be viewed as more similar to each other in a context that includes many Asian and African countries than in a context that includes only European countries.

How does the salience of features vary with changes in the set of objects under consideration? We propose that the salience of features is determined, in part at least, by their diagnosticity (i.e., classificatory significance). A feature may acquire diagnostic value (and hence become more salient) in a particular context if it serves as a basis for classification in that particular context. The relations between similarity and diagnosticity are investigated in several studies that show how the similarity between a given pair of countries is varied by changing the context in which they are embedded.

Study 4: The Extension of Context

According to the preceding discussion, the diagnosticity of features is determined by the prevalence of the classifications that are based on them. Hence, features that are shared by all the objects under study are devoid of diagnostic value, because they cannot be used to classify these objects. However, when the context is extended by enlarging the object set, some features that had been shared by all objects in the original context may not be shared by all objects in the broader context. These features then acquire diagnostic value and increase the similarity of the objects that share them. Thus the similarity of a pair of objects in the original context is usually smaller than their similarity in the extended context.

To test this hypothesis, we constructed a list of pairs of countries with a common border and asked subjects to assess their similarity on a 20-point scale. Four sets of eight pairs were constructed. Set 1 contained eight pairs of American countries, Set 2 contained eight pairs of European countries, Set 3 contained four pairs from Set 1 and four pairs from Set 2, and Set 4 contained the remaining pairs from Sets 1 and 2. Each one of the four sets was presented to a different group of 30–36 subjects. The entire list of 16 pairs is displayed in Table 4.3.

Recall that the features "American" and "European" have no diagnostic value in Sets 1 and 2, although they both have diagnostic value in Sets 3 and 4. Consequently, the overall average similarity in the heterogeneous sets (3 and 4) is expected to be higher than the overall average similarity in the homogeneous sets (1 and 2). The average similarity for each pair of countries obtained in the homogeneous and the heterogeneous contexts, denoted s_o and s_e, respectively, are presented in Table 4.3. In the absence of context effects, the similarity for any pair of countries should be independent of the list in which it was presented. In contrast, the average difference between s_e and s_o (.57) is significantly positive: $t = 2.11, df = 15, p < .05$.

Similar results were obtained in an earlier study by Sjöberg (1972) who showed that the similarities between string instruments (banjo, violin, harp, electric guitar) were increased when a wind instrument (clarinet) was added to

TABLE 4.3
Average Similarities of Countries in Homogeneous (s_1)
and Heterogeneous (s_2) Contexts

	Countries	$s_0(a, b)$	$s_e(a, b)$
American countries	Panama—Costa Rica	12.30	13.29
	Argentina—Chile	13.17	14.36
	Canada—U.S.A.	16.10	15.86
	Paraguay—Bolivia	13.48	14.43
	Mexico—Guatemala	11.36	12.81
	Venezuela—Colombia	12.06	13.06
	Brazil—Uruguay	13.03	14.64
	Peru—Ecuador	13.52	14.61
European countries	England—Ireland	13.88	13.37
	Spain—Portugal	15.44	14.45
	Bulgaria—Greece	11.44	11.00
	Sweden—Norway	17.09	15.03
	France—W. Germany	10.88	11.81
	Yugoslavia—Austria	8.47	9.86
	Italy—Switzerland	10.03	11.14
	Belgium—Holland	15.39	17.06

this set. Hence, Sjöberg found that the similarity in the homogeneous pairs (i.e., pairs of string instruments) was increased when heterogeneous pairs (i.e., a string instrument and a wind instrument) were introduced into the list. Because the similarities in the homogeneous pairs, however, are greater than the similarities in the heterogeneous pairs, the above finding may be attributed, in part at least, to the common tendency of subjects to standardize the response scale (i.e., to produce the same average similarity for any set of comparisons).

Recall that in the present study all similarity assessments involve only homogeneous pairs (i.e., pairs of countries from the same continent sharing a common border). Unlike Sjöberg's (1972) study that extended the context by introducing heterogeneous pairs, our experiment extended the context by constructing heterogeneous lists composed of homogeneous pairs. Hence, the increase of similarity with the enlargement of context, observed in the present study, cannot be explained by the tendency to standardize the response scale.

Study 5: Similarity and Clustering

When faced with a set of stimuli, people often organize them in clusters to reduce information load and facilitate further processing. Clusters are typically selected in order to maximize the similarity of objects within the cluster and the dissimilarity of objects from different clusters. Clearly, the addition and/or deletion of objects can alter the clustering of the remaining objects. We hypothesize that changes in clustering (induced by the replacement of objects) increase the diagnostic value of the features on which the new clusters are based and consequently the similarity of objects that share these features. Hence, we expect that changes in context which affect the clustering of objects will affect their similarity in the same manner.

The procedure employed to test this hypothesis (called the *diagnosticity hypothesis*) is best explained in terms of a concrete example, taken from the present study. Consider the two sets of four countries displayed in Fig. 4.3, which differ only in one of their elements (p or q).

The sets were constructed so that the natural clusterings of the countries are: p and c vs. a and b in Set 1; and b and q vs. c and a in Set 2. Indeed, these were the modal classifications of subjects who were asked to partition each quadruple into two pairs. In Set 1, 72% of the subjects partitioned the set into Moslem countries (Syria and Iran) vs. non-Moslem countries (England and Israel); whereas in Set 2, 84% of the subjects partitioned the set into European countries (England and France) vs. Middle-Eastern countries (Iran and Israel). Hence, the replacement of p by q changed the pairing of a: In Set 1, a was paired with b; whereas in Set 2, a was paired with c. The diagnosticity hypothesis implies that the change in clustering, induced by the substitution of the odd element (p or q), should produce a corresponding change in similarity. That is, the similarity of England to Israel should be greater in Set 1, where it is natural to group them together, than in Set 2 where it is not. Likewise, the similarity of Iran to Israel should be greater in Set 2, where they tend to be grouped together, than in Set 1 where they are not.

To investigate the relation between clustering and similarity, we constructed 20 pairs of sets of four countries of the form (a, b, c, p) and (a, b, c, q), whose elements are listed in Table 4.4. Two groups of 25 subjects each were presented with 20 sets of four countries and asked to partition each quadruple into two pairs. Each group received one of the two matched quadruples, displayed in a row in random order.

		a ISRAEL	
Set 1			
	b	*p*	*c*
	ENGLAND	SYRIA	IRAN
	37.5%	25%	37.5%
Set 2		*a* ISRAEL	
	b	*q*	*c*
	ENGLAND	FRANCE	IRAN
	24.2%	30.3%	45.5%

FIG. 4.3. An example of two matched sets of countries used to test the diagnosticity hypothesis. The percentage of subjects that ranked each country below (as most similar to the target) is presented under the country.

TABLE 4.4
Classification and Similarity Data for the Test of the Diagnosticity Hypothesis

	a	b	c	q	p	$b(p) - b(q)$	$c(q) - c(p)$	$D(p, q)$
1	U.S.S.R.	Poland	China	Hungary	India	6.1	24.2	66.7
2	England	Iceland	Belgium	Madagascar	Switzerland	10.4	-7.5	68.8
3	Bulgaria	Czechoslovakia	Yugoslavia	Poland	Greece	13.7	19.2	56.6
4	U.S.A.	Brazil	Japan	Argentina	China	11.2	30.2	78.3
5	Cyprus	Greece	Crete	Turkey	Malta	9.1	-6.1	63.2
6	Sweden	Finland	Holland	Iceland	Switzerland	6.5	6.9	44.1
7	Israel	England	Iran	France	Syria	13.3	8.0	87.5
8	Austria	Sweden	Hungary	Norway	Poland	3.0	15.2	60.0
9	Iran	Turkey	Kuwait	Pakistan	Iraq	-6.1	0.0	58.9
10	Japan	China	W. Germany	N. Korea	U.S.A.	24.2	6.1	66.9
11	Uganda	Libya	Zaire	Algeria	Angola	23.0	-1.0	48.8
12	England	France	Australia	Italy	New Zealand	36.4	15.2	73.3
13	Venezuela	Colombia	Iran	Brazil	Kuwait	0.3	31.5	60.7
14	Yugoslavia	Hungary	Greece	Poland	Turkey	9.1	9.1	76.8
15	Libya	Algeria	Syria	Tunis	Jordan	3.0	24.2	73.2
16	China	U.S.S.R.	India	U.S.A.	Indonesia	30.3	-3.0	42.2
17	France	W. Germany	Italy	England	Spain	-12.1	30.3	74.6
18	Cuba	Haiti	N. Korea	Jamaica	Albania	-9.1	0.0	35.9
19	Luxembourg	Belgium	Monaco	Holland	San Marino	30.3	6.1	52.2
20	Yugoslavia	Czechoslovakia	Austria	Poland	France	3.0	24.2	39.6

Let $a_p(b, c)$ denote the percentage of subjects that paired a with b rather than with c when the odd element was p, etc. the difference $D(p, q) = a_p(b, c) - a_q(b, c)$, therefore, measures the effect of replacing q by p on the tendency to classify a with b rather than with c. The values of $D(p, q)$ for each one of the pairs is presented in the last column of Table 4.4. The results show that, in all cases, the replacement of q by p changed the pairing of a in the expected direction; the average difference is 61.4%.

Next, we presented two groups of 33 subjects each with 20 sets of four countries in the format displayed in Fig. 4.3. The subjects were asked to rank, in each quadruple, the three countries below (called the *choice set*) in terms of their similarity to the country on the top (called the *target*). Each group received exactly one quadruple from each pair. If the similarity of b to a, say, is independent of the choice set, then the proportion of subjects who ranked b rather than c as most similar to a should be independent of whether the third element in the choice set is p or q. For example, the proportion of subjects who ranked England rather than Iran as most similar to Israel should be the same whether the third element in the choice set is Syria or France. In contrast, the diagnosticity hypothesis predicts that the replacement of Syria (which is grouped with Iran) by France (which is grouped with England) will affect the ranking of similarity so that the proportion of subjects that ranked England rather than Iran as most similar to Israel is greater in Set 1 than in Set 2.

Let $b(p)$ denote the percentage of subjects who ranked country b as most similar to a when the odd element in the choice set is p, etc. Recall that b is generally grouped with q, and c is generally grouped with p. The differences $b(p) - b(q)$ and $c(q) - c(p)$, therefore, measure the effects of the odd elements, p and q, on the similarity of b and c to the target a. The value of these differences for all pairs of quadruples are presented in Table 4.4. In the absence of context effects, the differences should equal 0, while under the diagnosticity hypothesis, the differences should be positive. In Fig. 4.3, for example, $b(p) - b(q) = 37.5 - 24.2 = 13.3$, and $c(q) - c(p) = 45.5 - 37.5 = 8$. The average difference across all pairs of quadruples was 11%, which is significantly positive: $t = 6.37$, $df = 19$, $p < .01$.

An additional test of the diagnosticity hypothesis was conducted using a slightly different design. As in the previous study, we constructed pairs of sets that differ in one element only (p or q). Furthermore, the sets were constructed so that b is likely to be grouped with q, and c is likely to be grouped with p. Two groups of 29 subjects were presented with all sets of five countries in the format displayed in Fig. 4.4. These subjects were asked to select, for each set, the country in the choice set below that is most similar to the two target countries above. Each group received exactly one set of five countries from each pair. Thus the present study differs from the previous one in that: (1) the target consists of a pair of countries (a_1 and a_2) rather than of a single country; and (2) the subjects were instructed to select an element of the choice set that is most similar to the target rather than to rank all elements of the choice set.

Set 1		a_1 PORTUGAL	a_2 SPAIN
	b FRANCE 45%	p ARGENTINA 41%	c BRAZIL 14%
Set 2		a_1 PORTUGAL	a_2 SPAIN
	b FRANCE 18%	q BELGIUM 14%	c BRAZIL 68%

FIG. 4.4. Two sets of countries used to test the diagnosticity hypothesis. The percentage of subjects who selected each country (as most similar to the two target countries) is presented below the country.

The analysis follows the previous study. Specifically, let $b(p)$ denote the proportion of subjects who selected country b as most similar to the two target countries when the odd element in the choice set was p, etc. Hence, under the diagnosticity hypothesis, the differences $b(p) - b(q)$ and $c(q) - c(p)$ should both be positive, whereas under the assumption of context independence, both differences should equal 0. The values of these differences for all 12 pairs of sets are displayed in Table 4.5. The average difference across all pairs equals 10.9%, which is significantly positive: $t = 3.46, df = 11, p < .01$.

In Fig. 4.4, for example, France was selected, as most similar to Portugal and Spain, more frequently in Set 1 (where the natural grouping is: Brazil and Argentina vs. Portugal, Spain, and France) than in Set 2 (where the natural grouping is: Belgium and France vs. Portugal, Spain, and Brazil). Likewise, Brazil was selected, as most similar to Portugal and Spain, more frequently in Set 2 than in Set 1. Moreover, in this particular example, the replacement of p by q actually reversed the proximity order. In Set 1, France was selected more frequently than Brazil; in Set 2, Brazil was chosen more frequently than France.

There is considerable evidence that the grouping of objects is determined by the similarities among them. The preceding studies provide evidence for the *converse* (diagnosticity) hypothesis that the similarity of objects is modified by the manner in which they are grouped. Hence, similarity serves as a basis for the classification of objects, but it is also influenced by the adopted classification. The diagnosticity principle that underlies the latter process may provide a key to the understanding of the effects of context on similarity.

DISCUSSION

The investigations reported in this chapter were based on the contrast model according to which the similarity between objects is expressed as a linear combination of the measures of their common and distinctive features. The results provide support for the general hypothesis that the parameters of the contrast

TABLE 4.5

Similarity Data for the Test of the Diagnosticity Hypothesis

	a_1	a_2	b	c	p	q	$b(p) - b(q)$	$c(q) - c(p)$
1	China	U.S.S.R.	Poland	U.S.A.	England	Hungary	18.8	1.6
2	Portugal	Spain	France	Brazil	Argentina	Belgium	27.0	54.1
3	New Zealand	Australia	Japan	Canada	U.S.A.	Philippines	27.2	−12.4
4	Libya	Algeria	Syria	Uganda	Angola	Jordan	13.8	10.3
5	Australia	New Zealand	S. Africa	England	Ireland	Rhodesia	−0.1	13.8
6	Cyprus	Malta	Sicily	Crete	Greece	Italy	0.0	3.4
7	India	China	U.S.S.R.	Japan	Philippines	U.S.A.	−6.6	14.8
8	S. Africa	Rhodesia	Ethiopia	New Zealand	Canada	Zaire	33.4	5.9
9	Iraq	Syria	Lebanon	Libya	Algeria	Cyprus	9.6	20.3
10	U.S.A.	Canada	Mexico	England	Australia	Panama	6.0	13.8
11	Holland	Belgium	Denmark	France	Italy	Sweden	5.4	−8.3
12	Australia	England	Cyprus	U.S.A.	U.S.S.R.	Greece	5.4	5.1

model are sensitive to manipulations that make the subject focus on certain features rather than on others. Consequently, similarities are not invariant with respect to the marking of the attribute (similarity vs. difference), the directionality of the comparison [$s(a, b)$ vs. $s(b, a)$] , and the context (i.e., the set of objects under consideration). In accord with the focusing hypothesis, Study 1 shows that the relative weight attached to the common features is greater in judgments of similarity than in judgments of difference (i.e., $\theta > \lambda$). Studies 2 and 3 show that people attach greater weight to the subject of a comparison than to its referent (i.e., $a > \beta$). Studies 4 and 5 show that the salience of features is determined, in part, by their diagnosticity (i.e., by their classificatory significance).

What are the implications of the present findings to the analysis and representation of similarity relations? First, they indicate that there is no unitary concept of similarity that is applicable to all different experimental procedures used to elicit proximity data. Rather, it appears that there is a wide variety of similarity relations (defined on the same domain) that differ in the weights attached to the various arguments of the feature-matching function. Experimental manipulations that call attention to the common features, for example, are likely to increase the weight assigned to these features. Likewise, experimental manipulations (e.g., the introduction of a standard) that emphasize the directionality of the comparison are likely to produce asymmetry. Finally, changes in the natural clustering of the objects under study are likely to highlight those features on which the clusters are based.

Although the violations of complementarity, symmetry, and context independence are statistically significant and experimentally reliable in the sense that they were observed with different stimuli under different experimental conditions, the effects are relatively small. Consequently, complementarity, symmetry, or context independence may provide good first approximations to similarity data. Scaling models that are based on these assumptions, therefore, should not be rejected off-hand. A Euclidean map may provide a very useful and parsimonious description of complex data, even though its underlying assumptions (e.g., symmetry, or the triangle inequality) may be incorrect. At the same time, one should not treat such a representation, useful as it might be, as an adequate psychological theory of similarity. An analogy to the measurement of physical distance illustrates the point. The knowledge that the earth is round does not prevent surveyors from using plane geometry to calculate small distances on the surface of the earth. The fact that such measurements often provide excellent approximations to the data, however, should not be taken as evidence for the flat-earth model.

Finally, two major objections have been raised against the usage of the concept of similarity [see e.g., Goodman (1972)] . First, it has been argued that similarity is relative and variable: Objects can be viewed as either similar or different depending on the context and frame of reference. Second, similarity often does not account for our inductive practice but rather is inferred from it; hence, the concept of similarity lacks explanatory power.

Although both objections have some merit, they do not render the concept of similarity empirically uninteresting or theoretically useless. The present studies, like those of Shepard (1964) and Torgerson (1965), show that similarity is indeed relative and variable, but it varies in a lawful manner. A comprehensive theory, therefore, should describe not only how similarity is assessed in a given situation but also how it varies with a change of context. The theoretical development, outlined in this chapter, provides a framework for the analysis of this process.

As for the explanatory function of similarity, it should be noted that similarity plays a dual role in theories of knowledge and behavior: It is employed as an independent variable to explain inductive practices such as concept formation, classification, and generalization; but it is also used as a dependent variable to be explained in terms of other factors. Indeed, similarity is as much a summary of past experience as a guide for future behavior. We expect similar things to behave in the same way, but we also view things as similar because they behave in the same way. Hence, similarities are constantly updated by experience to reflect our ever-changing picture of the world.

REFERENCES

Goodman, N. Seven strictures on similarity. In N. Goodman, *Problems and projects*. New York: Bobbs-Merril, 1972.

Hosman, J., and Kuennapas, T. On the relation between similarity and dissimilarity estimates. Report No. 354, Psychological Laboratories, The University of Stockholm, 1972.

Quine, W. V. Natural kinds. In W. V. Quine, *Ontological relativity and other essays*. New York: Columbia University Press, 1969.

Restle, F. *Psychology of judgment and choice*. New York: Wiley, 1961.

Rosch, E. Cognitive reference points. *Cognitive Psychology*, 1975, 7, 532–547.

Shepard, R. N. Attention and the metric structure of the stimulus space. *Journal of Mathematical Psychology*, 1964, 1, 54–87.

Shepard, R. N. Representation of structure in similarity data: Problems and prospects. *Psychometrika*, 1974, 39, 373–421.

Sjöberg, L. A cognitive theory of similarity. *Goteborg Psychological Reports*, 1972, 2(No. 10).

Torgerson, W. S. Multidimensional scaling of similarity. *Psychometrika*, 1965, 30, 379–393.

Tversky, A. Features of similarity. *Psychological Review*, 1977, 84, 327–352.

5 Aspects of a Stimulus: Features, Dimensions, and Configurations

W. R. Garner

Yale University

ABSTRACT

Several necessary distinctions about properties of stimuli are made. Component properties (attributes) consist of either dimensions or features. Dimensions are variables for which mutually exclusive levels exist, and quantitative dimensions are distinguished from qualitative dimensions on the basis of the role of zero: Zero is a positive value for quantitative dimensions but simply indicates absence of dimension for qualitative dimensions. Features are variables that exist or do not exist, so that zero is confounded as a level on a variable and as absence of the feature. Wholistic properties can be simple wholes, templates, or configurations, with simple wholes (and possibly templates) not being more than the sum of the parts; configural properties are emergent properties, thus other than the sum of the parts. Component and wholistic properties are different aspects of the same stimulus, because they coexist and are not independent. Implications of these distinctions for several cognitive tasks are made, including free classification, concept learning, decision and choice, and speed and accuracy of stimulus identification. Implications for modes of processing are also discussed.

ASPECTS OF A STIMULUS:
FEATURES, DIMENSIONS, AND CONFIGURATIONS

In the beginning is a stimulus. At least a stimulus is at the beginning of nearly every experimental procedure designed to tell us about human information processing, or cognitive psychology, more broadly speaking. But a stimulus is not just a vacuous entity; it has properties, and these properties have a great influence on the type of process that can be or is carried out by the humans we use in our experiments.

Unfortunately, the language used by psychologists to describe different properties of stimuli is so poorly differentiated that it is difficult at times to avoid the feeling of chaos. One writer refers to dimensions that have levels (values to another writer), and another talks of variables and their aspects (e.g., Restle, 1961). The confusion is easily illustrated by quoting Reed (1973): "Patterns consist of various elements which we can call features, attributes, cues, dimensions, or components. These words will be used interchangeably [p. 4]." Reed might have added to his list variables, aspects, and parts without doing an injustice to current usage. And, of course, there is another set of terms for noncomponent properties of stimuli — words such as template, whole, gestalt, configuration. These terms are equally inept in making the differentiations we need.

A great deal of this ambiguity is inherent in the language itself. In preparation of this chapter, I did a fairly thorough dictionary search in the hope that the distinctions I wanted to make were best exemplified by the use of some of these terms rather than others. Possibly, for example, some terms might be the best to use as the generic terms within which to include other terms. But the dictionary did not help; rather, it unfortunately confirmed that the confusion is indeed in the language itself.

Despite this confusion in the language, there are real differences in the properties of the stimuli used by different psychologists in their various experiments. However, the confusion in the language has led to minimal attempt to make the differentiations clear, with the result that it is frequently assumed that the stimulus properties in two different experiments are logically and functionally the same when they are not; we simply have not had a proper language to label the differences efficiently and without ambiguity.

One possible solution to this linguistic ambiguity is to invent some neologisms, which have no prior semantic meaning (thus no pre-existing ambiguity), and to define the new terms to suit our present purposes. I have not chosen that route in this chapter because I cannot feel sure that we know the kinds of differentiations needed sufficiently well that the meanings of the neologisms will not themselves soon become confused. In other words, I do not think we have as yet a sufficiently closed system of meanings to allow us to define a closed system of terms.

The alternative solution is to use the words that come closest to current modal usage in making the differentiations I want to make. Thus, in the title itself, I have used four terms that have been used as stimulus descriptive terms, because it seems to me that common usage (amongst the pertinent psychological scientists) comes close to the meanings I want to emphasize. These particular terms are defined in the main body of the text, but some prefatory terminological remarks can be made now.

A stimulus has properties, and that term will be used as a very general term, relatively undifferentiated. There are two major classes of stimulus properties: *component properties and wholistic properties.* Component properties are called *attributes,* and two major subclasses of attributes are called *dimensions* and *features.* Wholistic properties are subdivided into *simple wholes, templates,* and *configurations. Aspect* is again a fairly general term but is intended to emphasize the multiplicity of different properties of the same stimulus. Thus a given stimulus has both wholistic and component properties, and these are different aspects of the same stimulus. The term *variable* is used occasionally, and it means only that something (the attribute) varies within a set of stimuli.

Stimulus or Organismic Properties?

Are terms such as *component* and *wholistic* relevant to properties of the stimulus, or are they simply alternative modes by which an organism processes stimuli? The answer is both. There are many possible properties of a given stimulus, but psychologists are interested only in those that are at least potentially pertinent to the kinds of processes that the human organism can engage in. But this limit in our interest to those properties that are pertinent to the organism does not mean that the properties themselves are simply organismic properties that are in some sense imputed to the stimulus.

There is a necessary mutual interplay between stimulus and organismic properties. An organism cannot engage in pattern recognition, for example, based on a feature analysis unless there are in fact features in the stimulus to be analyzed. On the other hand, there is no need to attempt pure stimulus descriptions in terms that are inappropriate to the processing organism. So the properties of the organism limit the properties of the stimulus to which we pay attention; at the same time, the properties of the stimulus limit what the organism can do with the stimulus.

It is this latter point that provides the focus of this chapter: I attempt to differentiate some properties of the stimulus insofar as possible without regard to the nature of the processor of the stimuli. But the intent of these differentiations is to show how these stimulus properties limit or predispose the processing organism to deal with the stimulus in particular ways. In other words, properties of the stimulus provide a limiting condition for the processing organism, but at the same time, the stimulus properties do not completely determine mode of processing at all. Prinz and Scheerer-Neumann (1974), for example, in making some distinctions similar to some that I make in this chapter, show experimentally that humans may process stimuli as composed of features even though the stimuli have been generated dimensionally.

So the point of view in this chapter is not that knowing the properties of the stimulus allows us to know how the stimulus is processed; rather, it is that we can know some processing predispositions and some bounds on the type of processing if we know the properties of the stimulus. With this in mind, I define some stimulus properties, and I then discuss some probable consequences of these properties on different types of cognitive process.

ATTRIBUTES: FEATURES OR DIMENSIONS

As mentioned earlier, an attribute is a component property of a stimulus, a property that helps to define a particular stimulus but that is not synonymous with the stimulus. It often is thought of as an abstracted property of the stimulus in the sense that the attribute exists without any particular manifestation of it. Thus such things as color, size, form, brightness, and linearity are component properties of a stimulus, thus attributes.

Some Further Definitions

There are two major subtypes of attributes: dimensions, and features; and there is an intermediate type that I call a *pseudodimension.* There are further possible differentiations, although it is not obvious that further differentiations are psychologically meaningful. However, in all of the distinctions, a very important consideration is the role that the concept of zero plays for the attribute.

A *dimension* is an attribute of a stimulus such that if the dimension exists for the stimulus, it exists at some positive level (or value), and these alternative possible levels are mutually exclusive. To illustrate, if hue is an attribute of a stimulus, there must be some particular hue for each stimulus, and the stimulus cannot be two or more hues simultaneously. Thus the attribute of hue exists at some positive level, and the levels are mutually exclusive. Likewise, brightness or loudness are dimensions, because they must exist at some level, and the levels are mututally exclusive. And so also is form a dimension, because it must exist at one of several mutually exclusive levels. In terms of the kinds of attributes used to describe alphanumeric symbols (e.g., E. J. Gibson's list of distinctive features for a set of graphemes, 1969, p. 88), I would consider curvature of a line to be a dimension, because if the line exists, it must exist with one of several mutually exclusive curvatures. Others of Gibson's properties I would not consider dimensions, however, because there is no need for mutual exclusion.

In terms of information-processing notions, the proper interrogation with respect to a stimulus attribute that is a dimension is: At what level is this dimension? In some circumstances, it might be necessary to ask a prior question: Does this dimension exist for this stimulus? If the answer is yes, then a second question must always be asked concerning the level at which it exists.

The concept of zero is important in understanding the difference between a dimension and a feature, and it has two possible meanings with a dimension. With some dimensions, zero is one of the possible mutually exclusive levels on the dimension, as with zero brightness or loudness. In these cases, zero is a positive level on the dimension. Such dimensions might be considered a subclass of *quantitative dimensions.* For other dimensions, zero really means the non-existence of the dimension, and even the nonexistence of the stimulus. Thus a single visual stimulus has to have some form, and zero in this case would not ordinarily be a level on the dimension (yet see pseudodimensions later) but would simply indicate nonexistence of the dimension. Such dimensions might be considered a subclass of *qualitative dimensions.*

E. J. Gibson (1969) is one of the few authors to distinguish between features and dimensions, and for her, the defining property of a dimension is that it is a continuous and ordered attribute. I could consider continuous and discrete dimensions as further subclasses of dimensions, orthogonal to the distinction between quantitative and qualitative, but these distinctions go beyond the functional differences I want to emphasize in this chapter. Yet both the quanti-tative—qualitative distinction and the continuous—discrete distinction may, in some circumstances at least, play an important role in cognitive processes.

To summarize this point, however, the two most important defining charac-teristics of a dimension are: (1) the mutual exclusion of the levels on the dimen-sion; and (2) the role of zero as a positive level on quantitative dimensions or as indicative of nonexistence of the dimensions for qualitative dimensions.

A feature is an attribute of a stimulus that either exists or does not exist, but if it exists, it has only a single level; thus the idea of positive levels as mutually exclusive is inappropriate. A feature might be called a dissociable element in that it can be taken away from the stimulus without otherwise affecting the rest of the stimulus. As an example, the horizontal line in the middle of the upper case letter E is a feature of the stimulus (as is every other component, of course), and it can be removed without otherwise affecting the rest of the stimulus. In contrast, if the dimension of color is removed from a stimulus, the stimulus itself ceases to exist.

In terms of information-processing notions, the proper interrogation with respect to a stimulus attribute that is a feature is: Does this stimulus contain feature X? Most information-processing models incorporate this type of interro-gation and are thus appropriate to features rather than to dimensions, but many of the stimuli to which the models are applied are actually generated from dimen-sions rather than from features.

Once again, the concept of zero is crucial in understanding the nature of a feature and its difference from a dimension. With a feature, zero means simply that the feature doesn't exist in this particular stimulus. One way of conceptual-izing a feature is as a variable with just two levels, one of which is zero and the other of which is the positive feature itself. The importance of this concept is that when a feature does not exist in a given stimulus, there is no information in the stimulus that indicates the potentiality of the feature; whereas with a dimension, because it always exists as a positive value in any stimulus, the full set of dimensions is knowable from any single stimulus. This is one of the most important distinctions between a dimension and a feature: In every relevant stimulus, the full set of dimensions is always knowable; but the full set of features is knowable only if all features exist in the particular stimulus. With features, the role of zero is confounded, because it may mean nonexistence of the feature as a variable in a set of stimuli, or it may simply mean that the feature does not exist in this particular stimulus.

The Functional Context

In the abstract, the distinction between dimensions and features is fairly easy: A dimension is an attribute that exists for each stimulus in the relevant set and at some positive, mutually exclusive value; a feature is an attribute that does or does not exist for each stimulus in the relevant set. Thus zero may be a positive level on a dimension or may indicate nonexistence of the dimension; but if the set of features is considered to define the set of possible stimuli, then zero has to be considered a level on a variable, the other level being the feature itself.

In many actual stimuli, the distinction is easy to maintain. For example, if a set of stimuli is generated by the use of four forms and four colors in all 16 combinations, then we are unambiguously dealing with two dimensions with four positive levels on each dimension. And if the stimuli are generated by using a vertical line as a handle on which to attach features (a common device in generating actual stimuli), and the features are a horizontal right-hand line at the top, middle, or bottom of the handle, then we are dealing with three features, which can generate eight possible stimuli, several of which are identifiable as block upper-case letters, especially the F, E, L, and block C.

In other stimulus sets, the distinction depends on the functional nature of the attributes used in generating the particular set of stimuli. Suppose, to illustrate, that we use the vertical line as a handle but allow the horizontal line to appear at the top, middle, or bottom. In this case, we generate only three alternative stimuli, and the location of the line now functions as a dimension. Perhaps we should call such an attribute a *pseudodimension,* because it acts as a dimension only by the arbitrary imposition of the mutual-exclusion rule, which is a property of a dimension but which is not an inherent property of the particular form of attribute used. In still other stimulus sets, we can generate attributes with, say, two positive levels and arbitrarily designate the absence of either positive level as a third level. Such dimensions would also be pseudodimensions, or in a given context they might be considered pseudofeatures, because they use the zero as a level on a variable as is true with features, while at the same time using three mutually exclusive levels within the context of the set of stimuli generated. To illustrate, J. R. Whitman and I (Whitman & Garner, 1962) generated visual figures that used zero, one, or two vertical lines as three levels on a dimension, and a dot above the figure, below the figure, or absent as three levels on another dimension. Because of the inherent confusion in using such dimensions, we (e.g., Whitman & Garner, 1963) used only truly positive levels in generating our stimuli for later experiments.

Thus feature-like properties can be treated like dimensions, especially if, in the stimulus context, zero is arbitrarily defined (by either the experimenter or the experimental subject) as a positive level on an attribute that would otherwise be simply a qualitative dimension. On the other hand, dimensions can be treated as features, especially by the human information processor whose preferred mode of processing is a feature-type interrogation even when doing so may be inappropriate or unnecessary. To illustrate, consider stimuli generated from four forms and four colors. There is nothing to prevent the human information processor from asking a series of yes—no questions such as: Is the stimulus red, is the stimulus green, is the stimulus square, etc? If the information processor asks such questions, the dimensions are being treated as features. This particular point was made by Prinz and Scheerer-Neumann (1974). They generated stimuli from dimensions, but the speeds of classifications in their experiments indicated that subjects were treating the levels on the dimensions as features that either exist or do not. As a comment, these authors used dichotomous dimensions, and it is quite possible that such dimensions are more easily treated as features than dimensions with more levels. However, it is entirely possible that the more natural way for humans to process stimuli for many different tasks is to use a feature system of processing insofar as possible, regardless of whether the stimuli are generated from dimensions or from features.

Processing Implications

As these examples have shown, the nature of stimulus generation does not completely determine the nature of the processing: Dimensionally defined stimuli can be processed as features, and feature-defined stimuli can, under some circumstances at least, be processed as dimensions. However, the properties of dimensions and features are meaningfully different, and these differences will make one form of processing more efficient than another, will predispose the subject to use a particular form of processing, or may in some circumstances limit processing to a particular mode. Although the number and subtlety of processing concepts is too great for a thoroughly detailed treatment of several different cognitive tasks, this section is used to illustrate how the difference between dimensions and features could influence performance in several different experimental situations.

Inferred Stimulus Sets.   The difference between dimensions and features is of importance to several cognitive tasks primarily because of the confounded role of zero with feature-defined stimuli. The first of these tasks is almost a simple demonstration of the fact that when a feature is missing in a particular stimulus, the stimulus provides no information about what alternative stimuli there are in the meaningful set. The task is to present one or more stimuli from a defined set to a subject and to require the subject to generate other stimuli that could be presumed to go with those presented. I have argued and shown (Garner, 1962, 1974a) that the properties of any single stimulus are determined by the properties of the set within which it is contained. In fact, there is no way to describe a stimulus without reference to the set of alternatives (see Garner, 1974a). If the full set of relevant stimulus alternatives is not known to an observer, then the alternatives are inferred from the available properties of the stimulus itself. This concept of the inferred stimulus set has been most successful in relation to visual pattern goodness, pattern goodness being inversely related to the size of the inferred set of alternatives. (Again, see Garner, 1974a, for a review of this literature.)

With regard to the differences between dimensions and features, the point is that stimuli generated from dimensions easily imply their alternatives, because dimensions always have a positive level in any stimulus generated. Thus the dimension can be known to be at least potentially functional on the basis of any single stimulus. On the other hand, if stimuli are generated from features, then if the feature is not present in any single stimulus, the stimulus does not imply the existence of the feature in alternative stimuli, and the observer cannot accurately infer it.

Consider the sets of 16 stimuli in Figs. 5.1 and 5.2, as well as the sets of four stimuli in Figs. 5.3 and 5.4. (These four figures are used as illustrations throughout this chapter.) In Fig. 5.1, there are four dimensions, easily labeled as top, right, bottom, and left. Each dimension is a line with two levels of curvature, in or out. All 16 stimuli that can be generated with these four dichotomous dimensions are shown. Each stimulus in the set has a positive level on each dimension, and except for stimuli 1a and 4d, both levels are shown in the stimulus.

In Fig. 5.2, the 16 stimuli are generated from features, again labeled as top, right, bottom, and left. The feature is a single out curvature. Stimulus 4d in this case is indicated as a dot to give it some positive property, because this stimulus is generated by the absence of all four features. This stimulus, of course, does not imply any reasonable alternatives, even though its counterpart in Fig. 5.1 at least gives some information about the kinds of alternative stimuli that might occur.

The dimensions in Fig. 5.1 are somewhat arbitrary in that they can be omitted without destroying the rest of the stimulus and thus can easily be converted to the feature system of Fig. 5.2. But the dimensions used to generate the four stimuli in Fig. 5.3 are not easily converted to features. Size and form are two dichotomous dimensions that generate four stimuli, and every such stimulus has to have both a size and a form. Thus any single stimulus has the potential of indicating the nature of its alternatives quite effectively.

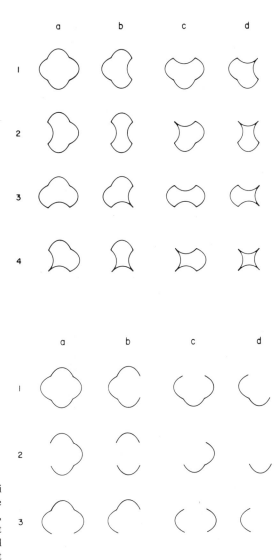

FIG. 5.1. A set of 16 stimuli generated from four dichotomous dimensions. The dimensions are top, right, bottom, and left; the levels on each dimension are in and out. The individual stimuli are identified in the text as located in rows and columns (e.g., the top left figure is 1a).

FIG. 5.2. A set of 16 stimuli generated from four features. The features are top, right, bottom, and left, and the features exist or do not exist. The individual stimuli are identified in the text by rows and columns, and stimulus 4d is shown as a dot because all features are missing in it.

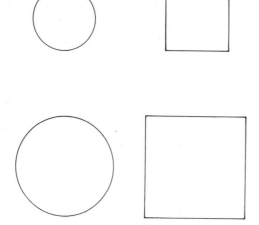

FIG. 5.3. A set of four stimuli generated from the dichotomous dimensions of form and size. The individual stimuli are identified in the text as large square, etc.

A counterpart set of four stimuli generated from features is shown in Fig. 5.4. Here the "I" stimulus is essentially a handle to which two features can be attached, a top horizontal line or a bottom horizontal line. These features allow the four stimuli to be identified as I, T, L, and a block C, for purposes of reference. Once again the featureless stimulus implies little about its alternatives.

In one sense, this lack of accurate stimulus inference with feature-generated stimuli is little more than a restatement of the fact that features are attributes for which one of the two levels is zero. However, there are many psychological processes that are a function of the nature and number of inferred stimulus alternatives (see Garner, 1974a, especially Lecture 2), ranging from paired-associate learning to simple two-choice discrimination. Furthermore, the confounding between zero as absence of an attribute and as a level on an attribute is a major factor in other cognitive processes that I discuss here.

Concept Learning. In concept learning or identification experiments, concepts are ordinarily defined in terms of logical rules or relations, such as affirmation (e.g., the concept is "red"), conjunction (e.g., the concept is "red and square"), or biconditionality (e.g., the concept is "either red and square or round and green").

The concepts may be defined in positive or in negative form. For example, the concept may be "A" or "not A", or it may be the conjunction of "A and B" or the conjunction of "not A and not B". Stimuli, then, in the language of concept research, are positive instances of the concept if they satisfy the rule and are negative instances if they do not.

Stimuli generated from features rather than dimensions seem more compatible with the nature of concepts themselves. If the concept is stated in the positive form, then the feature, or combination of features, exist in the positive form, and the negation of the concept (its complement) is represented by the appropriate absence of the positive features. Likewise, if the concept is stated in the negative form, then the absence of the feature seems cognitively appropriate to a concept stated in terms of the absence of a property.

Despite this natural relation between the rules used to define concepts and features, by far the greatest majority of concept experiments have used dimension-generated stimuli rather than feature-generated stimuli. But with stimulus instances defined by dimensions, negative concepts such as double negation can readily be translated into a positive form. To illustrate, consider the stimuli of Fig. 5.3, with a concept defined as "not large and not circle." This negatively defined concept is readily translated into the positive conjunction, "small and square."

With feature-defined stimuli, such a translation of a negative concept is much more difficult, being possible only if a "handle" exists. For instance, in Fig. 5.4, the concept "not top horizontal line and not bottom horizontal line" can be translated into the letter I. But consider the four lower-right stimuli in Fig. 5.2. The concept "not left feature and not right feature" is not readily translated into a positive stimulus and would have to be learned as a negation. That fact in itself may be important, in the sense that it is cognitively more difficult to deal with the absence of properties rather than the presence of properties. In addition, however, the fact that stimuli having only the absence of features are less informative about the stimulus alternatives than are stimuli having one level on each dimension may also be of cognitive concern.

Is this difference between features and dimensions actually important in concept learning? I know of no experiment that deliberately varied this factor within a single experiment, and as I remarked previously, most experiments have used dimension-defined stimuli whether the concepts were defined in terms of presence or absence of the pertinent properties. There is one experiment, how-

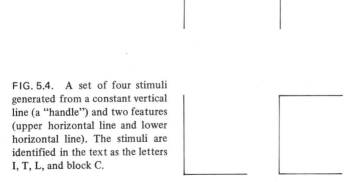

FIG. 5.4. A set of four stimuli generated from a constant vertical line (a "handle") and two features (upper horizontal line and lower horizontal line). The stimuli are identified in the text as the letters I, T, L, and block C.

ever, that does show that learning is more difficult when the concepts are defined in terms of negation and when the pertinent stimulus itself has the absence of a pertinent property as the appropriate exemplar. The experiment of interest was carried out by Neisser and Weene (1962). Their stimuli were strings of upper-case letters: JQVXZ. The concepts were defined in terms of the presence or absence of one or two of the letters. The letters could occur in any order and in any number per letter (e.g., VZZQ), but the only pertinent properties were the presence of absence of any single letter. The concepts used ranged from simple presence (or absence) through conjunctive and disjunctive concepts on to biconditional concepts. Although there is not space here to go into all the details of this experiment, a major factor in its design was that every concept was used in both its positive and negative form. Thus conjunctive presence was used (e.g., both V and Q, with a stimulus like VXZQ being a positive instance) but so also was conjunctive absence (e.g., neither V nor Q, with a stimulus like JXXZ being a positive instance).

The results of primary interest are simply that equivalent concepts stated in their negative form were more difficult to learn than when they were stated in their positive form, for every form of concept. This difference disappeared for most of the concepts in a second stage of learning, after opportunity for learning all the stimulus alternatives, but concepts of simple presence remained easier than concepts of simple absence even in this second stage of learning. Some years ago, shortly after the article appeared, I did a formal informational analysis of the learning task in this experiment to try to understand why it was more difficult to learn negative concepts with negative instances than positive concepts with positive instances. The result was clear: The concepts whose instances were the absence of letters provided less information than the concepts whose instances were the presence of letters, for the reason being discussed here, namely, that such stimuli do not imply their alternatives accurately. In other words, if the stimuli had been generated with upper and lower cases of letters as two levels on a dimension (e.g., VZqxJ) rather than as presence or absence of a letter (e.g., VZJ), this informational disadvantage of the negatively defined concepts might not have occurred. These authors' stimuli were fairly complex in allowing different orders and repetitions of letters, so I cannot be positive that the only factor operating was this lower information content of featureless instances, but the suggestion is certainly strong that it is an important factor.

In summary, then, it seems clear that difficulty of concept learning is influenced by whether the stimuli are generated with dimensions or with features. We have very little information on the specific effects, but I would conjecture the following: Overall, concept learning is easier with stimulus instances that are generated from dimensions rather than from features. And overall, concepts defined in positive form are easier to learn than those defined in negative form. However, this difference between negative and positive concepts is slight for stimuli generated from dimensions but is greater for stimuli generated from features. This interaction could be so substantial that the easiest task of all might be to have a positive concept in which positive instances correspond to the presence of features and negative instances correspond to the absence of features. And likewise, the most difficult concept task might be a negative concept such that positive instances are the absence of features and negative instances are the presence of features. Thus this interaction might well obscure any overall effects of either type of concept or type of dimension.

Selective Attention.   Selective attention tasks may require attention to quite different properties of the stimulus. In terms appropriate to this discussion, Treisman (1969) and later I (Garner, 1974b) distinguished between selective attention to a dimension and selective attention to the levels on a dimension, or some conjunction of them. To illustrate, stimuli such as those in Fig. 5.3 may be used, and the subject may be required to classify a set of stimulus cards as fast as he or she can on the basis of size. In other words, the subject is instructed to consider size as the relevant dimension and form as the irrelevant dimension and to attend only to size in carrying out the classification task. This task requires selective attention to the dimension itself, with later processing of both levels (or all, if more than two levels per dimension) also being required.

Alternatively, the subject may be required to attend selectively to just one level on the dimension of form, being required, for example, to put all the circles in one pile (or to respond positively to them in some other way), while discarding all noncircles. In this case, selective attention to the level on a dimension is required. It is, of course, also possible to require selective attention to some conjunction of levels, such as large square.

This distinction between selective attention to the source of variation and selective attention to the level on a dimension is quite meaningful when the attributes are dimensions with positive values on them. The distinction is even more meaningful if the dimensions are multileveled rather than dichotomous. For example, if the stimuli can be red, yellow, green, or blue, then to require selective attention to red stimuli, with no differentiation between yellow, green, and blue, is quite different from a requirement to selectively attend to the dimensions. In the latter case, all levels on the dimension must be processed.

This distinction becomes almost meaningless if the stimulus attributes are features rather than dimensions, because each source of variation has only a single positive value. Thus to require selective attention to the upper horizontal line in the feature-generated stimuli of Fig. 5.4 is the same as to require selective attention to the attribute as a variable, because the level and the feature are one and the same. If the feature is considered as a variable with two levels (the feature and its absence), then it is logically possible to require a subject to attend selectively to each of these levels. However, to require selective attention to the absence of a feature is meaningless, because the positive feature must in effect be processed in order to assert its absence.

So, once again, the confounded role of zero with features makes distinctions between the source of variation and levels on the variable attribute meaningless, whereas the distinction is very meaningful wtih stimuli generated by dimensions. At least the distinction is potentially meaningful in terms of the logical properties of dimensions and of features. There is, of course, always the interesting question of how the actual processing is carried out when selective attention to a level on a dimension is required. If human processors are indeed capable of dealing with levels on dimensions as features that either do or do not exist, then the mode of processing may not in fact be different in the two cases. However, even if processing of the level on a dimension is done the same way as processing of a feature, it is still clear that selective attention to dimensions is possible (at least if the dimensions are separable; see Garner, 1974a, Lecture 6), and that attention to a dimension is different than attention to a level on a dimension. On the other hand, the distinction between selective attention to a feature as a level on a variable and attention to a feature as a variable itself is simply not meaningful.

Decision and Choice.   Another area in which the confounding of zero as absence of a variable and as a level on a variable limits processing options is in the area of decision and choice. There are many models of choice behavior in which it is assumed that choices between stimuli are made on the basis of information about one property at a time rather than on a composite evaluation of all properties of all stimuli available. In any model of this sort, there must be some basis for deciding the order in which the properties will be evaluated, and this order will, of course, have considerable influence on the final choice outcome. And the question of concern here is: What are the kinds of properties that can be or are ordered for evaluation, and what determines the order?

Coombs (1964) describes sequential choice models (which he terms *lexicographic*), and although he does not specifically differentiate between dimensions and features in the sense that I do here, it is clear from his discussion that he is thinking in terms of dimensions. And the property that is ordered in the lexicographic model is the dimension itself, not the levels on the dimension. Furthermore, the factors that determine the order of processing the dimensions need not be related at all to the number or particular levels on the dimension. A dimension can be salient or preferred, and this preference might well be for a dimension on which two levels can be barely discriminated. (See, e.g., Imai and Garner, 1965, for evidence that the preference for a dimension is not necessarily related to the discriminability of the levels on the dimension.) To illustrate, in choosing an automobile for purchase, our chooser might decide to consider body style first but then finds that the alternative body styles available are barely different, in fact are so similar that on successive choices of body style a probability distribution across styles is obtained rather than a clear preference for just one style. But even if a single body style is easily chosen, the point is that processes having to do with the dimension itself are quite separate from processes having to do with the levels on the dimension, just as they are in selective attention.

Alternatively, consider that the properties of the items to be chosen are features. In this case, no distinction between the feature as a variable and as a level on the variable can be made, so choosing a particular feature as the first to be considered is the same as choosing that particular feature, even though the choice may be probabilistic. Tversky (1972) presents a theory of sequential choice (called by him *elimination by aspects*) that is based on the feature idea rather than the dimension idea. Thus the choice sequence is made by asking a series of yes—no questions such as: Does this automobile have automatic transmission? The order of questioning concerning aspects (features) is determined probabilistically by a weight given to each aspect. The important point here is that there cannot be a separate weight for the feature as variable and the feature as level.

Incidentally, it is of interest that many of the illustrations used by Tversky, including the illustration used here about the automatic transmission, really refer to dimensions rather than features. An automobile must have a transmission. Tversky's use of the feature-type interrogation, however, once again illustrates the point that choice makers may use a feature system of processing even though the properties being processed are dimensional. In general, of course, if the properties of the stimuli or choice objects are features, then feature processing must be used; if the properties are dimensions, then processing may be done dimensionally or as though the levels on the dimensions are features. It is an open experimental question as to how the processing is actually carried out.

Accuracy of Stimulus Identification.   I turn now to several problems encountered in relation to stimulus identification, problems of accuracy, speed, and forms of processing. The task to be considered is this: A total set of stimuli is formed from dimensions or features, one stimulus is presented to a subject at a time, the subject has to identify (i.e., label uniquely) each stimulus, and we measure accuracy and/or speed of identification. For the moment, I consider accuracy, and the question is whether there should be differences in the types of errors made due to inherent differences between dimensions and features. There are indeed distinct differences in error distributions when stimuli are generated from dimensions rather than features.

The concepts of state and process limitation (Garner, 1970, 1974a) are important in understanding the nature of identification errors, because this distinction interacts with that between dimensions and features. Errors occur because there is some inadequacy in the processing system; there is, in other words, a limitation. State limitation exists when sufficient information about the stimulus fails to get into the organism. The most usual ways in which experimenters produce state limitation are to use very short exposure durations, or very low intensities. Process limitation occurs when alternative stimuli to be identified are confused for some reason. They may simply be too similar, or there may be too many to carry in memory, etc. The term *state* implies that there is some general inadequacy in the organism to receive information, even if the inadequacy is in the "amount" of the stimulus available. The term *process* implies that there is some inadequacy with respect to the process that the experimenter, in setting the task requirements, requires of the subject.

First, let us consider stimuli generated from dimensions and how errors occur if the stimuli are state limited. (And, incidentally, state limitation is by far the most usual way in which experiments concerned with errors are carried out; that is, errors are produced by state limitation of the stimulus input.) If the stimuli are generated from dimensions, as in Fig. 5.1 and 5.3, all stimuli have an equivalent status in that the "amount" of stimulus is essentially the same for each particular stimulus. That is, to illustrate in Fig. 5.1, there is as much of stimulus 3a as of stimulus 4b, and state limitation will have no differential effect on different stimuli.

When errors are made, they are made on the basis of similarity, stimuli differing on a single dimension being more similar than those differing on two dimensions, etc. For example, in Fig. 5.3, if the small circle is identified incorrectly, we would expect that more erroneous identifications would be small square or large circle than large square, because large square differs from small circle in two dimensions, whereas the other two stimuli differ from it in only one dimension. Furthermore, if large circle is used in error to small circle, then small circle will be used in error to large circle, and except for possible response bias, we would expect an equal number of each type of error in a long series of identifications. In other words, the error distribution between all possible pairs of stimuli should be symmetric. Furthermore, exactly the same symmetric distribution of errors occurs if the errors are produced by process limitation.

Now consider stimuli generated from features as in Fig. 5.2 and 5.4, with state limitation the cause of errors. Once again, if an error is made, the incorrect identification tends to be one differing from the stimulus on only a single feature. For example, in Fig. 5.4, if an incorrect identification is made to the C, it is the T or the L, not the I, because the I differs from the C more than the T or L differ from the C. However, the error distribution is not symmetric in this case, because errors always tend to be made in the direction of fewer features. In state limitation, something is lost, and if stimuli are generated by features, then the loss is of features. To be specific, consider stimulus L. If an error is made in responding to it, the most likely error is I, certainly not C; yet the L is a very likely identification when the stimulus is C. So L is used as an erroneous identification to C, but C is not used erroneously to L. In general, the error distribution is very asymmetric and tends toward the stimulus with the fewest features. Alternatively, if errors are used to provide a sequential task, each identification becoming the stimulus for the next identification, ultimately the stimulus identification is the I in Fig. 5.4, or stimulus 4d in Fig. 5.2, that is to say, it becomes the featureless stimulus.

On the other hand, there is little reason to expect this asymmetry in error distribution if the stimuli are process limited, because simple stimulus similarity operates in determining errors, not loss of features.

A simple kind of operational demonstration can illustrate the difference between state and process limitation and their effects on error distributions. Let us produce state limitation by directly eliminating one dimension or one feature in Fig. 5.1 or 5.2. To illustrate, assume that the top dimension is eliminated in stimulus 2b, the one shaped like an hourglass. If that dimension is eliminated, then the possible stimuli are 2b or 2d: In other words, only stimulus 2d is used as an erroneous identification. If the top dimension is eliminated in stimulus 2d, then the possible stimuli are again 2b or 2d, and only stimulus 2b is used as an erroneous identification. So the error distribution is symmetrical.

If the top feature is eliminated in stimulus 2b in Fig. 5.2, then the stimulus is always erroneously identified as 4d. However, if the top feature is eliminated in stimulus 4d (a redundant elimination because the feature is already missing), then no error of identification is made. So the error distribution is asymmetrical.

Now let us produce process limitation in the same stimuli and on the same dimensions and features not by eliminating the dimension or feature but by reversing its level. In Fig. 5.1, a reversal of the top dimension in stimulus 2b produces stimulus 2d; and a reversal of the top dimension in stimulus 2d produces stimulus 2b. So the error distribution is symmetrical.

In Fig. 5.2, with feature-generated stimuli, the reversal of the top feature in stimulus 2b (reversal in this case means elimination of feature) produces stimulus 2d; but also a reversal of the top feature in stimulus 2d (adding the feature) produces stimulus 2b. So the error distribution is symmetrical.

To summarize, error distributions can be expected to be symmetrical for both types of stimuli when identification is process limited, but when identification is state limited, the error distribution is symmetrical if the stimuli are dimensionally generated but is asymmetrical if the stimuli are feature generated.

Are there any data to support these expectations? The best available are some provided by Townsend (1971) on upper-case letter identifications. Letters, of course, in the terms I have been using, consist of both features and dimensions, so data on letter identifications should be of some help. Townsend used all 26 upper-case letters as stimuli, and his subjects were required simply to identify the letters. He used two different presentation conditions in order to produce errors: In Condition 1, a very short exposure was used (producing unequivocal state limitation); and in Condition 2, both short duration and poststimulus noise were used (producing state limitation plus possibly some process limitation).

For each letter as stimulus, I noted the most probable letter used as an incorrect identification (the modal error), using data from both conditions combined. I then classified the error in relation to the stimulus, and 12 of the modal errors were best described as a loss of features, and only five could reasonably be described as an increase of features.

To examine the relation between errors and features, I selected six pairs of letters that seemed most unambiguously to be related to each other in terms of simple loss or gain of features. These pairs are shown in Table 5.1. To clarify, consider the letter pair E–F. These letters are identical except for the presence

TABLE 5.1
Number of Times One Letter of a Pair Was Incorrectly Used
as Response to the Other Letter Presented as Stimulus[a]

	Stimulus Letter	
Letter Pair	First	Second
E – F	16	7
E – L	20	3
T – I	24	14
G – C	19	6
Q – O	60	16
R – P	18	8

[a]Data from Townsend (1971).

or absence of a single feature, the bottom horizontal line. When E was presented as the stimulus, then F was used erroneously as a response 16 times; when F was presented as the stimulus, E was used erroneously as a response 7 times. In every pair in Table 5.1, the letter with fewer features was used more often as a response to the letter with more features than in the reverse direction.

That these asymmetries represent true perceptual processes and not simple response bias is fairly self-evident from the data. Response bias almost certainly follows frequency of usage in ordinary English, but these data do not follow frequency of usage at all. F is less frequent than E, and L than E, yet each is used erroneously more often. When the more frequent letter is also the one with fewer features, as with Q and O, then the asymmetry becomes even greater. To illustrate further that these effects are not simple response bias, it can be noted that the letters I and L were used as responses in Townsend's data overall about twice as often as the letters E and F. Clearly, the way for a letter to be used often when the stimulus is state limited is to have few features.

Evidence that symmetrical error distributions occur when there is a difference in levels on a dimension (such as curved-straight) was impossible to obtain, because there were simply too few errors for a meaningful analysis. Overall, however, these data lend support to the idea that error distributions are different as a function of the dimension–feature distinction and that this difference is probably related to whether errors are produced because of state limitation or process limitation.

Asymmetry in Redundancy. Another type of asymmetry occurs when redundant stimuli are generated with features rather than with dimensions. For this illustration, Figs. 5.3 and 5.4 are most useful although the four stimuli in the upper left or in the lower right quadrants of Figs. 5.1 and 5.2 can also be used But I refer to Figs. 5.3 and 5.4.

First, let me be explicit about what I mean by redundancy. In Fig. 5.3, there are four stimuli produced by orthogonal combinations of the two dimensions of size and form. From these four stimuli, six pairs of stimuli can be obtained. Four of these pairs involve a difference between stimuli on a single dimension (e.g., the two stimuli on the right differ only in size). Two of the pairs differ on both dimensions at once, these pairs being small circle and large square, or small square and large circle. Such stimulus pairs are redundant, because they differ in more ways than minimally necessary in order to have two different stimuli. At least with some stimulus dimensions (Garner, 1974a, Lecture 6), speed of discrimination if faster with the redundant pairs than with the nonredundant pairs.

However, whatever the effects on performance are, measured by accuracy or by speed, there is no reason to expect that one of the redundant pairs would give different performance than the other redundant pair. When stimuli are generated with positive levels of dimensions, the different redundant pairs are all equivalent. Furthermore, with reference to the previous section, there would be no differential effect produced by the use of state rather than process limitation to produce inadequate performance.

The situation is quite different for the four stimuli shown in Fig. 5.4, those generated by combinations of presence or absence of two features. Once again, there are four pairs of stimuli that differ on a single feature, and performance with each of these pairs would, with state limitation, show the asymmetry of errors discussed in the preceding section. But consider the two redundant pairs: I and C or L and T. Now the use of features to generate the stimuli provides two pairs of redundant stimuli that are functionally quite different.

The pair I and C will, of course, be highly discriminable, and they are still most easily differentiated on the basis of number of features. Thus state limitation would once again produce asymmetry of the error distribution, and the letter I would be used as a response in a simple identification task much more often than would the letter C.

But the pair T and L will almost certainly be dealt with differently. The redundancy is functionally in this pair of stimuli, but this pair of stimuli differ only in which of the two features is present. Thus it is possible to redefine this pair of stimuli by asking simply which feature exists. Such a redefinition in effect makes these two stimuli differ as levels on a dimension (albeit a pseudodimension), and there are natural consequences of this redefinition. For example, there would be no reason at all to expect an asymmetric distribution of errors in differentiating the T and L stimuli, with state limitation. This loss of asymmetry can be thought of as due to the loss of any stimulus alternatives that have fewer features than the stimuli actually used. But this interpretation in turn suggests that such a pair of stimuli would not be perceived as feature generated.

Although I know of no data on this point, I expect speed of discrimination to be greater for the C vs. I pair than for the T vs. L pair, because the two stimuli differing by two features seem more different than the pair differing on which feature exists, or alternatively as two levels on a single pseudodimension. Thus both error distributions and speed of discrimination could be expected to differ for the two pairs of redundant stimuli if they are feature generated, although not if they are dimension generated.

Speed of Identification.   These differences between the two pairs of redundant stimuli suggest that there may be very important differences in mode of processing of dimensions or features in stimulus identification, differences of the sort that are most readily reflected in speed of identification. In this last section concerning attributes, I discuss some processing implications of the difference between dimensions and features, particularly with regard to whether processing is exhaustive and whether serial or parallel processing is likely to be used.

First, consider 16 stimuli that are generated from four features, such as those shown in Fig. 5.2. A particular stimulus is presented, and the identifier needs to decide which particular stimulus it is. If the stimuli are nonredundant, as in our example, then the feature search or interrogation must be exhaustive. That is to say, four yes–no questions must be asked, and none of the questions may be omitted. So our identifier (experimental subject, that is) must ask: Is the top feature present? Is the right feature present? Etc., until interrogation has proceeded with regard to all four features. Such an interrogation could be carried out in either serial or parallel mode, but in whichever mode, it must be exhaustive if no errors of identification are to be made. If the interrogation is carried out in the serial mode, it would not matter whether a random or fixed order of interrogation is used because of the need for the interrogation to be exhaustive. And this exhaustive requirement also means that identification times will be quite stable from stimulus to stimulus and from trial to trial.

Now consider 16 stimuli generated from two dimensions: four forms times four colors. (Momentarily I use dimensions with four levels to sharpen the distinction between features and dimensions.) Because there are still 16 alternative stimuli, we know that complete identification can be accomplished once again with four dichotomous questions. The form these questions must take to be efficient are: Is it either red or green? If yes, then: Is it red? If no, then, is it yellow? And: Is it either a circle or a triangle? If yes, then: Is it a circle? Etc. In other words, each question must be framed in order to produce one bit of information in the answer. If this efficient interrogation procedure is used, processing is again exhaustive. And thus for every stimulus, there are exactly four questions, and speed of identification is stable from one stimulus to another and from one trial to another.

A comment about the nature of exhaustive search is required. When talking about feature-generated stimuli, to state that the interrogation procedure is exhaustive is relatively unambiguous, because each feature is a single positive property. Thus an exhaustive interrogation is one that asks one question for each possible feature. When talking about dimension-generated stimuli, the situation is more complicated, because now the search may be exhaustive for the levels on a dimension as well as for the dimensions themselves. In the illustration just used, the efficient interrogation procedure must be exhaustive both with respect to the four levels on each dimension and with respect to the two dimensions. Other forms of processing, however, may involve self-terminating search for the levels on a dimension, even though interrogation must be exhaustive with regard to the dimensions themselves.

Suppose, for example, that a form of interrogation is used with these dimension-generated stimuli that treats the levels on the dimensions essentially as features. For the dimension of color and form, in the illustration we have been using, the questions are: Is it red? Is it green? Is it square? Etc. This interrogation should proceed only until a positive answer is obtained; that is, interrogation should be self-terminating rather than exhaustive with respect to levels on each dimension, although exhaustive with respect to dimensions themselves. If there are four levels on each dimension, and interrogation proceeds until a positive answer is obtained, then the number of questions required per dimension ranges from 1 to 4, for an average of 2.5 questions per dimension and 5.0 questions for both dimensions combined. A slightly more efficient procedure does not require a further question if three negative responses have been obtained; in this case, the number of questions required per dimension ranges from 1 to 3, for an average of 2.25 questions per dimension and 4.50 questions for both dimensions combined.

How does speed of identification compare with these different systems of information processing? If time of processing is even reasonably proportionate to the number of interrogations required, then we can make the following inferences: As mentioned previously, for the exhaustive interrogation required of features and for the efficient processing of the dimension-generated stimuli, exactly four questions must be asked on every trial. Thus these two systems have low variability of identification as well as an equal average identification. If the less efficient feature-type interrogation is used for the dimension-defined stimuli, then there is high variability of identification from trial to trial (because of the high variability in number of questions required), and speed of identification is slower on the average.

The difference between the two types of attribute in respect to identification is potentially less important if the dimensions are dichotomous. Identification of the 16 dimension-defined stimuli in Fig. 5.1, to illustrate, is easily carried out by the use of four dichotomous questions, by asking a series of questions equivalent to those used with the feature-defined stimuli of Fig. 5.2: Is the top line curved out? Is the right line curved out? Etc. If such an interrogation is used, with termination after one question per dimension, processing of the dimension-defined stimuli will be as efficient as processing of the feature-defined stimuli. Yet the dimension-defined stimuli, even with dichotomous dimensions, can still tempt the identifier to use an inefficient feature-type interrogation if the fully exhaustive interrogation is used. To illustrate: Is the top line curved out? Is the top line curved in? Etc. Such a procedure requires a grossly inefficient twice as many questions as minimally necessary.

So far in this section I have been concerned about whether information processing is exhaustive or self-terminating, without yet raising the further (and at least equally important) question concerning whether processing is done in serial or parallel mode. In the analysis carried out here, it is natural to think in terms of serial processing in estimating either average or variability of identification time. However, parallel processing gives similar results as long as there is reasonably high variability in processing time between dimensions, levels, or features. Nevertheless, it is now appropriate to address more directly the question of serial vs. parallel processing, and whether the form of processing should be influenced by the differences between feature- and dimension-generated stimuli.

Consider once again the nature of the questioning required if four levels exist on each dimension used to define stimuli. If a proper (i.e., efficient) question is asked, it must be of the form: Is it either red or green? Is it red? The first question asked in this case does require parallel processing of the levels on the dimension if the question is to be efficient. If each question, in other words, is to be equivalent to every other question, then the first question requires the information processor to divide the alternative levels into two subgroups, and the processor in effect has to ask a simultaneous question about two or more levels on a dimension. If the dimension in question is an ordered continuum, such as size, the equivalent of parallel processing can be accomplished, to illustrate, by asking: Is the stimulus larger than one foot? That is, the question dichotomizes the dimension. If such an interrogation is used, then to say that parallel processing has occurred is to bastardize the meaning of the concept of parallel processing. However, with dimensions that have nominal levels on them, such as form and probably color, the processing would have to be parallel in the true meaning of the term.

So parallel processing of the levels on a dimension is required for the efficient interrogation procedure with dimension-defined stimuli. If serial processing is actually used, so that the question "Is it either red or green?" is decomposed into "Is it red? Is it green?," then the interrogation has simply reverted to a serial feature-type interrogation, which is, as we have seen, inefficient with dimension-defined stimuli.

Is there any evidence that parallel processing of levels on a dimension is difficult or easy? Not much, but some, and it suggests that parallel processing is difficult when what must be processed in parallel are the levels on a dimension. I might just remark that the long-known low level of performance with absolute judgments of stimuli differing on a single dimension (see Garner, 1962, chap. 3) implies that levels on a dimension cannot be processed in parallel. But there is some more direct evidence, even though I have to reinterpret the data to make them completely appropriate to this argument. Marcel (1970) reported data from a recognition experiment in which subjects had to report whether a stimulus was or was not in the defined positive set. His stimuli were generated from four dichotomous dimensions: color, shape, orientation of a bar, and continuity of the bar. The targets were defined conjunctively (e.g., "red square"), and the positive sets contained one, two, or four stimulus targets. The question of interest to us is what happens if the subject must attend to (be prepared to recognize as in the positive set) more than one stimulus when the stimuli are defined in different ways. The result of interest is that if two targets in the positive set involved no difference in levels on the same dimension, then they could be processed in parallel, with two targets being processed as fast as one. If however, the alternative targets involved two levels on the same dimension, then the evidence was for serial processing, with more processing time required for more targets. For example, subjects could handle two targets in parallel if they were defined as "red square or horizontal broken line," but could not if they were "red square or green circle." For my purposes, this result can be interpreted to mean that ordinary subjects cannot simultaneously interrogate for the color green and for the color red, or for two levels on any other dimension. And, of course, the research of Prinz and Scheerer-Neuman (1974) mentioned earlier argues that dimensions are processed as features, and the main evidence for that conclusion is that interrogation is serial with regard to levels on a dimension.

No further analyses are attempted here. These illustrations and examples are enough to indicate that with a process as simple as stimulus identification, the differences between features and dimensions almost certainly produce differences in mode of processing, differences that are reflected in speed of identification. Stimuli generated from features require exhaustive processing of the features (unless redundant features are used) and seem to lend themselves to parallel processing. Stimuli generated from dimensions should require exhaustive interrogation of levels on dimensions, as well as the dimensions themselves, and should require parallel processing of levels on a dimension in order for processing to be efficient. Evidence suggests that parallel processing of levels on a dimension is not possible and that inefficient feature-type interrogation is used with dimension-defined stimuli. Thus there is some suggestion that feature-defined stimuli are more efficiently identified than dimension-defined stimuli.

WHOLISTIC PROPERTIES: SIMPLE WHOLES, TEMPLATES, OR CONFIGURATIONS

Component properties are one major subclass of stimulus properties; wholistic properties are the second major subclass of properties, and although *attribute* seems like an acceptable term for component property, there seems to be no reasonable single term to use for wholistic property. [And, incidentally, I have followed increasing custom, specifically Neisser (1967), in using the English wholistic rather than the Greek holistic.] The distinctions I want to make with regard to wholistic properties are functionally less sharp than the distinction between dimension and feature, but there are nevertheless at least three separate concepts involved in the idea of wholistic property.

Simple Wholes

One concept that clearly is used in psychology is what I call a *simple whole*. Any stimulus can be described in terms of its components, but if we describe all of the components, then we have in some sense described a whole. Yet there is no assertion involved that the whole is in any way more than or different from the sum of its parts; thus the term *simple whole*.

This is a very minimal concept, and it is not clear that in purely stimulus terms it has any real meaning at all. A simple whole is primarily an information-processing concept, and it implies that parallel rather than serial processing has been used in a particular experimental situation (i.e., all of the parts have been processed together, thus as a whole). To illustrate, Bamber (1969) showed that experimental subjects can say that two strings of letters are the same nearly as fast if there are four letters in the strings as if there is one letter in each string. This result implies that the letters are being processed in parallel. Alternatively, we can say that the letters are being processed as a whole. But in this context, whole means little more than parallel processing. Lockhead (1972) has proposed the term *blob processing* for such wholistic processing, and Lockhead's blob is not too different from what I am calling here a simple whole.

If we can indeed find stimulus properties that differentially allow parallel processing of the properties, the concept of a simple whole may become quite useful. At the moment, however, it has somewhat of a negative connotation in that it makes no attempt to describe the stimulus in terms other than its component properties.

Templates

In psychology's information-processing literature, the term *template* is used to exemplify wholistic processing as contrasted with component processing more frequently than any other term, and yet it has never achieved a very satisfactory definition. Like a simple whole, its definition is somewhat negative in that it does not ascribe clearly positive stimulus properties to the template that are different from the sum of the component properties. Nevertheless, there is the essence of a concept involved in the term *template* that is different from a simple whole and also from a configuration. Thus it needs to be kept in our lexicon of stimulus terms.

The difficulty with the term's definition lies in the fact that in ordinary use a template is a device for drawing an exact replica, but nobody can claim that any human being processes a stimulus by checking for an exact match with an item held in memory. So in practice there must be some limit on what is meant by exact, and with the visual figures for which the term *template* is most appropriate, certainly such attributes as brightness, orientation, size, and lateral and vertical location must be understood not to be relevant. Yet if there is a set of attributes understood not to be relevant, then the kind of definition of template used by Neisser (1967) can be very useful. He alludes to templates as "prototypes" or "canonical forms" and describes the process of template-matching as identification by coincidence or congruence with a basic model. It seems to me that there are two meaningful stimulus properties involved in Neisser's usage and that these are of positive value in asking experimental questions about cognitive processes. The first stimulus property is that of a canonical form, or possibly a schema. That is to say, there exists a modal, or average stimulus, that is defined by the relevant attributes, the values of the irrelevant attributes being averaged out. The second stimulus property is that the canonical form is capable of measurement of amount of coincidence or congruence.

The first of these two properties does not imply that the stimuli must be geometric forms, only that it is possible to differentiate the relevant from the irrelevant attributes in deciding what the canonical form or schema is. In this respect, incidentally, a template becomes much like a concept, perhaps rightly so. The second property, however, with its measurement of overlap requirement, implies something like geometric forms unless we provide a very definite rule for measurement of overlap with nongeometric forms.

Certainly there is evidence that something like template processing occurs under some circumstances. In an experiment logically similar to Bamber's (1969) experiment, Sekuler and Abrams (1968) required a same-or-different judgment for pairs of visual patterns and found that the number of elements (blackened cells in a matrix) had little effect on decision time as long as "same" meant complete identity rather than partial identity. Thus their subjects certainly were using something like a template-processing mechanism in this task.

Is a template really different from a simple whole? This last experimental example is a statement that parallel processing of elements occurs, as in the Bamber (1969) experiment. Furthermore, there was no manipulation of a purely stimulus property in the experiment; only the processing task was changed. So with this illustration, there is the same sense of negative connotation with template as with simple whole. Yet it still seems to me that template is a potentially more positive stimulus concept than is simple whole.

Configurations

Of the three types of wholistic property, that of configuration is to me the one with clearly positive stimulus properties. In this case, the whole is indeed more than, at least other than, the sum of the parts, and to a considerable extent these configural properties of the stimulus can be expressed without reference to an experimental outcome. In other words, the implicit circularity of definition that occurs with the ideas of simple wholes and templates is easily avoided.

Two illustrations of configural properties are symmetry and repetition, both of which are in Gibson's (1969) list of features for upper-case letters, although she refers to repetition as cyclic change. These types of properties, however, are different from features and dimensions in two important respects: First, both of them refer to relations between other parts of components of the stimulus; and second, neither symmetry nor repetition can be changed without changing some of the other stimulus components. This last point is, I feel, especially compelling for considering that configural properties are of a different kind than component properties. With either a feature or a dimension, the level on the attribute can be changed without changing other component properties of the stimulus, but if symmetry is changed to asymmetry, then other (component) properties are also changed.

To illustrate, consider the stimuli in Figs. 5.1 and 5.2. Each of these stimuli is symmetric about one, two, or four axes. For example, stimulus 1a in each figure is symmetrical about the horizontal, vertical, and both diagonal axes; stimulus 2b is symmetric about the horizontal and vertical axes; and stimulus 3b is symmetric about its left diagonal axis. If we want to change either the axes of symmetry or the number of axes of symmetry, we must change the level on either a dimension or a feature.

An even simpler illustration is contained in Fig. 5.4, in which stimulus C is symmetrical about the horizontal axis (and is also repetitive). In order to eliminate the symmetry, a feature has to be removed. So properties such as symmetry are not independent of the component properties and thus are configural properties. On the other hand, the dimensions of size and form in Fig. 5.3, as well as the two features in Fig. 5.4, can be changed so that a change in one dimension or feature does not affect the level of the other dimension or feature. Thus these properties are independent of each other.

Symmetry and repetition therefore are properties that are more than the sum of the component properties; they are emergent properties. In a broader sense, both symmetry and repetition are manifestations of stimulus redundancy, and although such properties are most easily found with visual figures, they are not at all restricted to such stimuli. Certainly the concept of redundancy itself is applicable to a wide class of stimuli, and the specific properties of symmetry and repetition are applicable to any type of sequential stimulus.

Are configural properties important in information processing and other cognitive processes? And how do they relate in importance to attributes, the component properties? There are strong suggestions that the emergent configural properties tend to dominate perception of stimuli, overriding component properties, when they are available.

Perceptual Classification.   One of the simplest ways to determine the importance of any type of stimulus property is to ask subjects to put a set of stimuli into different classes, with the object of determining which properties of the stimulus set form the basis of the classifications. To illustrate, consider the stimuli in Fig. 5.1 once again. If we were to give these 16 stimuli to subjects and ask them to form classes any way they wanted, one very possible classification scheme would be to divide the stimuli into two classes according to the two levels on one dimension. Thus a decision would be made that one dimension is relevant and the other three are irrelevant, and the stimuli would be divided into two groups on the basis of levels on the relevant dimension. If, in Fig. 5.1, the top dimension is considered relevant, then the eight left-hand stimuli would be put into one class and the eight right-hand stimuli would be put into a second class. Of course other dimensions could be considered relevant; so if the bottom dimension were considered relevant, then the top eight stimuli would go into one class, and the bottom eight stimuli into another. Completely equivalent classifications could occur on the basis of presence or absence of features for the stimuli in Fig. 5.2. And classifications might be based on the use of two relevant dimensions, so that four classes would be formed.

Let us consider another possible basis of classification, one based on the configural property of redundancy. The 16 stimuli of Fig. 5.1 easily form six groups based on the configural equivalence of the stimuli to each other, and the stimuli are arranged according to this classification in Fig. 5.5. The top stimulus (1a in Fig. 5.1) is symmetric on all four major axes, with the result that any reflection or 90° rotation of the stimulus simply reproduces itself. It is, in this sense, unique, and would be classed alone. The second stimulus is also unique and would be classed alone. On the third row are two stimuli that are symmetric about two axes (the horizontal and vertical), with the result that rotations of 90° allow either of these stimuli to produce the other. So they would be classed together. The next three rows each contain four stimuli, each of which is symmetric about a single axis. This lower amount of symmetry (and redundancy) means that four stimuli are the equivalent of each other when rotated and/or reflected, and they would probably be classed together.

So these stimuli can be classified either on the basis of the dimensional properties or on the basis of the configural properties. I think it highly likely that they would be classified on the basis of the configural properties. And, of course, a completely equivalent classification contrast is available for the stimuli in Fig. 5.2, those generated with features. They too can be classified by features or by configural properties and would almost certainly be classified by the configural properties.

One reason for expecting classification to be done on the basis of configural properties is the earlier work of myself and a colleague (Garner & Clement, 1963).

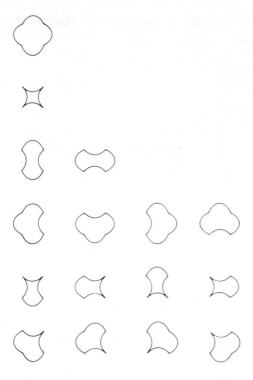

FIG. 5.5. The 16 stimuli from Fig. 5.1 grouped according to their occupancy in equivalence sets defined by rotations and/or reflections.

We used as stimuli dot patterns formed by locating five dots in the cells of a 3 x 3 matrix. Such patterns also allow classification by equivalent stimuli based on rotations and/or reflections (R & R subsets). Although there was no simple contrasting classification based on dimensions or features available with those stimuli, classification was definitely done on the basis of the configural equivalences like those of Fig. 5.5 here. Furthermore, they showed that the stimulus patterns with few equivalences were rated as good patterns in the gestalt sense of good.

Similarity Judgment. Presumably when subjects carry out a classification task, they do so on the basis of similarity. That is, they put similar stimuli in the same class, so if they put stimuli that are configural equivalents of each other in the same class, we can assume that they are considered similar.

Recently, however, Glushko (1975) has shown another interesting property of the dot patterns used previously (Garner & Clement, 1963) with a direct similarity-scaling technique. He used 17 different patterns from the Garner–Clement study, and no two patterns came from the same equivalence set. However, the patterns differed in the size of the equivalence set from 1 to 4 to 8. Glushko's subjects were required to select the more similar pair from a standard and two-comparison stimuli, and these data were used to carry out a nonmetric, multidimensional, scaling procedure. The result of interest here from this analysis is that the most important single derived dimension was easily identified as having to do with the size of the equivalence set. This result states that stimuli having the same amount of redundancy (easily translated as number of axes of symmetry) were judged as more similar than stimuli having different amounts of redundancy. Thus not only are stimuli from the same equivalence set highly similar but so are stimuli having the same amount of redundancy or symmetry. If such a result had been obtained with the stimuli in Fig. 5.5, it would mean that all 12 of the bottom stimuli would be rated as more similar to each other than any would to the two top stimuli, because all of the 12 bottom stimuli have a single axis of symmetry, whereas the two top stimuli have four axes of symmetry. Would such a result actually occur? It is at least possible.

Speed of Discrimination.   One last cognitive process is discussed — that in which speed of discrimination or classification of stimuli is used. In an experiment using the Garner–Clement dot patterns, Clement and Weiman (1970) required discrimination of various pairs of the patterns. In such experiments the good patterns (i.e., those with few configural equivalences) are more easily discriminated than poor patterns (see Garner, 1974a, Lecture 2, for review of this literature). Clement and Weiman used pairs of stimuli that allowed discrimination to be done on the basis of a single dot location to see if the advantage of the good patterns in speed of discrimination would disappear when discrimination could be carried out on the basis of a single component or element. The advantage did not disappear until it was made impossible for the subjects to use the configuration. Thus the configural property dominated the component property.

Pomerantz and Garner (1973) measured speed of classification with four stimuli generated from the two parentheses on a typewriter: ((,)), (),)(. Of the six possible pairs of stimuli, the first two were the most difficult to discriminate and the last two were the easiest to discriminate. How is such a result to be explained? If we consider these stimuli as generated from two dimensions (the right and left parentheses), each with two levels (right and left curvature), then each of these pairs is a redundant pair, with the other four pairs differing on a single dimension only. But one redundant pair gives faster discrimination, and the other redundant pair gives slower discrimination. So dimensional redundancy is not a good explanation of the process.

However, consider the stimuli in terms of their configurations: The first two stimuli come from the same equivalence set, one being a reflection of the other. Such equivalent configurations are very similar, thus difficult to discriminate. The last two stimuli come from different equivalence sets and are furthermore symmetric in two dimensions (compared to one for the first stimulus pair). Both of these conditions are good for discrimination, so speed is faster. The point once again is that configural properties seem to dominate component properties when both types are available for performance of a given experimental task.

COMPONENT AND WHOLISTIC
PROPERTIES AS ASPECTS

The data I have cited for these three experimental tasks suggest that wholistic configural properties are cognitively more important than the component attribute properties. If such a conclusion were drawn without further qualification, a quite inadequate picture of the situation would have been painted.

In a given set of stimuli, such as upper-case English letters, it is obvious that dimensional differences exist in the set along with feature differences. Furthermore, these can coexist in many structural forms. For example, features can be orthogonal with dimensions or nested within the levels of a dimension, or dimensions can be nested within features. To illustrate, consider the letters C, O, I, and L. This set can easily be described in terms of features within levels of a dimension, with the following interrogations for an identification task: Is the letter straight or curved? If curved, then: Is it closed or open? If straight, then: Does it have the bottom horizontal line? Notice that two dichotomous questions must always be asked, but never more than two, a state of affairs quite appropriate for identification of four alternative letters. I do not give illustrations of all the ways in which features and dimensions can be used in a mixed fashion to specify the component properties of English letters. Rather, I make the point that just as dimensions can operate independently of other dimensions, and features can operate independently of other features, so also can dimensions and features operate independently of each other. They are both attributes and provide component properties of stimuli.

On the other hand, attributes and wholistic properties are not independent of each other, especially if the wholistic properties are configural. Configural properties are a consequence of the interrelation of attributes, whether dimensions or features. Thus they exist along with attributes and are in a very real sense simply a different aspect of a stimulus or set of stimuli. A square is a square while at the same time having four lines of equal length and at right angles to each other so as to close the figure.

To use letters once again as an example, this time consider a set of four lower-case letters: b, d, p, q. This set of letters can easily be described in terms of an orthogonal combination of two dimensions: loop on the right or on the left, and loop at the top or at the bottom. In other words, all four letters have both a straight line and a loop, and the two dimensions are the up—down and right—left location of the loop's attachment to the line. If these four letters are considered to be adequately described in terms of dimensions, then of the six possible pairs, two of them are dimensionally redundant: b, q and p, d. These two pairs should then be discriminated more accurately than the other four pairs, in which the pair differs in only a single dimension. Whether such a potential advantage would actually occur would depend, of course, on the integrality of the dimensions (Garner, 1974a, Lecture 6).

Suppose, however, that the coexisting configural properties of these four letters are important in their perception and processing rather than the dimensional properties. These four letters share a configural property in that they are all in the same equivalence set (i.e., each can produce any of the others by rotation and reflection). If this is so, then discrimination between all pairs should be equivalent. Perhaps this example is not very good, because each of the nonredundant pairs requires only a simple reflection for one to produce the other, whereas each of the two redundant pairs requires either two reflections or a rotation of 180°. Nevertheless, this set of letters does illustrate that dimensional and configural properties coexist in the same set of stimuli and that these two types of property are different aspects of the same set of stimuli.

Configural Properties as Positive.   Very often (if not usually), the evidence for the use of wholistic properties in perception is essentially negative in nature. For example, in the Bamber (1969) and the Sekuler and Abrams (1968) papers cited previously, the evidence for wholistic processing was the failure to find any change in processing time as the number of items to be processed was increased. Other than the awkwardness of dealing with the null hypothesis as a positive property of a set of data, this type of negative evidence is esthetically unsatisfactory. Is a simple whole that which exists when you have no evidence that something else does? Is template processing what happens when you find no evidence that number of features or dimensions does not influence processing? There are some positive experimental operations that can be used to show that template processing occurs if we accept Neisser's idea of template as prototype or schema rather than as some sort of absolute entity. For example, if processing time increases with amount of deviation of the particular stimulus from the prototype, then there is positive evidence that schema or prototype processing is occurring.

However, of the three types of wholistic property I have enumerated, configural properties most nearly satisfy the need for properties that are positive, that can be defined independently of a processing outcome, and that are easily manipulated in an experiment. As a prime example, we can easily generate stimuli such as those in Figs. 5.1, 5.2, and 5.5 that not only have symmetry but that have different amounts of symmetry and that also have different axes of symmetry. Still further, stimuli such as these can be described either in terms of their component properties (dimensions or features) or in terms of the configural property of symmetry. So both component and wholistic properties of the stimulus set can be described, varied in an experiment, and the differential consequences determined. It is not always easy to pit the two types of properties against each other as independent properties, because they are truly different, but not necessarily independent, aspects of the same set of properties. Indeed, notice that the use of the four letters b, d, p, and q did not allow an unconfounded manipulation of the two types of properties.

But there are, usually more artificial, stimuli that can be generated that do pit dimensions or features against configural properties of symmetry, or equivalence set occupancy, more broadly speaking. For example, the four stimuli generated from two parentheses (Pomerantz & Garner, 1973), ((,)), (),)(, do provide a fair opportunity to disentangle the dimensional from the configural properties as they affect different types of information processing. So also do any number of subsets of stimuli from Figs. 5.1 and 5.2. For example, the four stimuli in the lower left corner provide two pairs of dimensionally redundant stimuli (3c, 4d and 3d, 4c). But one of these pairs has stimuli that are reflections of each other and the other does not. Many such subsets of stimuli can be selected from those of Figs. 5.1 and 5.2 including each of the subsets of four defined by the four quadrants.

Processing Options

Because component and configural properties are two aspects of a set of stimuli does not mean that in processing they are mutually exclusive. In fact, I used the term *aspect* deliberately to connote the idea of simultaneous coexistence. It is even possible that both properties are used at the same time, although not necessarily with the same efficiency.

Even more likely is that one property will be used for one type of cognitive task and another will be used for still a different task. To illustrate, consider once again the stimuli in Figure 5.1. These have configural properties as well as dimensional properties, and I have suggested that in a classification task the configural properties would most likely be used. But in free recall of these figures, I know from a great deal of personal experience in generating such sets of stimuli that the dimensional properties are much the easier to use, because the use of dimensions allows a more systematic production procedure than does trying to remember all the unique stimuli, and then rotating or reflecting them as necessary to generate the additional stimuli. In other words, I do not try to free recall (i.e., generate) these stimuli as in Fig. 5.5, but rather as in Figs. 5.1 or 5.2.

An interesting experimental contrast, the outcome of which does not seem obvious to me, would be the use of a concept learning experiment for the stimuli of Figs. 5.1 and 5.5 A four-stimulus positive set can be defined easily by a conjunctive rule (e.g., out at the top and out at the bottom), a rule that makes the four stimuli in the upper-left quadrant the positive instances. Alternatively, a four-stimulus positive set can be defined as one of the equivalence sets in Fig. 5.5. Would it be easier or more difficult to learn such a set than to learn the positive set defined by a conjunctive rule? As I look at the patterns, I think that the use of configural properties would be much easier than the use of dimensional properties.

Are configural properties, then, somehow psychologically more fundamental? Possibly so, but I do not feel ready to accept that conclusion because of the obvious effect of specific task on the utility of the two types of property.

Possibly the concept of primary and secondary process, which I have used previously (Garner, 1974a) in dealing with a problem of dual properties or aspects of stimulus sets, would be more useful. If there is some reasonable way to decide which is primary and which is secondary, then that differentiation would be useful. My own inclination is to consider as primary those properties that are processed under a speed stress. So if, for example, in a speeded classification task the configural properties are used, while the dimensional properties are used in a nonspeeded free recall, I would be willing to state that configural properties are primary (i.e., dominate) and that dimensional properties are secondary.

CONCLUSION

In recent years, psychologists have come to accept the idea that how humans (or other organisms) process information is not a very simple question; certainly it is not a question of seeking an invariant law about human behavior. Although few psychologists have attempted to provide a clear definition of what cognitive psychology is today, or even why the term has come to designate most human experimental psychologists, I suspect that this acceptance of the complexity of human mental activity is one of the underlying characteristics of people who consider themselves cognitive psychologists. Psychologists, naturally, have come to terms with the reality of this human complexity in various ways. Anderson and Bower (1973) express concern about the fact that organisms change memory retrieval strategies to suit different task demands. Simon and Newell (1971) state this lack of invariance of human information processing as simply a conclusion to be drawn from their own research.

Overall, psychologists have simply accepted this state of affairs, usually with good grace if not enthusiasm, and have gotten on with the business of determining the entire set of circumstances that lead to a particular type of information process. Of the classes of factors that can influence the form of information processing, the fact of individual differences is becoming accepted; and it is ironic that I should have to say accepted, because the study of individual differences has long been one of the most respected areas of psychology. But it has not been accepted so readily by those who have worked in the experimental tradition, where nomothetic laws have been sought, and where individual differences have simply constituted an irritating source of error.

The class of factors that we might call *task definition* are also becoming accepted as important determiners of information or cognitive processing. We no longer assume that all memory processes are alike but that what the experimental subject will do depends on the specific memory task assigned. And we certainly no longer assume that people perform the same way in a speeded classification task as they do in a concept-learning experiment, even though these two tasks have considerable superficial similarity.

The class of factors that I have emphasized are the stimulus factors. My own feeling is that stimulus factors have been less readily accepted as a class of factors whose effect on information processing must be understood. Possibly this reticence is due to our long-standing behaviorist tradition, which has emphasized the nature of behavior and has considered the stimulus simply to be the instigator of behavior, not a major causative agent.

I hope, of course, that I have made the point that we need as much sophistication in our understanding of stimulus concepts as we do in our understanding of processing concepts, because the nature of the stimulus must necessarily have a great influence on how information is processed. We can no longer assume that anything the experimenter varies is a variable and that no further specification of the nature of the variable is required. Nor can we assume that all wholistic properties are equivalent. Although I have made several distinctions about both component and wholistic properties of stimuli, I suspect that even finer distinctions than I have made may turn out to be important. For example, the various subclasses of property I have called *dimensional* may be more important than is now apparent; certainly the difference between quantitative and qualitative dimensions, with their quite different roles of zero, could be most important. And I still hope that better positive operations for defining templates and differentiating them from simple wholes will emerge.

What is also important, however, is that we understand these to be properties of the stimulus, properties that can be manipulated without regard to the processing organism. Only when we have constructs about the stimulus that are quite independent of the information processor can we ask meaningful experimental questions about the effects of these stimulus properties on the processor. But to define such properties, even if only tentatively, and to ask how information processing is affected by different stimulus properties, is a productive approach to the study of cognitive psychology.

ACKNOWLEDGMENT

Preparation of this paper was supported by Grant MH 14229 from the National Institute of Mental Health to Yale University.

Requests for reprints should be addressed to W. R. Garner, Department of Psychology, Yale University, New Haven, Connecticut 06520.

REFERENCES

Anderson, J. R., & Bower, G. H. *Human associative memory.* Washington: V. H. Winston, 1973.

Bamber, D. Reaction times and error rates for "same"–"different" judgments of multidimensional stimuli. *Perception & Psychophysics,* 1969, *6,* 169–174.

Clement, D. E., & Weiman, C. F. R. Instructions, strategies, and pattern uncertainty in a visual discrimination task. *Perception & Psychophysics*, 1970, *7*, 333–336.

Coombs, C. H. *A theory of data*. New York: Wiley, 1964.

Garner, W. R. *Uncertainty and structure as psychological concepts*. New York: Wiley, 1962.

Garner, W. R. The stimulus in information processing. *American Psychologist*, 1970, *25*, 350–358.

Garner, W. R. *The processing of information and structure*. Potomac, Md.: Lawrence Erlbaum Associates, 1974. (a)

Garner, W. R. Attention: The processing of multiple sources of information. In E. C. Carterette & M. P. Friedman (Eds.), *Handbook of perception* (Vol. 2). New York: Academic Press, 1974. (b)

Garner, W. R., & Clement, D. E. Goodness of pattern and pattern uncertainty. *Journal of Verbal Learning and Verbal Behavior*, 1963, *2*, 446–452.

Gibson, E. J. *Principles of perceptual learning and development*. New York: Appleton-Century-Crofts, 1969.

Glushko, R. J. Pattern goodness and redundancy revisited: Multidimensional scaling and hierarchical clustering analyses. *Perception & Psychophysics*, 1975, *17*, 158–162.

Imai, S., & Garner, W. R. Discriminability and preference for attributes in free and constrained classification. *Journal of Experimental Psychology*, 1965, *69*, 596–608.

Lockhead, G. R. Processing dimensional stimuli: A note. *Psychological Review*, 1972, *79*, 410–419.

Marcel, A. J. Some constraints on sequential and parallel processing, and the limits of attention. In A. F. Sanders (Ed.), *Attention and performance III*. Amsterdam: North-Holland, 1970.

Neisser, U. *Cognitive psychology*. New York: Appleton-Century-Crofts, 1967.

Neisser, U., & Weene, P. Hierarchies in concept attainment. *Journal of Experimental Psychology*, 1962, *64*, 640–645.

Pomerantz, J. R., & Garner, W. R. Stimulus configuration in selective attention tasks. *Perception & Psychophysics*, 1973, *14*, 565–569.

Prinz, W., & Scheerer-Neumann, G. Component processes in multiattribute stimulus classification. *Psychological Research*, 1974, *37*, 25–50.

Reed, S. K. *Psychological processes in pattern recognition*. New York: Academic Press, 1973.

Restle, F. *Psychology of judgment and choice*. New York: Wiley, 1961.

Sekuler, R. W., & Abrams, M. Visual sameness: A choice time analysis of pattern recognition processes. *Journal of Experimental Psychology*, 1968, *77*, 232–238.

Simon, H. A., & Newell, A. Human problem solving: The state of the theory in 1970. *American Psychologist*, 1971, *26*, 145–159.

Townsend, J. T. Theoretical analysis of an alphabetic confusion matrix. *Perception & Psychophysics*, 1971, *9*, 40–50.

Treisman, A. M. Strategies and models of selective attention. *Psychological Review*, 1969, *76*, 282–299.

Tversky, A. Elimination by aspects: A theory of choice. *Psychological Review*, 1972, *79*, 281–299.

Whitman, J. R., & Garner, W. R. Free-recall learning of visual figures as a function of form of internal structure. *Journal of Experimental Psychology*, 1962, *64*, 558–564.

Whitman, J. R., & Garner, W. R. Concept learning as a function of form of internal structure. *Journal of Verbal Learning and Verbal Behavior*, 1963, *2*, 195–202.

6

From Perceived Similarity to Dimensional Structure: A New Hypothesis about Perceptual Development

Bryan E. Shepp
Brown University

The concept of stimulus dimension is central to most theories of information processing, but it is seldom analyzed systematically. More often than not, the experimenter assumes that the dimensions he or she varies are perceptually independent for the subject and proceeds to ask questions about the manner in which these dimensions are processed. The hazards of this approach have been pointed out by Garner (1970, 1974), who argues that by ignoring the nature of the input, conclusions about processing may be erroneous or incomplete.

In support of this argument, Garner and his associates (e.g., Garner, 1974; Garner & Felfoldy, 1970) have shown that differences in the structure of stimuli do lead to different forms of processing. Their analysis is based on a distinction between two fundamentally different combinations of stimulus dimensions, integral and separable. Phenomenologically, integral dimensions (e.g., hue and brightness) are perceived as unitary wholes, whereas separable dimensions (e.g., size of circle and angle of a radial line) are seen as perceptually distinct components. Operationally, integral dimensions produce a Euclidean metric in multidimensional scaling, lead to redundancy gain when correlated and some measure of accuracy or speed is used, and produce interference in speeded classification when the dimensions are orthogonal and selective attention is required. By contrast, separable dimensions produce a city-block metric in direct distance scaling, lead to no redundancy gain, and produce no interference in speeded classification that requires selective attention. In short, these results show that integral dimensions are perceived in terms of a similarity structure and do not permit selective attention. Separable dimensions, on the other hand, are perceived in terms of a dimensional structure and do allow selective attention.

The work of Garner and his colleagues has, thus far, had its major impact on theories concerned with processing by adult subjects (e.g., see Nickerson, 1972).

Most of these theories have ignored the nature of the stimulus, and they face some obvious difficulties. Similar problems may also be posed for developmental theories of selective processing (e.g., Hagen & Hale, 1973; Zeaman & House, 1963), and broader implications may be entertained. The analysis provided by Garner (1974) speaks not only to questions about developmental changes in selective processing, as processing relates to the type of stimulus input, but it also speaks to a fundamental question about the ontogeny of perceived structure.

The nature of perceived structure and selective processing are both central to the problem of perceptual development, and there is an extensive literature (e.g., Bruner, Olver, & Greenfield, 1966; Gibson & Olum, 1960; Gibson, 1969) documenting developmental changes in both types of process. Two important conclusions are suggested by this literature. One concerns the nature of representation and indicates that the young child perceives stimuli in a diffuse, global, or undifferentiated manner, whereas the older child perceives input in an articulate, specific, or differentiated fashion (e.g., Bruner, Olver, & Greenfield, 1966; Gibson, 1969; Werner, 1948). The second points to age-related differences in selective attention and suggests that the young child exhibits poorly focused attention and is unable to ignore irrelevant information, whereas the older child focuses attention and can successfully ignore irrelevant input (e.g., Crane & Ross, 1967; Hagen & Hale, 1973; Maccoby, 1969; Pick & Frankel, 1973; Strutt, Anderson, & Well, 1975; Smith, Kemler, & Aronfreed, 1976).

Although a case can be made for each of these trends in perceptual development, most investigators have stressed one process to the virtual exclusion of the other. Moreover, theories that assume developmental differences in perceived structure are often viewed as competing with those models that posit developmental differences in selective attention (e.g., Tighe, 1973). A major reason for this situation is the failure to develop converging operations for representational concepts, on the one hand, and for processing concepts on the other. Frequently, the validity of both concepts depends on results from the same paradigm, and there are few paradigms that are accepted as uniquely implicating either of the concepts. Thus there has been little effort to integrate the concepts within a single theory.

Gibson's (1969) work is an important exception, and she clearly recognizes the significance of the developmental changes in selective attention as well as changes in perceived structure. Gibson assumes that the young child perceives input in an undifferentiated fashion, whereas older children analyze stimuli into their constituent features or dimensions. This progression is accomplished through perceptual learning, which includes the basic processes of abstraction and selective filtering. Through abstraction, the child learns to extract features or dimensions from a stimulus, and by selective filtering, the child learns to ignore features that are irrelevant to a specific abstraction. Clearly, Gibson has attempted to specify both the developmental changes in perceived structure and selective processing, and she makes an effective argument as to the importance of both concepts (Gibson, 1969).

There are, however, two fundamental issues on which Gibson has remained uncommitted, and which must be clarified if differences between perceived structure are to be effectively delineated from differences in selective processing. First, there is the relation between perceived structure and selective attention. Quite clearly, if dimensions are separable for the child, selective attention is possible, and developmental differences in selective attention can be identified quite independently of perceived structure. But what principles of attention apply to the undifferentiated stimulus that is perceived by the young child? This question leads to the second issue — namely a specification of the nature of an undifferentiated stimulus. On this issue, Gibson (1969) has suggested that dimensions of variation may go undetected in an undifferentiated stimulus but otherwise leaves the specification open.

A Separability Hypothesis

In reviewing the two trends in perceptual development, the young child was described as perceiving stimuli wholistically and failing to attend selectively, a description that closely resembles that of an adult subject who is processing integral dimensions. This similarity suggests the hypothesis that dimensions perceived by the older child and the adult as separable are perceived by the younger child as integral, and it is through perceptual learning that dimensional structure is extracted from the stimulus.

This view differs from that of Garner (1974), who considers integral and separable dimensions to be pure stimulus concepts. Although not discounting the importance of stimulus properties, we are suggesting the importance of a process whereby a wholistic stimulus becomes divided into its constituent dimensions. Moreover, this view also implies that some tasks either promote or demand the division more so than others, because it seems unlikely that all tasks are equally good for perceptual learning (Gibson, 1969). That these assumptions are not implausible is shown by Lockhead (1972), who points out that both integral and separable dimensions are analyzable. Multidimensional stimuli are analyzable if the subjects can respond accurately to the values of one dimension while values of the other dimension are varied orthogonally. He further shows that although integral dimensions are initially processed as single "blobs," they may be analyzed into their constituent dimensions should the task require analysis.

Garner has also recognized that integral dimensions can be analyzed; and to accommodate the possibility that the same stimuli are sometimes perceived as wholes and sometimes decomposed into their component dimensions, he has proposed a distinction between primary and derived processes. For integral dimensions, perceived similarity is the primary process; the extraction of a dimensional structure is derived. For separable dimensions, the situation is reversed (Garner, 1974). In these terms, we are suggesting that the primary process for young children is perceived similarity for both types of dimensional combinations and that dimensional structure is derived through perceptual learning.

A separability hypothesis, not incompatible with Gibson's theory (1969), suggests an interpretation of perceptual development that differs in several important respects from that of Gibson. First, by assuming that young children perceive dimensional combinations in terms of overall similarity, the nature of the stimulus is specified clearly and is subject to specific evaluations. By contrast, the perception of an undifferentiated stimulus by young children often seems to be inferred by the absence of behavior that serves as the criterion to identify the perception of dimensions. Second, if the young child perceives dimensional combinations as integral, the suggestion that such children show an inability to attend selectively may often be erroneous. Selective attention to integral dimensions is not a logical possibility, and the young child's failure to attend selectively to integral dimensions is in no sense different from that of the adult confronted with integral dimensions. Third, because separable dimensions are necessary for selective attention, it would seem that Gibson's processes of abstraction and selective filtering cannot occur concurrently in early development. Abstraction would come first, followed by selective filtering. Thus the development of selective attention would lag the development of perceived dimensional structure.

Some Evidence for Developmental Differences in Perceived Structure

In addition to the two developmental trends cited earlier, there is other evidence that can be interpreted to mean that young children perceive dimensional combinations as integral. For example, Wohlwill (1962) and Bruner, Olver, and Greenfield (1966) provide evidence that the performance of younger children is facilitated more by increasing redundancy in the stimuli than is the performance of older subjects. Increased redundancy with integral dimensions leads to an increase in dissimilarity between stimuli and could account for the improved performance of younger children. Evidence to support a separability hypothesis also comes from dimensional shift studies, which show consistently that young children have more difficulty in analyzing multidimensional stimuli than do older children (e.g., Wolff, 1967) and usually require overtraining in order to do so successfully (e.g., Shepp & Turrisi, 1966, 1969).

Perhaps the most direct support for a separability hypothesis comes from the work of Tighe and his associates (Tighe, Glick, & Cole, 1971; Tighe & Tighe, 1972). These investigators have proposed that subjects may solve standard discrimination tasks by either of two alternative modes. Consider Table 6.1, which shows a simultaneous discrimination task. From the experimenter's point of view, color is the relevant dimension, and form and position are irrelevant. One mode of solution in this task is consistent with the experimenter's point of view; subjects learn that color is the relevant dimension and consistently choose red. In this case, the different arrays are treated as instances of the same problem, and the solution is governed by some form of dimensional learning.

Tighe, Glick, and Cole (1971) point out that there is another equally plausible description of the task and suggest an alternative type of solution. Notice in Table 6.1 that two stimuli, red square and red circle, lead to a correct response. The subject could, in principle, treat each stimulus as a separate object, in which case each array of the task constitutes an independent subproblem, and the solution is based on the choice of specific objects.

The type of solution adopted by the subjects can be revealed by an examination of performances on reversal and nonreversal shift tasks. If subjects have learned the initial task on the basis of object—reward relations, both subproblems must be relearned in the reversal shift, and the errors committed on each subproblem should be equivalent. In the nonreversal shift, however, the object—reward relation remains unchanged in one subproblem (Array 1) and is reversed in the second (Array 2). Only the reversed subproblem must be relearned, and the errors committed on the reversed subproblem should exceed those committed on the unchanged subproblem, which ideally would be zero. "Dimension—reward" learning (Tighe & Tighe, 1972) would, however, lead to a very different outcome in the shift tasks. Because each array is perceived as an instance of the same problem in both types of shift task, error rates should be equivalent for the arrays within each shift task. In particular, the changed and unchanged subproblems of the nonreversal shift should be learned at the same rate.

The work of Tighe and his colleagues is germane to the present discussion because of the assumptions made about the type of solution adopted by children of different ages. They have assumed that children perceive both modes of repre-

TABLE 6.1
Reversal—Nonreversal Shift Paradigm

Array	Original	Learning[a]
1	Red [+] square	Green [−] circle
2	Red [+] circle	Green [−] square

Array	Reversal shift		Array	Nonreversal shift	
1	Red [−] square	Green [+] circle	1	Red [+] square	Green [−] circle
2	Red [−] circle	Green [+] square	2	Red [−] circle	Green [+] square

[a]Only two of the possible four arrays are shown. In practice, two additional arrays, in which the positions of the stimuli are interchanged, would also be presented. The symbols "+" and "−" indicate that a choice of a particular stimulus is rewarded or nonrewarded respectively.

sentation but that younger children are more likely to learn object—reward relations than dimension—reward relations, whereas the reverse is assumed for older children. Tighe & Tighe (1972) and Tighe (1973) report results that support these assumptions. Younger children typically show the distributions of errors on the subproblems of the nonreversal shift that would be expected for an object—reward learner. Older children, however, show equivalent error rates on the two subproblems of the nonreversal task. The perception of stimuli as objects would correspond to what the present analysis has described as integral dimensions, whereas the perception of dimensions implies that the dimensions are separable. Thus, with an appropriate translation, the data from an analysis of subproblem learning lend support to a separability hypothesis.

Although evidence exists for a separability hypothesis, it is indirect and clearly post hoc. Moreover, it is doubtful that advocates of other views will readily accept the analysis favoring a separability hypothesis. In order to establish the validity of the hypothesis and to sharpen the contrast between it and other interpretations, some direct tests are required. In the remainder of this chapter, some results from two different paradigms — speeded sorting and free classification — are offered.

SOME DIRECT TESTS OF THE SEPARABILITY HYPOTHESIS: SPEED SORTING

The properties of integral and separable dimensions are clearly illustrated by the performances of adults on the speeded-sorting task employed by Garner and Felfoldy (1970). In this task, subjects are required to sort a deck of cards into two piles as quickly as possible. On each card, one value on each of two dimensions is displayed, and the subject is instructed to sort on the basis of one of the dimensions. During the course of the experiment, subjects perform on each of three different tasks: one-dimension, correlated-dimensions, and orthogonal-dimensions. In the one-dimension task, the values of the target dimension (X) are varied such that all cards bearing X_1 are placed in one pile, and those bearing X_2 are placed in the other. The value of the second dimension (Y) is held constant. In the correlated-dimensions task, the values of X and Y are redundant; $X_1 Y_1$ are sorted in one pile, and $X_2 Y_2$ are sorted in the other. In the orthogonal-dimensions task, Y_1 and Y_2 are paired equally often with X_1 and X_2; $X_1 Y_1$ and $X_1 Y_2$ are placed in one pile, and $X_2 Y_2$ and $X_2 Y_1$ are placed in the other.

Differences in the perceived structure of integral and separable dimensions can be observed by comparing performances on the one-dimension and correlated-dimensions tasks. Because the perceived differences between stimuli composed from integral dimensions are described by a Euclidean space (Hyman & Well, 1967, 1968; Handel & Imai, 1972), the redundancy introduced in the correlated-dimensions task serves to increase the judged distance between the stimuli. Thus the stimuli in the correlated-dimensions task are more dissimilar to each other than are the stimuli of the one-dimension task. In contrast, the perceived differences between stimuli composed from separable dimensions are best described by a city-block metric (Shepard, 1964; Handel & Imai, 1972), which implies a perceived dimensional structure and no increase in dissimilarity with redundant stimuli in the speeded-sorting task. Thus subjects sorting integral dimensions should show facilitation on the correlated-dimensions task as compared with the one-dimension task, whereas subjects sorting separable dimensions should show no differences in sorting times on the two tasks. This pattern of results was reported by Garner and Felfoldy (1970).

Differences in selective attention are implied by differences in perceived structure and are revealed by comparing performances on the orthogonal-dimensions and one-dimension tasks. For integral dimensions, with their underlying similarity structure, attention is nonselective. No selective filtering is possible, with the result that interference should occur on the orthogonal-dimensions task. On the other hand, the dimensional structure of separable dimensions allows selective attention. Consequently, subjects sorting separable stimuli on an orthogonal-dimensions task should sort as quickly as on a one-dimension task. As predicted, Garner and Felfoldy report interference on orthogonal-dimensions tasks with integral stimuli but none with separable stimuli.

Experiment I

In our first experiment (Shepp & Swartz, 1976), first- and fourth-grade children were instructed to sort drawings of houses in a speeded-sorting task. The basis of all sorts was a property of the door of the house. The door was either composed of integral dimensions — hue and brightness — or dimensions that could be separated — hue (or brightness) and shape of door window. Three different types of tasks were used: sorts with one dimension, sorts with correlated or redundant dimensions, and sorts with orthogonal dimensions.

According to a separability hypothesis, first- and fourth-grade children should perform the sorting tasks with integral stimuli in a manner not qualitatively different from that of the human adult. Compared with single-dimensional sorts, correlated sorts should be facilitated, and interference should occur in that task with orthogonal-dimensions. Quantitative differences would be expected in that first-graders should sort on all tasks more slowly than fourth-graders because of differences in perceptual experience, motor skills, or both.

In contrast to sorts with integral dimensions, age-related differences in sorting times should appear between the different tasks when separable dimensions are presented. If first-grade children are processing separable dimensions as integral, facilitation should be observed in the correlated-dimensions task, and interference should occur in the orthogonal-dimensions task. Fourth-graders, on the other hand, should have abstracted the separable dimensions and, provided that subjects of this age exhibit selective attention, should perform on all three tasks equally well.

Method

The subjects were 40 first-grade children and 40 fourth-grade children selected either from a summer day camp or from the East Providence, R. I., school system. Eight subjects of each grade level were assigned to tasks with integral stimulus; the remaining subjects were assigned to tasks with separable stimuli.[1]

The stimuli were 18 × 13 cm line drawings of a house that contained one 2 × 4 cm door within the outline of the house. Integral dimensions were hue and brightness of the door and were produced by attaching Munsell glossy chips, 2 × 4 cm, to the door. Two levels of hue, Munsell 5R and 10R, and two of brightness, Munsell values 4 and 6, were used. When neutralized, hue was 7.5R, and value was 5. The chroma of the chips was held constant at 12.

The separable stimuli were color of the door (hue or brightness) and the shape of the door window (square or circle) placed in the upper third of the door. The square (1.61 sq cm) and the circle (1.27 cm in diameter) were cut from white paper and superimposed on the Munsell chips. The perimenter of each shape was emphasized with a thin black line. On single-dimension tasks with hue or brightness, the door window was removed. On the single-dimension task with door window, no Munsell chips were used, and the door remained a black outline on a white background. Each card was placed in a plastic envelope for protection.

The subject was required to sort a deck of 32 stimulus cards into two piles. For this task, three types of stimulus sets were used. In the first, only one dimension varied in its two designated values, and the second dimension was constant or absent (one dimension). In the second type of set, one value on one dimension was consistently paired with one value on the other, resulting in two unique stimuli with 16 of each in a deck (correlated dimensions). Finally, in the third set, both values of one dimension were paired with each value of the other, yielding four stimuli, with eight of each in a deck (orthogonal dimensions).

Each subject was run on six trials, three on each of two consecutive days. A trial consisted of six sorts; each of two dimensions was designated as the target in each of the three stimulus sets. The order of the sorts within a trial was determined by a Latin Square.

The subjects were instructed that the purpose of the "game" was to determine how fast they could separate the houses with the two types of doors. Depending on the group to which they were assigned, subjects were told that sometimes the

---

[1] Shepp and Swartz (1976) conducted two experiments. To simplify presentation, partial results of Experiment I are compared with the results of Experiment II. The reader interested in additional details of the results or procedure is referred to Shepp and Swartz (1976).

doors were red or orange (hue), sometimes they were dark or light (brightness), and sometimes they had square or round door windows (door window). At the beginning of a sort, the 32 cards were shuffled and shown to the child with the instructions to place, for example, "red doors on one side and orange doors on the other." The deck of cards was placed in front of the child, and the child picked up each card individually and placed it on the appropriate pile to the left or right of the deck. The subject was permitted to look through the deck before beginning, to choose on which side to place each pile, and to pick up each card in any manner, but no subject was permitted to hold the deck of cards while sorting.

The sorting times were recorded to the nearest .2 second. Errors were recorded, but no feedback on errors occurred; rather, constant encouragement to sort quickly was given, and caution to sort accurately was given only when more than one error occurred. At the end of the second session, the subject was praised and received a small bag of candy.

Results

The major results of the experiment are presented in Tables 6.2 and 6.3. Before considering these results, however, two other features of the data deserve mention. First, errors on the task were minimal, and no analyses were performed; first-graders committed .08 errors/deck, and fourth-graders made .06 errors/deck. Second, there was a clear practice effect on Trials 1–3, but the effect was negligible on Trials 4–6. Thus, each subject's scores on Trials 4, 5, and 6 were averaged such that the mean of each sort in Tables 6.2 and 6.3 is based on a single score contributed by each subject. The sorting times were analyzed in a 2 x 3 x 2 mixed factorial design (age x stimulus set x dimension) for both the integral and separable conditions.

TABLE 6.2
Mean SortingTime for Integral Dimensions

Grade	Dimension Sorted	One Dimension	Correlated Dimensions	Orthogonal Dimensions
1st	Hue	37.84	33.50	47.09
	Value	31.26	30.41	35.08
4th	Hue	25.81	24.44	37.97
	Value	24.82	24.42	28.09

TABLE 6.3
Mean Sorting Times for Separable Dimensions
(Experiment II)

Grade	Dimension Sorted	One-Dimension	Correlated-Dimensions	Orthogonal-Dimensions
1st	Color	37.15	34.78	42.46
	Form	38.72	34.61	47.60
4th	Color	22.92	23.03	23.05
	Form	23.73	23.09	23.01

In the integral condition, reliable effects due to age $(F = 9.01, df = 1/14, p < .01)$, dimension $(F = 12.51, df = 1/14, p < .005)$, stimulus set $(F = 37.12, df = 2/28, p < .001)$, and the interaction between stimulus set and dimension $(F = 15.13, df = 2/28, p < .001)$, were observed. Generally, fourth-graders sorted faster than first-graders, brightness sorts were made faster than hue sorts, and single-dimension and correlated dimensions sorts required less time than orthogonal sorts. The stimulus set x dimension interaction is easily observed in Table 6.2. Orthogonal sorts require more time with both dimensions than do one dimension or correlated sorts. However, correlated sorts are facilitated only when S is instructed to sort on the basis of hue. A comparison of the correlated sorts with the one-dimensional sorts reveals significant facilitation for both first-grade $(t = 4.06, df = 7, p < .01)$ and fourth-grade $(t = 3.06, df = 7, p < .01)$ subjects. Similar comparisons for value revealed no reliable differences $(p > .05)$.

In the separable condition, there were significant main effects due to age $(F = 161.21, df = 1/46, p < .001)$, stimulus set $(F = 163.71, df = 2/92, p < .001)$, and dimensions $(F = 4.93, df = 1/46, p < .05)$. Not surprisingly, first-graders sorted more slowly than fourth-graders, and color sorts were easier than form sorts. The effect of stimulus set is due to the fact that relative to the one-dimension task, the correlated-dimensions task shows facilitation, whereas the orthogonal-dimensions task shows interference. There was also an interaction between stimulus set and dimension $(F = 5.35, df = 2/92, p < .01)$, which is easily seen in Table 6.3. In the correlated-dimensions task, sorting times were virutally equal for both color and form. In the one-dimension and orthogonal-dimensions tasks, however, form produces slower sorting times than does color.

The most important effect is revealed by a reliable interaction of age x stimulus set $(F = 167.83, df = 2/92, p < .001)$. As shown in Table 6.3, the performances of fourth-graders are very similar in all three tasks. This result indicates that color and form are separable dimensions for the older child and that for these subjects selective attention is possible.

In contrast, first-grade subjects show reliably faster sorting times on the correlated-dimensions task and reliably slower times on the orthogonal-dimensions task as compared with the one-dimension task. Taken at face value, these results indicate that color and form are integral for first-graders. Garner (1974), however, has pointed out that the correlated-dimensions task with separable dimensions can show facilitation if the dimensions are not of equal difficulty. He has dubbed this effect *selective serial processing*. In this case, when the subject is performing the correlated-dimensions task, with the instruction to sort on the more difficult dimension, and sorts on the easier dimension instead, selective serial processing occurs. When compared with performances on the one-dimension task with the more difficult dimension, the correlated-dimensions task shows facilitation, but these facilitated sorting times are no faster than times on the one-dimension task with the easier dimension. In the present study, the first-graders were faster on the correlated dimensions task than on either of the one-dimension tasks $[t(23) = 5.31, p < .001]$.

It should be pointed out, however, that not all subjects show the same effect. Sixteen subjects showed interference on the orthogonal-dimensions task and facilitation on the correlated-dimensions task that rules out selective serial processing. For these subjects, then, it appears that color and form are integral. The remaining eight first-graders show a pattern of results that is consistent with the conclusion that some children of this age perceive dimensional structure but fail to attend selectively. These subjects show facilitation on the correlated-dimensions task but only when required to sort on the more difficult of the two dimensions. These sorting times are not faster, and are often slower, than the sorting times on the one-dimension task with the easier of the two dimensions. This result, and the fact that the sorting times on the correlated dimensions and one-dimension tasks do not differ on the easier dimension, suggests selective serial processing and perceived dimensional structure. The added observation of interference on the orthogonal-dimensions task implies a failure to attend selectively.

Discussion

Generally speaking, the results of Experiment I support the distinction between integral and separable dimensions and provide strong evidence that younger children perceive dimensional combinations that are separable for older children as integral. Moreover, it appears that whereas attention is nonselective for the younger child, the process becomes selective for the older.

Consider first the performance of subjects on the tasks with integral dimensions. Both first- and fourth-graders performed on the sorting task in a manner not qualitatively different from that of the adult (Garner & Felfoldy, 1970). Interference was observed in the filtering task, where selective attention is required, and a redundancy gain was observed on hue sorts with value correlated. These performances indicate that the processing on integral dimensions is mandatorily distributed. Interference is produced, because the orthogonal dimension cannot be filtered out, and a redundancy gain occurs, because the inter-stimulus difference is greater in the correlated-dimensions task than in the one-dimension task. Age-related differences in sorting performance appear only to be quantitative and may be due either to differences in previous perceptual learning, to motor skills, or to both.

It is somewhat surprising that the correlated sorts with value were not facilitated, because these specific values produced redundancy gains in the work of Garner and Felfoldy (1970). What is probably true is that children of these ages are extremely cautious about making errors. The fourth-grade subjects averaged only .08 errors/deck, which is less than those made by Garner and Felfoldy's adults (.22 errors/deck). The tendency to be cautious would inflate all sorting times, but differences between easy tasks might be more easily obscured than between difficult tasks.

In contrast to performances on tasks with integral dimensions, the performances with separable dimensions suggest age-related differences in perceived structure as well as selective attention. The performances of fourth-graders on tasks with separable dimensions resemble those of the adult (Garner & Felfoldy, 1970). Color and form have been differentiated, so there is no redundancy gain in the correlated-dimensions task. Moreover, because the older child can focus attention, there is no interference in the filtering task, where selective attention is required.

The performances of first-grade subjects on tasks with separable dimensions are mildly problematic in that these subjects appear to be of an age that is transitional. Clearly, the majority of these subjects performs in a manner that is consistent with our hypothesis. In comparison with one-dimension sorts, correlated-dimensions sorts are facilitated, and orthogonal-dimensions sorts are impaired. Because selective serial processing is ruled out for these subjects, the pattern of results indicates that color and form are integral. In contrast, the remaining first-graders perform in a manner that indicates some perception of dimensional structure but a failure to attend selectively. These subjects show no redundancy gain in the correlated-dimensions task other than what can be attributed to selective serial processing, but they do show interference on the orthogonal-dimensions task.

Although the results of Experiment I clearly support a separability hypothesis, the question as to their generality surely could be raised in at least two different senses. First, are other dimensional combinations (e.g., size and brightness) integral for younger children? This question is addressed later in the chapter. Second, in proposing the separability hypothesis, are we speaking to a form of perceptual learning that leads to the separability of physical dimensions like color and form, or are we suggesting that separability is important to broader questions of categorizations such as Rosch's basic-level categories (Rosch & Mervis, 1975) or the abstraction of arbitrary classes such as letters and digits? The contention is that learned separability applies to both types of perceptual learning, and Experiment II examines the processing of letters in a speeded-sorting task. This work is being conducted in collaboration with Peter Eimas, and although it is quite preliminary, it suggests some additional directions for a separability hypothesis.

Experiment II

In acquiring the skill of recognizing and processing letters, the child appears to be confronted with several learning tasks. Individual letters must be discriminated, and stimuli classified as letters must be distinguished from other forms such as numbers. In addition, the child must learn that the same name applies to a particular letter despite differences in size (A vs. A) or differences in both size and form (A vs. a). As previously described, a separability hypothesis speaks to such learning in a very limited fashion. For the young child, letters that vary in size should be like any other form that varies in size and should be perceived in terms of overall similarity; these combinations should be processed as integral dimensions. The hypothesized progression from perceived similarity to dimensional structure does not simply apply, however, to learning about letters. Even if form and size were to become separable with increasing age (which we do not know), the dimensional structure would appear to be irrelevant to much of what the child must learn about letters. In addition to dimensions, the child must also learn about specific features [e.g., straight lines (Gibson, 1969)] which may have structural properties that are very different from dimensions (see Chapter 5). This possibility raises a critical question for a separability hypothesis: If variations in letter and size are perceived as integral by young children, what structures are perceived by older children, who, as a result of perceptual experience, learn about both features and dimensions?

This question is undoubtedly not a simple one, but fortunately some interesting alternatives are suggested by the work of Posner and his associates (e.g., Posner & Mitchell, 1967; Posner & Keele, 1967; Posner & Boies, 1971). They have devised a letter-matching task in which pairs of letters are presented to the subject who is instructed to respond "same" or "different" as quickly as possible. The criterion for same can be a physical match (A, A) or a name match (A, a). Reaction times to physical matches are faster than to name matches, a result that has led these investigators to conclude that different levels of processing are involved. Physical identity is encoded first with name identity following, and the difference in level produces a difference in reaction time. They also identified an intermediate "analog" level applicable to instances were upper- and lower-case letters are of the same shape (e.g., C, c).

According to this theory, the physical stimulus undergoes a series of transformations, with deeper levels of processing becoming more conceptual in nature. Thus, at the level of a name match, the only relevant aspect of the stimulus pair is a common name; all other aspects are irrelevant. An implication of this argument is that irrelevant variations in the stimulus should not affect reaction time at the level of a name match. Recently, Corcoran and Besner (1975) have shown such an effect in that variations of size and/or brightness do not affect reaction time of name matches (i.e., A, a). Although this result is clearly important for the view of Posner and his colleagues, it does not speak to our primary question of perceived structure.

Fortunately, other conditions run by Corcoran and Besner do. Subjects were also presented with physically identical pairs of letters (A, A) and pairs where identical shapes varied in size (A, A). Both types of pairs showed faster reaction times than name matches, but reaction times to the latter were consistently slower than to the former. The fact that a size variation in identical shapes slowed processing indicates that the dimensions were not separable (Garner & Felfoldy, 1970). Rather, an interactive structure would appear to be implicated.

The fact that the variation of size produces differences in reaction time for letters of the same shape could result from the perception of the stimuli either as asymmetric separable dimensions or as configural dimensions. Consider first the possibility that variations in size and letter are asymmetrically separable. Given the results of Corcoran and Besner (1975), this would suggest that variations in size affect processing of letters but that variation of letter would not affect a classification based on size. In terms of speeded sorting, one would expect a redundancy gain in the correlated-dimensions task, whereas asymmetric interference would be expected in the orthogonal-dimensions task; size should interfere with letter classification, but size classifications would not be affected by variation of letter (see Garner, 1976).

If variations in size and letter result in configural dimensions, a very different outcome would be anticipated in the speeded-sorting task. Because configural properties result from a relation between components of a stimulus (see Chapter 5), no redundancy gain would be observed in the correlated-dimensions task, but mutual interference would be expected in the orthogonal-dimensions task.

In Experiment II, these alternatives were evaluated in the speeded-sorting task, in which the letters A and E were varied in size. Our separability hypothesis assumes that young children would perceive these stimuli as integral, but it does not specifically predict either of the previous alternatives with increasing perceptual learning. If these stimuli are asymmetrically separable, the redundancy gain would be maintained with increasing age, and an asymmetry would appear in the orthogonal-dimensions task. If, on the other hand, these stimuli are perceived as configural with increasing perceptual learning, the redundancy gain in the correlated-dimensions task would be lost for older children and adults, and mutual interference would occur in the orthogonal-dimensions task.

Method

The subjects were kindergarten, second-grade, and fifth-grade children attending school in East Providence, R. I. There were 16 subjects at each grade level. In addition, there were 12 undergraduates from Brown University, who were paid for their participation.

The stimuli were capital letters E and A taken from the 60 pt UNIVERS 75 series of Letraset usa, Inc. The large letters were 1.6 cm high, whereas the small letters were 0.9 cm high. The letters were centered on 3 x 5 plain white cards and laminated for protection.

For the adult subjects, the same design used in Experiment I was repeated in Experiment II. However, a modification was introduced for the children. Eight subjects were assigned randomly to each of two groups. One group received one-dimension and correlated-dimension tasks, whereas the second received one-dimension and orthogonal-dimensions tasks. Thus, for these subjects, a trial consisted of four sorts. For example, a subject in the first group would receive: (1) a letter sort (one-dimension); (2) a size sort (one-dimension); (3) a letter sort (correlated-dimensions); and (4) a size sort (correlated-dimensions).

The adult subjects were run in a single session. The children, however, were run for two sessions on consecutive days. Three trials occurred on each day. The order of the tasks within a trial was determined by a Latin Square. Two subjects were assigned to each of the four different orders. One Latin Square was used for Trials 1, 3, and 5; and its reverse was used for Trials 2, 4, and 6.

All subjects held the deck of cards in one hand and sorted with the other. Some children did not know the names of the letters; these subjects were told the letter names and shown which letters would go together. Otherwise the procedure was the same as in Experiment I.

Results and Discussion

The sorting times for Trials 4—6 were taken as the measure of performance for both the adult and kindergarten subjects. Practice effects were minimal on these trials, and there were no effects due to order. Although the children made more errors than the adults, errors were negligible and were not analyzed.

The mean sorting time for each condition at each age level is shown in Table 6.4.[2] Due to the nature of the design, performances on the correlated-dimensions and orthogonal-dimensions tasks were compared separately to performances on the one-dimension task using a 4 x 2 x 2 (age x stimulus set x dimensions) mixed factorial design. For the correlated-dimensions task, this analysis yields significant effects due to age ($F = 27.03$, $df = 3/32$, $p < .001$), stimulus sets ($F = 11.33$, $df = 1/32$, $p < .005$), and stimulus sets by age ($F = 5.02$, $df = 3/32$, $p < .001$). An inspection of Table 6.4 suggests that each successive age level improves in speed of sorting, an impression that is confirmed by post hoc analysis.

Although performances on the correlated-dimensions task were generally superior to those on the one-dimension task, only kindergarten children showed

---

[2]In a previous version of this chapter, speeded-sorting results for the adult differed from those presented in Table 6.4. The earlier results did not replicate. The results presented for the adult in Table 6.4 have been replicated with different letter—size combinations in the speeded-sorting task and with A and E in a discrete trial-classification task.

TABLE 6.4
Mean Sorting Times for Letter and Size
(Experiment II)

Age	Dimension Sorted	One-Dimension	Correlated-Dimensions	Orthogonal-Dimensions
Kindergarten	Letter	40.92	38.87	44.83
	Size	41.67	39.54	44.21
2nd Grade	Letter	34.79	33.51	35.46
	Size	34.15	34.11	35.19
5th Grade	Letter	25.19	24.42	27.11
	Size	25.06	25.31	26.17
Adult	Letter	14.99	15.09	15.54
	Size	15.00	14.67	15.94

reliable facilitation. Furthermore, a comparison of the average sorting time of the correlated-dimensions task with the faster of the one-dimension tasks indicates that the facilitation shown by kindergarteners can be attributed to the presence of integral dimensions $[t(7) = 4.93, p < .01]$.

Consider now the performances on the orthogonal-dimensions task. Again, sorting time improves with age ($F = 22.61, df = 3/32, p < .001$), and orthogonal-dimensions tasks require more time than do one-dimension tasks ($F = 36.27, df = 1/32, p < .001$). Moreover, as indicated by a reliable age x stimulus sets interaction ($F = 6.02, df = 3/32, p < .001$), orthogonal dimensions produce less interference with increasing age. Kindergarteners show the greatest interference, and adults show the least. Second- and fifth-graders show an equivalent amount of interference, and although they show less interference than kindergarteners, they exhibit more than the adult.

The results of Experiment II agree with those of Experiment I in showing that young children perceive dimensional combinations as integral. Kindergarteners show genuine facilitation on the correlated-dimensions task and interference with orthogonal dimensions. The results of Experiment II also indicate that, with perceptual learning, the perceived structure of size and letter variations becomes configural rather than asymmetrically separable. There was no evidence of any facilitation due to correlated dimensions beyond the kindergarten level, but orthogonal dimensions interfered at all ages including the adult.

Although the results of Experiment II do provide support that older children perceive size–letter variations in terms of configural properties, there is the strong possibility that letter–size combinations other than those employed in the present experiment will yield different perceptual organizations. By Garner's analysis (see Chapter 5), the stimulus aspects of letters may involve features and dimensions as well as configural properties. A configural pattern of results may have been favored in the present experiment, because A shows symmetry and E shows repetition and symmetry, properties that are configured (see Chapter 5).

Taken together, the results of Experiments I and II provide strong support for a separability hypothesis. In both experiments, younger children do show a pattern of results indicating that dimensional combinations are perceived as integral. The results of Experiment II show clearly that perceptual development is not simply a matter of some dimensions becoming separable. Other patterns emerge as well. We return to this question later.

FREE CLASSIFICATION

One of the paradigms that clearly reveals differences between integral and separable dimensions is the free classification task (Garner, 1974). In this task, the subject is presented with several stimuli and is instructed to put together the ones that go together. Consider the triad of stimuli illustrated in Fig. 6.1. Stimulus A is a combination of value 1 on dimension 1 and value 1 on dimension 2; stimulus B is a combination of value 1 on dimension 1 and value 4 on dimension 2; stimulus C combines value 2 on dimension 1 and value 3 on dimension 2. Stimuli A and B are the only pair of the triad that show an identical value on at least one dimension, whereas stimuli B and C are the pair that are nearest in overall similarity.

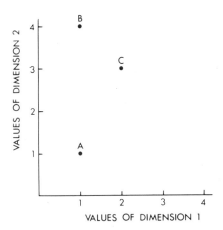

FIG. 6.1   An   illustration   of an informative triad for free classification.

By Garner's (1974) analysis, stimuli *A* and *B* will be classified together if dimensions are separable, and *B* and *C* will be put together if the dimensions are integral. This prediction has been confirmed by Handel and Imai (1972) in an experiment where adults were instructed to classify various subsets of stimuli composed of either chroma and value of the Munsell series or size and brightness of square. Their results were clear. Stimuli composed of chroma and value were classified according to similarity, and stimuli composed of size and brightness were classified by dimension.

According to a separability hypothesis, if children of differing age levels are instructed to classify stimuli composed of dimensions that are separable for the adult, young children should classify the stimuli according to overall similarity, and with increasing age, one would expect an increasing tendency to classify according to dimensional structure. Specifically, if the stimuli represented in Fig. 6.1 were composed of size and brightness, younger children should classify stimuli *B* and *C* together, and with increasing age, there should be an increase in the frequency with which *A* and *B* are classified together.

Smith and Kemler (1977)[3] have recently conducted two free-classification experiments in which kindergarten, second-grade, and fifth-grade children were presented with either a series of triads (Experiment III) or tetrads (Experiment IV) and instructed to partition each subset according to which stimuli "go together." The stimuli varied in size and brightness, which for the adult are separable dimensions (see Handel & Imai, 1972). In both experiments, the important stimulus arrangements are those that put similarity classifications in conflict with dimensional classifications. By hypothesis, the kindergarten children, perceiving the stimuli as integral, should classify by similarity; with increasing age, there should be a shift in the direction of dimensional classifications.

Experiment III

Method

The subjects were 30 children who were attending kindergarten, second, or fifth grade at a suburban Philadelphia elementary school. Five males and five females were chosen randomly from each grade to participate in the experiment. The mean age was 68 mo (range: 62.2—73 mo), 95 mo (range: 87—99 mo), and 131 mo (range: 122—138 mo) for kindergarten, second, and fifth grades, respectively.

The stimuli consisted of an irregular quadrilateral that varied only in brightness and size. The forms were cut from six sheets of Coloraid paper that ranged

---

[3]I am especially indebted to Linda Smith and Deborah Kemler not only for providing me with a copy of their manuscript but for their permission to include their work in this chapter.

from almost white to black (Coloraid numbers: 1, 2, 5, 7, and black) and were mounted on 4" x 5" white cards. Six different sizes were used and had the following areas: .42, .72, 1.00, 1.28, 2.59, and 3.88 sq in. Adjacent values on each of the dimensions were discriminably different from one another.

In order to achieve equal intervals of psychological distance on each of the dimensions, eight undergraduates rated the similarity of pairs of stimuli differing by one dimension. The method of magnitude estimation was used, and from these data, 16 different triads were arranged.

As shown in Fig. 6.2, three different types of traids were presented. In Type I and Type II traids, similarity relations are pitted against dimensional relations. Each contains two stimuli (*A* and *B*) that share an identical value on one dimension but differ substantially on the second. One of the two stimuli (*A*) differs only slightly from the third stimulus (*C*) in the triad, but it differs on both dimensions. Based on the adult similarity judgments, the sum of the difference between *A* and *C* in each triad is always smaller than the one dimensional difference between *A* and *B*. Type I and Type II triads differ from each other only in the noncritical relation between stimuli *B* and *C*.

There are three types of classifications that can result from Type I and II triads. The subjects can: (1) make a dimensional classification (DIM) by putting

Triad Type	Grade	Classification
I A •, • C, B •	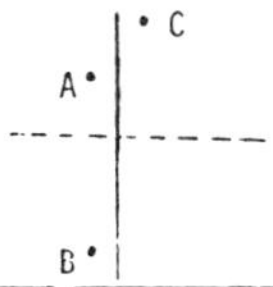 K 2 5	DIM .40 (.109) .57 (.185) .66 (.250)
II A •, • C, B •	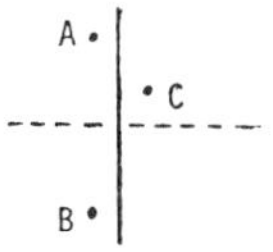 K 2 5	DIM .34 (.069) .50 (.217) .68 (.215)
III A • • C, B •	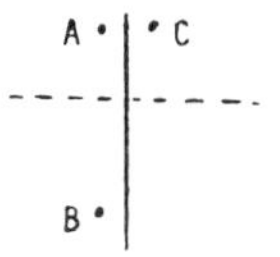 K 2 5	DIM ONLY .34 (.116) .41 (.088) .41 (.172)

FIG. 6.2.   Size-*X* brightness triads. In the left column are shown schematic representations of the size-*X* brightness triad types, drawn so that values of the two dimensions are represented along the horizontal and vertical axes. Distances along the axes represent perceived psychological differences. The solid line in each schematic indicates a dimensional partition; the dashed line, a similarity-maximizing partition. In the right column are given mean proportions of systematic classifications that were dimensional for each type and grade level. Standard deviations are in parentheses.

together the two stimuli that share an identical value in the same group; (2) make a similarity classification (SIM) by putting together the two stimuli that differ only slightly on both dimensions in the same group; or (3) classify stimuli haphazardly by putting together the two stimuli that differ considerably on both dimensions.

In Type III triads, both the pair A and B and the pair A and C share a value. This arrangement makes possible two dimensional classifications for these triads. In one classification, subjects can put together the two stimuli that share a value on one dimension and differ substantially on the other (DIM ONLY) or subjects can group together the two stimuli that share one value and differ only slightly on the other dimension (DIM + SIM). Again, subjects could classify stimuli haphazardly by putting together two stimuli that differ considerably on both dimensions.

There were six unique Type I and four unique Type II triads. Specific triads were constructed by selecting a specific value on the shared dimension and the appropriately constrained values on the nonshared dimensions. For half of these triads, the shared dimension was size; for the remaining half, the shared dimension was brightness. There were six unique Type III triads. For half of these triads, the two stimuli that shared a value of size were also the most similar pair; for the remaining half, the opposite arrangement was employed.

The triads were randomly ordered in a series of 58 trials. Each Type I and Type II triad was repeated four times, and each Type III triad was repeated three times within the series. The experimenter and subject sat facing each other across a table. Three stimuli were placed in front of the subject, either in a row or as if at the vertices of a triangle, and the subject was told to "put together in one group the two that go together." "Which two most go together?" The words "most alike" or "most similar" were not used. The experimenter occasionally encouraged the subject, but no specific feedback was given.

Results

Fortunately, haphazard responses were rare even for kindergarten children. In no case within any age group did the frequency of haphazard responses account for more than 10% of the observations.

The proportion of systematic classifications (SIM or DIM) that were dimensional was computed for each subject. For Type III triads, the DIM ONLY classification is counted as dimensional. The mean proportions of such classifications for each grade level and type of triad are shown in Fig. 6.2. Because Type III triads offered two dimensional solutions and did not therefore put a similarity solution in conflict with a dimensional solution, they were analyzed separately from Type I and Type II triads.

Type I and Type II Triads.   The proportions of DIM classifications for Type I and Type II triads were analyzed by an analysis of variance for a 3 × 2 × 2 (age x type of triad x dimension that shared a value) mixed factorial design. This analysis revealed a significant mean effect of age $[F(2, 27) = 6.93, p < .01]$. As indicated in Fig. 6.2, the proportion of dimensional classifications increases reliably with age for both Type I and Type II triads. No other main effects or interactions were reliable.

In order to determine if similarity or dimensional classification predominated at each age level, the mean proportion of DIM classifications for each age on each type of triad was compared with the value expected (.50) if subjects were dividing their responses equally between SIM and DIM classifications. On both Type I and Type II triads, kindergarteners produced the DIM classifications significantly less than 50% of the time $[t(9) = 2.90, p < .05$, and $t(9) = 7.33$, $p < .001$, respectively, for Types I and II]. The proportion of responses for second-graders did not differ reliably from the chance value. Fifth-graders gave DIM responses significantly more than 50% of the time $[t(9) = 3.16, p < .05$, and $t(9) = 2.64, p < .05$, respectively, for Type I and Type II triads]. These results clearly indicate that kindergarteners gave a similarity classification more often than a dimensional classification on both Type I and Type II triads, whereas fifth-graders responded most often with a dimensional classification on both triads. The responses of second-graders appeared to be equally divided between two types of classifications.

Type III Triads.   The proportions of DIM ONLY responses were analyzed in a 3 x 2 (age x dimensions shared by most similar pair) mixed factorial design. The analysis revealed no main effects or interactions. As may be observed in Fig. 6.2, the predominant response at all age levels was the dimensional classification that maximized the similarity of the stimuli on both dimensions $[t(29) = 3.14, p < .01]$. This result is interesting because it shows that even older children use overall similarity as an ancillary determinant of classification as long as it is not in conflict with a dimensional partition.

Discussion

The results of Experiment III, like those of Experiments I and II, provide strong support for a separability hypothesis. Size and brightness are perceived by kindergarteners as integral dimensions and, as a consequence, are classified according to overall similarity. In contrast, the dimensional classifications by fifth-graders indicate that size and brightness are perceived as separable. The intermediate performances by second-grade children do not seem to result from any particular systematic trend. Two of these subjects classified by dimension and two by similarity, whereas classifications for the remaining six second-graders were divided evenly between similarity and dimensional classifications.

Smith and Kemler also point out two other aspects of their data that deserve mention. First, systematic classifications, as opposed to haphazard responses, are produced even by young children. Thus, although the logic of classification does improve with age in some situations (e.g., Bruner, Olver, & Greenfield, 1966), free classification with structured stimuli does not appear to tap logical abilities that exceed those of young children, and it seems, therefore, to be a particularly useful technique for assessing principles of perceptual development. Second, kindergarteners' responses tend to be consistent across stimulus variation. Especially important is the fact that kindergarteners predominately use a SIM classification even though the dimension in a set that presents the shared value is varied. A few subjects at all ages show some preference to sort on the basis of one dimension relative to the other, but the group data clearly indicate that systematic responses to stimulus structure dominates kindergarten and fifth-grade classifications.

Smith and Kemler observed that the young children, more than older, relied on "first impressions" to generate their classifications. Because the role of mental set on perceived integrality and separability seems especially important in studies of perceptual development, they raise the question as to whether a more difficult task, requiring children to be more reflective, would yield the same results as a classification task with triads. To answer this question, their second experiment presented stimulus sets of four stimuli (tetrads) to be sorted into two groups of two.

An interesting feature of their second experiment was an attempt to discover if children perceive both types of stimulus structure. After subjects had generated one classification, they were instructed to generate a different one. If subjects successfully generated two sorts, they were asked to pick the "best" one. If a subject can generate both a similarity and a dimensional classification, this raises the interesting question as to whether the younger children will prefer the similarity classification while older ones will prefer the dimensional classification. Experiment IV describes this work.

Experiment IV

Method

The subjects were 10 kindergarten, 10 second-grade, and 10 fifth-grade children who attended the same elementary school as those of Experiment III. Their mean ages were 69 mo (range: 66–76 mo), 102 mo (range: 92–101 mo), and 130 mo (range: 126–139 mo) for kindergarten, second-grade, and fifth-grade children, respectively. Five males and five females were chosen randomly from each grade to participate in the experiment.

The specific stimuli were identical to those of Experiment III, but they were arranged in tetrads rather than triads. Fourteen unique tetrads were composed and arranged in four different types of tetrads. The four types of tetrads are illustrated in the far left column of Fig. 6.3. Specific instances of each type of tetrad were devised in a manner analogous to the formation of triads in Experiment III.

In tetrad Types I and II, similarity and dimensional classifications are put in conflict. For Type I tetrads, a similarity response results if two groups are formed such that the two members of each group differ slightly on both dimensions. For Type II tetrads, a similarity response consists of forming one group in which the two members share a value on one dimension and differ slightly on the other. A similarity classification for these tetrads maximizes intergroup similarity while minimizing intragroup similarity. There were four unique Type I and four unique Type II tetrads. For each type, one-half of the potential dimensional classifications require partitioning on the basis of shared sizes, and one-half require partitioning on the basis of shared brightness value.

In Type III tetrads, two dimensional solutions are possible. Each is constructed as a set of all combinations of two specific values on each dimension. One-dimensional classification maximizes both similarity within groups and dissimilarity between groups relative to the other classification (see Fig. 6.3). Two unique Type III tetrads were arranged. In one, size maximized intragroup similarity, whereas in the other, brightness maximized intragroup similarity.

In Type IV tetrads, one-dimensional classification is provided, but there is no clear similarity classification. This tetrad was included to check on subjects'

Tetrad Type		Grade	Classification	
I			DIM	SIM
		K	.34(.161)	.58(.153)
		2	.36(.244)	.58(.230)
		5	.80(.190)	.18(.161)
II			DIM	SIM
		K	.28(.200)	.61(.261)
		2	.35(.213)	.57(.237)
		5	.68(.165)	.31(.180)
III			DIM ONLY	DIM + SIM
		K	.20(.197)	.70(.204)
		2	.19(.114)	.75(.160)
		5	.28(.175)	.72(.175)
IV			DIM	ONE-SIDED
		K	.53(.143)	.29(.166)
		2	.70(.213)	.18(.149)
		5	.90(.166)	.05(.104)

FIG. 6.3.   Size-X brightness tetrads. In the left column are shown schematic representations of the four size-X brightness tetrad types. Representation is as in Figure 6-1. For each type, two partitions are shown. That indicated by the solid line refers to the partition named in the next-to-last column. That indicated by the dashed line refers to the partition named in the last column. In the right columns are given mean proportions of various classifications for each type and grade level. (See text for further clarification of classification types.) Standard deviations are given in parentheses.

abilities to follow instructions. The principal concern was whether subjects would form two groups of two stimuli or whether, contrary to instruction, subjects might choose the two most similar stimuli for one group and leave the other two as "leftover." The latter "one-sided" response is put in conflict with the dimensional classification in the arrangement of Type IV tetrads. There were four unique Type IV tetrads. For two of them, size could be partitioned dimensionally; for the remaining two, brightness could be partitioned dimensionally.

The tetrads were presented in a series of 42 trials, where each unique tetrad was repeated three times. The series was randomly ordered with the exception that during the last third of the trials each of the 14 unique instances was presented once.

The experimenter and the subject sat facing each other across a table top that was bisected by a red line. On each trial, the subject was given a stack of four stimulus cards, haphazardly ordered, and instructed to "make two groups": "Put two over here (on one side of the red line) so that they go together, and put two over here (on the other side) so that they go together." The experimenter periodically encouraged the subject on the first two-thirds of the trials, but no specific feedback was given. On the last third of the trials, the subject was asked to justify his or her first (primary) classification and to give another (second) classification. The following series of questions was used. Indicated in parentheses are the type of follow-up questions that were asked if the subject failed to answer or comprehend the first form of the question.

1. *Is this a good way* (relative to the primary response)? *Why? How come you did it this way? Why do these two go together* (indicating one group)? *Why do these go together* (indicating another group)? *Is there anything alike about these two?*
2. *Could you do it another way? How? How might somebody else do it? Try it another way.* (If a subject strongly asserted that there was only one way to do it or offered a justification for that assertion, he or she was not prodded further to produce a second classification.)
3. Repeat of Questions 1 above in relation to the subject's second classification, if produced.
4. *Which way is the best way? This way or the one before? Are you sure? Why? Show me the best way again* (as the experimenter restacks the stimuli and presents them again for classification).

Results and Discussion

Type IV Tetrads.   Before considering the data of major interest, it is important to consider classifications on the Type IV tetrads. The results on these tetrads provide a check as to whether the children follow the instruction to classify the tetrads into two groups of two as opposed to the lesser demand of choosing one pair of stimuli that go together, leaving the remainder as the second pair. For the Type IV tetrads, the act of producing a partition of the set such that consistent relations hold within both groups (a DIM response, in this case) is put into conflict with a classification whereby the pair of stimuli that are most similar overall are put together (a one-sided response). The primary classificatory responses for the Type IV tetrads are presented in the bottom rows of Fig. 6.3. The proportions of DIM classifications were analyzed in a 3 x 2 (age x dimension that had two values) mixed factorial design. Only a reliable mean effect of age was observed $[F(2, 27) = 11.69, p < .01]$. Pairwise contrasts indicates that the proportion of DIM responses increases reliably with age. Yet, as can be observed in Fig. 6.3, the DIM classification predominates at all age levels, indicating that the subjects tend to follow instructions. As additional supporting evidence, when the dimensional classification was given, it was judged as the "best" classification on 70%, 74%, and 100% of the trials by kindergarten, second-grade, and fifth-grade subjects, respectively.

Type I and Type II Tetrads. Similarity and dimensional classifications are put in conflict in both Type I and Type II tetrads and thus provide the most critical information about a separability hypothesis. The proportions of total primary responses to these tetrads that were DIM classifications are shown in the top rows of Fig. 6.3. An analysis of variance of these data in a 3 x 2 x 2 (age x type x dimension that shared two values) revealed a significant main effect due to age $[F(2, 27) = 6.93, p < .01]$. No other effects were significant.

Inspection of Fig. 6.3 indicates that the age trends of classification of tetrads parallel those that were observed with the triads in Experiment III. With tetrads, kindergarteners give SIM classifications reliably more often than DIM classifications $[t(9) = 2.25, p < .05]$. Fifth-graders, on the other hand, make DIM classifications reliably more often than SIM classifications $[t(9) = 4.25, p < .01]$. As in Experiment III, second-graders appear to divide their responses evenly between the two types of classifications.

Subjects tended to produce both SIM and DIM classifications when, on the last third of the trials, they were asked to give two classifications. The mean proportion of trials on which both classifications were given are .67, .71, and .56 for kindergarten, second-grade, and fifth-grade children, respectively. A single-criterion analysis of variance indicates that there is no reliable effect of age $[F(2, 27) = .62]$. Table 6.5 shows the conditional probabilities of "best" judgments on Type I and Type II tetrads. Four separate single criterion (age) analyses of variance were conducted on these data. Because there were unequal *n*s due to the nonoccurrence of some solutions in some subjects, the analyses were run using the least squares method for unequal group sizes. All four analyses showed a reliable effect of age. Clearly, as shown in Table 6.5, the probability that a dimensional classification is judged "best" increases with age, whereas the probability that a SIM response is judged "best" decreases with age.

TABLE 6.5
Conditional Probabilities of "Best" Judgments
(Type I and Type II Tetrads)[a]

	Grade	Type I	Type II
Prob (DIM Best | DIM and SIM	K	.31 (.194)	.33 (.267)
	2	.47 (.350)	.56 (.351)
	5	.86 (.258)	.71 (.317)
Prob (SIM Best | DIM and SIM	K	.64 (.227)	.60 (.376)
	2	.40 (.353)	.30 (.337)
	5	.13 (.258)	.03 (.168)

[a]Conditional probabilities for the classification that was considered the "best" (e.g., the first conditional probability reads: The probability that a dimensional classification was best, given there were both dimensional and similarity classifications given on that trial). Standard deviations are given in parentheses.

Type III Tetrads. Two dimensional solutions are offered for Type III tetrads. One solution (DIM + SIM) maximizes overall similarity within each grouping more than does the second (DIM ONLY). An inspection of Fig. 6.3 suggests that all subjects tend to classify these tetrads to maximize overall similarity. A single-criterion (age) analysis of variance on the proportions DIM + SIM classifications confirms this suggestion. There was no reliable age effect. It appears that all age groups are sensitive to the values on both dimensions, and even older children will maximize overall similarity as long as the classification produces a dimensional structure.

When asked to give a second response on the last third of the trials, all subjects tended to give the alternative dimensional classification. The mean proportions of such trials in which both dimensional classifications (SIM + DIM and DIM ONLY) are given, are: .65, .75 and .90 for kindergarteners, second-graders, and fifth-graders, respectively. A developmental change in the production of both classifications is consistent with a separability hypothesis. If dimensions are separable and the rule is to classify stimuli such that they share a value on a dimension, then the two dimensional classifications are equally good. If, on the other hand, dimensions are integral and the rule is to group stimuli on the basis of overall similarity, then one classification (DIM + SIM) is clearly better than the other (DIM ONLY). The data for "best" judgments on Type III tetrads is shown in Table 6.6. As one might expect, judgments of DIM + SIM classifications as "best" decrease with age, whereas judgments that both solutions are equally good increase with age.

Justifications of Classifications. When justifying either a dimensional or a similarity classification, all subjects tend to verbalize some criterion that is, in fact, true of the partition. In justifying DIM and DIM + SIM responses, subjects predominantly verbalize either the dimension that is shared (e.g., size) or the specific values that are shared (e.g., little and big). Given a dimensional classification, the mean proportions of such verbalizations are .78, .88, and .88 for kindergarteners, second-graders, and fifth-graders, respectively. In justifying SIM responses, the subjects predominantly verbalized the one dimension that maximized intragroup differences: .67, .70, and .60 of the verbalizations were of this type for kindergarteners, second-graders, and fifth-graders, respectively.

Surprisingly, developmental differences were minimal in the justification data. There was some tendency for the youngest children to mention both dimensions in the justification of similarity responses, and this tendency decreased with age. The proportions of such responses were .22, .15, and .00 for kindergarten, second-grade, and fifth-grade children, respectively. But perhaps what is more important is the fact that even the youngest subjects do use dimensional terms in their verbalizations. Given their preference for similarity partitions, more global descriptions might have been expected.

The verbalizations by young children in terms of dimensions might appear initially to contradict a separability hypothesis. Given that these children classify the stimuli in terms of overall similarity, how can they at the same time use dimensional terms to describe their classifications? Smith and Kemler provide a good answer. As they point out, overall similarity is the primary mode in perceiving integral dimensions. This does not mean that integral dimensions cannot be analyzed at a more derived or higher level of processing (Garner, 1974; Lockhead, 1972). Thus the classification data may be tapping the primary mode of perception in younger children, whereas the verbalizations are accessing a more derived perceptual mode.

In summary, the data from both free-classification studies support the argument that younger children perceive dimensional combinations as integral and that with increasing age some dimensions become increasingly separable. Moreover, despite the fact that many children at all ages could provide both types of classification, younger and older children showed a preference for the classifica-

TABLE 6.6
Data for "Best" Judgments
(Type III Tetrads)[a]

Grade	DIM + SIM	DIM ONLY	Both
K	.65 (.241)	.30 (.258)	.00 (.00)
2	.55 (.368)	.10 (.210)	.30 (.411)
5	.40 (.390)	.10 (.210)	.50 (.411)

[a]Mean proportions of "best" judgments for Type III tetrads, showing preferences for the DIM + SIM classification, the DIM ONLY classification, or a judgment that both were equally good. Standard deviations are given in parentheses.

tion predicted by a separability hypothesis. Finally, even though kindergarteners could provide a second classification and could verbalize their sorts dimensionally, this shows only that analysis of integral dimensions is possible. The primary perceptual mode for these children is one of overall similarity.

GENERAL DISCUSSION

This chapter describes four experiments. The results of three of them, using very different tasks, provide strong evidence that dimensional combinations that are perceived by older children and adults as separable are perceived by younger children as integral. It is also reasonable to suppose that the results of many experiments cited earlier as implicating a separability hypothesis can also be claimed by it. However, the results that speak to the development of selective attention, apart from the question of perceived structure, are less clear. Moreover, the results of Experiment II show that perceptual learning involves more than the abstraction of separable dimensions, as outcome that is hardly surprising in view of Gibson's (1969) work and the several alternative dimensional interactions described by Garner (1976). Thus it appears that some additional directions to a separability hypothesis need to be specified.

Consider first the evidence that supports the assumption of developmental differences in perceived structure. The results from the speeded-sorting task of Experiment I and those from the free-classification tasks clearly support the assumption. In speeded sorting, younger children show a redundancy gain when color and form are correlated, the typical result for integral dimensions (Garner & Felfoldy, 1970). In free classifications, younger children classify stimuli that vary in size and brightness according to overall similarity, which is the adult mode of classifying integral dimensions (Handel & Imai, 1972). Thus, in both experimental situations, dimensional combinations that are separable for the adult are treated by younger children as integral.

In contrast to the performances of younger children, older children perform on the same tasks with the same dimensions in a manner similar to the adult. In speeded sorting, there is no facilitation with correlated dimensions. Moreover, stimuli in free classification are grouped according to a dimensional structure. Both types of performances resemble those of the adult in analogous tasks (Garner & Felfoldy, 1970; Handel & Imai, 1972).

Developmental differences in perceived structure imply differences in selective attention. For younger children, stimulus dimensions are integral, and selective attention is not a logical possibility. Interference would be expected in the orthogonal-dimensions task and was observed in the performances of first-graders in Experiment I. Selective attention is not an optional process for these subjects, and it is erroneous to claim a process deficit. With separable dimensions, on the other hand, selective attention is possible, and as the performances of the fourth-graders with orthogonal dimensions in Experiment I revealed, color and form can be selectively attended by children of this age.

It is also possible, however, that even though dimensional structure is perceived, selective attention will fail. As we suggested earlier in the chapter, the child would need to perceive dimensional structure prior to acquiring the skill of selective attention. Developmentally, then, there should be a transition where the child perceives dimensions but cannot selectively attend. In this event, a specific pattern of performances should appear in the speeded-sorting task. There should be no redundancy gain with correlated dimension, which indicates perceived dimensional structure, but there should be interference with orthogonal dimensions, which means that the filtering of irrelevant dimensions has failed. Many of the first-graders in Experiment I showed this pattern of results, indicating that selective attention does lag the perception of dimensions in perceptual development. This conclusion is also supported by some results of Smith, Kemler, and Aronfreed (1976). In one of the conditions of their study, an auditory signal was presented while the subject was performing a visual matching task. These stimuli are clearly separable. Yet the auditory signal interfered with the performance of younger children but had no effect on the performance of older children.

Although there is some support for the assumption that the child must perceive dimensional structure before learning to filter irrelevant inputs, there are two aspects of the free-classification data that suggest an added complication. Recall that in Experiment IV many of the children at each developmental level were able to produce both similarity and dimensional classifications. Yet there was a clear trend toward increasing dimensional classification with increasing age. These observations indicate a change in the relative dominance of the two forms of perceived structure with increasing age and suggest that a component of perceptual learning is the learning to attend to a dimensional structure rather than a similarity structure. Thus the second-graders in Experiments III and IV divide their classifications between those that honor a dimensional structure and those that honor a similarity structure for the reason that on some occasions they attend to dimensions whereas on others they attend to overall similarity. The first-graders of Experiment I, who appear to be in a transition period, could be exhibiting the same attentional problem. Switches in attention between stimuli could eliminate a redundancy gain with correlated dimensions but not interference with orthogonal-dimensions.

We are suggesting, then, that selective attention serves at least two functions during the course of perceptual learning. First, the child must learn to attend to dimensional rather than similarity structures. Second, given perceived dimensional structure or other independent channels of input, the child must learn to filter irrelevant sources of input. The assumption that attention is not unitary is, of course, well documented (e.g., Posner & Boies, 1971), and Gibson (1969) has stressed multiple components of attention in her theory of perceptual development. Our argument is different in that selective attention is assumed to be implicated as dimensional structure achieves relative dominance over similarity structure.

The evidence thus far summarized indicates that a separability hypothesis provides an accurate account of a fundamental aspect of perceptual development. Yet, by stressing a progression from perceived similarity to perceived dimensional structure, the hypothesis fails to capture several stimulus structures that affect adult perception and does not speak to the processing options that such structures allow. As a consequence, the generality of the hypothesis is limited, and the processes of perceptual learning are undoubtedly oversimplified. Two issues serve to underscore these points.

First, by assuming that the result of perceptual learning is the appearance of separable dimensions, the importance of perceived similarity is overlooked. In some instances, dimensions may be present in the stimulus, but they may not provide the most useful organization for the subject. Rosch and Mervis (1975), for example, have argued that many natural concepts are structured by overall similarity rather than by a few criterial features or dimensions. In view of this evidence, it is unreasonable to suppose that perceptual development proceeds relentlessly in the direction of dimensional structure. As with integral dimensions, the primary mode of perception of some objects may be overall similarity.

In other cases, task demands may be such that attention to the similarity structure is advantageous to the observer. For example, it has been shown that the reaction to "same" in the same—different task is too fast by the adult to be accounted for by either serial- or parallel-processing models. This finding has led some investigators to propose that same responses are made to some wholistic property of the stimulus (see Nickerson, 1972). In such tasks, the subject could be using overall similarity for same responses and dimensional structure for different responses. Should this interpretation prove viable, a picture of perceptual learning that is different from the one we have presented might appear. Based on the observation in free classification that younger children could classify by either structure but preferred overall similarity, it was assumed that children would learn to attend to dimensional structure during the course of perceptual experience. We now add the possibility that attention to alternative structures may become more labile during the course of perceptual development.

Second, as shown by the results of Experiemnt II, a progression from perceived similarity to dimensional structure does not always occur. As with other dimensional combinations, younger children perceived combinations of letter (A and E) and size as integral; correlated dimensions produced a redundancy gain, and orthogonal dimensions did interfere. In contrast to our other results, however, older children and adults did not sort letter and size as though they were separable. There was no redundancy gain with correlated dimensions, but interference with orthogonal dimensions was shown by older children and adults.

Clearly, in this case, the developmental progression appears to go from perceived similarity to a configural structure.

We also have reason to believe that different letter—size combinations will produce still other developmental progressions. We have recently completed an experiment with the letters d and g combined with variations in size. They were presented in the speeded-sorting task, and adults were subjects. With these stimuli, no redundancy gain was observed in the correlated-dimensions task, and interference was asymmetrical with orthogonal-dimensions. Size variation did not interfere with letter classification, but letter variation did interfere with size classification. The developmental part of this study is not finished, but there is no reason to believe that young children would not sort these letters on the basis of overall similarity. Taken together, these results suggest the general picture that young children do perceive dimensional combinations as integral, but depending on stimulus structure, several different developmental progressions in perceived structure seem to occur. Moreover, each implies a processing option that has consequences for the acquisition of selective attention during the course of perceptual development.

In summary, we have shown that there is a clear developmental trend from perceived similarity to perceived dimensional structure. The effect is not confined to a single task nor to a single set of dimensional combinations. We have also shown that: (1) there are additional progressions in perceived stimulus structure that emerge in the course of perceptual learning; and (2) a promising direction for further study is the relation of perceived structure to the processing skills of the developing child. A separability hypothesis seems, in spirit, to be entirely consistent with Gibson's (1969) theory of perceptual development and is but one way to make more specific some of her basic principles.

Other interpretations that perceptual learning proceeds from wholistic to dimensional perception have been offered by Tighe (1973) and by Zeaman and House (1974). In some respects, both of these views are similar to a separability hypothesis. Both rely entirely, however, on the results of discriminative shifts for support. Discriminative shift effects occur with separable dimensions (see Wolff, 1967) and, as we (Shepp & Howard, 1973) and Tighe (1973) have shown, with integral dimensions as well. Thus these views neither appear to be a general nor to have as much promise as a separability hypothesis.

ACKNOWLEDGMENTS

The preparation of this paper was supported, in part, by Research Grant HD—04320, awarded by the National Institute of Child Health and Human Development. Requests for reprints should be sent to Bryan E. Shepp, Department of Psychology, Brown University, Providence, R. I. 02912.

We are indebted to the following for assistance in conducting Experiments I and II: K. Foote, D. Lamparski, K. Quaid, and J. L. Shepp. Special thanks are due to M. Furey, C. Groff, and J. L. Shepp in preparation of the manuscript. I would also like to thank the principals and teachers of the East Providence, R.I. school system as well as Edward Martin, Superintendent, and his staff for their continuing cooperation.

REFERENCES

Bruner, J. S., Olver, R. R., & Greenfield, P. M. *Studies in cognitive growth.* New York: Wiley, 1966.

Corcoran, D. W. J., & Besner, D. Application of the Posner technique to the study of size and brightness irrelevancies in letter pairs. In P. M. A. Rabbitt & S. Dornic (Eds.), *Attention and performance V.* London: Academic Press, 1975.

Crane, N. L., & Ross, L. E. A developmental study of attention to cue redundancy. *Journal of Experimental Child Psychology,* 1967, *5,* 1–15.

Garner, W. R. The stimulus in information processing. *American Psychologist,* 1970, *25,* 350–358.

Garner, W. R. *The processing of information and structure.* Potomac, Md.: Lawrence Erlbaum Associates, 1974.

Garner, W. R. Interaction of stimulus dimensions in concept and choice processes. *Cognitive Psychology,* 1976, *8,* 98–123.

Garner, W. R., & Felfoldy, G. L. Integrality of stimulus dimensions in various types of information processing. *Cognitive Psychology,* 1970, *1,* 225–241.

Gibson, E. J. *Principles of perceptual learning and development.* New York: Appleton-Century-Crofts, 1969.

Gibson, E. J., & Olum, V. Experimental methods of studying perception in children. In P. H. Mussen (Ed.), *Handbook of research methods in child development.* New York: Wiley, 1960.

Hagen, J. W., & Hale, G. H. The development of attention in children. In A. Pick (Ed.), *Minnesota symposia on child psychology* (Vol. 7). Minneapolis: University of Minnesota Press, 1973.

Handel, S., & Imai, S. The free classification of analyzable and unanalyzable stimuli. *Perception and Psychophysics,* 1972, *12,* 108–116.

Hyman, R., & Well, A. Judgments of similarity and spatial models. *Perception and Psychophysics,* 1967, *2,* 233–248.

Hyman, R., & Well, A. Perceptual separability and spatial models. *Perception and Psychophysics,* 1968, *3,* 161–165.

Lockhead, G. R. Processing dimensional stimuli: A note. *Psychological Review,* 1972, *79,* 410–419.

Maccoby, E. E. The development of stimulus selection. In J. P. Hill (Ed.), *Minnesota symposia on child psychology* (Vol. 3). Minneapolis: University of Minnesota Press, 1969.

Nickerson, R. S. Binary-classification reaction time: A review of some studies of human information-processing capabilities. *Psychonomic Monograph Supplements,* 1972, *4,* 275–317.

Pick, A. D., & Frankel, G. W. A study of strategies of visual attention in children. *Developmental Psychology,* 1973, *9,* 348–358.

Posner, M. I., & Boies, S. J. Components of attention. *Psychological Review,* 1971, *78,* 391–408.

Posner, M. I., & Keele, S. Decay of visual information from a single letter. *Science,* 1967, *158,* 137–139.

Posner, M. I., & Mitchell, R. F. Chronometric analysis of classification. *Psychological Review,* 1967, *74,* 392–409.

Rosch, E., & Mervis, C. B. Family resemblances: Studies in the internal structure of categories. *Cognitive Psychology,* 1975, *7,* 573–605.

Shepard, R. N. Attention and the metric structure of the stimulus space. *Journal of Mathematical Psychology,* 1964, *1,* 54–87.

Shepp, B. E., & Howard, D. V. Are differential orienting responses necessary for dimensional learning and transfer? *Journal of Experimental Psychology,* 1973, *100,* 122–134.

Shepp, B. E., & Swartz, K. B. Selective attention and the processing of integral and nonintegral dimensions: A developmental study. *Journal of Experimental Child Psychology,* 1976, *22,* 73–85.

Shepp, B. E., & Turrisi, F. D. Learning and transfer of mediating responses in discriminative learning. In N. R. Ellis (Ed.), *International review of research in mental retardation* (Vol. 2). New York: Academic Press, 1966.

Shepp, B. E., & Turrisi, F. D. Effects of overtraining on the acquisition of intradimensional and extradimensional shifts. *Journal of Experimental Psychology,* 1969, *82,* 46–51.

Smith, L. B., & Kemler, D. G. Developmental trends in free classification: Evidence for a new conceptualization of perceptual development. *Journal of Experimental Child Psychology,* 1977, *24,* 279–298.

Smith, L. B., Kemler, D. G., & Aronfreed, J. Development trends in voluntary selective attention: Differential effects of source distinctness. *Journal of Experimental Psychology,* 1976, *20,* 352–362.

Strutt, G. F., Anderson, D. R., & Well, A. D. A developmental study of the effects of irrelevant information on speeded classification. *Journal of Experimental Child Psychology,* 1975, *20,* 127–135.

Tighe, T. Subproblem analysis of discrimination learning. In G. H. Bower (Ed.), *The psychology of learning and motivation* (Vol. 7). New York: Academic Press, 1973.

Tighe, T. J., Glick, J., & Cole, M. Subproblem analysis of discrimination-shift learning. *Psychonomic Science,* 1971, *24,* 159–160.

Tighe, T. J., & Tighe, L. S. Stimulus control in children's learning. In A. Pick (Ed.), *Minnesota symposia on child psychology* (Vol. 6). Minneapolis: University of Minnesota Press, 1972.

Werner, H. *Comparative psychology of mental development.* (Revised edition). Chicago: Follett, 1948.

Wohlwill, J. From perception to inference: A dimension of cognitive development. *Monographs of the Society for Research in Child Development,* 1962, *72,* 87–107.

Wolff, J. L. Concept-shift and discrimination-reversal learning in humans. *Psychological Bulletin,* 1967, *68,* 369–408.

Zeaman, D., & House, B. J. The role of attention in retardate discrimination learning. In N. R. Ellis (Ed.), *Handbook of mental deficiency.* New York: McGraw-Hill, 1963.

Zeaman, D., & House, B. J. Interpretations of developmental trends in discriminative transfer effects. In A. Pick (Ed.), *Minnesota symposia on child psychology* (Vol. 8). Minneapolis: University of Minnesota Press, 1974.

7 Nonanalytic Concept Formation and Memory for Instances

Lee Brooks
McMaster University

In discussion of human conceptual behavior, a pervasive contrast is that drawn between analytic and nonanalytic thought. By reputation, analytic thought is reputed to belong in the scientific sphere of cold simplicity, in which individual cases are an inconvenience to be considered mainly for their capacity to elucidate a sweeping general principle. When successful, analytic processes are supposed to be precisely focussed and relentlessly powerful; in failure, they stand in gross violation of common sense. In contrast, nonanalytic processes are more at home in the poetic and richly textured world of individuals, of special cases, and of interesting exceptions. Successful nonanalytic processes are often held to be the source of deep wisdom, of insight and humane qualities; but in failure, they represent stubborn, unenlightened illogicality.

In studying concept identification, experimental psychologists have found it far easier to capture analytic than nonanalytic processes. In the sense of analytic that I define shortly, both the associationist theories of Hull (1920) and the cognitive theories of Bruner, Goodnow, and Austin (1956) deal with analytic processes, differing mainly in whether the analysis is passive and automatic or is active hypothesis testing. In this chapter, I discuss the possibility that this one-sidedness stems from the contrast alluded in the foregoing. The tasks and materials normally used in concept-learning research have induced subjects to concentrate on the extraction of generalities rather than on drawing analogies to individuals. As a result, these experiments have biased the subjects' processing toward analysis with various degrees of consequent success. However, in the research discussed later, we encouraged subjects to learn and use information about individuals and thereby have been able to observe and to some extent control a few of the phenomena on which the reputation of nonanalytic processes are based. This emphasis on special cases obviously interacts strongly with the type and structure of the stimuli used, and I hope that this interaction will provide the basis for the coordination of this work with that of several of the other members of this conference.

THE REFERENT PHENOMENON:
ARTIFICIAL GRAMMAR EXPERIMENTS

Let us begin with a description of an experiment that does emphasize the learning of specifics as a basis for the later generalization of an extremely complicated concept. The starting point for this experiment was the work of Arthur Reber (1967, 1969, 1976) on the implicit learning of artificial grammars. Reber used miniature Markov grammars similar to those shown in Fig. 7.1 (Chomsky & Miller, 1958). In such grammars, only those strings of letters that can be generated by following the arrows and loops are considered grammatical. The stimuli columns presented in the training phase design in Fig. 7.1 show strings that are acceptable for each of the grammars. In Reber's tasks, subjects memorized and produced in free recall short lists of grammatical strings from one grammar. They were then unexpectedly asked to discriminate new grammatical strings from strings using the same letters but which violated some of the sequential constraints of that grammar (similar for example to discriminating the members of column *A* in Fig. 7.1 from those listed for the test phase in column *N*). Subjects in these experiments protested that they did not have knowledge of any rules and did not know what they were supposed to be doing, but nonetheless they performed well above chance. Reber demonstrated convincingly that this above-chance performance was not based on any explicit knowledge (Reber, 1967) and that whatever it was based on generalized with apparently equal facility to the same sequential patterns using different component symbols (Reber, 1969).

In a sense, we could say that Reber's subjects were learning the concept "grammaticality" implicitly, because they were able to discriminate new instances of the grammar from noninstances. But, there are three differences between his experiment and the more usual concept-learning experiment that need to be cleared up before we can be completely comfortable with this analogy. First, Reber's subjects did not see noninstances during acquisition. It is just possible that there was some primitive form of recognition memory operating that would allow the nonverbalizable discrimination of "sort-of-like-old" items from novel items. This recognition memory might not operate, or at least not operate implicitly, if the two types of items were mixed in a single discrimination sequence. A second difference between Reber's procedure and the more traditional one is more interesting for our present purposes. In Reber's experiment, the subjects' only specified task was to memorize individual items. It was in fact a concept-learning experiment masquerading in the guise of a memory experiment, and this fact alone may have been sufficient to induce the subjects to learn the stimulus structure in a more implicit manner. Third, Reber's subjects were asked to reproduce the stimuli themselves rather than to associate them with some arbitrary response or course of action. This may have caused a difference in the subjects' strategy over and above the requirement of item memory, a difference that, if crucial, we need to know about.

Previous failures in pilot experiments to produce clear implicit concept learning with artificial materials led me to adopt tactics for the following experiment that were absolutely mundane; the artificial grammar materials that already

Grammar A

Grammar B

Training Phase

		Group 1 Responses	Group 2 Responses		Group 1 Responses	Group 2 Responses
	Stimuli from A	PAL: low category salience	PAL: high category salience	Stimuli from B	PAL: low category salience	PAL: high category salience
List #1	VVTRXRR	Paris	city	MRMRTTV	Montreal	animal
	VVTRX	zebra	city	VVT	moose	animal
	XMVTTRX	baboon	city	VVTRTTV	Chicago	animal
	VT	Cairo	city	MRRMRVT	possum	animal
	VTRR	tiger	city	MRRRM	Halifax	animal
List #2	VVRXRR	Oslo	city	MRRMRV	Vancouver	animal
	XMT	elephant	city	MRRRRRM	bison	animal
	XMTRRRR	Rome	city	VTTTTVT	Detroit	animal
	VVRMVRX	panda	city	VV	coyote	animal
	XMVRMT	Budapest	city	MMRTVT	rattlesnake	animal
List #3	XXRRR	giraffe	city	MMRVTRV	beaver	animal
	XMVRXRR	Moscow	city	MMRTV	Boston	animal
	VVTTRMT	Tokyo	city	VTTVTRV	Toronto	animal
	XXRRRRR	lion	city	VTTV	cougar	animal
	VVRMTR	aardvark	city	VVTRVT	New York	animal

Testing Phase

A	B	N
XXR	MRM	TRV
XMTR	MMRV	VVTVV
VVRX	MRMRV	MMMTV
VVRXR	MRMRTV	RMTTMR
VVTRXR	VTVT	VVVTVT
XMVRX	VVTRV	MTRVXT
XMVRXR	VVTRTV	RMRVTRR
VVRMT	VTVTRVT	TVTXTTR
VVRMTRR	MMRVT	VTRXMTM
XMVTRMT	MMRTTVT	XRXMVTV

FIG. 7.1.

had been shown to produce implicit learning were tried in a concept-discrimination situation. To accomplish this, a group of eight subjects were given three paired-associate lists in which one-half of the stimuli were generated from grammar A in Fig. 7.1 and the other one-half from grammar B. After these subjects, referred to in Fig. 7.1 as "PAL (paired-associate learning): low category salience," had met the criterion of one trial through without mistake for each of the three lists, they were asked if they had noticed that there were two different types of stimuli. As I hope will appear plausible from an inspection of the stimuli in Fig. 7.1, the answers to this question were uniformly negative.[1] They were then asked if they noticed that there were two different types of response. They either answered that they had not or (the more frequent reply) that the responses were all either cities or animals.

Up to this point in the experiment, we had been elaborate in our attempts to disguise the fact that this experiment involved concept learning. The subjects were told, and reported that they believed, that it was a paired-associate experiment. The categories of stimuli were not clearly distinguishable, and the only response category that the subjects noticed was one, as planned, that was un-related to the underlying categories. We were apparently successful in our scheme of having subjects learn items from two different categories in such a way as to emphasize individual items rather than the differences between two categories of stimuli.

We then confirmed our subjects' opinions about the forthrightness of psy-chologists by telling them that the distinction we were interested in was that between New-World items (associated with grammar B) and Old-World items (associated with grammar A). We went over the fact that all of the responses in the lists they had just learned were either clearly associated with the New World or the Old World, but we did not show them any of the stimuli again. Next we presented a stack of 30 cards on each of which was one of the items from the testing-phase list shown at the bottom of Fig. 7.1. The subjects were told that 10 of these cards contained a new string of letters that should be the name of an Old-World item, 10 that should be the name of a New-World item, and 10 that did not belong to either category. Their job was to sort them into these three categories. Their initial response was much like that of Reber's subjects: giggles or irritation together with an emphatic protestation that they didn't know what they were doing. Their performance, however, was also like that of

---

[1]Grammars A and B would be the same used by Reber if a final node were added in both cases. Reber did not design these grammars to be discriminated from one another, and the fact that all of the instances from each grammar ended in the same letter resulted in several of our subjects centering on that one letter. One of the unfortunate side-effects of this deletion was that the letter X was associated only with Grammar A. Curiously, none of our subjects reported this even when, in a variation not reported here, they were asked for their reasons for categorization after every test trial.

Reber's subjects: They were able to distinguish each of the three categories from one another at a level well above chance.

The data derived from this sorting of the cards, as well as a resorting of the same cards to establish consistency of response and a sorting and re-sorting of a second deck, are shown in Table 7.1 (Group 1). Also in Table 7.1 is a contingency table combined for the first sortings of both of the decks. The partitions of this table that tested the subjects' abilities to sort new grammatical items from nongrammatical items (A & B vs. N) and their ability to sort new items of one grammar from new items of another (A vs. B) were both significant (Castellan, 1965). Obviously the 60–65% correct performance is above the blind-chance level of 33%, although the subjects were utterly incapable in their general reports at the end of the experiment of accounting for the cues they had been using. One last feature of the data also resembles Reber's results: Only about 60% of the items were categorized the same way both times that they were sorted. With these results, we have extended Reber's results to a discriminative concept-learning

TABLE 7.1
Percent Correct on Transfer

	Stack 1	Stack 1 Repeat	Stack 1 Consist.	Stack 2	Stack 2 Repeat	Stack 2 Consist.	Stimulus Category		
							A	B	N
Group 1 PAL: low category salience	60.0	63.4	**60.2**	60.0	64.4	**62.3**	A 6.4 B 1.7 N 1.9	1.4 7.5 1.1	2.9 2.9 4.2
Group 2 PAL: high category salience	65.8	63.3	**72.1**	60.4	61.7	**75.0**	A 7.1 B 1.3 N 1.6	1.3 6.9 1.8	3.7 1.4 4.9
Group 3 Concept training	47.5	45.4	**60.0**	50.8	47.5	**66.2**	A 5.1 B 2.9 N 2.0	3.1 4.4 2.5	2.3 2.5 5.2
Group 4 Random-response assignment	40.4	45.0	**68.3**	47.5	47.9	**70.4**	A 4.5 B 3.1 N 2.4	2.3 4.2 3.5	3.3 2.4 4.3
Group 5 No training	37.1	42.8	**59.4**	44.4	51.1	**78.8**	A 4.3 B 3.0 N 2.6	2.9 4.8 2.3	3.6 2.5 3.1

[a]The consistency columns refer to the % of items that were sorted the same way for both trials on a given stack.

situation. Our subjects performed well above chance both on discriminating new instances of two different grammars (A vs. B) and on discriminating "sort-of-like-old" items from items that violated both grammars (A or B vs. N), although they could not even approximately account for their performance. This was accomplished under conditions in which the subjects did not know the relevant categories at the time of acquisition and in which they did not even know that there were any general rules to be learned.

However, the fact the subjects did perform above chance when they did not know the categories does not prove that they wouldn't do even better when they did know the categories. To evaluate this possibility, we ran the same paired-associate procedure except that we made the presence of two types of items quite obvious. All of the items in the paired-associate lists that were from grammar A were associated with the literal word "city" as a response; all of the items from grammar B were associated with the response "animal." The other details of the procedure were identical to those with the previous group: The experiment was presented as a memory experiment until all three lists had been learned, and then the same two stacks of new items were presented for sorting and re-sorting. The results of this groups, referred to in Table 7.1 as "Pal: high category salience," are very similar to that of the previous, low salience group. In some of the work discussed later, concealment of the response categories at the time of acquisition is important, but clearly in this case it is not. Subjects perform in very similar fashion whether or not they know the significance of the categories of response at the time of learning.

The comparison of real interest, however, is between both of these paired-associate groups and a group that was presented the task in the usual concept-learning manner (reception paradigm). The subjects in this group were told that they were to learn to distinguish strings of letters that were generated by two different sets of rules, or grammars. They were shown the 30 acquisition items one at a time, were asked to categorize each item into grammar A and grammar B, and were told whether they were right or wrong after each response. This training was continued for the same average number of stimulus exposures that were required by the "PAL: high category salience" group to reach criterion on the three lists. This matching for the amount of stimulus exposure is extremely crude, but there is no single clear way to solve the problem. Fortunately, these concept-learning subjects took approximately the same overall acquisition time as the PAL subjects, and the results are sufficiently clear that precise matching does not seem terribly urgent. The results for the test sorting done by this concept-learning group are also shown in Table 7.1. Their performance was obviously, and significantly, lower on A vs. B. Under these conditions, when subjects were trying to learn the concept, they did not do as well on generalizing to new items as when they didn't even know that there was a concept to be learned.

We can go a step further and make the argument that these concept-learning subjects were not performing on the discrimination they had been trying to learn at a level of performance above that expected if they had had no relevant training at all. To demonstrate this, we ran one group in which subjects were given no acquisition training but were simply handed the deck and told that it contained items that were generated from one set of rules, an equal number that were generated from another set of rules, and an equal number that violated both sets of rules. Their job was to sort these items into piles that they thought corresponded to these three types of items. Obviously, these subjects could not know which items we called "A," which items we called "B," and which items we regarded as violations of both, but they could group apparently similar items together. When we named the three piles that they produced "A," "B," and "N" in such a way as to maximize their accuracy scores, the results, shown in Table 7.1 for the training group, were very similar to those produced by the concept group for *A* vs. *B,* although the concept group was still superior on recognition of "sort-of-like-old" from violations (*AB* vs. *N*). This operation of favorably renaming the three test piles did not improve the scores of any of the concept-learning group. As a result, we can say that the performance of the concept-learning groups was not much better than that produced by appropriately naming groups of apparently similar items; that is, we cannot convincingly say that the concept-learning subjects profited much more from their acquisition experience than by learning names for the two a priori discriminable groups of test items. This conclusion was further reinforced by the results of a final control group. In this groups, the New-World–Old-World responses were randomly assigned to the acquisition items. After the same type of paired-associate training, they were given the instructions used for the no-training group and were asked to sort the test items. This procedure controls for the possibility that prior exposure to the acquisition items changes subsequent similarity judgments of the test items. The results, however, are very similar to the concept group for both *A* vs. *B* and *AB* vs. *N* partitions.

We have then a case in which emphasizing the learning of individual items produces better performance than does an emphasis on the extraction of regularities. The most obvious implication of this result is that the reception concept-learning paradigm (sorting successively presented items with feedback after each item) is in no sense an optimal situation for learning some types of concept material. I suspect that this result is dependent on several conditions:

1. The regularities in the material are so complex that the concept-learning subjects are unable to induce them in any reasonable amount of time, certainly not under the conditions of successive presentation.

2. The individual items are sufficiently similar to one another that a subject would be likely to have poor incidental memory for them. That means that if a subject were concentrating on inducing general rules to the partial or complete exclusion of learning individual items, he would be unlikely to incidentally remember many of the individual items. As I argue later, this poor incidental memory for instances is typical of the conditions that occur in a great deal of the concept-learning literature.

3. The stimulus material suggests to the subject that the categorization rules must be very complex. Consequently, subjects are not much tempted to analyze material for regularities either during acquisition (e.g., PAL: high category salience) or testing (both PAL groups) unless they are explicitly asked to. In the current material, the strings are made up of a small number of letters, and even a casual memory scan reveals that these letters are not exclusively associated with one or another of the response categories. This might suggest that the categorization is dependent on some combination of or sequential dependencies among letters. But again, even a casual scan suggests that there are a very large number of letter sequences, no one of which occur in a majority of the stimuli. Any sequential generation and testing of analytic hypotheses would seem to require more dedication and unquenchable enthusiasm than we have been able to generate in our subjects.

What then are the options open to these nonmaniacal subjects? The possibility that Reber has suggested as an explanation for his results is that the subjects are implicitly abstracting the underlying structure of the stimuli. In his view, it is important that this process of abstraction be done implicitly, because encouraging the subjects to look deliberately for regularities in the stimuli that they are memorizing decreases their speed of learning and accuracy of generalization (Reber, 1976). However, the present experiment was designed to make the notion of implicit abstraction of structure an unlikely explanation here. It is hard to understand how our subjects could have been simultaneously abstracting two different structures when apparently they did not know that there were two different types of items. If the two types of *stimuli* had been so obviously different, abstraction could have been taking place independently of the response categories. We would then have expected the random-response group to have done better than they did; after all, they were exposed to the same acquisition stimuli as were all of the other groups. But if instead it was important to have the *response* categories to help separate the two classes of stimuli, then it is hard to account for why the "PAL: low category salience" group, which, if anything, was at least partly working on the wrong classification of the stimuli, did as well as the "PAL: high category salience" group, which was given the correct categorization of the stimuli. Finally, if implicit abstraction is the basis of the New —Old discrimination (*AB* vs. *N*), then it is surprising that we got about the same level of performance as did Reber when surely the structure of *A* and *B* was more complex than either *A* or *B* alone, as Reber used.

Another possibility, and one for which I argue here, is that the subjects were drawing analogies between test items and individual, previously memorized instances. A subject might, for example, decide that the test item MRMRV looked similar to the MRRMRV that was associated with Vancouver, or that VVTRTV looked similar to the VVTRVT that was associated with New York. Because both Vancouver and New York are New-World items, the subject might decide to call the new strings New-World items by simple analogy. He has no clear basis for rejecting such an analogy, and, as mentioned previously, the job of analyzing all of these memory items for their common features seems substantially more discouraging. To use this kind of mechanism, he would not have to know what the response categories were at the time of item acquisition. Rather, once he was told the categories and shown a test item, he would only have to retrieve an analogous memory item and be able to interpret the information stored with it. On the other hand, if analogy is the road to success with this material, the subjects in the concept-learning group were in a much less enviable situation. They had been set to induce a set of rules that were too complicated for them to deal with under these circumstances, and, in the course of working on this procedure, they had not stored the individual items that later would have allowed them to draw analogies.

This combination of analytic complexity and poor item memory may also explain some of the difficulties that I had experienced in obtaining implicit learning in previous experiments. I had been interested in simulating the highly competent but inarticulate concept-identification performance that people commonly show with natural concepts, but which is extremely rare in the laboratory tasks that are supposed to be models of natural concepts. One obvious reason for the explicit, highly verbal learning typical of laboratory tasks is that the material used is very easy to analyze and to capture in a verbal rule. The obvious solution to this problem is to make the material more analytically complex. But the results of several experiments that adorn my filing cabinets and those of several other people to whom I have spoken are that the subjects simply stopped learning with fairly modest increases in complexity — an equally poor simulation of natural performance. What we had done was to introduce enough complexity to eliminate analysis by our subjects, retained counterbalanced stimulus sets, which had the effect of preventing the learning of prototypes, and used conditions of item repetition that prevented learning individual items on which analogies could be drawn. Reber's secret of success with complex material may have been that he had asked his subjects to memorize items that allowed them later to draw analogies.

My personal suspicion is that this analogy or proximity (Reed, 1972) strategy is a component of an interesting variety of everyday tasks but that its explanatory value has been underestimated recently in psychology. Results suggesting it have not appeared very frequently in concept-learning experiments, because the common procedures bias against it. To test this argument, I first examine the properties of an analogy strategy in a simplified situation and then suggest the natural situations in which such a strategy might be useful.

NONANALYTIC MECHANISM:.
A SIMPLIFIED EXAMPLE

Both the strength and the weakness of the artificial grammar experiments is their complexity. This complexity is helpful in that many natural situations that we are interested in are at least this complicated. The same complexity is decidedly unhelpful in that we have a much more difficult time trying to understand what is going on in them. I would like at this point to detour into a description of material that is deliberately simplified to make our own analysis of an analogy strategy easier.

Imagine that a subject was given the training list in Fig. 7.2 to learn in paired-associate fashion. In the course of this learning, no hint is given of any rules or response categorizations. He or she is then given the stimuli one at a time from the test list and is asked any of the four questions: Does it fly, is it big (weighs more than a pound), is it alive, does it attack? In fact, these four semantic bits are related to the stimuli by the four simple attributive rules shown at the bottom of Fig. 7.2, but let us suppose that our subject performs the task on a strictly analogical basis. That is, he did not induce any rules during the training task, because he accepted it as a paired-associate task and because there were so many ways to classify the stimuli and the responses that no one way seemed especially salient. He is now in the situation in which it is easy to retrieve the training responses because they are meaningful, but in which it is difficult to remember the stimuli because they are not meaningful; all of which makes it hard to do any post hoc induction of rules. He is faced with, let us say, the second test item

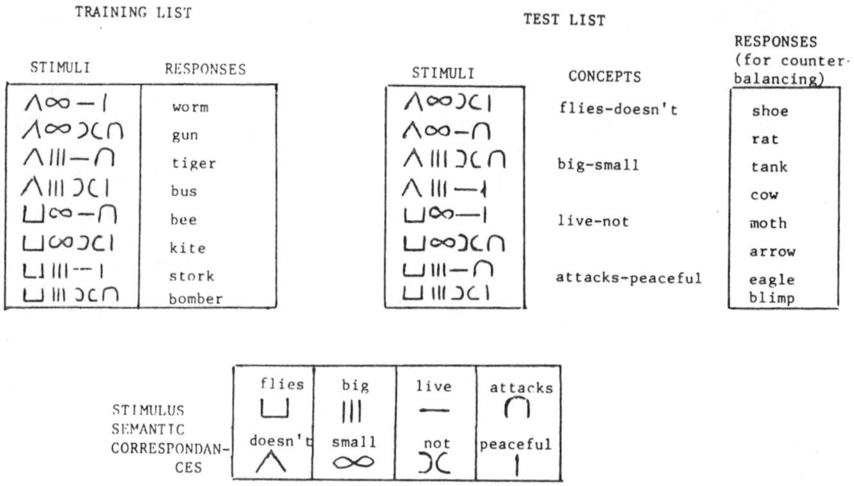

FIG. 7.2.   Demonstration material for nonanalytic concept identification.

and the question "does it fly?" This item might remind him of the item that was called worm in the training list, and because in this stable universe worms don't fly, he would say that this item probably doesn't either. There would be no need for him to be happy with this strategy of responding, but with no better strategy open to him, he might adopt it.

Aside from whether I have made it convincing that a subject would respond in this manner, let us examine what would happen if he did. As shown in Fig. 7.3, he would retrieve an item from his memory that resembled the test item. In this case, maximal similarity would be an item that resembled the test item in three out of the four characteristics. In fact, the list was constructed so that each test item maximally resembled four of the memory items. This peculiar similarity structure was designed to reduce the vulnerability of the experiments described later to the effects of poor memory. That is, the chances were maximized that the subject would be able to find a good analogy even if he were unable to retrieve several of the memory items. If he does in fact retrieve an item that maximally resembles the test item, then for any given question the odds are only one in four that the discrepant characteristic will be the one that is criterial for the question being asked. In the example shown, if he retrieves the items worm, gun, or tiger, he will correctly answer the question of whether it flies; if he retrieves the item bee, he will answer the question incorrectly. The same odds would also occur for any of the other test items or any of the other questions.

For our purposes, the crucial thing about this mode of responding is that the subject could achieve this 75% accuracy without being able to specify the criterial attribute. He might be able to say in exactly what regard the test and memory

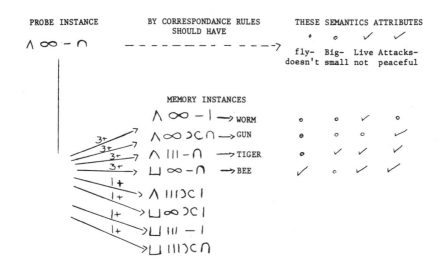

FIG. 7.3.   A hypothetical retrieval process for nonanalytic concept identification.

items resembled one another, but under the premise that he had not previously induced a rule, this would not allow him to single out any one of those resemblances as being more important than the others. Standing on the outside, we might be tempted to assert that his consistently above-chance performance, together with his inability to give a rule, indicated that he had implicitly abstracted a rule or had implicitly weighted different cues according to their validity for predicting category membership. But all we would in fact have observed was a consistency among separately operating instances rather than any differential weighting of the criterial feature. He might not be able to give a rule that relates a portion of the stimulus to the response categories, because he is not accomplishing the task in a manner that is describable that way; he might not be able to name the criterial feature, because he is not responding differentially to it.

In contrast, this example suggests what I think is a useful definition of analytic concept identification. Let us take *analytic* concept identification to mean a process whose direct effect is to separate aspects of the stimulus and evaluate their ability to predict category membership. The product of such a process is what is commonly referred to as a *rule,* that is, an explicit or an implicit summary of the aspects of the stimulus that are used to assess category membership of any item in which those aspects occur. Because this is the use of the word "rule" that has dominated the concept-learning literature, I will use it in this sense, not in the sense of being just any definite procedure whatever. In *nonanalytic* concept identification, on the other hand, the category membership of an item is inferred from its overall similarity to a known individual or low-level cluster of individuals, where similarity is judged on the basis of aspects or configurations of the stimulus that are *not* weighted for their criteriality for the particular concept being considered. If a person decided that a mystery beast was a dog rather than a cat because it looked remarkably like Lassie (as opposed to Fido, Rover, Fluff, or Puss), and Lassie was known to be a dog, then he would be using a nonanalytic process. If he decided that it was a dog because it had nonretractable claws, had circularly constricting pupils, or closely resembled the prototypical shape of a dog, then he would be using analytic processes in the foregoing sense. Note that the term *analytic concept identification* is being used in a relatively specialized sense. It is often used as a simple contrast to the term *configural,* but that is not what is intended here. If the person were categorizing the beast as a dog because its overall shape was similar to that of a prototypical dog, he would still be differentially weighting shape, as opposed to color or coat texture or activity, for its criteriality on the category dog. As such, he would be using in some form exactly the type of information that we would be seeking if we were trying to develop an explicit analytic rule for category membership. On the other hand, if he were responding on the basis of similarity to special cases, what I am referring to as nonanalytic, he would not be using that information in any form. I hope to demonstrate in this chapter that the present distinction between analytic and nonanalytic on the basis of the weighting of stimulus aspects for particular concepts captures the natural language distinction more accurately than does a distinction on the basis of elements versus configurations.

Let us look at three distinctive consequences that flow from the current characterization of nonanalytic concept identification. The first is that, assuming that the subject is able to retrieve a memory instance that has maximal similarity to the probe or test item, the more irrelevant dimensions the better. Recall that the reason we suggested that the subject would get 75% correct performance in the idealized situation we discussed earlier was that with four binary dimensions, an instance with maximal similarity would be identical to the test item on three out of four characteristics. This means that the chances are only one in four that the criterial characteristic differs between the two items and therefore that the appropriate categorization would differ for the two items. If we were considering material that only had three binary dimensions, then the appropriate figures would be two out of three aspects of identity for an item of maximal similarity, and therefore only two-thirds chance of correct categorization, because there would be two chances out of three that the differing aspect would be irrelevant to the correct categorization. On the same basis, we would expect 80% correct performance with five binary dimensions. Note that with the present material we are guaranteeing that the irrelevant dimensions are indeed irrelevant in the usual sense that by themselves (that is, knowing their values rather than knowing the items in which they occur), they do not improve the probability of correct categorization above chance. Also note that this expectation is not based on a particular selection of test instances; for example, the test list and memory list of Fig. 7.2 are exhaustive of all possible instances with four binary dimensions, and they are not partitioned in such a way as to avoid categorization errors.

Another interesting consequence is that the relative difficulty of different categorization rules changes when we are considering nonanalytic concept identification. For example, consider the illustrations of rules shown in Fig. 4.7. For the simple attributive rule shown, the characters in the first position are criterial, and those in the second and third are irrelevant. Assuming that the categorization of one of these eight items (rows) is known, let us consider the effect on correct categorization of changing one of the characters in this item to its opposite. This is equivalent to considering the chances of making a correct categorization by drawing an analogy from this known item to a new item of maximal similarity, that is, that differed from the known item by only one characteristic. If the change is introduced in the criterial characteristic, the categorization should change, and using the known items for an analogy would lead to an incorrect categorization. If the change is in an irrelevant characteristic, the categorization should be the same, and using the known item for an analogy would lead to a correct categorization. If the three changes are equally probable, then two-thirds of the responses based on analogy would be correct. But, on the same assumptions, we would also get the expectation of two-thirds correct when

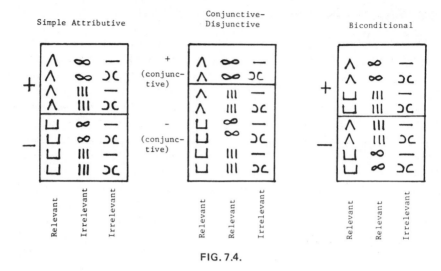

FIG. 7.4.

we are considering the conjunctive rule in Fig. 7.4. If the change came in the irrelevant dimension, an analogy would always be correct. If the change came in either of the two relevant dimensions, then the correct categorization would be the same for the two bottom items, change in one-half the cases for the middle four items, and always change for the top two items, for an average of 50% correct. With the biconditional rule, however, we would expect only one-third correct responses, which means that this rule would be the most difficult of the four for both analytic and nonanalytic processes [see Hunt (1962) for an argument regarding analytic processes]. In keeping with our previous discussion, the rates of success would increase to 80% for the attributive, conjunctive, and disjunctive rules and to 60% for the biconditional if we added two other irrelevant dimensions to our example.[2]

The third consequence of nonanalytic concept identification is that in some sense a learner can learn the physical correlates of several different concepts at once. In the current idealized example, the learner would be able to answer all four of the questions in Fig. 7.2 after the same amount of training. Of course, the current example leans on previous learning about the referents of the response terms, but there are natural examples in which learning about correlations between stimuli and categories is separate from learning about semantic or behavioral characteristics of individuals.

---

[2]The identical average performance with the conjunctive and attributive rules is, of course, dependent on using binary dimensions. The introduction of multivalue dimensions does not change the essential argument: namely, that complexity of categorization decreases in many cases when a nonanalytic strategy is used. The same comment can be made about several of the other simplifying assumptions in the examples used in this chapter; assumptions such as exhaustive memory search, complete and literal memory encoding, and perfect memory for prior instances are not essential to the contrast between analytic and nonanalytic strategies.

Simple Semantabit Experiment

In the next section, I argue that each of these three consequences of the non-analytic strategy of drawing analogies to special cases helps the learner to cope with the complexity of the natural world. But first, let us look at the results of encouraging such a strategy with the simple material that we have been considering. The experiment outlined in Fig. 7.2 was run with a group of eight McMaster graduate and undergraduate students. They were given paired-associate practice on the training list until they could go through the list three consecutive times without error. They were then presented the test list (the lists used for test and training were counterbalanced across subjects) and were asked one of the four questions (the order of questions was again counterbalanced) for each of the items of the list. Whatever question was asked was then repeated for each item to establish response consistency, and, finally on a third pass through the list with that question, the subject was also asked to give the reason why he responded as he did. This same three-pass procedure was then used for each of the other three questions. The stimuli themselves were deliberately designed to be the same completely counterbalanced, easily analyzed material that has been typical of concept attainment experiments. If a nonanalytic approach emerges with this material, then we can make the point forcefully that an analytic strategy is not completely under the control of the material itself. Further, I personally have the hope, which I do not pursue here, that studying material in which both analytic and nonanalytic strategies are viable will tell us something about transitions between the two.

Our principal question then is whether this procedure of paired-associate training followed by unexpected generalization trials would change the typical subject's manner of attack on the problem, and the answer was that in the main it did. I do not mean to claim that the subjects' behavior is well fit by the simple nonanalytic model that was described earlier. By making the material easy for us to analyze, we obtained the classic result that it was also easy for the subjects to analyze, and this was demonstrated by the persistent efforts of at least two of our subjects to figure out the rules. But I do mean to document that the paired-associate procedure radically changes the way many subjects approach the problem and that it is fair to characterize this approach as predominantly nonanalytic. Let us first examine the performance of the six out of the eight subjects for whom this is a reasonable description. These subjects reported after the experiment that their general method of responding was to think of a memory item that the test item reminded them of and respond on the basis of that; in addition, on 80% of the individual trials on which they were questioned, these subjects named a particular memory item as the reason for their response. Further, there was a curious reluctance to name the physical cues being used. These subjects had to be urged to specify their reasons in physical terms, and even then one of them steadfastly replied that she just didn't know. Other reasons given were much more subjective than one might have expected given the rather antiseptic nature of the stimuli: "It looks all cluttered up," "it looks like heavy machinery," "it looks gentle," "it looks like a vicious moth." When they did specify the physical elements that they used, they tended to give two or three of them rather than the one that would have sufficed. But, there was no indication that these physical specifications were purely fortuitous; when we treated each of these physical specifications as if it were a positive-only rule (that is, specified only a positive case, leaving the negative case unspecified) that could be used to sort all of the items in the test list, we obtained a predicted success rate of 72% when the actual success rate was 70% for those trials. If these subjects had been saying just any old thing just to get us off their backs, I doubt that the correspondance would have been quite as close. When treated as rules, however, these physical specifications had a rather restricted number of items to which they were applicable; whereas a complete (positive and negative cases) rule statement would have had a domain of eight instances on the test list and a positive-only rule a domain of 4, the average domain of these physical specifications was only 2.3. Finally, there is no reason to believe that these subjects merely selected a memory item to name that was consistent with a response that they had already decided upon. For over 50% of all items across all subjects, the same memory item was named as the reason for response for all four of the questions asked about a given item, and the success rate on these items was 74% as opposed to the 72% success rate on the other items for which analogies were named. That is, it looks as if a given test item typically reminded a subject of the same memory item each time that the test item was shown. If the memory items had been named ad hoc to fit a valid abstraction, then we should expect a greater variety of memory items used as an analogy for a given test item and a higher success rate when the memory item was allowed to vary.

In contrast to the boom or bust pattern often observed in experiments using simple rules, the accuracy of categorization by these subjects was clearly in between. The average accuracy on the two trials on which we did not ask the subject to state a reason was 67% and on the reason trials was 72%. The modal number correct was six out of eight across all three trials, with the whole distribution shaped reasonably like a binomial, thus indicating that most subjects were performing in the middle rather than either at chance or at perfect performance. This intermediate performance is not due to the subjects typically making a transition between chance and perfect performance halfway through an eight-item trial, as is indicated by the fact that the performance on the first no-reason trial was virtually identical to that on the second no-reason trial.

One of the two remaining subjects reported analyzing throughout the test trials and named a single stimulus feature as being the basis of his response for all trials on a given question. His responses and success rates were consistent with his claim that the feature he named was in fact in control. Two of the features that he named were in fact the ones that were criterial for the two concepts involved, with a resulting 100% accuracy; the other two were not, with resulting accuracy rates of 54% and 58%. The last subject was a split between these two modes of behavior. He correctly named the criterial feature for two of the questions and gave analogical reasons and responses for the other two, with resulting accuracy of 100%, 100%, 75%, and 75%. His description of his performance was that he tried to find what feature several of the memory items had in common, but if that failed, he responded as if the test item were the same as one of the memory items that looked like it.

I'm afraid that this whole discussion has been a rather bad compromise between too much and too little detail. But, the points that I mean to make are that the memory procedure leads to frequent reports by the subjects that they are using a nonanalytic strategy and that there is enough corroboration in their performance to suggest that we are not being too naive in believing them. Their performance, then, is a prime example of why we should be very cautious in inferring that a process of implicit abstraction underlies above-chance performance even when we know that a simple rule exists.

Complex Semantabit Experiment

We used the same type of material to provide a demonstration of the altered role of rule complexity when a nonanalytic procedure is adopted. Five McMaster students learned the paired-associate list shown in Fig. 7.5 to a criterion of three successive correct times through the list. The responses were related to the stimuli by the rules also shown in Fig. 7.5, but as with the previous experiments, the

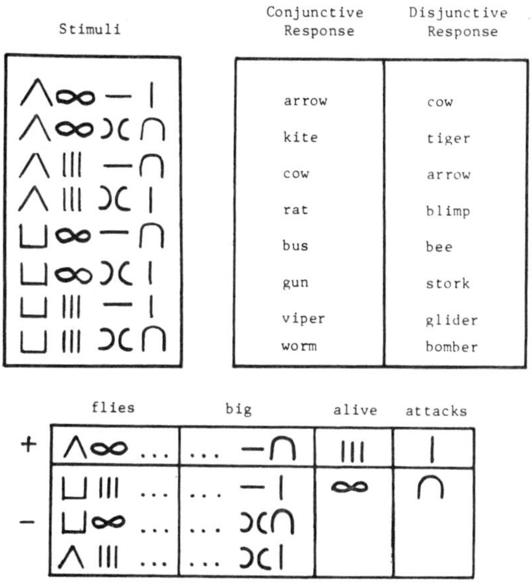

FIG. 7.5.

existence of rules or categories was not mentioned until after the paired-associate training. The test list was then presented, and the four questions were asked in a mixed sequence on four passes through the list. On the last two passes, the subjects were also asked to state why they answered as they did. In this procedure, the subjects were being asked to perform on two conjunctive and two simple attributive rules at the same time. An additional group of five subjects were given the same procedure with the exception that the positive and the negative values were interchanged, which resulted in them performing on two disjunctive and two simple attributive rules at the same time. Finally, two additional sets of four subjects each were run in the conjunctive-attributive and the disjunctive-attributive conditions, with the stimuli turned upside-down, both in training and testing. This procedure balanced the spatial distribution of the symbols that signaled the four concepts to reduce the effect of position-biased encoding on later categorization performance.

The results are to be viewed as being in the nature of a progress report. The most straightforward analysis, shown in Table 7.2, is consistent with the general expectations derived from the analogy mechanism described previously. There is no big advantage of simple over complex rules, and all of the values are in the neighborhood of 75%. However, there are two difficulties with this interpretation. The first is that analysis is clearly mixed into the performance of about one-half of the subjects. One of the reasons for being interested in material of this simplicity is that because both analysis and nonanalysis are feasible for this material, it should be possible to study the transition between the two. But, at the present time, I am restricting myself to the more limited objective of showing that nonanalytic mechanisms account for at least some of the results. The second difficulty is that these results could contain an unknown amount of response bias, because one of the values of each of the complex concepts occurred in only two out of the eight training or test items. There are not enough items in this rather restricted system to employ the usual control of selecting the items from the overall stimulus pool in such a way as to equate response frequency. The solution to both of these difficulties is to look for a more specific pattern of results than the alternative explanations can readily account for. To do this, we restricted our attention to those subjects who consistently claimed to be using an analogy strategy. The results for these subjects are shown in Table 7.3. As is shown, these subjects qualified for our special attention by mentioning a specific analogy on over 90% of all of the trials on which they were questioned (reason trials). On 62% and 81% of the total trials for a given test item, they mentioned the same analogy on both of the reason trials. Although there is still a chance that this use of the same analogy for the same item is a coincidence, we will treat these as items that readily suggested a similar item on the training list.

If these subjects were using analogy on the complex concepts, we would expect an average of 50% correct for the minority response (that is, for the positive response in the conjunctive problem and the negative response in the disjunctive problem) and 83% for the majority response. To see this, imagine

TABLE 7.2
Percent Correct in Test Phase of the
Complex Semantabit Experiments

Group	Concept Type	
	Complex	Simple
Conjunctive-attributive	77.8	70.1
Disjunctive-attributive	75.7	81.2
Biconditional-attributive	53.5	79.5

[a]The two complex and the two simple concepts were collapsed for each group.

TABLE 7.3
Performance of Analogy Subjects

		Conj.-Attrib. (N = 4)	Disj.-Attrib. (N = 5)
Mean % reason trials on which an analogy is mentioned		98	94
Mean % reason trials on which the *same analogy* is mentioned on both reason trials		62	81
Complex Concepts			
% correct on all trials	Majority response	80	83
	Minority response	73	56
% correct on same-analogy trials	Majority response	83	82
		($\bar{x}$ = 73)	($\bar{x}$ = 75)
	Minority response	42	52
Simple Concepts			
% correct on all trials		83	83
% correct on same-analogy trials		73	79

the center panel in Fig. 7.4 with one additional irrelevant dimension (column) added. For the minority response (top two rows), if the discrepant feature occurred in either of the two relevant dimensions, accuracy would be 0%, and if it occurred in either of the two irrelevant dimensions, accuracy would be 100% for an average of 50% for these items. For the first four items in the majority response, the corresponding accuracy would be 75% per item, and for the last two items, accuracy would be 100%, for a weighted average of 83%. These expectations are approximated for the disjunctive group on both the total trials and the same-analogy trials. It fits for the same-analogy trials for the conjunctive group but misses substantially for the minority response of this group. A post hoc rationalization of this latter miss is that attention was drawn to the minority response in the case of the conjunctive group but not in the case of the disjunctive group. As a result, the conjunctive group might have been more likely to have noticed and learned the common features while they were performing on an analogical basis. Finally, when we look selectively at the same-analogy trials, the average of the complex rules is similar to the average of the simple rules, which confirms the general expectation with which we started this analysis. The necessity of confirming this expectation on some of the trials for some of the subjects documents the horrible death of some of my more simple-minded versions of what went on in this experiment. I will most assuredly attempt to make this work less ad hoc in the near future, but I offer it now as a rather stark contrast to what we found in the next two groups.

The third group in this set of experiments was run under a slightly different procedure: namely, that used for the simple semantabit experiment described earlier. The stimulus set is shown in Fig. 7.6. The difference between it and the sets used for the other two groups makes comparison less neat than I like, but I prefer to tack down the interpretation with material that conforms to ideas that I describe shortly than to repeat the experiment with very minor variations. The results at least suggest the interpretation described earlier, that the biconditional rule would be more difficult than any of the other three. This expectation of only 50% accuracy was roughly confirmed for all groups of trials, including those on which the same analogy was given on all reason trials.

Finally, a group of eight subjects was run using all 16 stimuli possible with this stimulus material on a series of four reception procedures for the four rules shown in Fig. 7.5. The subjects were asked to categorize the stimuli for each problem into the categories *A* and *B*. They were given the standard concept instructions to the effect that there was a definite way to tell which stimuli went into which category and that it was possible to get all of them correct. Each problem was run until the subject got 10 categorizations in a row correct or to a maximum of 32 trials. After each problem, the subjects were told that a new problem was to begin and that the basis of categorization that they had been

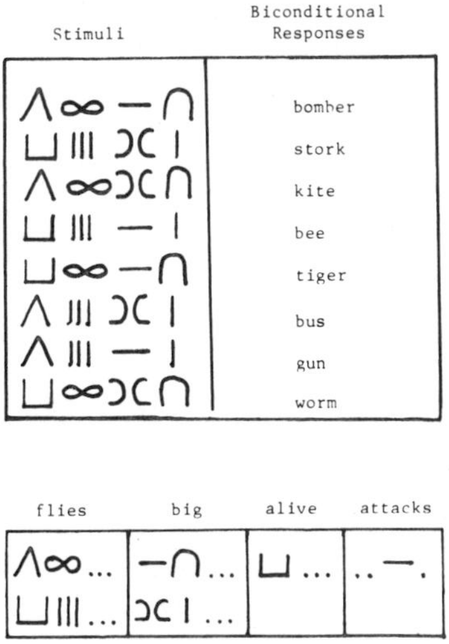

FIG. 7.6.

using or trying to find would no longer be in effect. This was an attempt to simulate roughly the four problems that were being taught simultaneously to the previous groups. Again, there is no neat way of matching the various groups, but the present experiment at least was sufficient to demonstrate that there is nothing so horribly peculiar about the present material that the usual rule difficulty results break down when using the reception procedure (Neisser & Weene, 1962). The trial on which the last error occurred was 14 for the simple attributive rules and 28 for the complex rules out of a maximum of 32 trials. Given two concepts of each type for each of eight subjects, there were 12 correct rules statements for the simple rules and two for the complex rules when the subjects were asked for a rule statement at the end of each problem. This difference between the simple and the complex rules would undoubtedly have been larger if we had run more trials, because most subjects had not solved most of the complex problems. But, this number of trials was sufficient to make the point that the complex rules are indeed more complex when run sequentially and with an emphasis on problem solving.

In sum, then, the results of all of these experiments support the interpretation that subjects use a nonanalytic strategy for determining their responses on a majority of the trials under this procedure (although their left hemispheres may still be privately busy) and that when they do, the relative difficulty of various categorization rules may be substantially different than under the more usual analytic conditions.

NATURAL CONCEPT-LEARNING SITUATIONS:
MULTIPLE-TASK CONTROL

So far we have discussed a complex situation and a relatively simple situation in which nonanalytic concept learning can plausibly be regarded as important. In the complex case, analysis was not the preferred or most effective mode of operating, an outcome that I suggest is due to the complexity of the material itself. In the simple case, analysis would have been more effective for the attributive concepts but was made less likely by having multiple bases of categorization and by not indicating the importance of these categories until after a set of individual items had already been learned. The question that we obviously must address next is whether these rather strained situations have anything to do with natural concept learning. Given the tone of the preceding discussion, I imagine that it will not come as a numbing surprise that I believe they have a very real applicability. In general, to make a nonanalytic strategy work, the learner has to store an adequate number of instances and then has to use them in an analogical rather than an analytic manner. I argue that: (1) there are many factors that encourage learning individual items, the most potent of which is that when the learner is presented with a series of individuals, he or she is generally under the demand of more tasks than just the directed learning of a single concept; and (2) many concepts are in fact so complicated that a nonanalytic strategy is at least an important preliminary step in concept learning. Let us first examine the reasons for storing individual instances.

Factors that Encourage Storage
of Information about Individuals

1. *Concurrent Task Requirement to Learn Individuating Information.* In natural situations, the number of ways that a learner can be required to concurrently learn about individuals is legion. A child needs to know not only that a given beast is a dog but also that this is the one that will let you pet him and the other one is the love that will take your arm off. Dogs can be treated as a class when deciding whether they belong on the dinner table but should be differentiated for decisions about which ones to let in the front door. Calling Lassie "Rin-Tin-Tin" or referring to her as a seasoned killer leads to a feeling of having committed a faux pas similar to that of calling her a cat. The only reason for even mentioning this point is that a common method of experimentally simplifying the study of concept formation is to isolate it from the concurrent learning of the characteristics of individuals. The assertion if often made that learning rules affords one the economy of not learning about individuals. This is clearly valid and often extremely important; but, it loses some of its point when applied to situations in which learning idiosyncratic information is independently re-

warded. Learning about individuals may be difficult and uneconomical, but once it has been done for other reasons, it provides a body of information to be reckoned with in the acquisition of categories. If we have designed an artificial task in which it is very difficult to recognize individuals, let alone associate distinctive information with them, then we obviously cannot assess the contribution of this influence even though it may be important in many natural acts of concept learning.

2. *Classification Under Conditions of Incomplete Information.* Classification of individuals is not always done under conditions in which people can sample all of the information they would like. As a result, they might rely on information that is specific to particular instances. For example, let us assume that the analysis of basic-level categories done by Rosch and her associates is applicable to dogs. Given an extended behavior sample of a newly arrived organism, the observer might be able to acquire the prototypical view, the barks, smells, and activity that would allow the assessment of dogness. But, are there sufficient cues emanating from a dog asleep under a table, a bad photograph of a dog, or from the first half-second after a dog has entered the room that would allow the observer to categorize it on the basis of the cues that would normally be sufficient to distinguish it from your average racoon? Without in any way denying the importance or validity of Dr. Rosch's arguments about cue validity and family resemblance, I would suggest that the observer in such circumstances might rely on much more particular information about known dogs than would be the case under optimal conditions. There is considerable pressure for people to perform quickly or with a small sample of information, and it is this pressure that is a major factor leading to the complexity stressed by writers on information processing (Neisser, 1967). One of the perplexing immediate reactions that I had after reading Dr. Rosch's and Dr. Berlin's account of fuzzy categories was that if natural concepts were generally that overdetermined, why had concept theorists and information processors so long stressed the disjunctive and particular nature of natural categorization? Part of the answer is probably a bit of theoretical bias. But, another portion of the answer is the quite valid insight that people must categorize dogs, capital letters, and the like under conditions of incomplete information. The effect of this is that people are probably rewarded for storing and using much more particular information about individuals than might be sufficient to get the job done under optimal conditions.

3. *Classification Under Memory Conditions that Favor Learning About Individuals.* If the conditions normally used in concept research were typical of natural learning situations, most learning would go on in zoos, museums, or department-store catalogs. In all of these situations, a wide variety of individuals appear in rapid succession, a situation that would make comparison easy and would reward the individual for reducing memory load by finding common

characteristics. However, when learning about dogs and chairs, if not fence posts and ants, the learner typically sees the same individuals many many times for every new instance that is seen. This affords the luxury of distributed, generous practice with individuals. Even if there is no pressure for producing individuating responses or for classification using incomplete information, incidental learning alone might lead to the accrual of a considerable number of specific details. Given the usual type/token ratios and pacing conditions, experiments in psychology (including my own) are evidently more influenced by the example set by ants and fence posts than by that set by dogs and furniture in the home. Procedures that provided more intensive experience with one individual before introducing the next might provide an interesting contrast in results.

4. *Classification Using Stimulus Structures with Sharp Similarity Gradients.* If a test item looks overwhelmingly like a small set of prior instances all of which were in the same category and irrevocably unlike all others, regardless of whether or not they are in the same category, then the learner could be rewarded for using whatever information he or she had stored about individuals and possibly even for storing more information at the next opportunity. The effect of such a stimulus structure would probably in many instances also be a result of the next point.

5. *Classification Using Stimulus Structures of High Analytic Difficulty.* Even if a learner were grimly determined to emerge from the task's tribulations with an explicit rule, there are at least three reasons why memorizing instances would be a means to that end.

1. If there is a large number of dimensions, then there is a very large number of potential hypotheses. One strategy the learner could adopt to reduce the number of hypotheses. One strategy the learner could adopt to reduce the number of hypotheses that must be tested is to look for common features across several memorized examples. If any are found in common, then it is probably a good bet that they belong to the same category. If the features common to those examples are low in frequency across the whole stimulus set, then the learner might even be able to get by without a memory of previously tested hypotheses, because the conjunction of low probability events would be so low as to make repeated testing of the same hypotheses unlikely.

2. If the learner codes the stimuli as made up of a few levels on each of a large number of dimensions, then he or she does have to keep track of which hypotheses have and have not been tested. One way of solving this problem is to focus on an instance and systematically test each feature for its categorical relevance. This, of course, is the focussing strategy described by Bruner, Goodnow, and Austin (1956). Although this does result in learning at least one instance, it is worth noting that this use of any such focal instances is quite different than in the analogy mechanism we discussed previously. In the case of

the focussing strategy, the instances that are recalled tend to be the same from trial to trial and are *not* selected on the basis of similarity to the current test instance. The comparison between these memory instances and the current instance, far from being nonanalytic, is exactly the device by which an organism with limited processing capacity can accomplish analysis.

3. If the dimensions of variation are not clear to the learner, then the only option available is to remember some instances and compare them for common types of variation, which can generate hypotheses to test. This is another reason why a stimulus structure with highly distinct and diverse instances might lead to the memorization of instances.

The three possible results of analytic complexity just mentioned are all cases in which the memorization of individuals is being used in the service of analysis. These considerations are relevant to this chapter only in that instances learned in the course of analyzing one concept could be used in an analogical manner on an independent concept or, more importantly, when the learner became discouraged with an attempted analysis of a complex concept. This latter consideration is what I would guess is the essential result of analytic complexity. The task of analysis may appear so formidable that the learner might relax into learning and generalizing around instances. Such a use of analogy might merely be a detour on the way to the Ultimate Analysis, but if it were accompanied by a high level of success, increasing familiarity with individual instances, and concurrent attention-consuming tasks, it might become the permanent solution.

6. *Multiple-Category Membership.*   The same individual might be an example of a dog, a gentle friend, and a potential source of fleas in one's bed. These categories do not necessarily imply one another, but each of them are potentially generalizable to new instances as is clear when one is regarding a snarling Doberman or thinking about the consequences of adopting a raccoon. Decisions about such categories as gentle animal friends or flea bags may be aided by general principles such as "all Dobermans are mean" or "any animal can have fleas," but I suspect that, at the very least, these general principles spring to mind at different rates in the presence of a Doberman puppy or an English sheep dog. In cases such as these, cognitive economy may be on the side of learning a few individuals and using them for many different decisions. This is likely to be particularly true for categories that do not have common single-word names (e.g., fierce beasts or flea bags). Information about these important but discursively named categories is more likely to be found at the level of the special case than at the level of the general principle, and this fact encourages storing information about special cases.

7. *Uncertainty About Future Task Demands.*   The very point about analysis is that it is analysis for a specific category. As was true of the subjects in the experiments in the first two sections of this chapter, if one does not know the

relevant categories, one cannot analyze for category membership. Yet it is exactly the uses to which information will be put in the future that is at least partly uncertain in many natural situations. One good solution for both uncertain or multiple-task demands is to learn a lot about individuals and to put the resulting information to flexible use later.

In summary, there is a wide variety of natural circumstances that encourage the storage of information about specific instances. These circumstances, however, are often not well simulated by concept-learning procedures. This is well attested by both an inspection of the procedures used and by the fact that memory for instances is often reported to be close to chance (Bourne & O'Banion, 1969; Coltheart, 1971; Dominowski, 1965; Esper, 1925; Trabasso & Bower, 1964). To provide a remedy for this, to provide a simulation of a wider variety of natural tasks, the acquisition phase of concept-learning experiments will have to be varied to include intensive practice with individuals, the provision if individuating information about individuals, speeded classification of noisy but identifiable individuals, interrogation about several different categories, and, as many members of this conference are already doing, more complex stimulus domains. The research that I have reported in the first part of this chapter serves any of these functions in only a rather crude way; the memorization of individual instances is provided for but only with the list-learning procedures of paired-associate learning. I suspect that far more interesting results will be obtained from procedures in which individual instances are presented in the context of the variety of tasks that normally typify our contacts with individual objects.

Factors that Encourage Decentralized, Nonanalytic Concept Performance

Storing information about individuals is only one condition for the occurrence of nonanalytic concept learning. The learner must also be in circumstances that encourage him to use the information in an analogical manner; that is, he must be in circumstances that encourage him to assess category membership by reference to any of a variety of special cases rather than by a more unified strategy of abstracting a prototype or by weighting and summing cues that predict category membership across all individuals. Some of the circumstances that I think are important for encouraging a nonanalytic concept-identification procedure have been implied in the previous discussion, but I now review them in this fresh perspective.

1. *Complex Stimulus-Category Relations.* If there is a very simple and salient feature that predicts category membership, then adult subjects will be strongly tempted to encapsulate it in an analytic rule. Indeed, some subjects made the effort even under the rather unfavorable conditions of post hoc induction that we used in the semantabit experiments. But, with material as complex

as that in the artificial grammar experiments, analysis seemed to run a poor second. The obvious question, then, is whether most natural categories have the degree of complexity of the artificial grammars, whether they have the complexity that gives nonanalytic mechanisms a viable permanent or an interim role to play in conceptual behavior. During the period in psychology in which natural categories were being characterized as being essentially arbitrary, the popular answer to this would almost certainly have been "yes." But since the work of Drs. Rosch and Berlin (as well as Evans, 1967) has demonstrated the inadequacy of the assumption of arbitrariness, we need to look at this answer more carefully. Their position is that natural basic-level categories are obvious to the perceiver in that they represent information-rich clusters of stimulus information. These categories are not arbitrary, as was implied by the learning theorists who stressed the importance of reinforced responses for category formation, but rather are a result of the learner perceiving strong correlations among the cues that characterize the members of the category. If in fact it is sufficient to say that most categories of concrete objects are obvious and overdetermined, then the nonanalytic mechanisms that I have been talking about would be an unnecessary complexity.

I personally believe that the data and ideas that Rosch and Berlin have contributed will be a permanent part of our notions about natural categories but that they are not (and were not claimed to be) sufficient to explain the entire process of natural object identification. The cues that have the correct stimulus structure to form a concept need not be the ones that are easily sampled and thus the ones that are generally used to provide an identification. We could assert this and yet agree that the cues that have sufficient salience and intercorrelation to form a category may still be very important in the person's subsequent notions about the category. The size, shape of head, gait, tail wagging, and noisemaking of a dog may be the characteristics that have enough intercorrelation to induce the observer to group these beasts in a single category and to make him regard a spaniel as having enough typicality to put an Afghan or Pekingese to shame. Further, these characteristics may become a part of the observer's concept of a dog such that they will be the first physical characteristics thought of when the word "dog" is spoken and the cues most heavily weighted when they are perceived. But none of this means that these cues are normally sufficient to identify quickly even the most mundane spaniel under the circumstances in which it normally presents itself. If we add all of the cues actually used, then the process of identification may have enough complexity to make a process of drawing analogies to individuals or special cases seem fairly economical.

If we assume that the highly centralizing tendencies of a family resemblance or a prototypical structure coexist with a decentralized set of analogies for a given concept, then we might ask which develops first. I think the answer is that it could go either way. We could imagine that the concept of "dog" originally develops because the child observes the first two or three referent beasts for long enough, from enough different angles, and has enough different interactions with them, that he or she would regard them as obviously being soul mates of one another. But then, under the pressure of trying to identify them within the first 500 milliseconds or of trying to decide which dormant beasts to let lie, the child might start using overall resemblance to *one* of his or her well-memorized dogs as a method of identification. On the other hand, the child might first learn each of them as a phenomenon unto itself and only gradually have the experiences and interactions with them that would make their common species membership obvious, a point effectively argued by K. Nelson (1974). Finally, to add one last complexity to the relations between prototypes and diverse analogies, I suspect that specific analogies are particularly important for instances at the fringe of a category. For example, the cues that are necessary to say "not man's best friend" to a wolf, fox, or coyote are probably rather important conditionals. It is likely that the structure of the category "dog" is based on the weighting and summing of a large number of trotting, shape, and size cues unless they are in the presence of the very specific fox-like, coyote-like, or wolf-like cues. Such an argument becomes especially compelling when one regards some of the more widely varied decorative items of our time, such as ashtrays, dessert plates, and candleholders.

   2. *Pressure for Accuracy.*   It is not enough that the structure of the world is complex; the learner must also treat it that way. Faced with a very difficult structure, the subject might be able and willing to settle for a fairly low rate of error by acting as if a simple rule or a simple prototype fit. In many natural cases, the feedback contingencies are tolerant of errors arising from this type of simplification, as with social stereotypes and with unnecessary avoidance responses. In other cases, such as the naming of concrete objects, a simplification will result in the guilty party being laughed around the block. To model the latter situations even when the stimulus structure favors the use of analogies, we might have to place heavy pressure for accuracy on the learner, possibly by some device such as manipulating payoffs. This might have two effects: to decrease satisfaction with approximations, and to punish long-shot experimenting that subjects sometimes use in the course of analysis.

   We all from time to time are inclined to force our hypotheses on the world whether it agrees or not, and I suspect that our subjects are no different. As experimenters, our grand simplifications often get brought to earth by results in which unappreciative subjects fail to recognize the magnificence of our schemes. Here is our opportunity to pass along this favor by insisting on their fidelity to a complex classification structure.

   3. *Highly Salient Similarity of Test Items to Subsections of a Stimulus Category.*   As Dr. Garner has pointed out in his discussion of secondary and

primary processes, there are times in which a perception of similarity seems to be primary, with the reasons trailing far behind. This is clearly not characteristic of any of the materials that I have used in this chapter, but it is the obvious area of application of analogical, nonanalytic processes. One of the contributions that I hope to make by the current discussion is to point out that nonanalytic processes are not limited to stimulus situations in which similarity is intuitively primary.

4. *Limited Time and Resources Available for Analysis.*   Accurate analysis, as opposed to analytic simplifications, is often experienced as time-consuming and effortful. I would guess that this means that in many natural situations, the analysis doesn't get done simply because the person's resources are directed toward dealing with the meaning of the current item rather than toward an analysis of the stimulus-category contingencies. Occasionally a procedure has been added to a concept task to provide distraction; but, more typically, by isolating concept attainment tasks from everything else, the learner is allowed to spend his or her full resources on analysis.

5. *Contextual Support that Decreases Errors.*   A likely signal for analysis is a high density of errors in categorization. But such a signal might not be frequent in many natural situations. A child can usually sit in cagey silence until someone else spills the beans about the labeling of the novel hairy organism in front of him. Or, more likely, because the world seldom requires immediate differential action to a new beast, the child does not feel any challenge to categorize until a great deal of supporting evidence has been acquired. If all this means that the child has a low probability of making a real gaff, then the signal for effortful comparison and analysis is much less prominent here than in the usual laboratory task. After the child has acquired considerable familiarity with an individual, then he or she might find some reward in a more rapid response, in keeping with our earlier conjecture. But rapid response is probably not a frequent requirement in the face of real novelty.

The ratio of conjecture to demonstration has become rather dramatic in the foregoing, but the point is to make a case for seeking out experimental situations in which the storage of information about individuals and analogy to them are prominent. The tension between regarding an item as an individual and an item as an instance of a category seems to be an obvious feature of everyday life. Thinking of my own pets as adaptive organisms is an activity in which I find myself leaving out considerations that I would readily think of with respect to just any old iguana; yet there is no question that I would categorize them as adaptive, in some annoying instances highly adaptive, organisms. The bias that cognitive psychology has recently had in favor of the general and the abstract has not encouraged the modeling of such situations in the study of concept attainment. Yet the interaction between the general and the particular, between the analytic and the nonanalytic, strikes me as intriguing a topic to stress in concept research as it has been in recent discussions of imagery and propositions.

The Prevalence of Imperfect Transfer

One objection to the general applicability of analogy mechanisms is that there is always some error built into them. that is, even with a large number of resemblances, one would have to predict that a completely nonanalytic subject would still make some level of error. In fact, this is not necessary. For example, a completely nonanalytic learner could conceivably avoid error by pooling semantic characteristics from several examples (a case considered by Reed, 1972) as would be true if a response were determined by a majority vote from one of the semantic columns in Fig. 7.3. Note that such a learner could in principle be 100% correct without being above chance in guessing what the criterial feature is. However, the more important point is that most of the transfer situations that we have to predict have a considerable amount of error in them, particularly if several values of the test stimuli have changed from normal. This error is often dealt with: (1) as an indication of goverance by internal rules that are imperfectly correlated with the experimenter's; or (2) as the operation of rules plus some other source of error. But, of course, one contention of this chapter is that there might not be a rule at all. Similarly, subjects do not even respond to an instance the same way every time that it is presented. Consider the case of what could be considered the eminently rule-governed behavior of pronouncing such pseudo-words as MIGH, PSOAL, and HAMB. These are pronounced neither errorlessly, consistently, nor particularly rapidly (Baron, 1977). This can be handled by modifications of a rule mechanism, but I don't believe that it is what one would expect from the usual rule formulation, and such expectations are a matter of heuristic importance. On the other hand, if one thinks of analogies as memory items with shifting accessibility, such phenomena seem quite natural.

The prevalence of imperfect transfer is even more apparent if one considers the case of problem solving in practiced situations such as chess or experimental design. In such cases the function of past experience may be to suggest several familiar courses of action that are then edited or modified by rational investigations of consequences. One could conceive of the process by which alternatives are suggested as being governed by fairly well-integrated rules, but if one does so, then there is the curious question of why those rules are so unavailable to explicit formulation. When one also considers such examples as speaking and writing, it almost seems that the more complex and subtle the behavior is, the more likely it is to be learned implicitly. If such a situation were limited to linguistic behavior or to the perception of qualities such as space and form, then we would be tempted to argue that we have species-specific preparation for these behaviors and that general intelligence is simply not competent to match it. Although this may in fact be partly true, the sufficiency of such an explanation is brought into question by the same trends in chess and scientific problem solving, where, if my theology is correct, species-specific preparation is highly unlikely. One interesting possibility that deserves more investigation than it is now getting is that the reasons for the difficulty that the subject (and computer programmer) have in formulating even heuristic rules is that rules in the analytic sense do not exist. Instead, the answer might be more familiar to a memory theorist: Possible categorizations come from analogies to instances with variable (and variable appropriateness in) encodings as well as variable accessibility.

Considering examples such as these also makes it clear why I prefer to refer to these nonanalytic mechanisms as analogy rather than similarity or proximity mechanisms. Such modes of exploration, particularly under the name "stimulus generalization," have traditionally been used by theorists who were interested in demonstrating just how simple an organism could be and still get by. When combined with narrow boundary conditions, this parsimony, Occum's myopia, was the whipping boy of a great deal of cognitive psychology. But there is no reason why analysis has to be so smart or nonanalysis so dumb. To me, the term *analogy* suggests a nonanalytic mechansim with a similarity device in which there is a control or editing stage to soften the blow of unrestrained physical resemblance. The chess master may not know how the two or three potentially interesting moves come to mind, but he or she does know that they will not all be good and that they do need critical examination. In the experiments in this chapter, we have not given the learner enough information to be able to use such a stage, but I think that the potential of such designs is as great in the areas of concept learning and familiar problem solving as it is in the area of novel problem solving.

An example of this explanatory potential is provided by the pronunciation of unfamiliar written words. First of all, the conditions of learning to pronounce fit the criteria discussed earlier in this chapter. Words must be individually identified, the "rules" of pronunciation of English orthography are surely sufficiently complicated, and learning is carried out under conditions and at an age not well-suited to analysis. Some deliberate pronunciation rules are taught explicitly and are learned in some form or another. But children and adults alike are notoriously unable to specify all of the rules that they do use in pronouncing nonsense words, leaving aside the question of whether the knowledge summarized by an explicit rule operates in that form in those cases that it does cover.

The simplest form of a similarity or generalization mechanism surely would not work, because each new word has a unique response rather than the categorical responses we have been considering. In addition, if unweighted physical similarity were operating, a person would in many cases draw an analogy to a word remote in pronunciation (RATE to RATS, instead of to MATE). However, if we think of a mechanism in which very modest orthographic skills were appended to an analogy mechanism, then we might be able to get more satisfactory results. Assume that a child knew just enough to see a rough correspondence between a word and a pronunciation of it. The child could then encode and store it roughly segmented in an orthograhpically appropriate manner. When a new item was to be pronounced, he or she would search out a word in memory that matched on as many segments as possible and then carry out a relatively simple phonemic substitution, possibly changing just the initial consonant. Such an operation would explain why children apparently need some orthographic knowledge to succeed in reading English but typically cannot either learn or express explicit rules that are sufficient to explain their competence. The point of such a mechanism is that it probably takes less knowledge and less time (Brooks, 1976) to segment a word orthographically than it does to pronounce a word from scratch, integrating separate components. Further, as mentioned earlier, such a mechanism would easily be able to handle familiarity effects and observed within-subject variation in the pronunciation of the same novel word. If all of this seems terribly far-fetched, ask yourself whether it seems more likely that you are pronouncing the following list by analogy to known words or by general rules (e.g., are not made up especially for this grand occasion): puch, hamb, dur, spoy, psoal, rotation (list due to Baron, 1977).

I would like to be very careful not to overdraw the issues involved. The main point of this chapter is my advocacy of considering an analogy mechanism to explain some types of natural concept attainment and problem solving and to seek out laboratory procedures that simulate key aspects of these natural situations. This does not mean that I am under the illusion that I have provided any way of choosing between rules and analogies as theoretical mechanisms. One could quite easily describe the results of any of the experiments in this chapter by saying that the learner has acquired a long list of highly conditional rules. But what rule-oriented theorists have apparently not felt compelled to do is to describe the conditions in which people have a strong tendency to acquire conditional rules and those conditions in which they have a tendency to learn general rules. My own tendency is to select as a first approximation the theoretical device that most nearly captures the experience of the learner, and in the current situation, that means selecting an analogy mechansim rather than a mechanism of implicitly abstracting a great number of conditional rules after the categories become known. Studies of the flexibility of various theoretical devices, such as provided by Reed (1972), are valuable and have made their point. But my own feeling is that our current most pressing need is to acquire the empirical control that would allow us to capture the variety of performance styles that we all believe to exist in natural conceptual behavior. In that regard, I hope this chapter adds to the recent work of Posner and Keele, Rosch, and Garner.

There are enough conjectures in the previous discussion to support a great deal more research than we have accomplished, but in the next section, two lines of work provide comment on the preceding.

Lepton Experiments

One obvious implication of our discussion of multiple-task control is that the specific task to which the learner is responding during acquisition influences how he or she encodes the items and thus his or her later generalizations. This study demonstrates an interesting instance of this. Subjects were presented a series of 10 animals, such as the six pairs shown in Fig. 7.7. These animals differed on five binary dimensions: length of leg, number of legs, number of angles in the body and head, length of neck, and presence of spots. Each animal was presented on a different background such as that shown in Fig. 7.8. The backgrounds differed from one another on a variety of dimensions including the presence of a large body of water and a warm climate, which are the two that were relevant to this study. The backgrounds were colored in green, blue, and brown washes, which are not shown in the accompanying figure but which went a considerable distance toward making up for defects of the art work. The dimensions of variation of both the animals and the backgrounds are obviously a mixed bag when considered for their formal qualities, a situation that was motivated by my interest in getting an impression of how such combinations might be dealt with. Each animal in the training series was presented in two views to deter subjects from thinking of such strictly formal properties such as orientation, particular posture, or apparent activity. Obviously, several of these properties are not important for the current experiment, but the stimuli were being developed for a series of experiments in which I would like the subjects to treat these stimuli as if they were pictures of real animals rather than as if they were formal designs.

FIG. 7.7

FIG. 7.8.

Three groups were run that differed in the acquisition task and hopefully in the encoding that the subjects employed. The first was the familiar reception procedure. These subjects were told that there were two kinds of animals, leptons and nonleptons, and that the subject's job was to learn consistently to tell them apart. The subjects were required to guess on each trial whether the animal that was presented was a lepton or a nonlepton, for a total of 10 times through a list of 10 animals. Categorization as a lepton was determined by a conjunctive rule on two dimensions of the animal (e.g., body shape and presence of dots) that were balanced across subjects. On the first trial, each of the 10 animals were presented on a different background; on alternate succeeding trials, each animal was presented either on the same background as they were on trial 1 or on a blank background. No mention was made to the subject of the variation among backgrounds, although the dimension warm/cold was related to two attributes of the animals by a conjunctive rule (e.g., length of neck and number of legs), and the dimension large-body-of-water/no-water was related to one attribute of the animal by a simple attributive rule (e.g., length of legs). Our original intention was to treat these two dimensions in the same way as in the simple—complex study described earlier. However, several subjects did not treat these as separate dimensions (including such gems of logic as "This one was on a warm dry island, so I guess there wasn't any water close"), so the dimensions were pooled for the following analysis. After the acquisition trials, a mixed list of 10 new items and the 10 old items was presented on blank backgrounds, and the subjects were asked for each animal to first indicate whether it was old or new, then whether it either had been or should be in a warm climate, and then whether it either had been or should be near a large body of water. Asking about climate was regarded as being dirty pool but was partially compensated by a succeeding trial on which they were asked whether each animal was or was not a lepton.

Our expectation was that these subjects would act as subjects often do in reception procedure experiments: namely, treat these animals as instances of categories, ignoring anything that they regard as irrelevant to the sorting task. The results, shown in Table 7.4, are consistent with this expectation. The animals, to which they presumably were paying attention, were recognized substantially above chance; the background information that was associated with these animals, which the subjects vowed they had not attended to, was not recalled above chance. The results for the transfer items, then, are not surprising: The subjects were able to successfully categorize the new items for leptivity but not for the background they belong in. Several of these subjects spontaneously expressed surprise at the extent to which they were unable to recall the association between the animals and backgrounds as distinctive as these.

A second group was presented with exactly the same material, but the task that they were to perform during the 10 acquisition trials was to associate each of the animals with a common masculine first name: Sam, George, Tom, John, etc. The transfer was handled exactly the same way for the recognition and the background questions. However, just before the trial on which they were to categorize for leptons, they were told that all of the animals that they had been working with were either leptons or nonleptons and were given a list of the names of the four acquisition items that happened to be leptons. On the next pass through the transfer list, they were asked to say which of the items were leptons regardless of whether they were old or new items. These subjects, then,

TABLE 7.4
Percent Correct Categorizations in Lepton Experiments

		Recognition of Animals	Background Categorizations	Lepton Categorization
Concept training	Memory items	72	56	88
	Transfer items	80	53	84
Learning names	Memory inst.	86	74	70
	Transfer inst.	78	64	68
Learning names and concept labels	Memory inst.	96	73	74
	Transfer inst.	88	50	66

did not know of the existence of the category lepton until after the acquisition trials and after they had already performed on recognition and the categorization of backgrounds.

As can be seen in Table 7.4, for both old and new items, this name-learning group did significantly better than the concept group on categorizing the backgrounds and significantly worse on categorizing the animals as leptons. The concept-training group seems to have performed better on the concept that they were concentrating on, leptons,but much worse on a task that involved information that they perceived as incidental to their main task.

A third group was taught both the first names of the acquisition items and whether or not they were leptons. They were required to guess both the concept label and the name for each item during the 10 acquisition trials and were given specific feedback on each of these pieces of information. The transfer tasks were handled exactly as they had been for the concept-learning group. The results underline the distinction between having the information necessary for transfer and using it. Although these subjects performed on memory for backgrounds at a level very similar to that of the name-learning group, they clearly performed at a chance level when attempting to categorize the new items for appropriate background. By report, these subjects were attempting to solve this task by deciding whether or not the new item was a lepton and then guessing whether in general leptons belonged in a warm climate or near a large body of water. In fact, there were both warm and cold weather leptons and wet and dry leptons, but these subjects reported perseverating on this line of attack.

The point of these experiments is to demonstrate that learning individuating responses rather than just categorical labels changes both what physical aspects of the stimuli are encoded and to some extent what use is made of this information. None of the groups was given any instructions regarding the background, but it was clearly to the advantage of the groups that were learning individual names to use any distinctive information that was associated with the individuals. The concept-learning subjects focused more narrowly on the properties of the animals themselves, although they could easily have assumed that the backgrounds had something to do with the lepton category. These analytic subjects seem to have cast a more tightly circumscribed net with resulting higher accuracy for the main target, leptons, but poorer results for a target that was still hiding in the background.

Analysis and Memory for Instances

Earlier in the chapter, I claimed that memory for instances was associated with the analysis of complex problems. As documentation of this, I now briefly describe a thesis done by a former student of mine, Mervyn Hislop (1970). The initial aim of Dr. Hislop's work was to find a way of varying the degree of control of concept attainment asserted by explicit verbal hypotheses. This was achieved by a variable that seems almost too simple to work: asking the subject to state a hypothesis before the instance was sorted on a given trial rather than after it was sorted. The general idea was that if the subject had to state a hypothesis before making a placement of the instance, he or she would be more likely to regard the entire trial as a testing of that hypothesis, whereas making the placement first might make the hypothesis more of an afterthought. I can think of no reason why such a variable had to work, and if it hadn't, I'm sure that no sleep would have been lost over it. But it did work, and the resulting data are useful in the present discussion.

Hislop's stimuli were 80 cards drawn in a counterbalanced fashion from a stimulus space of seven four-valued dimensions: size, shape, color, number, shading, background, and position. The conditions as well as the stimuli were ones that encouraged analysis. The subjects were told what the seven dimensions were and that the correct rule for classification involved only one of the seven dimensions. Four levels of complexity were produced by telling one set of subjects which dimension was the correct one (leaving the subjects only the task of assigning the values on that dimension to the two categories); another group that the correct dimension was either shape, number, or position; a third group that size and shading were irrelevant; and a fourth group that any of the dimensions could be relevant. Of the 30 subjects, 15 in each of these conditions were run under the rule-first procedure (RF), and the other 15 were run under the placement-first procedure (PF). The solution performance for each of the resulting eight groups is shown in Table 7.5 in the form of the mean trial of the last error. Because in all of these groups no gradual improvement occurred during the presolution period, the trial of the last error is an adequate summary of their performance. There is an obvious and highly significant interaction between the variable that were are calling emphasis on the verbal rule (RF–PF) and the complexity of the problem, with the RF–PF differences being individually significant at the 5D and 7D levels. If anything, the rule-first procedure is superior for the 1D subjects, which might be accounted for by the greater tendency of the rule-first subjects at all levels of complexity to adhere to a win–stay/lose–shift response pattern. The significant superiority of the placement-first groups for

TABLE 7.5
Mean Trials of the Last Error for Ss
Attaining Solution in Eight Groups

Number of Potentially Relevant Dimensions	RF	PF
1D	30.3	35.7
3D	30.8	29.5
5D	47.6	33.6
7D	68.2	17.4

5D and 7D was also found in a subsequent comparison with a group for which no rules were required and no feedback given. This latter finding establishes that the rule-first procedure suppressed learning, not just the suppression of performance on those trials on which a rule was required.

What might be causing this suppression of learning, in the rule-first group for complex problems? The interpretation that Hislop argued for was that the placement-first subjects had a much greater tendency to recall prior cards and scan for common features, whereas the rule-first subjects had a greater tendency to concentrate on the hypothesis that they had tested. This interpretation was supported in a variety of ways:

1. The hypotheses given by the PF subjects had a much higher probability of correctly sorting the immediately preceding items than items drawn from other places in the trial sequence; this tendency was much less marked in the RF subjects.

2. In a subsequent experiment using only the 7D condition, the PF subjects had a much higher probability of recognizing and responding correctly to repeated items than did the RF subjects.

3. The solution time tended to be shorter ($.05 < p < .10$) for PF subjects that had the individual items appearing twice than did a PF group that had all novel items.

4. When the items were repeated three times apiece and the subjects were instructed to try to scan past instances for common features, PF subjects attained solution faster than did subjects run under the usual PF conditions.

These effects of repetition are not the nonanalytic effects that we have been talking about previously, as is evidenced by the fact that novel items in the presolution trials were not responded to above chance.

We collaborated on some additional conditions in which the dimensions of stimulus variation were not as clear as they were in the studies just described, with results of even less influence of explicitly stated hypotheses for PF subjects. However, the experiments just described are the ones most relevant for the present discussion. There are three points that I think are worth mentioning in this context. These studies demonstrate that: (1) we cannot take a + effect of item repetition by itself as an indication of nonanalytic responding; (2) we cannot completely confuse the notion of analytic processes with the notion of control by explicit verbal hypotheses, as would be methodologically convenient; and (3) an analytic strategy can lead to the learning of individual items, which are potentially usable in other contexts.

FINAL COMMENTS

In this final section, let us take a moment to view the issues in a more general way. The Tantalus branch that provides my most general interest in this area is that which displays the contrast between deliberate, verbal, analytic control processes and implicit, intuitive, nonanalytic processes. At the present time, we do not have the control to be able to take a person into the laboratory and teach him or her a body of material in an explicit, direct, verbal manner or, at our choice, in an implicit manner. Yet something like this appears to be an issue in many educational disputes such as discovery versus directed learning or phonics versus look—say reading programs. Obviously, the same thing is not being learned in these alternative methods, yet they are meant to accomplish similar goals and are debated as alternatives. Similarly, we don't have a sufficient grasp of the representation of knowledge to provide a good answer as to why so many of our complex concepts and categories, such as those in grammar and chess, are so resolutely beyond explicit formulation by experts let alone the average practitioner. Problems of this scope are tantalizing and obviously have evaded my grasp. However, in sorting out this morass of explicit/implicit, analytic/nonanalytic, and deliberate/intuitive processes, I am sure that there are some types of prejudging of the issues that will not bring them into reach. For example, I am sure that it is not useful to initially define concept learning in a way that presupposes analysis: "Concept identification learning is a process in which a person learns which cues or combinations of cues that predict membership in a particular category." Such a definition leaves out the posssibility that the cues that are used are those necessary to identify a particular instance in memory and that those cues are not weighted for the particular category being assessed. In a sense, all I'm arguing is that much of the work of identification may be done at a very low level of a conceptual hierarchy and that the rest of the work is done by knowing the concept membership of these special cases. But this can be enough of a difference to get in our way if we stubbornly decide that the work of identification is being accomplished only at the level of generality we have described.

A second type of prejudging that seems likely to move the issue further from our grasp is to use the word "rule" to mean either any observed behavioral regularity or any definite procedure, both of which uses are ubiquitous in psycholinguistics. Such uses of the word are all right if the rules being referred to are strictly part of the apparatus of a theory. But when they are used as descriptions of people's knowledge, they swamp a useful natural language distinction. In common parlance, "rule" connotes a deliberate, usually verbalizable, control procedure. In this sense, a rule-governed process would be one in which the diverse instances suffer or enjoy a common fate, with the intended effect of reducing the control exerted by idiosyncratic information. For me, too loose a use of the word "rule" has served to submerge the likely fact that much of our knowledge is a looser confederation of special cases in which our knowledge of the general is often overridden by our knowledge of the particular. Again, the contrast between these two states is the point of controversy between different teaching methods. In our analysis of these controversies, I believe we are ill-served by a terminology that directs our attention away from this crucial issue of within-category integration.

Completely centralized, completely integrated control, as would be implied by a strict rule system, does not seem typical of a wide range of human behavior. Control by a general rule is at least occasionally overridden by information particular to instances, and people accept the rules they express as rules of thumb that do need local correction. Note that it is exactly this type of yielding to the exceptions that is not controlled in most concept-learning experiments. The subjects in our experiments are not directly given a model of the process by which the stimuli were generated. They know that they are not dealing with some natural process such as natural selection, which could be expected to produce instances that are difficult to summarize in a small rule set, and they think they know that they are not dealing with a process highly subject to local historical influences such as a natural spoken or written language system. Subjects who are influenced by the stereotypes of science could easily assume that the stimuli are a set piece made up by someone bent on intellectual intimidation and that the game is to find the completely consistent rule system contained in them. If we gave them some other scenario for the generation of the stimuli, we might direct them from the start toward looking for a more loosely integrated concept-identification structure.

Another way of describing this "loosely integrated" mode of concept utilization is to say that people's normal way of retrieving information relevant to novel complex stimuli is to use a combination of the two modes of memory search that we have talked about in this chapter, a point clearly made by Tversky and Kahneman (1973) in their treatment of subjective frequency. Our *analytic* subjects reported mainly relying on a category search of past instances. To find the "rule" that would allow them to categorize the new instances, they retrieved as many of the instances that they could think of that fell into the category "flies." If they found a common characteristic, they tried it out on succeeding instances or, with rare sophistication, also searched instances in the "doesn't fly" category to make sure that the common characteristic in fact differentiated the two categories. In the *nonanalytic* mode, their memory search was for items that looked like the current instance. This "similarity set" provides useful material for playing the odds but poor material for analysis. The similarity set shown in Figure 7-3 (worm, gun, tiger, bee) does provide the material for correct odds playing (in three out of four cases they don't fly, therefore guess that the probe instance doesn't fly) but obviously is perfectly useless for deciding which stimulus element signals flying. If one finds a beast that closely resembles Lassie on 199 out of 200 perceptual comparisons, then one has probably found a dog, possibly even loyal, trustworthy, and brave, but is probably not much closer to deciding what makes a dog a dog. If the stimulus field is large, complex, and heterogeneous, then this type of odds playing is much more within cognitive capacity than is an analytic category search — and the difficulty of such searchs, of course, is what gives us professional employment.

I have been arguing that an important constraint in many natural situations is that information is being acquired under the concurrent control of multiple tasks. When this constraint occurs in the presence of complicated material and heavy pressure for accuracy, the result might be loosely integrated, nonanalytic identification of concepts. Although it might be true that such concept-identification procedures eventually turn into something that is appropriately described by analytic, high-powered, large-domain rules, we cannot assume this and must be extremely cautious about such an inference. In essence, a nonanalytic approach stresses the importance of the frequency of individuals during acquisition rather than the frequency of isolated attributes. There are all stages of complexity in between which could also be important, but the issue of major importance is not to try to define closely the cut-off point; rather, it is to examine the factors that push a person's strategy toward one end of the scale or another — that is, toward learning individuals by codings that are designed to retain the item's individuality, or toward tracking the validity of characteristics of the stimulus with respect to specified categories. Stressing the nonanalytic, instance-oriented strategy could:

1. under some circumstances allow the learner to deal with more complicated problems than would an analytic strategy.

2. lead the learner to code different and more detailed aspects of the stimulus than would an analytic strategy.

3. change the relative difficulty provided by various categorization rules, by an increase in the number of irrelevant dimensions, or by the relevance of multiple categorizations.

4. lead to an increased sensitivity to standard memory factors such as number and repetition of individual items.

5. be easier with nonseparable dimensions and stimulus sets with multiple sharp-similarity gradients than with separable dimensions and evenly distributed stimulus sets.

6. provide the material for post hoc categorization and therefore give protection against unanticipated tasks.

7. provide a base of information that would aid later analysis.

8. explain the difficulty often encountered in answering the question, "How in general do you tell items in category *A* from those in category *B*?"

9. provide the basis for "global" reports such as, "It just looks like object *X*, which I am familiar with, but now that you point it out, all instances in that category do have property *Y* in common."

ACKNOWLEDGMENTS

The work in this chapter was supported by a grant from the National Research Council of Canada. I would like to thank Jan Szumski for running the artificial grammar experiments and Amina Miller for her exceptional assistance in all other phases of this project.

REFERENCES

Baron, J. Mechanisms for pronouncing printed words: Use and acquisition. In D. LaBerge & S. J. Samuels (Eds.), *Basic processes in reading: Perception and comprehension.* Hillsdale, N.J.: Lawrence Erlbaum Associates, 1977.

Bourne, L. E., & O'Banion, K. Memory for individual events in concept identification. *Psychonomic Science,* 1969, *16,* 101–103.

Brooks, L. R. Visual pattern in fluent word identification. In A. Reber & D. Scarborough (Eds.), *Toward a psychology of reading.* Hillsdale, N.J. Lawrence Erlbaum Associates, 1976.

Bruner, J. S., Goodnow, J. J., & Austin, G. A. *A study of thinking.* New York: Wiley Press, 1956.

Castellan, N.J. On the partitioning of contingency tables. *Psychological Bulletin,* 1965, *64,* 330–338.

Chomsky, N., & Miller, G. A. Finite state languages. *Inform. Cont.,* 1958, *1,* 91–112.

Coltheart, V. Memory for stimuli and memory for hypotheses in concept identification. *Journal of Experimental Psychology,* 1971, *89,* 102–108.

Dominowski, R. L. The role of memory in concept learning. *Psychological Bulletin,* 1965, *63,* 271-280.

Esper, E. A. A technique for the experimental investigation of associative interference in artificial linguistic material. *Language Monographs,* 1925, No. 1.

Evans, S. H. A brief statement of schema theory. *Psychonomic Science,* 1967, *8,* 87–88.

Hislop, M. *Cue sampling and verbal hypotheses in concept identification.* Unpublished doctoral thesis, McMaster University, 1970.

Hull, C. L. Quantitative aspects of the evolution of concepts. *Psychological Monographs,* 1920, *28,*(0, Whole No. 123).

Hunt, E. B. *Concept learning: An information processing problem.* New York: Wiley Press, 1962.

Neisser, U. *Cognitive psychology.* New York: Appleton-Century-Crofts, 1967.

Neisser, U., & Weene, P. Hierarchies in concept attainment. *Journal of Experimental Psychology,* 1962, *64,* 640–645.

Nelson, K. Concept, word, and sentence: Interrelations in acquisition and development. *Psychological Review,* 1974, *81,* 267–285.

Reber, A. S. Implicit learning of artificial grammars. *Journal of Verbal Learning and Verbal Behavior.* 1967, *6*, 855–863.

Reber, A. S. Transfer of syntactic structure in synthetic languages. *Journal of Experimental Psychology*, 1969, *81*, 115–119.

Reber, A. S. Implicit learning of synthetic languages: The role of instructional set. *Journal of Experimental Psychology: Human Memory and Learning*, 1976, *2*, 88–94.

Reed, S. K. Pattern recognition and categorization. *Cognitive Psychology*, 1972, *3*, 382–407.

Trabasso, T., & Bower, G. Memory in concept identification. *Psychonomic Science*, 1964, *1*, 133–134.

Tversky, A., & Kahneman, D. Availability: A heuristic for judging frequency and probability. *Cognitive Psychology*, 1973, *5*, 207–232.

Part III   REPRESENTATION

All discussion of psychological structures and processes lead eventually to the issue of representation. There are two aspects to the issue: How do we wish to say that the topic of research, in this case categories, are represented in the head of the processor, and the meta-issue of how we wish to represent that representation in psychological theory. In various ways, all three chapters in this section address these issues. Because the chapters themselves present meta-theoretical discussions, they provide their own introduction to a great extent and require less commentary than the chapters in Part II.

As a clear example of the manner in which the issue of representation is fundamental to the earlier discussions, let us take the case of Brooks' claim that learning of categories can occur by means of the storage of and later matching to particular examples rather than by means of the abstraction of attributes. Some principle of learning such as this is most useful in understanding how the prototype structure of a category might develop. But the concept of storage prior to analysis of a particular instance raised the difficult issue of how to understand the representation of such an instance. Our first impulse might be to claim that the instance was stored as an image. After all, images have traditionally been treated as the type of representation that was most concrete, nonlogical, wholistic, and unanalyzed.

Kosslyn's chapter should dispel any such notion about images. Although arguing that we do indeed wish to retain the concept of image as a type of representation separate from that of propositions, Kosslyn demonstrates that we cannot treat the concept of image as a way of avoiding issues concerning the nature of representation (a way of sneaking stimuli into the head without their becoming cognitive entities). Although we may eventually wish to treat images as at least one form of relatively less analyzed representation in storage, we must specify in what way analysis does and does not occur and the mechanisms for such storage.

Palmer's chapter is fundamental to an understanding of the issues raised in the earlier parts of the book. By distinguishing the information in theories from the notation in which they are stated, he has been able to clarify the difference between the issue of the structure of categories, to which Part I is addressed, and the processing issues discussed in Part II. That subjects make prototypicality judgments that must be based on consideration of more information about instances than are (by definition) contained in criterial attributes does not pre-determine whether categories are to be represented in a processing model as templates, feature lists, or structural descriptions. And prototype and criterial attribute theories of representation and processing are, like other categories, themselves not either/or categorizations; rather, there are extreme forms of both theories and a range of intermediate forms in between. Palmer's chapter provides an example of how the principles of categorization argued for in regard to an experimentally tractable set of stimuli, such as material objects, can operate reflexively back onto one's own metatheory. Thinking in terms of clear cases and intermediate forms with respect to prototype theories themselves has enabled Palmer to clarify many issues that were obscured by the attempt to treat proto-types and criterial attributes as though they were exclusive and clear-cut categories. We believe that such clarification might result for many theoretical issues were they considered in this light.

George Miller's chapter raises questions about representations in a format that is unique in our discussion of categorization. He asks his reader to consider the possibility of dividing categorical knowledge such that one part is contained in his knowledge about the world, in "practical knowledge," while the other con-cerns the kind of knowledge that results from labeling an object as a member of a particular category (i.e., "linguistic knowledge"). Within a theoretical frame-work that acknowledges that exemplars vary in their goodness as members of categories and that boundaries are vague and movable, Miller nonetheless proposes tests of category membership based both on perceptual and functional criteria.

Function tends to be a slippery concept in psychological research. All too often it is evoked as a wise, mysterious, and unanalyzed "right way" to look at objects, in opposition to a supposed analytic but inadequate "wrong way," which is called *form*. The chapters in this volume have demonstrated that func-tions can, indeed, be subject to analysis and that it is the interrelation between perceptual and functional aspects of objects, rather than their alleged opposition, that may be the fruitful line of study. Thus, Berlin analyzes both one role that perceptual attributes play in the formation of folk generics and one role that cultural usefulness plays in the formation of subgeneric classes. Rosch analyzes perceptually related aspects of the function of concrete objects in terms of the motor programs by which the objects are used. In addition, Rosch suggests that more general aspects of object functions be examined by means of the role of objects as props in cultural events. And Newport and Bellugi show the inseparability of function and perception for the visual—gestural language of ASL.

In the Aristotelian tradition of representational systems, category membership is based on a notion of truth or falsity. If certain criteria are met (certain attributes in a certain logical relationship present or absent), identification is certain. We suspect that Miller's suggestion that functional criteria be represented by a modal logic description of possibility may yield new insights about the nature of categories by leading investigators to pose new questions. Perhaps shortcomings of older functional approaches have arisen from their insistence on treating function as a single attribute in a truth table. The Miller and Johnson—Laird model goes beyond this older view, beyond a simple probabilistic model, and, we hope, generates a fruitful new attack on the complex problems of linguistic and cognitive representation.

8 Imagery and Internal Representation

Stephen Michael Kosslyn
Harvard University

This chapter explores the ways in which images may serve to represent and encode information about the properties of members of a category. Images are discussed in the context of a basic research strategy that has led to the development of a process model embodied in a computer simulation (Kosslyn & Schwartz, 1977, in press). Before turning to the substantive issues, we outline our research strategy and discuss why we adopted this tack. Following this, we discuss some basic issues about imagery; these issues are considered in the light of rational concerns, introspections, and empirical findings. Next, we describe our current model, showing how our positions on the issues considered earlier motivated our theorizing. Finally, we offer some possible extensions of the model and speculate about the representation of "prototypes" of categories in images and the uses to which these representations might be put.

A RESEARCH STRATEGY

The Inference Problem

To some, the study of imagery seems simple. All one needs to do is to introspect. This is equivalent to saying that in order to study visual perception, all one needs to do is look. Clearly, much processing goes on before we become conscious of an object, either when we are perceiving it or imaging it. An understanding of either phenomenon entails uncovering the mechanisms responsible for representing and processing the relevant information. Thus, in studying imagery, we must infer what transpires in the hidden reaches of the mind from

re

what percolates through to consciousness and the outside. This situation is rather like one where an unknown solid object is placed in a dark box and our task is to describe the surface of the object by shooting in BB's and observing how they bounce back. There are three important aspects to this situation: first, there is the nature of the hidden object of study; next, there is the data, the angle at which BB's bounce back when they are shot in at various angles; and finally, there is the systematic relation between the angle of incidence and the angle of reflection. It is clear from this example that one needs to know two of these things in order to determine the third. If one does not know that the angle of incidence equals the angle of reflection, one cannot use the data to deduce the shape. Similarly, if one wants to discover the incidence/reflection relation, one must have knowledge of both the data (the results of shooting BB's at particular angles) and the surface characteristics of the object. Consider the sorrow of one who knows only how BB's bounce out of our dark box, and knows nothing of the law relating the angles of incidence and reflection, nor anything about the concealed object. Somehow he must infer both the incidence/reflection relation and the nature of the surface of the object from the data, but he needs prior knowledge of the relation to infer the surface characteristics and vice versa! This pitiful creature is the cognitive psychologist.

Cognitive psychologists often try to study some particular aspect of cognition, like the nature of the internal representations. Unfortunately, any one aspect is embedded in a whole system of mechanisms. In order to examine any one component, we necessarily involve encoding, representation, computation, and response processes — all of which are reflected in our data. Before we can know how to use data to characterize the underlying phenomenon of interest, we must know how to "correct for" the effects of other components of the cognitive system; but before we can know how any of those components work, we first must know about all of the others — including the one we set out to study! The general situation is like one where there is a range (data), domain (mental phenomenon of interest), and mapping function (processes that translate the mental phenomenon of interest into observable effects), and we are trying to determine the characteristics of the domain from only a knowledge of the range. Obviously, there is a degree of freedom; any piece of data is a consequence not only of the underlying phenomenon of interest, but also of how it is translated into observable effects.

This "inference problem" is at its worst in the study of imagery. The structural properties of a representation derive in large part from how that representation is processed. For example, consider a case where some items are ordered into a list in a computer's memory. Say that the *only* way one can examine this material and its order is via the retrieval processes of the machine. Now, if these items were able to be retrieved only in one order on one day, and only in another order on another day, for all intents and purposes the order of the list itself would have been changed. One can argue that the actual list ordering had not been changed, but how would one ever know?? In studying imagery, one can only investigate the data structures in the context of having people *do* something with them. Thus, by its very nature we can never isolate an image in the pure, but can only study it as it relates to processes that operate on it (cf. Kosslyn, in press; Palmer, in this volume; Pylyshyn, 1975). As Anderson (1976) argues, numerous different representational structures, with different processes operating on them, can be formulated to explain any given research finding. In terms of our initial analogy, the situation resembles one where the hidden object in the box is now in motion. Even if we somehow were able to discover the incidence/reflection relation, we still could not determine whether a given bounce was due to characteristics of the surface, the direction of movement, or both.

Coping With the Inference Problem

What are we to do? The "inference problem" is a perfect case of a "Catch-22:" in order to study anything, we have to know everything to begin with! The only way I can think of to cope with the inference problem requires that we "pull ourselves up by our bootstraps". Newell (1973) discusses a way in which this might be accomplished: one should attempt to construct large models of cognitive systems. Whereas it is easy to formulate different explanations of the results of a given experiment (as one would expect, given number of factors that can be varied), it is much more difficult to explain large numbers of results in an explicit and elegant (i.e., parsimonious and straightforward) way. Further, the account should characterize not only the phenomenon of interest, but also the way in which it is processed in the context of the total system. It is hard enough to come up with even one comprehensive model for numerous and varied findings, let alone to conceive of alternative accounts (cf. Anderson, 1976). The results of different experiments come mutually to constrain each other: a principle or mechanism should be recruited whenever it *can* be used, if one is to avoid ad hoc special cases. When the assumptions about internal processes and structures become implausible in the face of data, revisions are necessary. Thus, progress is achieved not with a bang, but via a continual process of readjustment and reformulation.

It is important to recognize that the bootstrap approach hinges on the concept of "elegance." An elegant explanation is both parsimonious and straightforward (or "natural"). There are two glaring problems with this concept: First, we do not even know how to assess parsimony, let alone something involving parsimony plus "straightforwardness" or "naturalness". Nonetheless, our intuitions seem reasonably reliable on these matters. Most people can recognize an inelegant explanation when they see one. Not using the concept of elegance because it is not rigorously defined is a little like not using some new miracle drug simply because we do not know exactly how it works. Furthermore, some constructs will only become rigorously developed in the course of being used (cf.

Kosslyn & Pomerantz, 1977). Second, and perhaps more fundamental, why should we expect the mind to be best described in an elegant way? If the mind evolved in a piecemeal fashion, it may resemble a patchwork quilt more than a woven tapestry. Two responses to this worry come to mind: presumably evolutionary pressure selected for the most efficient mental machinery, and these in fact were most elegantly structured. Alternatively, perhaps the mind (or the Universe, Dr. Einstein) *is* a patchwork mess, and we never will be able to have a description of it that is any simpler than a description of the phenomena themselves. But we shall never discover this unless we try to prove otherwise.

Many people seem to recognize that something like the bootstrap approach is necessary in formulating theories, not only in psychology but in other sciences as well. The problem now becomes how to formulate a theory. One option is simply to use intuition as a guide; this rationalist approach has been fruitful in other sciences. At the present juncture, however, too many different sorts of models seem consistent with the data at hand; we simply do not know enough to get off on the right foot. The present approach is to attempt to gain a running start by first narrowing down the class of acceptable models. Only after we know something about the basic operating characteristics of imagery will we attempt to formulate an explicit model.

Phase I: Discriminating Among Alternative Basic Operating Characteristics

Many (e.g., Platt, 1964) argue that a systematic program of investigation should begin by defining "trees" wherein nodes correspond to issues and branches represent competing positions on them. One then supposedly performs "crucial" experiments that eliminate all but one position. This approach has apparently proven productive in fields like molecular biology, but cannot be adopted intact for present purposes. The inference problem seems to preclude the possibility of a truly crucial experiment, given that another interpretation of any given result is always lurking just around the corner. Instead, we are forced to adopt a method of "converging operations" (cf. Garner, Hake & Eriksen, 1956). At each node we will perform a number of different experiments, and hope that the results are most consistent with one position and inconsistent with the others. Again, elegance is the final arbiter: if numerous results can be explained by positing some given operating characteristic (i.e., basic sort of representation or process), whereas accounts not incorporating this are more complex and messy (i.e., inelegant), we shall adopt the elegant interpretation. We will not use this "tree" approach to try to discriminate among explanations for a given experimental result. Instead, we will try to discriminate among competing operating characteristics that define different classes of models. Our initial experiments will attempt to expose underlying "competences"; we will attempt to demonstrate that people have some capability or are able to preserve some sort of information. Each of these experiments is, of course, subject to the inference problem; other explanations are of course possible. If we have erred, we will discover this soon enough, when our assumptions are not borne out in further experiments. Detailed explanations of how people actually perform the tasks used in addressing these issues will be deferred until after an explicit model is cast.

The Value of Loose Conceptions in Casting Basic Issues

The problem now is one of delineating the competing classes of models, properties of which define the nodes and branches of a "tree". We began by formulating a model that seemed consistent with our intuitions and the available data. Our model was captured by a metaphor: images were hypothesized to be like displays on a cathode-ray tube that are generated by a computer program (plus data). This metaphor (described in detail in Kosslyn, 1974, 1975a, 1975b, 1976; and in Kosslyn & Pomerantz, 1977) suggested that there is a spatial representation that is generated from more abstract representations and that this spatial representation − the image proper − is processed by other mechanisms (a "mind's eye"). We used this metaphor to help us to generate competing alternative models, simply by positing different operating characteristics for the different components (including non-existent operating characteristics, as will be discussed shortly).

Although any sort of model could serve to direct one toward interesting research questions, we intentionally began by formulating our model in a loose, vague way; our metaphor is not so much a model as the beginnings of a model, a "protomodel". It seemed counterproductive to begin with a very detailed model. In fact, beginning with an elaborate, well-specified model seemed silly, because many of the decisions that must be made to fill in details would not be motivated by known properties of the phenomena under study. It also seemed a waste of time, because a few new findings might strongly contradict a basic assumption of the model, and all the effort spent in working out the minor flourishes would have been for naught. In addition, we felt that starting with a well worked out model could actually distract one from the basic issues. That is, one could be seduced into investigating details (e.g., estimating values of parameters of that model) that are only marginal to the basic principles that distinguish one's model from other classes. This tendency is not unknown in cognitive psychology and seems the next worst thing to an out-and-out "confirmation bias," wherein one merely seeks data consistent with one's model, without concern for predictions of competing conceptions. Only after we felt justified in taking our basic notions seriously − by attempting to eliminate reasonable counterconceptions − did we begin to develop these ideas into an explicit, detailed model.

Phase II: Constructing an Explicit Model

Loose notions — often cast in the form of metaphors — can help one to formulate a set of basic principles underlying a theory. But after a relatively short while, these sorts of vague formulations tend to lose force, to dry up. After one considers the obvious contrasts between several general notions, it is not clear how to proceed from there; further issues do not present themselves. It is at this point that it makes sense to consider how a real system might operate within the constraints posed by the inferred operating characteristics as well as the specific results of experiments used to discriminate among classes of models; in the course of working out the details of a model, many new questions present themselves. In a way, the current approach treats model building as being analogous to "multidimensional scaling" of the results of a set of experiments. The goal is to "derive the lowest stress, lowest dimensionality solution with interpretable dimensions" (see Shepard, 1962; Kruskal, 1964). Our model, then, should be elegant, should explain results in a straightforward way with as few assumptions as possible. Furthermore, the model should suggest new topics for research in the process of organizing the existing results into a coherent framework. It is analogous to scaling coffee preferences and then discovering a "hole" in the derived space — prompting invention of a new sort of coffee (e.g., freeze-dried) to fill the gap. But instead of searching for a way to make coffee that will fall into that part of the preference-space, we use our model to direct us toward interesting data to collect.

The model we constructed was "motivated" by data in two ways: First, the structure of the model was dictated by available research findings; our decisions were not made arbitrarily. Second, the model was created partly as an aid for collecting new data; when we reached a point where a decision might be made arbitrarily, we took this as a sign that an experimental investigation was necessary. Thus, details of the model are motivated by experiments, and the model itself then turns around and motivates further experiments; it serves a function previously served by our vague conception. The data thus gleaned must in turn be accounted for by the model, requiring further development that in turn produces more issues to be resolved, and so on. Thus we pull ourselves up by our bootstraps.

PHASE I: BASIC OPERATING CHARACTERISTICS

Our metaphor led us to define a set of basic issues, and led us to take very different positions on these issues than would competing conceptions that do not involve generation of a functional spatial "display." These issues are not independent from one another; a stance on one necessarily entails eliminating possible positions on the others. First we consider the most fundamental issue raised by considering our metaphor and alternative conceptions; this concerns the role of the experienced quasi-pictorial image. Radically different sorts of theories emerge depending on whether one treats the experienced image as a functional representation or as an epiphenomenal concomitant of underlying abstract representations. Next we consider the origins of experienced images, having argued that they are in fact functional and must be accounted for by a model of human imagery. This issue is broken into a sequence of three related issues. Following this, we discuss our assumptions about, and possibilities for, image processing.

Each of these basic issues is considered from three vantage points: from rational considerations, from introspections, and from results of experimental investigations. The first perspective bears on any theory, and we can save ourselves time and bother if we can eliminate some conception(s) on purely rational grounds. The second perspective cannot be ignored by a theory of imagery; obviously, a theory of imagery should be consistent with reliable introspective reports of imagery, and ideally should offer the basis of an account of these experiences. Finally, we will consider the implications of results of empirical investigations; when rational argument and reports of introspections do not seem very persuasive — as most often happens — we will be all the more concerned with the collection and interpretation of interesting behavioral data.

The Role of the Quasi-Pictorial Image

Perhaps the most fundamental question about imagery addresses the functional status of the quasi-pictorial, spatial image we experience.[1] On the one hand, virtually all of the current explicit theories of imagery (all of which are embodied in computer simulations) assign a purely epiphenomenal role to the percept-like experience of imagery. According to these theories, the functional components of imagery are abstract "propositional" structures; these structures do not differ qualitatively from those underlying all other cognitive processes (e.g., Anderson & Bower, 1973; Baylor, 1971; Farley, 1974; Moran, 1973; Pylyshyn, 1973; Simon, 1972). On the other hand, most of the vague, traditional theories of imagery imply that the percept-like mental image we experience is central to the function of the image. In this view, the experienced image is what the process of imagery is all about. This representation is more like that evoked when looking at a picture than that engendered when describing one (see Kosslyn & Pomerantz, 1977; Kosslyn, in press). Our cathode-ray tube metaphor would be meaningless if the display were not functional.

---

[1]An image is not a picture proper (i.e., one cannot hang it on a wall), and hence cannot have all of the properties of pictures. Thus, we use the term "quasi-pictorial" to refer to those properties of pictures that are shared by images. Presumably, images represent information about spatial extent, brightness, texture, etc. in the same way as they are represented (centrally) during perception proper. Thus, the "quasi-pictorial" properties of an image are those that characterize a visual percept, but not necessarily those that characterize the perceived object itself.

Rational Considerations

It is impossible to present a reasonable treatment of this debate in the available space. Kosslyn and Pomerantz (1977) present a detailed discussion of the issues and arguments and conclude that rational considerations alone will not prove decisive. The three paragraphs below serve merely to illustrate the flavor of the debate.

At first glance, it seems much more parsimonious and straightforward to view the experienced image as an epiphenomenon instead of as a functional representation. A host of underlying abstract processes are required in either case, and treating the experienced image as functional seems to add just so much more fat on the beast. But can we really construct strong arguments on the basis of relative complexity or parsimony? It is impossible to say a priori which sort of model will operate more efficiently or economically; although fewer sorts of representations seem required by the first conception, the representations that are utilized and the processes that work on them may be more complex than those required if a functional image is in fact generated and processed. For example, an experienced image makes many implicit relations available (e.g., the relative height of a horse's knees and the tip of its tail) that probably would have to be noted explicitly (or would be inferred only with great difficulty) in a pure propositional model. The efficiency of a representational system depends on the purposes to which it is put; for example, a map is more efficient if one wants to find three cities that fall on a straight line, but a mileage chart is more efficient if one wants to know precise distances between them.

It may seem as though inclusion of a "mind's eye" (i.e., special interpretive devices for classifying images or parts thereof) is even more excess fat, but any representational system must include some sort of interpretive device; a propositional system requires if not a mind's eye, a "mind's forelobe," if you will. The mind's-eye notion is interesting because this same mechanism might be utilized in perception. In this light, then, needing two different interpretive devices for images and propositions is not necessarily a drawback, because one would need both devices anyway if percepts are represented in a nonpropositional format. There is no guarantee, however, that percepts are not represented propositionally . . . .

It is worth noting that the experience of an image does not arise in a vacuum. Some very complicated mechanisms must underlie that experience, and it is difficult to imagine why they would have evolved if the resulting product were useless. The counterargument, of course, is that the mechanisms are important but the resulting experience is not, it being merely an incidental concomitant of their workings. If so, then any sort of byproduct presumably could have occurred, and it is merely coincidental that the epiphenomal experience seems intuitively to have the right characteristics (e.g., one can "see" parts of imaged objects) to be used in information processing.

Introspections

So striking is the notion that one "sees" an image that the term "the mind's eye" is common parlance. Anecdotal accounts of many scientists are replete with reports of "seeing solutions" represented in visual images and trying to "picture" various patterns (cf. McKim, 1972). The sorts of metaphors usually used when describing such experiences, like "scanning" an image or "zooming in" on it, do not seem to make sense if the image itself is not being processed. Unfortunately, it is not difficult to find someone somewhere who will disagree with any introspective claim about imagery. Furthermore, introspection by its very nature only exposes the tip of the iceberg, and we currently are also interested in submerged portions. Finally, these sorts of introspections do not really address the current issue, because it in large part is about the meaning of such introspections; to admit such evidence at this point is putting the cart before the horse. Our only salvation seems to lie in consideration of carefully collected data.

Relevant Data

Interestingly enough, much of the relevant data is just the "quantification of introspection," the translation of the sorts of introspections mentioned previously into observable behavior. Let us consider three classes of data that seem to indicate that the experienced image is in fact functional: time to "see" properties of objects that are imaged at relatively large versus small subjective sizes; time to scan across images; and the effects of expanding an image until parts of it seem to "overflow." These three classes of results taken together seem to indicate that a spatial, quasi-pictorial internal representation (i.e., structurally similar to those that underlie the experience of seeing a picture during perception) may in fact be processed.

Perceptually, parts of smaller objects are harder to see than parts of larger objects. If imagery representations are like those that underlie the experience of seeing, then we might expect similar effects when one examines an image. Kosslyn (1975b) tested this idea by asking people to picture mentally animals at various subjective sizes; the sizes corresponded to the sizes of colored squares that the subjects had learned to draw prior to the actual experiment. The basic finding was that when people pictured animals at increasingly smaller sizes, more time was required to "see" named properties on the imaged object (e.g., a rabbit's nose). This result was also obtained when size was manipulated indirectly; in one experiment, for example, a target animal was imaged either next to an appropriately scaled elephant or fly, making the target animal relatively small or large. In this case, more time was required to see properties of the target beast when it was pictured mentally next to an elephant instead of a fly. This finding was reversed in another experiment wherein people were asked to perform the same task but to image an elephant as if it were the size of a fly and a fly as if it were the size of an elephant.

Before continuing, let us first consider a counterexplanation for these findings: It could be argued that parts of "larger" images are more easily detected simply because more representations are activated in some sort of abstract list than when a person is asked to image an object at a smaller subjective size. If so, then there is a greater probability that a representation of a given probed part is activated at the time of query when a person is asked to image an object at a large size instead of a small size. Hence, more time is required when searching the representations corresponding to a "small" image, because more often the probed part will not be activated and will need to be retrieved. People who have proposed such list models (e.g., Anderson & Bower, 1973) usually posit that items on the list are ordered in accordance with association strength, more strongly associated properties being stored nearer to the top (the point of list entry). Presumably, strongly associated properties are more usefully considered when attempting to identify the object, are more frequently encountered in association with the object, or for some reason are given a high "access priority." The notion that the list is ordered in terms of association strength allows one to account for the well-known finding (e.g., Conrad, 1972) that the more highly associated a property is with an object, the more quickly a person can verify the appropriateness of that property for the object. This ordering claim also provides us with a way of disproving the non-imagery counterinterpretation just described.

The reason it takes longer to "see" the parts of subjectively small images of objects, I claimed, was because the parts themselves were small. If so, then it should take more time to "see" smaller parts of images, even when the size of the imaged object is not varied; furthermore, this effect should not depend on the relative association-strength of probed properties. If the list interpretation is correct, in contrast, association strength (indexing list position) — and not size — should determine processing times. In one experiment, two "true" properties were selected for each animal such that the smaller one (e.g., for cat, "claws") was also more strongly associated with the animal (as determined by normative ratings) than the larger property (e.g., "head"). If it takes longer to "see" a property because of size per se, we expected that the smaller property would take more time to detect — even though it also was the more strongly associated. If, on the other hand, the size effect is really due to the probability that the probed part is activated at the time of query, then the more strongly associated part — which also is smaller — ought to be faster. In fact, I found (Kosslyn, 1976) that people did require more time to "see" smaller parts of imaged objects in this experiment. Interestingly, when imagery instructions were not given, and people were simply asked to verify a property's appropriateness as quickly as possible in any way they wished, now the smaller, but more associated, properties were verified more quickly. These findings were replicated in a second experiment using regression techniques to discover the more important determinate of verification speed — size or association in strength — in imagery and nonimagery instructed conditions. Thus, it does not seem that a simple list-structure explanation can account easily for the effects of imaged size; rather, people reported having to perform a time-consuming "zoom in" in order to "see" the smaller parts but not the larger ones. One could, of course, claim that one has two different lists, one ordered in terms of size and one ordered in terms of association strength. This clearly is ad hoc, post hoc, and inelegant.

A second source of evidence that images are spatial representations is that images can be scanned, and that it takes more time to scan further distances across an image. In my initial experiment (Kossyln, 1973), people first studied a set of pictures. One group was then asked to image each picture and to focus mentally on one end of the drawing; a possible property was then presented, and the subject was asked to decide as quickly as possible whether or not he could "see" it on his image. Of the true properties, one was selected that was located on the extreme left, middle, and extreme right of the pictures (for horizontal objects; top, middle, and bottom for vertical ones). Interestingly, the further from the point of mental focus, the longer were the decision times. Another group was not asked to focus on any end, and these people showed no differences in time to "see" properties located at different positions. Unfortunately, there was a major flaw in this study (as Lea, 1975, points out): More items fell between parts that were separated by further distances on the imaged object. So, although the motor and anchor were further apart than the motor and cabin on an imaged speedboat, more properties of the object (e.g., the front deck) fell between the further pair. In order to ameliorate this situation, Kosslyn, Ball & Reiser (in press) asked people to image a series of letters of the alphabet. Three letters appeared at different points along a line, of which two were of one case, and one of the other case. A person studied a line, and then it was removed. The person was then asked to mentally focus on one end of an image of the line. Following this, one letter was named. The subject was to scan to this letter and push one button if it was upper case, and another if it was lower case. The stimuli were constructed such that people scanned three distances over 0, 1 or 2 intervening letters. Interestingly, times increased linearly with distance scanned when the same number of letters was traversed (times also increased as more letters were scanned over).

In a second experiment on scanning images, people learned to draw a map of a mythical island containing seven locations. These locations were selected such that there were different distances between each of the 21 different pairs. After learning to draw the map, people imaged it and focused on a named location. Following this they heard the name of a possible location and "looked for it" on their mental image. Time to see the second location, when it was in fact present, increased with distance from the focus point. In contrast, when people were asked to answer without necessarily referring to the image before responding, distance separating the pairs did not affect reaction time in the least. The actual effects of interval distance on time to scan an image, then, cannot be attributed to number of items separating representations on a list nor can they be ascribed to some sort of underlying memory organization that is present even when images have not been used.

The third source of evidence concerns the possibility that images "overflow" if they become too large. The spatial extent of images may be constrained by the "size" of the representational medium; if so, then an image of any object can only be "expanded" a maximal subjective size before parts of it seem to overflow, and this maximal subjective size should remain constant for different sized objects. We used the following paradigm in an attempt to test this idea: People were asked to image an object as if it were being seen from very far away. They then were to imagine that they were walking toward the object and were asked if it appeared to loom larger (all subjects replied that it did). At some point, we suggested, the images might loom so large as to seem to "overflow." At this point, the subject was to "stop" in his mental walk and to estimate how far away the object seemed at this point. That is, the subject was asked to estimate how far away the object would be if he were actually seeing it at that subjective size. We did this basic experiment in a variety of ways. We asked subjects to image various sorts of pictures or to image animals when just given their names and sizes; in addition, subjects estimated distance by verbally assessing feet and inches or by moving a tripod apparatus the appropriate distance from a blank wall. We computed the "visual angle of the mind's eye" from the estimated distances and longest axis of each imaged object. In all our experiments, the basic results were the same: People claimed that smaller objects seemed to overflow at nearer apparent distances than did larger objects (the correlation between object size and distance was always very high). Estimated distance usually increased linearly with the size of the imaged object. In addition, when people imaged pictures at the size actually presented and indicated distance estimates nonverbally (by positioning a tripod apparatus from a wall), the calculated "visual angle" at the point of overflow remained constant for different-sized objects. Interestingly, the definition of "overflow" affected the actual size of the angle at which an image was considered to have "overflowed": Images do not seem to overflow some rigidly defined edge but seem to fade off gradually toward the periphery (see Kosslyn, 1975a). These results support the claim that images are spatial entities and that their spatial characteristics do in fact have real consequences for some forms of information processing.

These three sorts of effects, on detection, scanning, and overflowing, converge to support the claim that the spatial, quasi-pictorial images we experience can in fact be used in cognitive processing. In the tasks just described, these spatial/pictorial characteristics affected behavior in systematic ways that are difficult to explain without positing a functional image. It makes sense, then, to suppose that because these images can be processed, because the mechanisms are clearly present to do so, any theory of imagery must somehow account for the origins and processing of such experienced images. The experienced image cannot simply be written off as "epiphenominal" and henceforth ignored.

Origins of Images

Image Construction

One's approach to the issue of the origins of images depends in large part on how one resolves the issue just discussed. If our evidence is accepted and an image is conceived of as a spatial/quasi-pictorial representation that is processed and utilized in cognition, then one is interested in the origins of this image. If the experienced entity is epiphenomenal, however, then one will not be at pains to account for the experienced representation (e.g., Baylor, 1971; Farley, 1974; Moran, 1973). In this case, one discusses generative processes in terms of how some abstract representation is generated from others. Given our position on the issue just discussed, however, we do not consider this alternative any further. Instead, we consider the present issue to be one about the origin of the images we experience.

If we consider the "image" to be the experienced entity, then there are two aspects to the internal representation of an image to be considered. First, there are the representations composing the image itself; we have argued that the representations underlying the spatial/quasi-pictorial experience are like those that underlie visual experience during perception. Second, we must consider what sort of representation of the image is stored in memory when we are not experiencing the image and how this representation is processed to produce an image proper. There are two basic alternatives to begin with: The image might be stored intact in long-term memory and simply activated when one experiences it, or the image may somehow be generated from the underlying representations.

Rational Considerations.   Basically, all of Pylyshyn's (1973) complaints about imagery are only relevant to the notion that images are stored purely in a rote form and then simply "replayed" at a later time. As we (Kosslyn & Pomerantz, 1977) point out, these criticisms are not relevant to the second conception. Pylyshyn's paper pointed out that the simple "playback" idea cannot account for the organization and interpretation of images or for the use of images as mnemonics. In addition, he theorized that a rote image would be very uneconomically stored given the richness of our sensory input (see his paper, or ours, for further detail).

Introspections.   It is difficult even to describe having an image without refering to some generative process. The simple fact that people forget portions of an image does not speak to this issue, however: Portions simply may not be encoded into memory initially. The introspection that portions of images may be momentarily forgotten and then filled in is relevant, however. In fact, some people describe imaging as a kind of juggling act, wherein parts are constantly fading and requiring regeneration. This sort of introspection would not be expected if images were simply "turned on" like a slide projected from long-term memory.

Relevant Data. Weber and Harnish (1974) provide evidence that more complex images are more difficult to generate; in their experiment, more time was required for subjects to generate images of longer words prior to searching these images for letters having certain physical characteristics. Similarly, Kosslyn, Reiser, and Greenbarg (1977) found that drawings of animals containing more details required more time to generate than other versions of the drawings that omitted details. Interestingly, in one of our pilot experiments, people did not require more time to image more detailed drawings. In this case, subjects were not urged to include all details. Although one could argue that these results are due to a floor effect or some sort of demand characteristics, the subjects' post-session self reports seem to indicate otherwise: These people claimed to "see" all of the details in a "single flash," although the details were not necessarily very clear. With more effort, some subjects admitted, they could elaborate some of the details on the image. This sort of introspection suggests that the image may consist of a more-or-less unitary "skeleton" that includes some indication of the details, but which can be fleshed out and elaborated.

We claimed earlier that more time was required to "see" parts of smaller images, or smaller parts themselves. If parts are difficult to see, we would expect that the places to which they are attached also would be difficult to detect. If so, then it may be difficult to fill out the details on smaller images. Because it seems to require time to fill out details on images, we might expect, then, that smaller images ought to be constructed more quickly than larger images. Kosslyn (1975b) reports an experiment that confirmed this prediction; in this experiment, subjectively smaller images of animals were in fact generated more quickly than subjectively larger images. Subsequent experiments using a variety of techniques have replicated this finding (and revealed additional complications not to be discussed here).

Finally, it is worth mentioning data on what seems to be a special case of image construction, namely that involved in maintaining an image. That is, images seem to fade with time. In order to maintain an image, one may need to regenerate it periodically. If so, then more complex images ought to be more difficult to maintain. I (Kosslyn, 1975b) asked people to image various animals as if they were next to either a four-cell or a 16-cell matrix; people participating in this experiment required more time to "see" parts of the imaged animal when the animal was mentally pictured next to a 16-cell matrix. The same basic result was found when people imaged four digits, instead of just two, as if they were painted on an imaginary wall next to an animal; now, more time was required to "see" animal parts — or individual digits — when four digits were present. The extra effort required to maintain a 16-cell matrix or four digits apparently left less available processing capacity for regenerating the image of the animal, resulting in the image of the beast being more degraded (and its parts being harder to "see") in these contexts.

Piecemeal Retrieval Versus Construction

The foregoing introspections, considerations, and data lean against assuming that images are simply played back from long-term memory. But what if images are in fact stored in a single unit, which then is simply retrieved a bit at a time? For example, if images are represented by filling in cells of a matrix to portray a picture, one could store the matrix and simply retrieve the filled cells one at a time (perhaps in a random serial order or in parallel, but with a distribution of retrieval times). This sort of model could explain the finding described in the last section. Alternatively, images could be stored in separate units that are composed during the act of generation.

Rational Considerations. One usually has more than a few hundred milliseconds to look at an object. Thus one probably encodes more than a single representation of an object. As one moves toward an object, one presumably notices details previously overlooked. If an image is to be an effective form of internal representation, it would be useful if information gleaned from multiple looks could be amalgamated into a single representation. That is, information encoded separately should be able to be integrated into a single image. In fact, most of the purported uses of imagery (e.g., in problem solving) depend on images being constructions from multiple, previously unintegrated, representations.

Introspections. As Pylyshyn (1973) points out, when we forget part of an image, it tends to be a whole object or property; it is not as if a corner were torn from a mental photograph. This sort of introspection may simply indicate that images are not perfectly encoded, are not "mental photographs", and may not bear on the question of retrieval and generation. Many people report, however, that they can retrieve a forgotten portion upon a prompt, and insert said material into their image. If so, then that portion must have been encoded. In this case, one merely neglected to include it in the initial image. Such introspections are counter to a simple piecemeal retrieval notion. The "imaging as juggling" introspection noted previously also speaks to the present issue; again, units seem to be composed in the act of imaging.

Relevant Data. Kosslyn, Reiser, and Greenbarg (1977) report two experiments that bear on the present issue. In one, people imaged animals as if they were next to patterns painted on a wall. These patterns consisted of six-columns composed of a given letter of the alphabet. These columns either were evenly spaced or were grouped to form two thick columns three letters wide. Interestingly, even though there were the same number of letters present in the two cases, when letters were placed to form fewer perceptual groups (as defined by the Gestalt law of proximity), less time was later taken to generate an image of the scene.

In another experiment, we had people first study pictures of animals and then later participate in a task that required imaging them. The animals were presented in one of three conditions (each subject received each condition equally often, and each animal appeared in each condition equally often over subjects, of course). Animals were presented drawn on a single page, separated into two portions drawn on different pages, or separated into five portions, each of which was presented on a separate page. The subject was allowed to look at only a single page at a time and was told to "try to glue the pieces together" such that a composite image was formed. Parts were placed in the correct relative locations in the multiple page versions, facilitating this "gluing together" process. As expected, even though the same material was present in the different learning conditions, more time was required later to image animals presented on two pages than on one, and the most time was required when they were presented on five pages. Apparently, we forced the subject to encode more units when pieces were distributed over more pages, which required more time to retrieve and compose.

These results, then, demonstrate that images can be generated from encoded units. If images cannot be composed from multiple representations, the results of the second experiment seem problematical. Further, images often may be spontaneously encoded in multiple units — if only a single integral representation were encoded, the results of the first experiment described previously would make no sense. Thus, it seems reasonable to reject the piecemeal-retrieval hypothesis and to speculate that a model of imagery should account for generation via retrieval and composition of organized units stored in long-term memory.

Types of Representations Used in Image Construction

All our considerations lead us to the conclusion that images are not simply retrieved, but this assertion is not particularly informative when one considers all of the different ways in which an image could be constructed. Thus, it is profitable to continue to consider this issue at a more subtle level. A basic issue about the generation process itself concerns the sorts of representations used in generating an image. There are two very distinct possibilities that seem to differ in important ways. On one hand, only "perceptual information" (i.e., memories of "literal appearances") may be involved in generating images. Most simple Dual Code notions seem to imply that images (or parts thereof) are tucked away in long-term memory and then simply "activated" upon retrieval; the constructive aspects of this process involve whether or not given parts are activated. On the other hand, non-perceptual information, like that contained in verbal descriptions (or abstract propositions) could be used in conjunction with perceptual information in generating images. In this case, one might arrange remembered parts according to descriptions of their relations or even "fill in" parts that are not remembered perceptually but are encoded in a description (e.g., although one may not really remember what the wheels of a particular car looked like, knowing what wheels look like and knowing that it is a car and that cars have wheels may allow one to "put" wheels in the appropriate place anyhow).

Rational Considerations

It makes sense that all forms of one's knowledge could potentially be brought to bear in constructing images. There must be times when a simple verbal description would be more economical than a complete "literal" memory, and it would be convenient if such a description could take part in reconstructing the appearance in a subsequent image. More compelling reasons why some sort of abstract information is used in constructing images seem to follow from a consideration of how information about seen objects or scenes is encoded. Presumably, one encodes information from more than a single glance. People look not only at the object as a totality but often study individual parts. This notion is commonly assumed when people discuss how certain objects in a scene or parts of an object may be omitted from an image; in such cases, they were not noticed, whereas the included objects were in fact taken in. If parts are encoded individually, all of the parts need not be perceptually apprehended at the same time. If they are not, the relations between parts cannot be encoded as are the relations between objects in a single photograph. Rather, if objects in scenes, or parts of objects, often are encoded separately, the appropriate analogy would be one of arranging a set of separate photos in the correct position on a table top. In this case, the relative positions of the parts are not necessarily dictated by the perceptual information in the photos (although certain shapes can sometimes indicate how parts fit together). The relations, then, must be represented in a more abstract way.

Perhaps the most compelling reason to posit that nonperceptual information is utilized on constructing images is the simple fact that novel images can be constructed. People can be given a description (e.g., "Jimmy Carter sawing a giant peanut in half") and then evoke a corresponding image. In this case, we know that the abstract description somehow made contact with the image material and that never-before-seen relations were included in the image. It seems clear that one could provide oneself with various verbal descriptions; if so, then there is no reason why such information should not be used regularly in storing and constructing images.

Introspections

This is one issue in which introspections may constitute important evidence. Galton long ago reported that people sometimes omitted objects from their images, and it often has been noticed that one can insert an overlooked component into an image upon verbal prompting. This sort of introspection suggests that verbal information can be used in image construction. But can introspections bear on the more subtle issue of what sorts of representations are utilized in internally instigated construction? People often seem to image remembered objects or scenes incorrectly. The errors are not due to random jumbling of components of the image, however; instead, people report putting a part behind another when it should have been in front, or one part to the left of another when it was really to the right, and so on. I was once asked to image a drawing of an airplane that had appeared as an illustration in Kosslyn (1973) and then was asked whether the cockpit of the plane was in front of or behind the wings. My answer was in fact incorrect, but was an accurate description of my image. It seemed clear at the time that I had an image of the general shape of the plane and another image of the cockpit region in isolation; in constructing the image, I really wasn't sure where the cockpit belonged and placed it incorrectly (as it turned out). This sort of introspection suggests that parts of images are not tightly bound to given positions, are not inextricably attached to each other. It seems like the relations between parts are often rather vague, as if relations incorporate notions like "above" and "to the right" instead of absolute coordinates.

Other sorts of introspections also suggest that nonperceptual information is used in constructing images. These introspections are about the effects of knowing the identity of an imaged object or part. For example, I once noticed that I actually recalled only half of a wheel of a bike I was imaging (the part that caught the sun along the rim), but because I knew it was a wheel and I knew that wheels are round, I could fill in the remaining half if I wanted to. People commonly report introspections of this sort if specifically asked about them.

Unlike the first basic issue, then, it seems as though rational considerations and introspections may have some value here. The oft-reported (c.f., Pylyshyn, 1973) observation that images may be misrepresentations of the referents, and the simple fact that one can use verbally delivered information in constructing an image, seem to indicate that images may be constructed on the basis of more than memory for "literal" appearance. Nonetheless, one can always find someone who disagrees with one's introspections. Furthermore, such introspections do not penetrate the mists very much, do not provide much insight on the actual workings of the mechanisms involved in image construction.

Relevant Data

Most of the data on constructing images simply serves to demonstrate that images are in fact constructed and that such construction takes time. In fact, as far as I know, only Weber, Kelley, and Little (1972) have published data that directly bear on the issue at hand. In their experiment, people imaged the letters of the alphabet (in a type font just shown to them) in order, classifying each letter in terms of whether it was high or not (e.g., t vs. o). Subjects either spoke the letters aloud or were not so instructed, and either spoke their classifications (yes/no) aloud or indicated them by drawing a "/" or a ".". Processing times were almost identical for spoken and unspecified scanning; in previous work, Weber and Bach (1969) found that people could speak (overtly or implicitly) about six letters per second in their task, but could only image about two per second. The finding that spoken and unspecified scanning required about the same time was taken, then, to be consistent with the notion that people automatically provided implicit "verbal prompts" when constructing images of the letters of the alphabet in sequence. This inference was supported by the finding that the spoken responses required more time than written responses for both scanning conditions — even though spoken responses in isolation seemed faster. This result was interpreted to indicate that having to say the response interfered with verbally prompting the successive images (c f. Brooks, 1967); the amount of interference was the same in the two scanning conditions, supporting the claim that people implicitly spoke the letters even when not required to do so.

Weber et al.'s results seem to indicate that internal speech is in fact used in some circumstances when people construct images. The sort of sequential imaging they studied, however, almost seems to require some sort of verbal coordination. In order to study the generality of the notion that verbal/abstract information can be used in constructing images, Louis Gomez and I recently conducted a very simple experiment. People first were shown a matrix of capital Xs and were told that they soon would read descriptions of similar matrices and would be asked to form mental images of these arrays. We asked our subjects to practice imaging the sample array (which was four rows by 5 columns). After this, the 12 subjects received two practice trials wherein they were presented with a card that read "two rows of five" followed by one reading "four columns of two." As soon as the subject read a card, he was to generate an image of Xs, like those in the sample, arranged as described; when he had the image clearly in mind, he was to depress a button. We measured the time necessary to generate the image from the moment the description was presented (in a tachistoscope). Descriptions were written on the very bottom of a card, leaving plenty of room to image the matrix. After the practice trials, we presented two test trials (the order being counterbalanced over subjects). One trial required imaging an array of Xs "three rows of six," and the other required "six columns of three." Both descriptions produced the same image (although most subjects did not seem to realize this). Interestingly, more time (4.076 versus 3.800 sec., 10 of the 12 subjects showing the effect) was required when the matrix was described in terms of six columns instead of three rows; we cannot say whether this was due to having to generate more units, or difficulty in generating columns instead of rows per se. In any case, the type of description clearly influenced how the image was generated.

The foregoing result is clear evidence that verbal/abstract information may work in conjunction with "literal appearance" information in image generation. However, this result does not demonstrate that *stored* verbal/abstract information is used in generating images. In order to demonstrate this, Phil Greenbarg and I used a variation of the foregoing task. Now, a subject first was shown a matrix of three rows of letters, each row containing six items. The letters were spaced equal distances from those above, below, right, and left of them. In this experiment, we used two different matrices, one being composed of Xs, and one being composed of Os. The subject first was shown one matrix and asked to study it until he thought he could remember what was present. Following this, the matrix was removed, and the subject was told that we wanted him "to think of that pattern as three rows of six" or as "six columns of three" of the letter. After the subject had seen a matrix and been asked to conceptualize it a given way, he heard a tone. At this point, he simply formed a visual image of the matrix and pushed a button when his image was complete. As before, a clock was started at the signal, and terminated upon his response – allowing us to measure generation time. All subjects received both matrices, one being described each way; both matrices were presented in both serial orders and with both descriptions equally often over subjects, all conditions being completely counterbalanced.

We had a reason for asking the subjects to conceptualize the matrix only after it was removed. If the label were given first, or along with the matrix, it might affect how people encoded the perceptual information. If so, then any later effects of description on time to generate an image might be due simply to how many perceptual units had been encoded – more units (as would occur with the columns description) requiring more time. We were interested in demonstrating that perceptual and conceptual (if you will) information both are used at the time of generation itself. Thus, by presenting the description only after a matrix was seen, any effects of the type of description can be ascribed to an interplay between perceptual and abstract memory representations per se.

The results of this simple study were clear: More time was required to generate matrices conceptualized as six columns instead of three rows [3.422 versus 2.989 sec; although only 13 of our 20 subjects, showed this effect, the result was nonetheless statistically significant, $t(19) = 2.27$, $p < .05$]. Thus, the way in which one conceptualizes an appearance seems to affect how one later regenerates that appearance in an image. Images are not simply tucked away in memory, in toto or in separate pieces. Instead, images are truly generated and may be formed by using perceptual memories in conjunction with more abstract information.

Processing Images

We have now descended four levels in a "decision tree," making choices among alternative "basic operating characteristics." Our positions on the issues just discussed are in fact positions on the properties of structure-process pairs. As noted earlier, the structural properties of a representation arise in the context of how the representation is processed. Just as an array in a computer derives its spatial properties (i.e., two cells may be "adjacent," separated by some "distance," etc.) from how "words" are accessed in sequence, so too does the spatial/quasi-pictorial nature of a surface image depend on the sensitivities and operating characteristics of a "mind's eye." Thus, processing considerations are not distinct from claims about representation. Nevertheless, it may be useful in this section to examine the processing assumptions we used in the foregoing treatments of the issues in their own right. We shall consider not only the assumptions about processing experienced "surface" images, but the implications about how the "deep" representations in long-term memory may be processed. In addition to this, we also will speculate about some additional kinds of processing that our assumptions about the structural properties of surface and deep representations imply may take place at each level of representation.

Processing Surface Images

Rational Considerations. Virtually all of our argument and evidence that surface images are functional entailed positing a processor that "looks" on the image much like the processor in visual perception deals with incoming sensory information. Some sort of interpretive procedures are necessary for classifying the spatial patterns composing an image into various semantic categories. It makes sense that the same procedures would be used both for classifying surface representations engendered during visual processing and for classifying those generated from memory. Winston's (1970) procedures for classifying a pattern as a representation of an arch, for example, could operate just as easily, in principle, on materials from a matrix filled in from stored information as one filled in via input from a camera. Thus, we argue that the same procedures are used to interpret parts of images and percepts on the basis of economy and parsimony (as was argued in the first section). The alternative, of course, is to have separate sorts of procedures for interpreting images and percepts; if images really are spatial/quasi-pictorial structures like those underlying visual experience during perception, then this position is uneconomical and unparsimonious.

Not all of the processing of surface images need be like that involved in perception, however. Although perceptual representations are tied to the nature of the sensory input, images are not so constrained. Images should be much more amenable to transformation from memory than should perceptual representations; after all, images are generated from memory in the first place. If the capability for transforming the image exists, it also seems reasonable that such capacities will be brought to bear in using the image, in "inspecting" (i.e., applying interpretive procedures to) an image. If an image is too small, subjectively, such that some parts are not "visible," there is no reason why the size scale of the image should not be adjusted until the sought property is "visible." Various other sorts of transformations also seem appropriately applied in special cases; if one wanted to "see" the rear of an imaged object, a "rotation" would be usefully employed. This sort of argument is uncomfortably thin, however; there is no logical reason why an event *will* in fact occur simply because it *could* occur. Nevertheless, from an evolutionary standpoint, we presume that our capabilities are available because they are in fact usefully employed. It is clear that simple rational argument cannot really tell us too much about imaginal processing, however, so let us turn to introspective observations and then consider data.

Introspections. So strong is the notion that one does something similar in examining images and percepts that people commonly speak of "seeing with the mind's eye." Clearly, people seem to feel that they "see" objects and patterns in their images. These patterns need not be semantically interpreted ahead of time. For example, when first asked to describe the shape of some animal's ears, most people report having to inspect an image of the beast and then classify the imaged ears. In this case, the classification procedures seem introspectively quite similar to what one would have done if the animal were physically present at the time of query. In addition, some of the same factors that influence ease of classifying percepts (like size) also seem to influence ease of classifying images.

The notion that various transformations are brought to bear when inspecting images seems clearly true. When asked to see a relatively small part of an imaged object (e.g., a cat's claws), most people report "zooming in" until the claws are clearly visible. Interestingly, many people report being able to scan while zooming in, rotate while zooming in and so on, combining operations together. These operations seem reversible; people report being able to "pan out" if too close, scan any which-way and rotate along various axes.

Relevant Data. Virtually all of the data supporting the claim that surface images are functional also supports the notion that parts of surface images are classified by the same sorts of procedures used in perception. Indeed, we implicitly assumed that this was true when we argued that the data presented earlier demonstrated that surface images are functional. If we had not made this assumption about processing, we could not have generated most of the predictions that seemed to follow from our claims about the structure of the representation: properties of structures arise only vis-a-vis the workings of interpretive processes that operate on the structure in some specified way.

The notion that various transformations are brought to bear in processing images has not been studied as such. The work of Cooper (1975) and Cooper and Shepard (1973) on mental rotation and of Shepard and Feng (1972) on mental paper folding may in fact provide support for this claim, but it is difficult to know whether images per se were operated upon (rather than some other "analogue" internal representation). Although many people report "zooming in" on an imaged object when searching for a small part, but not doing so when searching for a larger one, this is not the only reason why it may take more time to see smaller details. Smaller details may simply be more difficult to "see," to classify via application of interpretive procedures, than larger ones (as seems to happen in perception), or smaller details may not be well filled out during construction. If scanning images is regarded as a sort of imagery transformation (which turns out to be an interesting way of treating it), then we do have evidence that this transformation is utilized in searching images (as discussed earlier). There has not yet been research demonstrating that multiple transformations may be used at the same time when one is examining an image for a sought property.

Processing Deep Representations

Rational Considerations. The basic purpose of deep processing is to map information in long-term memory into a surface image. The more interesting sorts of processing involve presetting various transformations before actually generating an image. In order to generate an image containing numerous parts, one must be certain that the parts are imaged at the correct relative sizes (even if they were encoded at different times, distances, etc.). Much of the combinatorial, generative properties of imagery seem to depend on one being able to readjust components of an image or images to certain sizes and positions before actual generation occurs.

It is of interest to consider limitations upon processing of the deep representations. Presumably, all possible relations between parts of an object (or among objects in a scene) are not explicitly encoded; only one or two relations may be noted directly, the rest "emerging" when a surface image is constructed (e.g., a horse's tail may be noticed in relation to the animal's rear but not in relation to its head, hooves, etc.; these relations become available after constructing the image, however, even though they were not explicitly encoded). In addition, properties like the area of an object would be difficult to derive from a deep representation; not only may this representation be in the wrong format for determining such, but the emergent relations among the parts will in part determine how much area is occluded by the whole (e.g., depending on how much parts overlap). Further, any information not semantically interpreted in the deep representation should not be accessible without generating the image. In order to tell that the abstract representation underlying a part of an image corresponds to a "pointed ear," for example, one would need a set of specialized interpretive procedures that presumably would only be used for this purpose. This seems unnecessary when procedures already exist for processing surface images.

Introspections. I find that I can mentally adjust the subjective size of an elephant and then image a person I know riding on its back. The image of the person seems correctly scaled for size no matter how large is the elephant. Hence, I seem to be able to adjust the size of one image before placing it so that it is of the same scale as another image. Furthermore, I can image two objects in a variety of locations, without first having to picture one and then move it to the correct position. Thus it seems possible to preset size and location.

In regard to the limitations of deep representation processing, there are at least two sorts of tasks for which I seem to have to use surface images. If I try to compare the relative areas of two similar-sized objects for the first time, I seem to image them side by side (especially if the areas are rather similar). Once I have made a comparison, however, I no longer need have recourse to images to make it again. In addition, if I try to assess a precise spatial relationship (like how far above the knees of a horse is the tip of its tail) for the first time, I also necessarily seem to use imagery (again, especially if the relation requires a subtle discrimination, and only if the relation has not been assessed before — see Kosslyn et al., 1977).

Relevant Data. Kosslyn (1975b) found that people could in fact generate images at specified sizes. Instead of first generating an image at some standard size and then manipulating this size, people were able to generate images at specified relative sizes. Smaller images, which presumably had less detail, were mentally pictured more quickly than larger ones. No one has yet explored experimentally whether people can preset location prior to generating and manipulating a surface image.

The question of the limitations of processing deep representations is in part just the other side of the question of when surface images necessarily must be consulted. This question has been investigated within the context of the present model, so let us now briefly review the major features of our model before continuing further.

PHASE II: DEVELOPING AN EXPLICIT MODEL

We have now reached the point where we have tentatively adopted a few basic operating characteristics, have collected a body of data, and our metaphor no longer raises clear issues. Thus it now makes sense to attempt to model imagistic processes and to let the emerging theory guide our further investigations. Our model must account for the available data and incorporate the principles that seem dictated by them. Further, if it is to avoid sterility, our model should lead us to collect more data that further constrain an acceptable theory. We first outline the model and note how it accounts for the previously discussed findings in the process. Following this,we consider how the model functions as an aid to conducting empirical work. Finally, we conclude with some possible extensions of the model that deal with perception and the role and nature of "prototypes" in imagery and perception.

A Computer Simulation Approach

We have embodied our theory in a running computer program for six main reasons. First, this strategy allows one to theorize about complex phenomena while still being explicit. Second, when dealing with a complex theory, one cannot always be certain that all of the components of the theory are self-consistent. If one embodies the theory in a computer program, such inconsistencies will prevent the program from working as intended. Third, when dealing with a complex theory, it is difficult to be sure that the theory is sufficient to account for the specified range of phenomena; a running program provides a kind of "sufficiency proof." Fourth, in the act of constructing the model, one sometimes discovers new issues not previously perceived. If one is not to be arbitrary, these issues must be resolved by collecting new data (as discussed in the introduction). Fifth, while constructing the model, one also may discover internal constraints imposed by the principles dictating the form of the model. That is, in the act of making the model self-consistent (i.e., not adding "special exceptions" to the general principles supposedly being embodied in the model), sometimes one is forced to make new predictions that previously were not considered. Finally, the sort of process data we had collected appeared to be modeled best by a process model, rather than a more abstract axiomatic or mathematical model.

Our model is quite complex and detailed and is only briefly described here; a more comprehensive treatment appears in Kosslyn and Schwartz (1977, in press). The present treatment focuses on how images are generated, inspected, and transformed. It is most convenient to treat the model as if it were comprised of two main components, a structural one and a processing one. We consider these components in turn.[2]

---

[2]This chapter is a progress report, originally written in August and September of 1976, and revised in April 1977. If it is not out of date by the time it sees the light of day, something must have gone drastically wrong! In particular, the reader is reminded that the program is in a continual state of revision, and the current description is likely to become "inoperative" in the near future.

The Image Representation

Images (i.e., the spatial/quasi-pictorial entities we experience) are treated as surface representations generated from more abstract deep-level representations.

The Surface Representation

An image is represented as a configuration of points in a matrix. A "picture" is depicted by selectively filling in cells of the matrix. The representational medium is not equally activated throughout; instead, the central region is most sharply in focus, and activation tapers off until no cells are activated. This assumption was included in the model for three reasons: First, it seemed intuitively sound; the center of the image does seem most sharply in focus, and the images seem to fade off at the periphery. Second, we have evidence that although one cannot "see" portions of the image that seem to have "overflowed," those portions are still there. In a variation of the imaged-map scanning experiment described earlier, people "zoomed in" on the initial focus location in their image until all else had overflowed; following this, they heard the name of a possible location on the map, and were told to be sure to "see" this location in the image before responding "true". As when the image is entirely visible, response times increased with distance to be scanned. It was as if the various locations were reconstructed and available to be scanned, even though they were not visible at the time. Intuitively, when one zooms in on part of the image it doesn't seem as if the rest is simply lost; rather, it seems to be "waiting in the wings" (see Kosslyn, Ball, & Reiser, in press). In addition, we found that the absolute size of the angle obtained in the "estimated-distance-at-the-point-of-overflow" experiments described earlier was affected by the precise definition of what it meant for an image to "overflow"; when subjects were told that an image had "overflowed" when all of the edges were not sharply defined at the same time, images seemed to overflow at further distances. If the spatial extent of the surface representational structure were sharply delineated, such instructions would not be expected to affect the size of the angle. But if images simply became progressively more hazy toward the edges, then it makes sense that one can adopt different criteria for when an image has "overflowed." The third reason for positing a distribution of activation across the image was a rational consideration: The imagery system may have only a limited "processing capacity" with which to display images. If so, some sort of distribution of activation would be expected, and it makes sense that some region should be fully activated, rather than the entire image being degraded. If the entire image were degraded, it would not be a very effective representational device. If some portion is more strongly activated than the others, it is reasonable to posit that the central region would be allocated full capacity; if not, the distribution of activation would be nonsymmetrical around the area of highest activation (if it were symmetrical, of course, the point of the highest activation would be equivalent to the "center").

The Deep Representation

Surface images are derived from representations stored in long-term memory. We modeled these representations in terms of files addressed by the name of the to-be-imaged object. The image deep representation includes two types of representations: First, the "literal" perceptual memory of the appearance (which is not semantically interpreted but corresponds to the products of "seeing that," not the products of "seeing as") is stored in a file containing R, *Theta* coordinates. These polar coordinates specify locations where points should be placed in the surface matrix. A polar coordinate system was chosen because: (1) it allows easy placement of images at different locations in the surface matrix (by simple relocation of the origin); and (2) it allows images to be generated easily at different subjectives sizes (i.e., different sizes in the display).

Any given appearance may be encoded in multiple files. One file must, however, correspond to the skeleton upon which "details" may be placed; this skeleton usually is a "global shape." This sort of representation seemed to be suggested by our preliminary finding that people could image more detailed pictures of objects about as quickly as less detailed versions *if* they were not severely urged to be sure to see each and every detail. Subjects reported that the initial images, even of the most complex versions, seemed to have all of the details although not necessarily very clearly. The "skeletal" image, then, is usually hypothesized to be low-resolution representation of the general appearance, which may be embellished at will if ancillary files are available (these subfiles presumably are the encoding of "more careful looks" at parts of the object). In special cases, however, where an object has clearly definable parts, like the tail of an "L," the largest segment could serve as the skeletal image to which details (or other parts) are added. We do not have an algorithm that dictates when the skeletal image is global or simply the largest part. Nonetheless, both sorts of structures seem introspectively valid on occasion.

The second component of the image deep representation consists of stored facts about the image; these facts are represented in a "propositional" format. Facts include information about: (1) parts of an object (or names of ancillary encodings); (2) where and how a part is attached to the global image (e.g., a cushion is "flush on" a seat); (3) how to find a given part (i.e., a procedural definition of a part, like what sorts of patterns correspond to the "seat" of a chair); and (4) the optimal resolution of the image in order to "see" the object. Additional information is also stored in this format but is not used in any of the circumstances discussed at present. The definitions of parts and their locations are in terms of tests that can be performed on the surface image when attempting to "find" a given part.

Image Processes

There are basically two sorts of imagery processes in our model: There are routines for generating and classifying the image, and there are routines for transforming the image.

Image Generation and Classification

Images are generated by printing out points in the surface display. If no particular size value or location information is specified at the time of generation, our model simply relies on default values. Unless otherwise instructed, the model centers an image and prints it such that all parts of the image are "visible" at once. That is, the image is printed only so large as to fill the activated portion of the surface matrix; this default was used after we performed a variation of our "mental walk to the point of overflow experiment" described earlier. In this variation, people were simply asked to image an object and estimate the distance; no mention was made of "walking" or of "overflow." Interestingly, the angle obtained when we analyzed these data was of the same magnitude (although sometimes slightly larger) as those obtained in the earlier versions of the experiment (and in fact people report usually being able to see all of an imaged object at once, even when not explicitly instructed to ensure this).

For purposes of illustration, let us discuss how our program generates an image of a chair. The first points placed in the surface matrix are those specified in the "skeletal" file. The resulting image is a somewhat "sketchy" chair. This global image is sketchy because only a limited number of points are used to portray it; this is intended to reflect "processing capacity" limitations at the time of encoding, when attention was diffused and unfocused. If instructed to generate a detailed image, or if task demands require it, various subfiles may be activated to place more points in the surface matrix. These files represent higher resolution representations of details of the imaged object's appearance. Details are integrated into the image by use of several procedures: The IMAGE procedure looks up a location and a relation for a given part (e.g., for a chair's cushion, "seat" is the location, and "flush on" is the relation); this information is stored propositionally in the object's file. The location and relation are then passed to PUT. PUT then calls the FIND procedure, which locates the relevant part on the image (the seat portion of the skeletal image) via performing a specified sequence of operations. These operations constitute a "procedural definition" of a part, and their names are stored with the file headed by the part's name. FIND accesses this file, retrieves this definition, and then attempts to discover whether the specified tests can be successfully applied to the pattern in the surface array. If FIND can in fact locate the specified array of lines and shapes, it has "found" the defined part. If FIND does in fact locate the "foundation" portion of the image (i.e., the part upon which it will place the other), it passes back the Cartesian coordinates delineating the part's location in the image. PUT then checks the location relation ("flush on," in this case), and, if need be, adjusts the size of the cushion such that it will fit flush on the seat and then prints out the "detail" at the correct location on the skeletal shape.

This sequence of events is repeated until all stored subfiles are on the image. The more files there are, then, the longer it will take to generate an image. Furthermore, the smaller the image is, the fewer points of the skeletal image will be differentiated in the surface display; if the image is too small, multiple points may occupy a single cell. Hence, it will be more difficult for FIND to locate portions and to then place (via PUT) details on the image, resulting in a less-detailed, more quickly generated smaller image. These features of the model, then, account for the effects of the size and complexity on time to generate images.

In addition, if we posit that the surface image fades with time, which seems a reasonable assumption, we also can understand the effects of complexity on the ease of maintaining images. In this case, if images fade at a given rate, the longer it takes to finish construction, the more the initially constructed portions will be faded upon completion of the image. Each subfile requires time to activate; hence, with more subfiles to be maintained, each subfile will be regenerated less frequently, and any given part thus will be more likely to be faded in more complex images. The "processing capacity" of image display is exceeded when so much detail is placed that initial portions are no longer available by the time the image is completed.

The FIND procedure is used in two ways. As mentioned earlier, it is used in image generation. If a foundation part (e.g., seat) is not located during image generation (perhaps because the image is too small), the detailed part (cushion) is simply omitted. FIND also is used when the program is simply asked whether or not a given part is included in an image of an object. In this circumstance, FIND is called by a procedure called LOOKFOR. LOOKFOR operates in conjunction with various image transformations (discussed next) in an all-out attempt to locate the sought part. If at first glance (as it were) FIND cannot locate a part (i.e., the definitional procedures are not satisfied), it looks up the optimal resolution of the image (as indicated by dot density) in order to "see" the part (storing the optimal resolution is a kluge; eventually we will implement a routine for calculating it from a representation of the size — relative to the whole object, the size of which will be indicated relative to an absolute standard — and material out of which the part is made). If the present dot density of the imaged object is not within the optimal range, transformations are called up to expand or contract (as appropriate) the image until the resolution is correct.

These procedures accomplish "zooming in" on or "panning out" from the object; we discuss the nature of these transformations shortly. If the size of the image is correct and FIND still cannot locate the part, FIND checks the direction of the part implied by the procedural definition of it; if the image has overflowed at the specified edge, FIND then calls the SCAN procedure and scans in the specified direction. If the size and location are correct, and the classificatory procedures still are not satisfied (i.e., FIND cannot locate a configuration of points that would correspond to the sought part), the program will return a "CANNOT LOCATE" response; if it locates the part, it will respond by indicating the Cartesian coordinates of the sought part.

The operating characteristics of the program, then, depend in large part on the characteristics of the transformations. The program should account for the fact that more time is required to "see" increasingly smaller parts: The smaller a part is, the more likely it is to require some sort of transformation in order to be seen; how such "zooming in" occurs will dictate the effects of size on time to "see" parts of an image. Similarly, if the image is so large that parts have overflowed the activated region of the surface matrix, it should require time to contract the image until the sought part is in view. In addition, we must explain why more time is required to scan further distances. The actual effect of distance on time to scan also will depend on exactly how the scanning operations work. Thus, let us now consider the transformations themselves.

Image Transformations

Our program transforms images by shifting the points defining a surface image in some specified fashion. "Scanning" an image is treated as just another sort of transformation, wherein points are shifted across the surface matrix such that different portions of the depicted object seem to move under the center (the point of greatest focus). "Rotating" an image consists of moving the points around a specified pivot. "Expanding" or "contracting" an image consists of migrating points away from or toward a pivot (at present always the center of the object). This operation is equivalent to "zooming in" or "panning out," because the texture, the level of resolution (as indicated by dot density in a given area), covaries with size; as the size increases, the dots become less densely packed, details may become more distinct, and the object seems to move closer.

It seems as though images are moved continuously, according to our model, because they are transformed in many small steps. Only a part of an image is moved at one time, the image caterpillaring along one portion at a time. This technique eliminates the necessity for a special buffer to store new locations of points while others are still being calculated, and it may be more economical than other techniques by spreading processing over time. The effect of small shifts is to require more such operations for large transformations; hence, it should require more time to perform larger transformations, which in fact is true. The actual magnitude of a given step is constrained, however: We did not want points shifted so far that a noticeable gap would be created in the image. This maximal step distance depends on a variety of factors, most notably the subjective size and internal complexity (as defined by the density of internal details in an imaged object) of an image: If an image is very small and complicated, points can only be moved relatively short distances before the image will seem to fragment, whereas if the image is subjectively larger and/or more simple, points may be moved further at each increment. The speed with which the image can be shifted across the matrix corresponds to the rate with which it may be scanned.

The Role of the Model in Furthering the "Bootstrap Procedure"

I argued earlier that model construction is like multidimensional scaling, where "holes" in the space could lead one to investigate new issues — producing new data requiring an account. This function is critical for the success of the bootstrap method, which requires a sizable corpus of interesting data to be explained. When one reaches a juncture in constructing the model where things can be done in more than one way, this quandary serves to motivate interesting research; in addition, the model itself should make predictions — leading to collection of the most interesting data of all, that which can disconfirm a theory. The remainder of this chapter explores how our model serves these functions. We will consider first a few implications from the model as it now stands and then consider ramifications of possible extensions in the next section.

The model seems to have some interesting implications for how imagery transformations might operate. Let us consider three of these implications. The notion that scanning is another form of imagery transformation leads us to expect that the more material in an image, the longer it should take to scan it, even if the additional material is not scanned over. Furthermore, the more similar scanned-across items are to a sought target, the more time should be taken to "inspect them," but this factor should not matter if additional items are merely scanned by. Thus, if we find that the more items there are in an image the longer it takes to scan to a given target, but that perceptual similarity only affects times when items are scanned over, we can infer that the additional time incurred when items are added off the scan path is not due to one searching among them for the target (if it were, perceptual similarity should matter with these items too). This result was in fact obtained in a preliminary experiment conducted by Baha Fam.

The fact that transformations work by shifting portions of an image in sequence leads us to expect "acceleration" when one "zooms in" on (expands) an image. In this case, the points can only be shifted outward a relatively small amount when the image is very small; as the image becomes larger, the points can be moved further at each iteration without disrupting the image: hence, one seems to be zooming in more quickly as it expands. Although we have not yet experimentally investigated this claim, it does seem consistent with my introspections.

Our model also suggests another possible way in which images may be transformed. A "blink" transformation, unlike a "shift," is not iterative. In this transformation, an initial image would be "erased" (either actively or simply allowed to fade without regeneration) and a new version, exhibiting the required transformation, would be generated. Although this "erase-and-regenerate" process requires effort, the amount of effort does not depend on the size of the transformation to be performed as it does with iterative shift transformations. Instead, it depends purely on the effort to delete and regenerate an image; if so, then it should be increasingly easy to use this sort of transformation in further reducing the size of an object. In this case, the smaller the final version, the less effort is required to generate it. If a shift transform were used, in contrast, the greater the transformation, as is involved in progressively shrinking an image, the more time will be required. These contrasting predictions for the two sorts of transforms have yet to be tested. Nor have we assessed the relative difficulties of the two sorts of transformations, which should allow us to predict when one sort will be used rather than another.

In order to account for the ease with which people can preset the size of images, and also seem to be able to preset the apparent location of imaged objects, we used $R, Theta$ coordinates in the deep representation. By specifying the value of R (the distance from the origin), size was easily adjusted; by specifying the location of the origin itself, location was easily altered. This representation also allows angular orientation to be easily adjusted, however. We did not bargain on this. However, the way PUT works would lead us to expect that people would have great difficulty in adding details to images generated at nonstandard orientations. PUT uses FIND to locate a foundation part (e.g., seat, when trying to place a cushion); the procedures incorporated in FIND, however, are rather orientation-specific and have difficulty in locating parts of rotated images. Thus, although one should be able to generate the skeletal image at different orientations with little difficulty, it should be quite difficult to flesh out this form with details. Introspecting, I notice that I seem to be able to preset orientation for only relatively simple things, like the letters of the alphabet. Even here I notice some problems in knowing which direction parts (e.g., the tail of an "L") ought to face; sometimes I seem to glue the parts on the wrong way when imaging even a letter at a nonstandard orientation. With more complex images (e.g., the White House), I have great difficulty in generating a clear, detailed image at a nonstandard orientation from the onset (although I can generate one at the usual orientation and then rotate it with some success); a somewhat fuzzy version may, however, be projected on command pointing at various numbers of a giant imaged clock. This fuzzy image may in fact correspond to the "skeletal" image we have hypothesized. These problems in generating images at nonstandard orientations, then, lead us to expect that blink transformations will not be used often in performing mental rotations. If the imaged object is very simple (e g., a broomstick), a blink transformation will be more likely than if the imaged object is more complex. These notions were not considered until the simulation was constructed.

The model raises a whole host of other sorts of issues and questions. Notably, we commonly are faced with the question of what the "default value" should be for some procedure. For example, should the model always fill in all of the detail when generating an image? In addition, we are faced with questions about how various components ought to fit together; should scanning and rotation transformations occur in some order, or in parallel? The simulation technique seems to help us progress in our bootstrap efforts, providing a way to conceptualize large numbers of results and acting as a spotlight, drawing our attention to further interesting empirical questions. In the course of following up its implications, we eliminate other possibilities, and this (as slow and discouraging as it may be) is probably the way to progress.

FURTHER DEVELOPMENTS

A good theory should be as general as possible, and it may be useful to think ahead about how to extend the present one. This section sketches out some possible extensions of our model.

When are Images Consulted?

So far we have only considered how images act as representational structures; we have not discussed when these representations are accessed in the course of cognition. A reasonable supposition is that the only time images must be consulted (if available) is when some sought information is not explicitly entered into the propositional files. For example, if one is asked what shape are a poodle's ears and one has never considered this before, it is unlikely there will be an entry "has round ears" stored in the Poodle file. In this case, one may be able to generate an image and inspect this representation. Similarly, if asked which is larger, a mouse or an elephant, one presumably can look up category information stored propositionally with the corresponding concepts. Whereas a mouse may be categorized as a "small" creature, an elephant probably is categorized as a "large" beast. This information alone is enough to allow one to assess relative sizes. But what if one is asked to compare from memory the sizes of a mouse and a hamster? In this case, the animals both may be categorized as being "small." If so, then comparison of propositionally represented information may not be enough to allow a decision, and images of the two creatures may need to be compared.

Before beginning to extend our model to deal with this situation, we tested this idea by using a size-comparison task wherein people assess the relative sizes of named objects as quickly as possible (see Kosslyn et al., 1977). In this task, people are first given the name of one object and asked either to image it at a "normal" size or at a "subjectively small" size. Some seconds after this, the name of a second object is presented, and subjects are simply to decide as quickly as possible which of the two named objects is the larger. No mention is made of using the first image, and subjects are not told how to arrive at their decisions. We reasoned that if images were in fact compared, then more time ought to be required when the subject starts off with a subjectively small, instead of normal-sized, image. In this case, he either has to "zoom in" on the animal before being able to compare it with an image of the second (both animals must be at the same size scale, as reflected by dot density in our model, before being compared) or must generate a new image at the correct size scale. In contrast, if the initial image is "normal" size to begin with, no transformation or regeneration should be necessary, and the comparison process should finish sooner than when subjectively tiny images are generated initially.

Our first experiment had two groups. People in the first group evaluated pairs that were composed of objects either of disparate or similar sizes (e.g., mouse/elephant versus mouse/hamster). The pairs were presented in a random order. People in the second group also participated in this task but received training in categorizing the stimuli beforehand. The stimuli were divided into two sets, the larger being categorized as "large" and the smaller as "small." Subjects in the second group learned to categorize each stimulus upon hearing its name. Our hope was that when pairs were composed of stimuli from different categories, imagery would not be used, and there would be no effects of the subjective size of the initial image. Interestingly, there were effects of initial image size in *both* groups: More time was required when starting with subjectively small images instead of normal-sized ones, regardless of whether pairs were composed of different-category items. Not only that, but these results occurred even when pairs were composed of objects of very disparate size. Discussions with subjects after the experiment led us to believe that they just "got into the habit" of using imagery, even if it was not absolutely necessary. That is, upon discovering that imagery was sometimes necessary (half of the pairs were composed of very similar-sized things), subjects may simply have decided always to use imagery. We conducted a second experiment to try to discourage this.

Our second experiment on imagery use in size comparison was exactly like the first except that the different types of pairs were now presented in separate blocks. Pairs that were composed of items within the same size category (for the second group) were presented in a block, and pairs composed of objects in different categories were presented as a block. In this case, the size of the initial image did not affect decision times when pairs included objects categorized differently; when pairs were composed of objects in the same category, initial image size was in fact important. Thus, we received support for our hypothesis: When category information was not helpful, people did seem to use images in making decisions about relative sizes of named objects. The results also underscore how flexible people's strategies are, how many options there are for how one may perform a given task.

The foregoing results suggest that we ought to implement a process whereby information is looked up directly in the propositional files and compared and a process whereby images are generated and compared. We currently are attempting to discriminate among more detailed accounts of these processes; in particular, we are studying how propositional information is accessed and compared and whether such processes usually occur prior to, during, or after image generation and comparison. Kosslyn et al. report the beginning stages of this project.

It is worth pausing for a moment to consider how we might account for the fact that images seem to preserve information about the actual size of an object. The problem is that when smaller objects are seen close at hand, more spatial extent may be encoded than when larger objects are seen at further distances. Thus, simply noting the extent represented in the deep representation will not necessarily indicate anything about actual size. Furthermore, generating the images themselves will not automatically help one to assess the actual relative sizes of two objects seen at different times and distances. We plan to solve this problem by making use of an introspection that "distance" in an image is reflected by level of resolution: Further things are "fuzzier," whereas nearer images have more detail. If "level of detail" could be used as an index of distance, then one could derive relative sizes by first adjusting the images so that they seemed to be at the same distance and then by simply assessing apparent sizes. In our model, dot density could be taken as a measure of resolution; the smaller an image gets, the more crammed together the dots become and the most indistinguishable are small details. Simple dot density is not enough, however, as different objects are composed of different materials — a mirror even very close up will not have as many visible surface perturbations as a tree trunk some distance away. We hope to solve this problem by having a parameter that will allow the program to adjust the dot densities so that they are comparable when the nature of the material composing the imaged object is taken into account (this information will be stored propositionally). Prior to generating images, then, dot densities will be appropriately adjusted by setting the R values for each image such that the number of dots within a given distance from the origin are equated (after weighting for material is performed). R values will be set in exactly the same way that they are in preparation for integrating a part into an image (e.g., when placing a cushion on a seat, one first assesses the size of the seat in the image and adjusts the cushion so it fits flush on it). Once the R values are set, surface images can be generated and compared vis-a-vis relative area, breadth, etc. Furthermore, any error in estimating densities in the deep representations can then be corrected when the actual image is reconstructed.

The way in which our model allows deep representations to be adjusted suggests that under some circumstances deep representations alone may provide the information necessary to make some decision about an object's appearance. If one sees a set of stimuli that are all at the same distance and orientation, and these stimuli vary only in terms of height, there seems no reason why the underlying representations could not be consulted directly when comparing relative heights. In this case, one would need only to discover the sum of the largest R values for points falling directly above and below the origin for each figure and then to compare these total R values. We have yet to investigate this notion, but it stands as another inspiration offered by our simulation approach.

Imagery and Perception

Imagery and like-modality perception intuitively seem to have much in common, and many researchers have explored this possibility (e.g., Brooks, 1967; Segal & Fusella, 1970). It is commonly asserted that imagery and perception share some of the same processing mechanisms, but rarely has any attempt been made to develop the details of this claim. Let us consider two possible loci where imaginal and perceptual processing might utilize the same structures.

First, it may be that the representations underlying the visual experience of perception and imagery occur in the same structure. That is, the surface display mechanism could conceivably be used to support representations generated from memory (imagery) or derived from sensory input (perception). This notion was basic to our entire discussion of image processing at the surface level and provided the grounds for most of our predictions for the experiments described in the discussion of the first issue. In addition, this notion would account for the finding that imagery selectively disrupts perception in the same modality (see Kosslyn & Pomerantz, 1977). Virtually all of the discussion about imagery/perception commonalities are concerned with shared surface level processing (see Paivio, 1971).

A second shared structure could occur at the deep level; this possibility has not been considered to date, as far as I know, but is suggested by our model. Brooks (Chapter 7) suggests that much of concept learning occurs via a process of encoding exemplars of the category and then using these exemplars to determine whether a new instance is or is not a member of the category. It seems entirely possible that a similar process occurs in pattern recognition. In this case, it may be that something like our stored imaginal deep representations are somehow "correlated" with the encoded deep representation of a stimulus. That is, some measure of similarity is obtained between the file(s) of R, *Theta* coordinates derived from encoding a new stimulus with those stored in memory. One interesting consequence of using R, *Theta* representations is that they would be relatively easily processed such that size constancy would be maintained. The memory representation most similar to the encoded one would then instigate an "hypothesis-testing" procedure. In this case, the procedures that define parts of the object (e.g., for a chair, seats, arms, cushions, etc.) would be invoked in an effort to classify parts of the surface representation. If a given number of parts were found, the object would be "recognized." Furthermore, some tests could be weighted more heavily than others (e.g., a seat may be considered more important for a chair than arms), and when a sum weight is reached, regardless of which successful tests contributed to this sum, the object is considered "recognized." If enough categorical procedures were not satisfied, tests could be executed for the object associated with the deep representation next most similar to the encoded one (i.e., a new hypothesis could be tested).

Images and Prototypes

Numerous theorists (notably Eleanor Rosch) have discussed prototypes of categories in terms of "prototypical images." The prototypical dog, for example, might be imaged as a black, medium-sized, not especially long-haired canine. What one does with this image, however, is not clear; one certainly does not seem to image a prototype and then use the image as a template during pattern recognition. The present speculations suggest a mechanism to account for the formation of prototypical images and their role in perception. Brooks' proposal implies that numerous exemplars are stored in memory, and it is difficult to imagine how this could not be true (no matter how concepts are learned). As noted previously, the same representations that serve as deep representations of images also could perform double duty in pattern recognition. Let us consider this claim in a little more detail.

We assume that more than a single file is encoded when one looks at an object: One file serves as the skeleton; the rest function as details. However the details are segmented and encoded, we would expect the same rules usually to result in a similar "parsing" (loosely defined) whenever the same object or scene is encountered. For example, if portions that are differently colored are encoded separately on one occasion, the same property should result in them being separately encoded later as well. Hence, one presumably has a set of files in long-term memory and a set of files in an encoding buffer that are compared with each other. In the last section we assumed that these sets were treated as units. But that does not have to be so; the skeletal file and subfiles encoded during perception could be compared independently, in which case they might be best matched to files and subfiles stored with different exemplars of the same class of objects. Over a course of time, some files and subfiles will prove to be more useful than others, will tend to correlate highly with encoded representations more often than others. These most-highly-similar portions stored in memory may then be given high accessing priority; perhaps the different files and subfiles may be ordered as if they were on an Anderson and Bower (1973) "GET list," with the most useful near the top of the list. These most easily accessed parts, then, would be used to generate a composite image when one is simply asked to image a named object. Alternatively, a special file could be set up that contains copies of these most useful image files and subfiles. In this case, this would be the file accessed when one is asked simply to image a given object. Either way, the composite image should have all of the properties of a prototype, and its deep representation would be most commonly used to instigate hypothesis testing of a newly encounted exemplar of that kind of object. These notions obviously leave much to be desired in the way of details, but seem promising and could be developed.

CONCLUDING REMARKS

Two fundamental points are made in this chapter—one general and one particular. The general point concerns the study of imagery and visual memory. Not only does imagery seem amenable to systematic study, but the study of imagery may well provide a gateway into understanding many memory and perceptual processes. There does not seem to be anything mystical about the notion that people have mental images, nor does it seem to require "hocus pocus" in order to talk about how images might function in the storage and processing of information. It seems clear that our understanding of imagery depends on collection of interesting behavioral data; rational considerations and introspections taken alone usually did not provide compelling motivations for adopting a given position (although they sometimes provided valuable converging arguments for particular positions when considered in conjunction with behavior data).

The particular point made here is that it is useful to attempt first to discriminate among alternative basic operating characteristics and then to construct a model that incorporates the most reasonable inferred principles. The model is intended to provide accounts of numerous and varied data, and also should motivate further research, producing new data to be explained. Further, the accounts of these results should be parsimonious and straightforward. Although the present beginnings seem promising in these regards, it is still much too early to utter glowing pronouncements and offer overly optimistic prognoses. At present, our enterprise has two glaring deficiencies: First, the accounts of the data are somewhat loose; as more constraints are built into the model, however, our explanations should become more precise (and ultimately include predictions of actual response times and the like, instead of just qualitative trends). Second, we have not modeled the entire cognitive system, and hence still suffer from some of the perils of the "inference problem." We have tried to place constraints on the interfaces with the missing components of the system, however. In particular, a perceptual system must have as its output data structures in the form of our long-term memory files. We have not begun to specify how such a parser would work, however, nor have we studied how imagery is used in problem solving and the like. In addition, the entire issue of how remembered perceptual and conceptual information interact is not treated very well at present. But at least the questions and issues are becoming clearer, and this is no small thing.

ACKNOWLEDGMENTS

This work was supported by NIMH Grant 1 RO3 MH 27012–01 and NSF Grant BNS 76–16987. The author wishes to thank Bob Abelson, Al Collins, Steve Pinker, Howard Egeth, Beth Loftus, Dedre Gentner, Reid Hastie, Pierre Jolicoeur, and, of course, Eleanor Rosch for helpful suggestions and insightful comments on this chapter. In addition, I most especially wish to thank Steven Shwartz, without whom the present project would not have progressed nearly so far nor so well as it has at this date. Finally, I wish to acknowledge that the physics of the useful analogy developed in the first section depend on some additional assumptions, but I'll leave it as an exercise for the reader to figure out how!

REFERENCES

Anderson, J. R. *Language, memory, and thought.* Hillsdale, N.J.: Lawrence Erlbaum Associates, 1976.
Anderson, J. R., & Bower, G. H. *Human associative memory.* New York: V. H. Winston & Sons, 1973.
Baylor, G. W. *A treatise on the mind's eye.* Unpublished doctoral dissertation, Carnegie-Mellon University, 1971.
Brooks, L. The suppression of visualization by reading. *Quarterly Journal of Experimental Psychology*, 1967, *19*, 289–299.
Conrad, C. Cognitive economy in semantic memory. *Journal of Experimental Psychology*, 1972, *92*, 149–154.
Cooper, L. A. Mental rotation of random two-dimensional shapes. *Cognitive Psychology*, 1975, *7*, 20–43.
Cooper, L. A., & Shepard, R. N. Chronometric studies of the rotation of mental images. In W. G. Chase (Ed.), *Visual information processing.* New York: Academic Press, 1973.
Farley, A. M. *VIPS: A visual imagery and perception system; the result of protocol analysis.* Unpublished doctoral dissertation, Carnegie-Mellon University, 1974.

Garner, W. R., Hake, H. W., & Eriksen, C. W. Operationism and the concept of perception. *Psychological Review*, 1956, *63*, 149–159.

Kosslyn, S. M. Scanning visual images: Some structural implications. *Perception and Psychophysics*, 1973, *14*, 90–94.

Kosslyn, S. M. *Constructing visual images.* Unpublished doctoral dissertation, Stanford University, 1974.

Kosslyn, S. M. *Evidence for analogue representation.* Paper presented at the conference on Theoretical Issues in Natural Language Processing. Cambridge, Mass., June 1975. (a)

Kosslyn, S. M. Information representation in visual images. *Cognitive Psychology*, 1975, *7*, 341–370. (b)

Kosslyn, S. M. Can imagery be distinguished from other forms of internal representation? Evidence from studies of information retrieval time. *Memory and Cognition*, 1976, *4*, 291–297.

Kosslyn, S. M. The representational-development hypothesis. In P. A. Ornstein (Ed.), *Memory development in children.* Hillsdale, N.J.: Lawrence Erlbaum Associates, in press.

Kosslyn, S. M., Ball, T. M., & Reiser, B. J. Visual images preserve metric spatial information: Evidence from studies of image scanning. *Journal of Experimental Psychology: Human Perception and Performance*, in press.

Kosslyn, S. M., Murphy, G. L., Bemesderfer, M. E., & Feinstein, K. J. Category and continuum in mental comparison. *Journal of Experimental Psychology: General*, 1977, *106*, 341–375.

Kosslyn, S. M., & Pomerantz, J. R. Imagery, propositions, and the form of internal representations. *Cognitive Psychology*, 1977, *9*, 52–76.

Kosslyn, S. M., Reiser, B. J., & Greenbarg, P. E. *Generating visual images.* Manuscript in preparation, 1977.

Kosslyn, S. M., & Shwartz, S. P. A simulation of visual imagery. *Cognitive Science*, 1977, *1*, 265–296.

Kosslyn, S. M., & Shwartz, S. P. Visual images as spatial representations in active memory. In E. Riseman & A. Hanson (Eds.), *Machine vision.* New York: Academic Press, in press.

Kruskal, J. B. Multidimensional scaling by optimizing goodness of fit to a nonmetric hypothesis. *Psychometrika*, 1964, *29*, 1–27.

Lea, G. Chronometric analysis of the method of loci. *Journal of Experimental Psychology: Human Perception and Performance*, 1975, *2*, 95–104.

McKim, R. H. *Experiences in visual thinking.* Monterey, Calif.: Brooks/Cole, 1972.

Moran, T. P. *The symbolic imagery hypothesis: A production system model.* Unpublished doctoral dissertation, Carnegie-Mellon University, 1973.

Newell, A. You can't play 20 questions with nature and win. In W. G. Chase (Ed.), *Visual information processing.* New York: Academic Press, 1973.

Paivio, A. *Imagery and verbal processes.* New York: Holt, Rinehart & Winston, 1971.

Platt, J. R. Strong inference. *Science.* October 16, 1964, pp. 347–352.

Pylyshyn, Z. W. What the mind's eye tells the mind's brain: A critique of mental imagery. *Psychological Bulletin*, 1973, *80*, 1–24.

Pylyshyn, Z. W. *Do we need images and analogues?* Paper presented at the conference on Theoretical Issues in Natural Language Processing, Cambridge, Mass., June 1975.

Segal, S. J., & Fusella, V. Influence of imaged pictures and sounds on detection of visual and auditory signals. *Journal of Experimental Psychology*, 1970, *83*, 458–464.

Shepard, R. N. The analysis of proximities: Multidimensional scaling with an unknown distance function. I. *Psychometrika*, 1962, *27*, 125–140; II. *Psychometrika*, 1962, *27*, 219–246.

Shepard, R. N., & Feng, C. A chronometric study of mental paper folding. *Cognitive Psychology*, 1972, *3*, 228–243.

Simon, H. A. What is visual imagery? An information processing interpretation. In L. W. Gregg (Ed.), *Cognition in learning and memory*. New York: Wiley, 1972.

Weber, R. J., & Bach, M. Visual and speech imagery. *British Journal of Psychology*, 1969, *60*, 199–202.

Weber, R. J., & Harnish, R. Visual imagery for words: The Hebb test. *Journal of Experimental Psychology*, 1974, *102*, 409–414.

Weber, R. J., Kelley, J., & Little, S. Is visual imagery sequencing under verbal control? *Journal of Experimental Psychology*, 1972, *96*, 354–362.

Winston, P. H. *Learning structural descriptions from examples* (MIT AI-TR-231). Cambridge, Mass.: M.I.T. Artificial Intelligence Laboratory Project, 1970.

9 Fundamental Aspects of Cognitive Representation

Stephen E. Palmer
University of California, Berkeley

This chapter was born of an ill-defined but definite feeling that we, as cognitive psychologists, do not really understand our concepts of representation. We propose them, talk about them, argue about them, and try to obtain evidence in support of them, but we do not understand them in any fundamental sense. Anyone who has attempted to read the literature related to cognitive representation quickly becomes confused — and with good reason. The field is obtuse, poorly defined, and embarrassingly disorganized. Among the most popular terms, one finds the following: visual codes, verbal codes, spatial codes, physical codes, name codes, image codes, analog representations, digital representations, propositional representations, first-order isomorphisms, second-order isomorphisms, multidimensional spaces, templates, features, structural descriptions, relational networks, multicomponent vectors, and even holograms. This abundance of language for talking about representation would be a good thing if all the distinctions were clear and if they fit together in a systematic way. The fact is that they are not clear and do not fit together. Different people use the same term in different ways and different terms in the same way. These are not characteristics of a scientific field with a deep understanding of its problem, much less its solution. This chapter is an extended inquiry into the nature of the problem of cognitive representation. The rationale is that a solution is more likely to be achieved if the problem is understood properly.

In order to make systematic progress on problems concerning cognitive representation, we must begin at the beginning: *What is representation?* This is a question few psychologists have ever asked and even fewer have made any serious attempt to answer. It is so basic a question that one might wonder whether its answer would be of any value to cognitive psychology. It is the main thesis of this chapter that the answer is enormously important and will change our understanding of both theories and experiments concerned with cognitive representation.

Let us assume that our goal is to specify as clearly as possible the nature of people's internal representations of the world. That is, we want to construct clear, concise theories of cognitive representation that can be evaluated using the methods of psychology as a behavioral science. The standard method of evaluation is to ask questions by experimental hypothesis testing. The answers to these questions delineate the nature of an adequate theory. If this is a reasonable characterization of the situation, is there any reason to believe that knowing (or having a theory of) what representation is will help us in either the theoretical or experimental enterprise?

Trying to determine the nature of cognitive representation without first knowing about representation as a general construct is much like trying to determine the nature of oak trees without first knowing about trees as a general class of objects. Suppose there are two botanists whose task is to describe the essential characteristics of oak trees by performing a series of tests on a given specimen. Botanist A has a thoroughgoing knowledge of trees: what their defining characteristics are, how types of trees differ from one another in ways that are relevant to classification, and how they differ in ways that are irrelevant. Botanist B knows none of these things. Botanist A works quickly and efficiently. She makes the measurements necessary to describe oaks versus other types of trees and only those measurements. She does not bother to note that oaks have bark and leaves because she knows that all trees have these attributes. Nor does she bother to count the number of branches on this particular tree, because she knows this to be irrelevant to her task. When she is done, she describes oaks as, say, trees with properties a, b, and c. Botanist B, however, necessarily performs many more measurements than A. If he is diligent enough, he eventually discovers the defining characteristics of oaks, but these are mixed together with properties that are relevant only to treeness and with other properties that are relevant only to this particular specimen. When he is done, his description might be that oaks are objects with properties a, b, c, d, ... Obviously, A has an advantage over B in knowing something about the general nature of trees. She is able to make fewer empirical tests, and her description is simpler and more specific to the relevant factors.

Although the analogy is rough, the major point is clear. If representations, like trees, have certain defining characteristics, certain relevant dimensions of variation, and certain irrelevant dimensions of variation, then knowledge of these things (or at least some working hypotheses about them) should be important to psychologists for very tangible reasons. It defines the kind of experiments that are deemed important and relevant. It specifies the general form of our theoretical descriptions and separates essential aspects from nonessential ones. In fact, without some "metatheoretical" framework of this sort, it is not clear that the theoretical and experimental enterprises are meaningful at all. In short, the answer to the representational question provides the larger framework for research that Kuhn (1962) has called a "paradigm."

If this is so, then we must currently have something that serves the function of a representational metatheory. As far as I can tell, the present framework for representations is a loose system of distinctions and classifications. Representational theories are defined by descriptive terms like those mentioned earlier: templates, features, structural descriptions, and so forth. Therefore, psychologists do experiments that purport to test these alternatives. Such experiments abound in the psychological literature. The issue is whether these are sensible questions to ask in our experiments. Ultimately, this boils down to asking whether our current framework for representation is sensible.

There are several observations suggesting that it is not. First, the distinctions we make do not follow from or lead to any coherent view of representation in general. This is why the basic question − what is representation − is so hard to answer. Second, virtually none of the current distinctions have ever been explicitly defined. We can point to some samples of each concept, but this ability is something less than a proper definition. Part of the reason they have not been defined is that good definitions are much easier to construct within a larger framework. Third, the distinctions do not relate to each other systematically. Is the template/feature distinction independent of, the same as, or otherwise related to the analog/propositional distinction? How do templates relate to prototypes? Our inability to provide good answers to such questions is symptomatic of our understanding of the concepts themselves. Fourth − and perhaps most apparent to experimental psychologists − the empirical tests of such distinctions rarely, if ever, lead to conclusive results. There always seem to be ready explanations from the allegedly discredited theoretical position. This fact can be partially ascribed to complications such as processing differences, because both representation and processing assumptions are required to predict performance. But often I suspect the problem is that many of the distinctions we purport to test are not mutually exclusive at a level that is meaningful for our goals and methods.

As Kuhn (1962) has noted, a scientific discipline does not abandon a reigning paradigm simply because it is seen to be defective. Rather, another must emerge to take its place. The new paradigm should be able to make sense of things that were formerly puzzling and bring a more elegant and coherent view to the domain of the field. In the rest of this chapter, I propose a new view of cognitive representation based explicitly on an answer to the general representational question. This view is developed informally with an emphasis on noncognitive representation. It is then applied to the concepts of the older framework. As far as possible, definitions are provided for constructs like templates, features, structural descriptions, prototypes, isomorphisms, propositions, and analogs. Relationships among them are clarified, and relevant aspects are separated from irrelevant ones. The results show that many of the mistakes we have made in understanding representation are alarmingly fundamental.

REPRESENTATIONAL METATHEORY

Let us turn now to the basic question: What is representation? The first problem is how to attack this question without considering cognitive representation itself. The answer, of course, is to examine noncognitive forms of representation, either real or artificially constructed for this particular purpose. Cognitive representation is exceedingly complex and difficult to study. Other sorts of representations are simple and easy to study. The plan is to move from simple representations to complex ones so that the basic issues are clear from the outset.

Some Examples of Representation

A representation is, first and foremost, something that stands for something else. In other words, it is some sort of model of the thing (or things) it represents. This description implies the existence of two related but functionally separate worlds: the *represented world* and the *representing world.* The job of the representing world is to reflect some aspects of the represented world in some fashion. Not all aspects of the represented world need to be modeled; not all aspects of the representing world need to model an aspect of the represented world. However, there must be some corresponding aspects if one world is to represent the other. In order to specify a representation completely, then, one must state: (1) what the represented world is; (2) what the representing world is; (3) what aspects of the represented world are being modeled; (4) what aspects of the representing world are doing the modeling; and (5) what are the correspondences between the two worlds. A representation is really a *representational system* that includes all five aspects.

Figure 9.1 shows some simple examples of representational systems that illustrate the previous points. In all cases, the represented world is the set of four rectangles shown in Fig. 9.1A. These drawings, simple as they are, contain many aspects that could be modeled in a representation. The representing Worlds B, C, and D show how different aspects of the same represented world can be modeled by the same representing world. World B reflects the relative height of the rectangles (a, b, c, d) by the relative length of the corresponding lines (a', b', c', d'). In other words, the fact that a is taller than b in World A is reflected by the fact that a' is longer than b' in World B. Similar statements can be made for any pair of rectangles in World A and the corresponding lines in World B. It is always true that if x is taller than y in World A, then x' is longer than y' in World B. One could describe this representational system by saying, "World B is a representation of World A in which the relative length of lines in B corresponds to the relative height of rectangles in A." The implication is that any question that could be answered about relative height in A could be equally well answered by considering relative length in B as long as the mapping of rectangles to lines were known.

World C reflects the relative width of rectangles in A by the relative length of lines. For example, the fact that d is wider than any other rectangle in World A

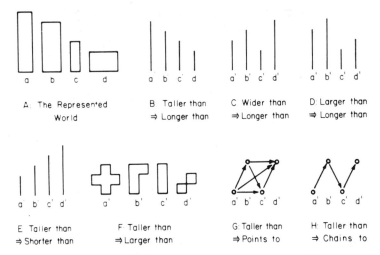

A: The Represented   B Taller than   C Wider than   D: Larger than
World   ⇒ Longer than   ⇒ Longer than   ⇒ Longer than

E Taller than   F: Taller than   G: Taller than   H: Taller than
⇒ Shorter than   ⇒ Larger than   ⇒ Points to   ⇒ Chains to

FIG. 9.1. Examples of representation. The represented world in each case consists of the objects shown in A. For each representing world, the correspondence of objects is indicated by the letters beneath them, and the correspondence of relations is indicated by the expression beneath each world.

is reflected in the fact that d' is longer than any other line in World C. World D performs the same kind of representational function for relative size of the rectangles in World A. These examples demonstrate that one cannot specify a representation simply by pointing to a representing world of objects. Without knowledge of the represented world, its modeled aspects, and the correspondence between the two worlds, representations B, C, and D are identical. Given this information, however, it is clear that they are quite different.

Worlds B, E, F, G, and H illustrate how the same aspect of a represented world can be modeled using different representing worlds. World B models height of rectangles in terms of line length; the taller the rectangle, the longer the line. World E also models rectangle height in terms of line length; but here, the taller the rectangle, the shorter the line. This representational system differs from that of B only in that a different relation ("shorter" rather than "longer") is used to model the represented relation ("taller").

World F reflects the height of rectangles by the size (area) of closed geometric forms. Note that object shape has no correlate in the represented world. In addition to using a different relation to represent "taller than," this example illustrates that there may be other aspects of the representing world that are irrelevant to its modeling function.

World G embodies a rather different way of preserving height relations among the rectangles in A. Here, the fact that a is taller than b in A is reflected in a' pointing to b' in G. What makes this kind of representation different from those discussed previously is that: (1) the representing objects corresponding to the rectangles are identical; and (2) new elements (the arrows) have been added that correspond explicitly to the relation being modeled ("taller than"). It is important to notice that the arrows of World G are not "object elements" but "relational elements." That is, the presence of a given arrow in the representational world does not correspond to any single object in the represented world. It is tempting to characterize the difference between representations B and G by saying that B represents relations ("taller than") by relations ("longer than") while G represents relations ("taller than") by elements (the arrows). The real difference is more subtle, however. "Points to" (more accurately, "is arrow-connected to") in World G is a relation just as "longer than" is in World B. The difference is that although "longer than" is a relation that can hold between an ordered pair of objects, "is arrow-connected to" is a relation that can hold between an ordered pair of objects only by virtue of each being related to a third element (the relational arrow) in a particular way.

World H illustrates yet another type of representation. Like World G, it contains explicit relational elements, but the arrows are not sufficient to model the "taller than" relation in A. "Is arrow-connected to" models some other, more restricted relation that might be called "next-taller than." In order for "taller than" to be represented, the "points to" relation must be made transitive. The solution is to use the "chains to" relation (more accurately, "is arrow-path-connected to"), which is essentially a transitive version of "points to." It is easy to see that if all the "chains to" relations were made explicit in World H by arrows, the resulting representation would be identical to World G.

Intuitively, what all these representations have in common is that they contain information that reflects some information about the world they represent. The information contained by the representing worlds can be the same yet can reflect different information about the represented world. Worlds B, C, D, and E of Fig. 9.1 are examples of this situation. In contrast, the information contained by the representing worlds can be quite different, yet can reflect the same information about the represented world. Worlds B, E, F, G, and H are examples of this possibility. No two representational systems in Fig. 9.1 are exactly the same, but some are more similar than others. We examine these similarities and differences in more detail shortly.

Operational Relations

Thus far a representing world has been treated as a "thing" that stands for a represented world that is also a "thing." It does so by virtue of certain relationships between it and the world it represents. But the concept of representation also includes an operational component. The representing world can be used for certain purposes instead of the represented world. In order for this to happen, there must be processes to operate on the represented world. We now consider briefly the interdependence of representation and its processing environment.

It is axiomatic within an information-processing framework that one cannot discuss representation without considering processes. The role of processing operations in the present analysis is that they functionally determine the relations that hold among the object elements. Consider World G of Fig. 9.1. The arrows connecting the circles in the diagram are only meaningful and useful if there are operations for finding them and the circles they connect. The operations of finding an arrow and its associated circles *define* the "points to" relation. Similarly, in World B, some operations define the "longer than" relation between pairs of lines, and other operations define the "chains to" relation in World H.

In these cases, we relied on our intuitive notions of "longer than," "points to," and "chains to." This works because we all have more or less the same operational concepts for these relations. In constructing processes to use these representations, however, operational definitions must be specified in terms of what the processes *do* to determine whether or not a particular relation holds. It is possible to have a representation that seems nonsensical by intuitive notions but is appropriate and sensible given the processses that operate upon it. The height of rectangles, for example, might be represented by line length where there is no intuitively obvious relationship (such as our usual concepts of "longer than" or "shorter than") to model "taller than." But if there is a process that *interprets* the length of lines — whatever they may be — such that corresponding lengths are *functionally* ordered just as the rectangle heights are ordered, then there is an *operational relation* defined by this process that corresponds to the "taller than" relation in the represented world.

A more familiar example of the same general concept is the "next" element of a list in list-processing computer languages. There is no necessary relationship between one element of a list and the next element in terms of physical location in memory or their numerical addresses. The list-processing language operationally defines the "next" element as the one "pointed to" (i.e., addressed indirectly) by the current element. Thus the "next" element is *functionally* next to the current element in terms of access order by the interpretive process. In an array-processing language, the situation is different. The "next" element of an array is defined such that it is also the next numerical address in memory. This does not mean that "next" is any less operationally defined in the array-processing language but only that it is more intuitively obvious what the relationship is. "Next" is completely defined by the operations in both cases.

The importance of this argument is that the relations in a representation are operational relations rather than apparent relations. Operational relations are simply those defined by the processes that interpret the representation. [Pylyshyn's "semantic interpretation function" is very similar to the present concept of operational relations (Pylyshyn, 1975).] Thus, in talking about operational relations, we implicitly include certain aspects of processing operations in the representation itself. Without those processes, the representation is meaningless.

The dependence of representation on processing goes even deeper. There is an important sense in which the only information contained in a representation is that for which operations are defined. In other words, it does not matter whether certain relationships could, in principle, be derived from a given representing world if there are no methods for doing so. A good example is Shepard's (1962a, 1962b) multidimensional scaling procedure. Suppose there is a matrix that tables the ordinal distances among, say, 30 cities in the United States. It is obvious to everyone that this representation contains weak information about relative distances between cities. What is not so obvious — indeed, what was not known until recently — is that this matrix contains a great deal more information about distance and some information about direction as well. In fact, the matrix contains enough information to produce a reasonable approximation to a map containing those cities. The proof that such information exists is that Shepard's scaling algorithm (and its descendants) is able to recover it from the original matrix. We now know that a great deal of locational information is implicitly contained in an ordinal matrix of this sort, but prior to Shepard's demonstration, this was not thought to be the case. More to the point, however, is that simply knowing it is theoretically there is not sufficient for it to be considered part of the represented information. No person or machine can derive it without actually performing the operations. In short, the implicit locational information is *not there at all* except for the computer programmed to extract it, and for that computer, it *is there* even though it does not seem to be.

This rather esoteric example illustrates a very simple fact. The only information contained in a representation is that for which operations are defined to obtain it. When stated in this way, the point seems almost trivial, but it is not. As we see later, the representational nature of several kinds of theories have been universally misunderstood precisely because this fact is not appreciated. In general, we must be very careful about deciding just what information is contained in a representing world. The notion of operational relations changes the way we view our constructs of representation.

The Nature of Representation

Let us stop now and consider what we have learned from the analysis thus far. First, a representation requires a certain kind of relationship between two functionally separate worlds. Each world consists of objects that are characterized by relations that hold among them. These relations are operationally defined. The function of a representing world is to preserve information about the represented world. We can tie all of this together by assuming that the information contained in the two worlds is the set of operational relations among objects. Preserving information, then, is equivalent to having corresponding relations in the two worlds.

The nature of representation is that there exists a correspondence (mapping) from objects in the represented world to objects in the representing world such that at least some relations in the represented world are structurally preserved in the representing world.[1] In other words, if a represented relation, R, holds for ordered pairs of represented objects, $<x, y>$, then the representational mapping requires that a corresponding relation, R', holds for each corresponding pair of representing objects, $<x', y'>$. This is just a very abstract and general way of describing situations like those shown in Fig. 9.1. The "taller than" relation in World A is preserved by the "longer than" relation in World B, by the "shorter than" relation in World E, by the "bigger than" relation in World F, by the "points to" relation in World G, and by the "chains to" relation in World H.

The same sort of representational relationship can hold for properties of individual objects. All objects in the represented world that are, say, 2 feet tall must correspond to objects in the representing world that have whatever property corresponds to 2-feet-tallness. This fits our description of representation if we view properties of individual objects as relations that hold for single objects. In fact, this is just the way properties are modeled in set theory — as "unary" relations (defined for individual objects) that are no different in principle from "binary" relations (defined for pairs of objects) or "n-ary" relations (defined for sets of n objects). We use the terms "unary relations" and "properties" interchangeably.

We now have at least an informal answer to the basic representational question. A world, X, is a representation of another world, Y, if at least some of the relations for objects of X are preserved by relations for corresponding objects of Y. The second goal is to characterize the ways in which two representations can differ from one another. A "representation" obviously refers to a representing world in relation to its represented world. The question of how two representations can differ, then, is really a question about how two worlds can differ from one another in the way they relate to their respective represented worlds. Given our definition of representation, it is clear that two representations can differ in the objects and/or the relations they represent. Having noted that two representations can differ in the objects they represent, we focus our attention on how two representations can differ when the objects they represent are the same.

If a pair of representations model the same set of objects, then there are two major kinds of differences to consider. First, two representations can model different relations of the represented objects. This is the case in Worlds B, C, and D of Fig. 9.1. Second, two representations can model the same relations, but in different ways. This is the case in Worlds B, E, F, G, and H of Fig. 9.1. Because representation is concerned with preserving information, and information consists of relations, we call the latter situation *informationally equivalent representation*

---

[1]This definition has a straightforward formalization in terms of model theory (Tarski, 1954). The represented and representing worlds are relational systems, each consisting of a set of objects and sets of relations. A representational system is an ordered triple consisting of the two relational systems and a homomorphic function that maps the represented objects into the representing objects. The basic approach is similar to that used in measurement theory for numerical representation (Krantz et al., 1971; Scott & Suppes, 1958; Suppes & Zinnes, 1963). This formalization, however, is beyond the current level of discussion.

and the former *nonequivalent representation*. The only remaining cases are those in which the same relations are modeled in the same way. This situation is called *completely equivalent representation*.

Nonequivalent Representations

Two representations that reflect different relations of the same objects are not equivalent in the sense that they do not preserve the same information. In other words, given two such representations and their processing systems, one could not answer the same questions about the represented objects from both representations. There are many possible differences that could result in this situation.

Type of Information. The most obvious condition for nonequivalence is that two representations can model qualitatively different dimensions of variation in the represented world. For present purposes, a "dimension" is just a set of mutually exclusive relations, only one of which is true for each object or set of objects on which the relations are defined. Properties of individual objects like height, length, size, and so forth are unary dimensions, because each individual object has only one value for each. The "values" along a dimension are simply the relations that comprise the dimension. Thus, "being two feet tall," "being red," and "having a hand" are possible values for unary dimensions of height, color, and handedness. Binary dimensions are defined just as unary dimensions except that they can hold only for ordered pairs of objects. The distance between two objects and their relative sizes are examples of binary dimensions, because one-and-only-one of the component relations can hold between each ordered pair. Similarly, *n*-ary dimensions can be defined for larger sets of objects — e.g., the relative distance between an object and two others.

The intended notion of differences in type of information represented is that one representing world may preserve some (but not necessarily all) information about a given dimension, whereas the other representing world may preserve no information about that dimension. In other words, one world represents that dimension somehow, but the other does not. Worlds B and C are examples, because B represents relative height information whereas C does not, and C represents relative width information whereas B does not. Clearly, this is an important way in which two representations can differ, because they cannot be used to answer the same *kind* of questions about the represented objects, much less the same specific questions.

Resolution. If two representations model the same dimension, they can still differ in many ways. The dimensional representation in one world may contain just a few relations, whereas in another it may contain many. The limiting cases are two relations and an infinite number. Consider some possible representations of the length dimension. In one representation, all lengths are categorized into just two values: "short" or "long." In the other, they are categorized into, say, 100 values. There will be many objects having the same representation of length in the first system that have different representations of length in the second. These two representations are nonequivalent, because there are questions for which they provide different answers. For example, two objects both classified as "long" in the two-valued system might fall in two different length categories within the 100-valued system.

In general, any dimension can be described as containing m relations. The number of relations comprising the dimension is one important aspect of its *resolution* or *grain*. The larger the number of relations in a dimension, the higher the resolution and the finer the grain. We are presently assuming that the assignment of relations (values along the dimension) is completely deterministic, but it need not be. One could define a probability distribution over the m dimensional values for each object to construct a probabilistic representational system. This possibility, however, is beyond our present level of inquiry.

The other aspect of resolution is concerned with the particular relations that are preserved. Two representations might each have the same number of levels without those levels containing objects that correspond to the same objects in the represented world. Two maps, for example, might have three levels of dot-size to represent city-size. If they used different criteria for assigning city-size to dot-size, the same city might be represented as a large dot in one map and a medium dot in the other. In order for the resolution of two representations to be identical for some dimension, then, they must not only have the same number of levels but must classify the represented dimension in the same way.

Uniqueness. If two representations represent the same dimension with the same resolution, they can still be nonequivalent in the sense defined earlier. Consider two maps again with three levels for their representation of city-size. In one map, the cities are represented as black dots of three different sizes such that the larger the city, the larger the dot. In the other map, the cities are represented as red, blue, and yellow dots of the same size. Using the first map, one can tell which of two cities is the larger if they are represented as different sized dots. That is, the ordering of dot sizes preserves the ordering of city sizes to some extent. In the second map, this is not obviously true. One can tell whether two cities are generally the same in size or different, but their order is not necessarily represented. If there is a "key" on this map that indicates the size-to-color mapping, one can figure out the relative sizes. The key provides what is needed — an operational ordering relation for the colors. Without the key, however, the two maps are not equivalent, because questions about relative size of cities could be answered from the first map but not from the second.

We call this kind of difference the *uniqueness* of a dimensional representation, because it is analogous to the concept of uniqueness in measurement theory

(Krantz et al., 1971; Suppes & Zinnes, 1963). In the case where the levels of a dimension are not functionally ordered, only same/different relations are defined for pairs of dimensional values. This kind of representation is called *nominal*, after the similar case of measurement scales. It might be thought that nominal representations are so weak that they are uninteresting, but this is not so. Nearly all current theories of language representation are exclusively nominal, and many theories of perceptual representation contain substantial nominal components. Any dimension in which only identity is preserved is nominal.

If the relations of a dimension functionally order the representing objects as the represented objects are ordered, then order information is preserved as well as identity information. Such representations are called *ordinal*, after the corresponding type of measurement scale. Ordinal representations preserve more information than nominal ones in the sense that additional higher-order relations are meaningful; "different" relations of nominal dimensions are divided into "more" and "less" relations in ordinal dimensions.

It is not clear how to describe other types of uniqueness properties for non-numerical representation (e.g., interval, ratio, or absolute representations corresponding to those types of scales). Certainly, when the representation is numerical, these concepts are meaningful. Perhaps they are in other kinds of representation as well if the correlates of numerical transformations can be identified. For present purposes, we simply note that such an analysis seems plausible.

Informationally Equivalent Representations

Two representations that preserve the same relations about the same objects are called *informationally equivalent*, because they are indistinguishable in terms of the information they preserve *about the represented world*. This does not mean that the representations are identical, of course. They can preserve the same information in many different ways. The fact that their methods of representation differ should not obscure the fact that they provide essentially the same view of the world they represent.

There are countless ways in which informationally equivalent representations can differ. These differences may be subtle (e.g., Worlds B and E of Fig. 9.1) or obvious (e.g., Worlds B and G of Fig. 9.1). No attempt is made here to catalog all the possibilities. Rather, I focus on two distinctions that seem to be important.

Intrinsic Versus Extrinsic Representation. The first distinction is most clearly exemplified by the contrast between Worlds B and G as representations of rectangle height in Fig. 9.1A. Consider two facts about the nature of the represented relation "taller than." First, if an object x is taller than an object y, it cannot also be true that y is simultaneously taller than x. In the language of logic, this fact defines "taller than" as an *asymmetric relation*. Second, if x is taller than y, and y is taller than z, than it must be true that x is taller than z.

This fact defines "taller than" as a *transitive relation*. The asymmetry and transitivity of "taller than" seem to be inherent constraints in the physical world.

It follows from our present definition of representation that if "taller than" is to be represented by some other relation, it too must be functionally asymmetric and transitive. There are two quite different ways of achieving this result. In World B, for example, the "longer than" relation seems to have the same inherent constraints. It is asymmetric, because if line x is longer than line y, then y cannot be simultaneously longer than x. It is transitive, because if x is longer than y, and y is longer than z, then x must be longer than z. We call this method of preserving structure *intrinsic representation*. Representation is (purely) intrinsic whenever a representing relation has the same inherent constraints as its represented relation. That is, the logical structure required of the representing relation is intrinsic to the relation itself rather than imposed from outside. The representation of "taller than" would be intrinsic if it were modeled by "shorter than" (World E), "larger than" (World F), "brighter than," "more numerous than," or any other relation that is inherently asymmetric and transitive.

The situation is strikingly different in World G, however. Here, "is arrow-connected to" represents "taller than," but there seem to be no inherent constraints on this representing relation. If x is arrow-connected to y, then y might be arrow-connected to x, or it might not. If x is arrow-connected to y, and y is arrow-connected to z, then x might be arrow-connected to z, or it might not. Thus arrow-connectedness is not *necessarily* either asymmetric or transitive, although it is *possible* for it to be either or both. Its ability to represent "taller than" follows directly from this fact. Asymmetry and transitivity can be literally imposed on it by requiring that it preserve the structure of its represented relation. We call this method of preserving structure *extrinsic representation*. Representation is (purely) extrinsic whenever the inherent structure of a representing relation is totally arbitrary and that of its represented relation is not. Whatever structure the representing relation has, then, is imposed on it by the relation it represents.

There are two ways in which intrinsic and extrinsic representation can be mixed. Obviously, one relation in a given representation can be modeled intrinsically and the other extrinsically. Not so obviously, both can be used in modeling the same relation. World H is an example of this. The "is arrow-path-connected to" relation is inherently transitive, because if there exists a path of arrows from x to y and another from y to z, then there must be a path from x to z. It is not inherently asymmetric, however. If there is a path of arrows from x to y, then there is no reason why there could not be one from y to x as well. Thus the transitivity of the "taller than" relation is represented intrinsically, whereas its asymmetry is represented extrinsically.

A word of caution is necessary about the distinction between intrinsic and extrinsic representation. The caution is that it rests on the concept of "inherent structure," a notion fraught with deep philosophical problems. After a moment's reflection, it is seen that "inherent structure" is closely related to the philosophical concepts of "a priori knowledge" and "analytic and synthetic statements." In fact, intrinsic representation could just as well be called "analytic" and extrinsic representation called "synthetic." These are ideas about which philosophers have been arguing for centuries (e.g., Grice & Strawson, 1956; Quine, 1951). Despite such problems, I think the intrinsic–extrinsic distinction and the underlying notion of inherent structure are intuitively clear enough to be useful. As we see later, the distinction lies at the heart of a current psychological controversy.

Direct Versus Derived Representation.   Another way in which two informationally equivalent representations can differ is in terms of how basic the information is within the representations. Intuitively, the distinction is between representing a relation so that it is a representational "primitive" and representing it so that it must be computed from other, more primitive relations. In World G, for example, the representation of "taller than" by "is arrow-connected to" seems more basic than in World H, where it is represented by "is arrow-path-connected to." The reason is that the latter relation relies on the former relation for its definition. In other words, one must make use of the "is arrow-connected-to" relation in order to evaluate the "is arrow-path-connected to" relation.

We call a representation of a relation *direct* if its operational definition relies on no other relations. Otherwise, the relation is *derived.* Any derived relation could be based on relations that are themselves either direct or derived. The dependencies that exist among relations determine the *derivational structure* of the system. Each relation can be specified in terms of how it is computed from other more basic relations.

There are some sticky problems involved with claiming that derivational structure is a representational issue. Strictly speaking, it is a question about how the representation is processed, because the definitions of relations are claimed to be operational. Still, there are cases in which it is obvious that one relation is derived from another – e.g., in World H of Figure 9.1. Direct representation is especially clear when representation is extrinsic, for reasons that become obvious later. With intrinsic representation, derivational structure is often obscure.

Completely Equivalent Representation

There is not a great deal to say about completely equivalent representations. They are simply informationally equivalent representations in which the same relations are modeled in precisely the same way.

It is worth mentioning, however, that no form of representational equivalence guarantees that performance characteristics will be the same for two representations embedded in process models. Even two completely equivalent representations may not have the same temporal characteristics, because a set of operations performed sequentially in one model may be performed simultaneously in the other. Error characteristics are similarly opaque without considering the processing environments for the representations in detail. The simple fact is that there are a multitude of nonrepresentational factors that contribute to performance characteristics, and these can differ no matter how similar the representations might be.

Complex Representations

Thus far we have been discussing "simple" representations that model a single dimension of their referent world. The situation is far more complex in cognitive representation and in most real-world representations. Many different dimensions of the represented world can be modeled in the same system. This allows for the possibility that different aspects of the represented world may have qualitatively different representations. Consider a typical road map. Dots representing cities and lines representing roads are laid out in a spatial arrangement that simultaneously preserves a number of different dimensions of the real world. The location of cities is represented by the location of dots. The population of cities is represented by the size of dots. The condition of roads (paved, unpaved, highway, etc.) is often represented by the color of lines.

From the view of representation developed here, such a map is not representationally homogeneous. Representing city-location by dot-location provides a very high resolution, whereas representing city-size by dot-size generally has very low resolution. It seems, then, that the best way to characterize complex representations is in terms of the simpler dimensional representations that we have been considering. There is no single, acceptable description of the map as a whole, but we can say sensible things about it when broken down into dimensional components.

Interdimensional Structure.   The separate dimensional pieces of a complex representation do not tell the whole story, however. When a representation contains more than one dimension, there is the possibility that pairs of them will not be independent. To the extent that this is true, there is interdimensional structure that must be preserved in the representing world. To use our familiar example, the height, width, and area of rectangles are not independent dimensions. If a rectangle is both tall and wide, it cannot be small. Height and width determine area in a fundamental way that prohibits such a combination.

Whatever interdimensional structure is present in the represented world must be preserved in the representing world for the modeled dimensions. This is not much of a problem if only a basic set of completely independent dimensions are represented directly and all others are derived from them. In such cases, the derivation generally takes into account the interdimensional structure. Otherwise, there is potentially a problem in preserving this information.

Once again, we can distinguish between intrinsic and extrinsic methods of preserving structure. If the height of rectangles were modeled, say, by the volume of spheres, and if the width of rectangles were modeled by their density, then the area of rectangles would be intrinsically represented by their mass.

This is so because the mass of spheres bears the same relationship to their volume and density as the area of rectangles does to their height and width. In other words, the inherent structure among dimensions in the representing world is the same as the inherent structure of dimensions in the represented worlds. The problem with this solution is that it very quickly becomes difficult to find analogous physical systems with all the required dimensional structure. For sufficiently complex representations, the constraints become so fierce that only a scaled model of the represented world will suffice. Although this is a satisfactory solution in some applications, it is not tractable for mental representation.

The other solution is to represent interdimensional structure extrinsically. That is, one could choose representing dimensions that are inherently independent and make them dependent by virtue of building in that structure. For example, the height, width, and area of rectangles could be represented by the length, brightness, and orientation of lines. Because length and brightness do not in any sense determine orientation, it would simply have to be the case that in the representing world, long, bright lines are oriented more vertically than are short, dark lines. Note that even though the individual dimensions involved are largely intrinsic representations of their referent dimensions, they are extrinsic at the higher level of interdimensional structure. Naturally, a representation can be extrinsic for both unidimensional and multidimensional structures.

Our hope that complex representations would be analyzable into simple representations turns out to be only partly realized. As more and more dimensions are added, higher-order structure increases drastically. Still, this general approach seems preferable to an unsystematic one. More importantly, by having considered simple representations first, we have come a long way toward our goal of a general framework — a metatheory, if you will — for representation. At least we have a coherent set of assumptions about what representation is and how representations can differ from one another at different levels.

COGNITIVE REPRESENTATION

We now turn our attention to the form of representation in which we were interested all along — cognitive representation. The plan is to use the framework developed for representation in the previous section to analyze the problem of cognitive representation. It must be clear from the outset that the goal is not to present a new and better theory of cognitive representation. Rather, it is to understand in a new and more fundamental way how cognitive psychology should approach mental representation and how we have been doing it for the past decade or so.

The discussion focuses on perceptual representation for two reasons. First, the concepts of perceptual representation currently in use are more confused and confusing than for any other cognitive domain. Second, the range of different proposals about perceptual representation seems greater than any other.

In fact, some are very similar to forms of representation currently in use in other domains such as language and various kinds of memory. In short, it is a microcosm of the state of cognitive representation as a whole.

Representation and the Cognitive Approach

The first thing about which we must be clear is exactly what we are doing when we construct a model or theory of mental representation from a cognitive point of view. Following Weizenbaum (1976), we make a distinction between theories and models. A theory of something is essentially a description of it at some level of analysis. It expresses the structural laws that hold in the object of study at a level of abstraction appropriate for the goals and methods of the scientific enterprise for which it is constructed. A theory, then, does not include aspects that are more concrete than can be verified by empirical observations of the sort indigenous to the science. A model is a concrete embodiment of a theory. Its relationship to its theory is that it satisfies the assumptions of the theory. Because there are many ways in which a given theory may be satisfied, there are many models that are consistent with it. All of these are described equally well by the theory. Thus the theory is simultaneously a description of its object of study and its many models.

For the current discussion, the object of study is mental representation of the world, perceptual representation in particular. The scientific field is cognitive psychology complete with its goals and methods. The question at hand is how cognitive theories and models relate to mental representation and its referent, the real world. Further, we want to know the scope of cognitive psychology in characterizing the nature of mental representation.

The proposed view of the situation is diagrammed in Fig. 9.2. To begin with, the "mental world" in which we are interested is some kind of representation of

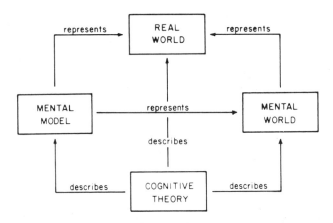

FIG. 9.2. A view of cognitive representation. Relationships among constructs are indicated by labeled arrows. See text for discussion.

the "real world." This is indicated by the "represents" arrow pointing from the mental world to the real world. A cognitive model of this mental world (the "mental model") is, in turn, a representation of that mental world. Thus the mental model is a representation of a representation of the real world. Almost by accident, the mental model is a representation of the real world in its own right.[2] This situation should begin to sound familiar. Both the mental model and the mental world are representations of the same represented world — the real world. This is just the case we considered earlier when discussing equivalence of representations. A relevant question, then, is what sort of equivalence can be achieved between the mental world and our hypothetical cognitive model of that world. The answer is that they should be as equivalent as is meaningful for the goals and methods of cognitive psychology. Not accidentally, this kind of equivalence is also the level of abstraction appropriate for the cognitive theory of mental representation. The theory should simultaneously be the proper description of both the mental world and the mental model. Indirectly, the cognitive theory is also a description of the real world, although it will differ substantially from, say, a physicist's. The fact that a cognitive theory also provides a description of the real world is significant. It explains why some theorists — notably Garner (1974) and J. J. Gibson (1966) — have been able to make important contributions to cognitive psychology by analyzing aspects of the world (the stimulus) rather than the representation of that world.[3] Note that they do not talk about the world in physical terms (like frequency and amplitude of mechanical deformations) but in psychological correlates of physical terms (like pitch and loudness of sound). Thus they are essentially describing the world in a way that is equally applicable to a mental model or mental world in an abstract sense.

---

[2]This idea can be demonstrated as follows. Suppose that the objects of the real world are a, b, c, and d and that those of the mental world are a', b', c', and d'. Because the mental world is a representation of the real world, there exists a mapping function (correspondence) from the real world objects to the mental world objects that could be expressed as $x' = f(x)$. Because the model of the mental world is also a representation of the mental world, its objects, a'', b'', c'', d'', can also be considered part of a similar mapping function from the mental world, $x'' = g(x')$. Now we see that the objects of the mental model can also be expressed by a mapping function from the objects of the real world, $x'' = g[f(x)]$ or $x'' = h(x)$, where h is just the composite of functions g and f. Thus, h is the representational mapping from the real world to the mental model. Although it is not universally true that this will result in the same relations being preserved in the mental model as in the mental world, it will be true if the mental model is an isomorphic (rather than homomorphic) representation of the mental world.

[3]The fact that Gibson does not acknowledge the existence of mental representation is irrelevant. His claims about the information available in the real world are still important for psychologists who postulate mental representations.

Following Neisser's (1967) classical statement, let us assume that the goal of cognitive psychology is to describe the "software" rather than the "hardware" of the mind. This assumption is justified by the kinds of experiments we perform. By and large, they are behavioral, not physiological, even when their object of study is a physiological distinction like hemispheric function. Even more to the point, scalpels are not included in our apparatus, and surgery is not part of our training. This means that neither cognitive theories nor experiments are properly concerned with the concrete way in which mental representation is accomplished within the brain and nervous system. Our theories and experiments *are* concerned with the nature of the information represented about the external world. Moreover, we want our models to be as equivalent to the mental world as possible in terms of the information contained about the world. In the language defined earlier, cognitive psychology can aspire only to informational equivalence between its models and actual mental representation inside the head.

This fact determines the proper level of discourse for cognitive theory as the level of abstraction defined by informationally equivalent systems. The representational issues of concern for cognitive theory are things like the types of information represented, the resolution of the dimensions represented, their uniqueness properties, and the higher-order structure that exists among different dimensions. These are our tools of analysis for dealing with mental representation from a cognitive approach. Questions about the concrete physical aspects of the mental world are inappropriate and irrelevant. The distinction between intrinsic and extrinsic representation is also beyond our reach. Derivational structure is somewhat unclear, because it is irrelevant as a representational construct alone but probably is relevant as a processing construct. Within this framework for cognitive representation, let us try to understand our current concepts of perceptual representation.

Notation and Illustration

When a theorist proposes a theory of representation, he or she usually draws one or more diagrams to illustrate the nature of the theory. These diagrams are essentially small pieces of a model of the theory being proposed. One problem with the current view of representation is the pervasive belief that these diagrams can be taken uncritically as the theory being put forth. A more subtle form of the same mistake is to assume that even though the figures are not the theory, they are intuitively transparent to the theory.

To demonstrate the flaw in this way of thinking, Fig. 9.3 shows seven standard, easily recognizable types of representation for a diagonal line. Within the usual classificational system, there is a template (A), a neural network (B), a digital matrix (C), a multicomponent vector (D), a binary feature set (E), a list of propositions (F), and a relational network (G). Most of these are currently thought

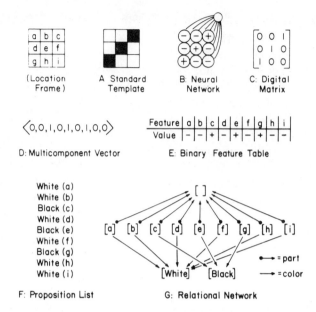

(Location Frame)   A: Standard Template   B: Neural Network   C: Digital Matrix

⟨0,0,1,0,1,0,1,0,0⟩

D: Multicomponent Vector

Feature	a	b	c	d	e	f	g	h	i
Value	−	−	+	−	+	−	+	−	−

E: Binary Feature Table

White (a)
White (b)
Black (c)
White (d)
Black (e)
White (f)
Black (g)
White (h)
White (i)

F: Proposition List

●—▸ = part
——▸ = color

G: Relational Network

FIG. 9.3.   Seven standard cognitive representations of a diagonal line. The letters *a–i* in Representations E, F, and G refer to the locations indicated in the Location Frame in the upper left corner. In Representation D, the vector components are in alphabetical order of the location-frame letters (*a, b, c, ...*).

to be different theories of representation. What are the differences, and are they meaningful for cognitive theory? They look different, and we talk about them differently. But these things may or may not reflect substantive differences at the level of cognitive theories of representation.

Let us examine them from the new view of representation. Each one consists of nine components, where each component represents a point (or, equivalently, a point's location) in the pattern. What dimensions are represented? Each representation contains information about the location and color of the individual points. In A, B, and C, location information is preserved by spatial location, in D by position in the vector, in E by identity of the feature, and in F and G by identity of the arguments of the relations. In A, color is represented by color, in B and E by "+" and "−", in C and D by "1" and "0" entries, and in F and G by the labels "white" and "black." In each case, then, color is a two-valued dimension, and location is a nine-valued dimension. The representation of both color and location is nominal in most cases, although A, B, and C seem to contain more information about location. As argued earlier, one must consider the processes that operate on the representations to determine what information is actually included in the representation. As we see later, the processing assumptions for standard templates, neural networks, and digital matrices reveal that location is represented nominally.

If this is a reasonable analysis, all seven representations in Fig. 9.3 are informationally equivalent but not completely equivalent. That is, they differ only in the concrete way information is preserved, not in what information is preserved about their referents. This means that they are all models of the same cognitive theory. In fact, they all turn out to be models of standard template theory.

I have obviously taken some liberties in constructing these drawings. No one has ever (to my knowledge) proposed a feature theory quite like the one shown. But why not? It is against the rules of feature theories? If so, why? These are questions that must be answered in order to understand our theories properly. The pictures we draw must not be confused with the representational assumptions contained in the theory itself. We must see *through* the surface form of those pictures to the information they contain about the represented world. That is what cognitive theories of representation are all about.

Templates

Until recently, templates have been the perennial "straw men" of perceptual representation. Discussions by Neisser (1967) and Lindsay and Norman (1972) have succeeded in convincing a whole generation of cognitive psychologists that templates — whatever they are — are useless representations for pattern-recognition systems. Two developments have brought about a resurgence of interest in templates. One is the construct of "prototypes" in representing categories (Rosch, 1973; Chapter 2 of this volume). The other is recent work on image rotation (Cooper, 1975; Cooper & Shepard, 1973; Shepard & Metzler, 1971) and image scanning (Kosslyn, 1973; 1975a; Chapter 8 of this volume). Rightly or wrongly, these phenomena have been seen as possible evidence for the existence of template-like representations. In addition, templates seem to be good candidates for the kind of low-level visual information storage studied by Sperling (1960).

The construct of templates has been with us for a long time, but no one has ever really defined it properly. Perhaps the most common "definition" is to point to a figure that displays a digitized pattern overlapping to a certain extent with an input pattern (Neisser, 1967, p. 51; Lindsay & Norman, 1972, pp. 2–6). The figure and accompanying text provide the reader with an intuitive feel for how template matching systems work but no real definition of the representations on which they operate. Worse still, processing assumptions that are totally independent of representational assumptions (e.g., parallel matching) are often confused with the form of representation.

The basic problem in understanding the fundamental nature of templates is that they are displayed as *pictures* of the patterns they are intended to represent. These pictures have all the information in their referents, at least implicitly. The template-picture has lines and angles plus properties like closedness and symmetry. It is not at all transparent to the nature of the underlying theory. Only when the operations performed on templates are considered do the assumptions about representation become clear.

Standard Templates.   The simplest case is a standard template match without any "preprocessing operations" (Neisser, 1967). Consider what happens when a template match is performed. The template in memory is compared to the input pattern in a point-to-point fashion, where location determines the correspondence of points. For each pair of corresponding points that have the same color (both white or both black), a match is registered. If there are n locations, then the number of matches can vary from no points to all n points. This defines a similarity dimension with $n + 1$ values for pairs of templates. It is used to classify patterns according to some decision strategy, usually of the best-fit variety.

There are two important things to notice about this process. First, no components are considered except individual points, and no dimensions are considered except location and color. Thus angles, lines, closedness, and all the rest of the information in the template-picture are irrelevant. They are not represented information, because there are no operations that define them or use them. Second, the matching process requires only information about the identity of locations and colors. It does not matter in the slightest whether one location is above, below, or close to another location, as long as it is matched to the corresponding point in the input pattern. In sum, both location and color are nominally represented dimensions.

Standard templates, then, are defined as follows. Templates are representations in which each pattern is composed of n points, and each point is defined by just two dimensional values: one from an n-valued, nominal dimension representing location and the other from a two-valued, nominal dimension representing color. Thus, all of the illustrations shown in Fig. 9.3 are surface variations (i.e., informationally equivalent models) of standard template theory when the usual processing operations are employed. Notice that many of the bizarre forms are far more revealing of the essence of templates than is the usual form.

Preprocessed Templates.   The problems with standard templates are well known. Because they are position-, orientation-, and size-specific, trivial changes in these parameters of the input pattern have catastrophic consequences for classification performance. To correct these difficulties, Neisser (1967) suggested "preprocessing operations" to normalize (translate, rotate, dilate, and "clean up") the input pattern prior to matching. The extent to which such operations actually solve such problems is not at issue here. The important point is that these preprocessing operations require a significant change in representational assumptions.

It is still true that points, locations, and colors are the basic kinds of information represented. But the representation of location cannot be nominal. In order to "fill in" a light point surrounded by black points, relations like "between" must be operationally defined. In a nominal representation of location, "filling in" operations could not be performed. Similarly, shifting a pattern x units in a given direction cannot be done with nominal representation of location. In fact, the usual preprocessing operations seem to require that location be represented at least intervally, because units of locational dimensions must be constant.

Similar changes could be made in the representation of color. The resolution of the color dimension could be greatly increased, and its values could be made ordinal or interval. Such information could be used to construct more powerful matching procedures that include partial matches for intermediate levels of grayness. In any case, the representational assumptions of preprocessed templates differ significantly from those of standard templates.

Hierarchical Templates. A slightly more deviant type of template theory is what might be called "hierarchical templates" or "minitemplates." The basic notion is that the components of a complex pattern might be a set of simpler templates rather than just a set of points. The simpler templates would then be defined by either even-simpler templates or by a set of individual points. Thus this representation is a hierarchy with individual points at the terminals. Such representations border on structural descriptions in that they have an articulated structure of higher-order parts.

The general nature of templates, then, rests largely on the kind of information represented: points, locations, and colors. There seems to be some agreement on color being represented as a nominal, two-valued dimension, but that could be relaxed. Note that the assumptions are actually of the sort that should be important for a cognitive theory of representation. Once the surface form is disregarded, templates are a fairly well-defined theory. Perhaps this is why template theory is so easily and frequently shown to be false. As we see later, most other purported theories are so vauge that they cannot really be tested.

Features

Feature representations were invented as an alternative to templates. As initially proposed, features were things like horizontal lines, angles, curves, and so forth. Since then, many additional features have been postulated for special purposes: closedness, complexity, wiggliness, and height of forehead, to name just a few. They are probably the most widely used form of representation. A large part of their popularity stems from their flexibility; anything can be a feature. This is simultaneously their greatest strength and greatest weakness. It makes them convenient to use to explain data, but it makes them inherently ill-defined as a theory.

There are a number of feature theories in current use. The three most popular seem to be binary features, multidimensional spaces, and hierarchical features. We consider the representational assumptions of each in turn and clarify some of the relationships among them.

Binary Features.   Perhaps the most common type of feature theory is sets of binary features. Prominent examples include E.J. Gibson's (1969) distinctive feature theory of letters and Jacobson, Fant, and Halle's (1961) distinctive feature theory of phonemes.

Binary feature theories operate more or less as follows. A set of n operational feature tests are applied to an input pattern — either serially or simultaneously. Each test has two possible outcomes, one for presence of the feature and the other for absence of the feature. (Precisely how this happens is seldom discussed.) In Gibson's theory, for example, letters are defined by presence or absence of properties like having horizontal lines, being closed, and being symmetrical. The results of these tests are compared to a set of stored representations of pattern types, each one being defined by the outcomes of the same feature tests. For each feature, a match is registered if the input pattern has the same value as the stored representation — i.e., both have the feature, or both fail to have it. Some measure of similarity is computed according to a function that integrates the matching results for each feature. The simplest computation is the number of matches, although various weighting parameters can be introduced to reflect the saliency of different features. The resulting similarity dimension is then used to classify the pattern according to some decision strategy. The most frequently employed rule is a 100% threshold, requiring that the input pattern have all the same features as the memory representation of the pattern type. Other more complex decision strategies are sometimes used (e.g., Smith, Shoben, & Rips, 1974).

The representational assumptions of standard binary feature theories are quite clear. Patterns are represented along n different unary (property) dimensions. Each dimension has just two values defined by the results of their operational definitions. The dimensions are nominal in that only same/different relations are defined for the matching procedure. Thus each pattern is a set of values along n different, two-valued, nominal, unary dimensions.

Although these assumptions are clear, they are not very specific. Because the informational nature of the dimensions is unspecified, the range of possible theories within this class is enormous. Note that if the features are exclusively location-colors (see Figure 9.3E), the result is a standard template theory. In other words, if the features are strictly of the form "is dark at location x" (where x is identified as a different location for each feature), the foregoing procedure would operate exactly as the template matching system described earlier. Thus standard templates are a special case of binary features.

An obvious extension of standard binary feature representations would be nominal m-valued feature systems. All that changes is the resolution of the dimensions. An example would be a set of color names (red, blue, yellow, green), in which each object has one color only and the only information in the color values is whether they are the same or different.

Multidimensional Spaces.   Another common form of feature representation is a multidimensional space. The basic metaphor is that mental objects can be modeled as points in a metric space of n dimensions. Relations among groups of objects are preserved by spatial relationships among sets of points. For example, overall psychological similarity is usually assumed to be reflected in distance relationships. The illustrations used to depict such representations are usually low-dimensional spaces with points labeled by object names and with coordinate axes labeled by dimensional feature names. Most multidimensional space representations are derived from the nonmetric scaling techniques originally developed by Shepard (1962a, 1962b). Prominent examples include spatial representations of animals (e.g., Rips, Shoben, & Smith, 1973), states (Shepard & Chipman, 1970) and numbers (Shepard, Kilpatrick, & Cunningham, 1975).

Multidimensional space representations are used to classify patterns in the following way. A set of n operational feature tests are applied to the input pattern. Each test has m possible outcomes, where m is a relatively large number usually assumed to approach infinity. The outcomes generally represent the *degree* to which the instance has that feature and are interpreted as interval representations. The results of these tests specify the point within the n-dimensional space occupied by the input pattern. The point is then compared to a set of stored representations of pattern types defined for outcomes of the same feature tests. At this stage, two different classification methods diverge: the point method and the region method. In the point method, the stored representations of pattern types are single (or sometimes multiple) points in the metric space. The input pattern point is compared to the category point(s) using some form of distance metric, usually Euclidean or city-block. This metric is taken as a representation of psychological similarity, and the pattern is classified with the category to which it is closest (most similar). In the region method, the representation of pattern types is in terms of a region with in the space. The input pattern is then classified as an instance of the category within whose region it falls. [See Reed (1973) for a more comprehensive treatment of spatial models of categorization.]

Notice that the basis for multidimensional space representations is essentially an analogy. It specified that a possible *model* for cognitive entities is a spatial one. But the spatial aspects of the model cannot be taken as part of the underlying cognitive theory, because the medium of representation is not within the cognitive level of analysis. That is, the "space" is metaphorical. The essence of multidimensional spaces as a *theory* of representation must lie elsewhere.

Without loss of generality, each point in an n-dimensional space can be described by a vector of n ordered values. Each component of the vector specifies the projection of the point on one of the axes of the space. Spatial relationships like distance are mathematical relations on vectors. Because the vector form of multidimensional feature theory contains the same information as the spatial form but without the spatial assumptions, it is more transparent to the underlying theory of representation. This theory assumes that there exists some number of highly resolved, interval, unary dimensions in a mental representation. In practice, the number of dimensions represented in multidimensional spaces is small. This is more a constraint of illustrating the representation than of the underlying theory itself, however.

Multidimensional spaces and binary feature theories seem very different from each other. Binary feature models are presented as tables, whereas multidimensional spaces are presented as spaces. These surface differences are not very revealing of the underlying similarities and differences. The commonality that seems to make them both versions of feature theory is that they both represent unary dimensions (properties of individual objects). The differences are that binary feature dimensions are two-valued and nominal, whereas multidimensional spaces are multivalued and at least interval.

Having noticed these relationships between binary features and multidimensional spaces, a number of other things become clear. For example, the language we use to talk about these models becomes as arbitrary as their surface form in illustrations. Consider the following spatial characterization of templates: "A template is a point in a discrete dimensional space. Each dimension represents the color of a particular location of the pattern, and if there are n locations, there are n dimensions in the space. For each dimension, there are just two values: 0 if the pattern is light at the location and 1 if it is dark. Thus, the input pattern and each memory representation occupies a point in this discrete space. The input pattern is then classified as an instance of the pattern type to which it is closest according to a city-block distance metric." On the surface, this seems very different from the usual description of templates, yet the theory described is the same. Because templates are a special case of binary features, the same sort of translation could be done for any standard binary feature theory.

The point of this discussion is not to argue that templates, binary features, and multidimensional spaces are all the same. As these concepts are *used*, they are certainly not. But they do have similarities as well as differences. These relationships are not obvious from the pictures used to illustrate them or the language used to talk about them. They are found in the basic representational assumptions.

Hierarchical Features.   Another version of feature theory is that in which feature dimensions are structured according to their interrelationships. The basic idea is that complex features can be defined in terms of more primitive ones. A familiar example is found in Lindsay and Norman's (1972) pandemonium model. At a concrete level, each pattern is defined by a number of orientation-specific features such as the number of horizontal lines, the number of vertical lines, and the number of oblique lines. At an abstract level, patterns are defined by orientation-free features such as the number of lines of any orientation. The higher-order dimension of number of lines is the sum of the values for the lower-order dimensions that comprise it. Thus, heirarchical feature theories are one way to specify logical dependencies that exist among different dimensions.

There are other relationships among dimensions that are more psychological than logical. Many of these concern what Garner (1974, 1976; Chapter 5 of this volume) calls "integrality" and "separability" of dimensions. As a paradigm case of integrality, hue, saturation, and brightness seem to be closely related psychological dimensions. We even have a name for this set of dimensions — "color." There seems to be a level of analysis at which these three dimensions combine into a unitary aspect of the stimulus. People can make separate judgments about the component dimensions, but it is difficult. This is a facet of dimensional representation that cannot be modeled in either standard binary feature systems or multidimensional spaces. Hierarchical features provide a mechanism for doing so by allowing structural relationships among different dimensions to be represented. It is not clear whether this violates the assumptions of feature theory in general. Just as hierarchical templates are deviant versions of template theory, so are hierarchical feature theories deviant versions of feature theory.

Structural Descriptions

Some theorists came to reject both features and templates as representations for pattern recognition because of their poor modeling of structural interrelationships among patterns and their parts. For example, although a feature theory can represent a given pattern having three lines and three angles, there is no representation of which lines are part of which angles, nor of how the lines are connected to form the angles. A more powerful representation is needed for such information, because a pattern is no longer defined solely by unary dimensions (properties). One must represent facts such as that Pattern P contains X and Y as parts and that the top of X is joined to the middle of Y — i.e., that X "is top-middle-connected to" Y.

The initial attempts at structural description theories followed the formalisms of generative grammars (Narasimhan, 1969; Narasimhan & Reddy, 1967). The representation of a pattern was the set of production rules required to generate it from primitive patterns. The production rules specified the manner in which parts were to be combined into wholes. Since then, grammatical formalisms have largely disappeared, but the legacy of representing *n*-ary relations has remained. It is essentially the power of representing relations on more than single objects that differentiates structural descriptions from features.

Simple Structural Descriptions.   Simple structural descriptions are closely related to hierarchical templates. The basic idea is that a pattern is defined by relationships among subpatterns. Each subpattern can be thought of as a minitemplate. The specified relationship among the minitemplates is satisfied by moving and turning the minitemplates until the proper relations hold. Each of the subpatterns, of course, could be either a primitive (usually, points or lines) or relationships among further subpatterns. Simple structural descriptions differ from hierarchical templates in that the relations among subpatterns are subject to variation. It is this variation in relationships that is represented by the structural relations in the representation.

In a structural description, each pattern is represented by a set of values for *m* *n*-ary relational dimensions. Each value of an *n*-ary dimension is a relation among *n* subpatterns. Because this is a rather complex concept, let us consider an example. The letter "T" might be defined in the following kind of structural description: "T" is the connection of the middle of a horizontal line to the top of a vertical line. This description actually contains three components: "T" contains a horizontal line, "T" contains a vertical line, and the horizontal line is middle-top-connected to the vertical line. The first two are binary relations between T and its subpatterns, and the third is a binary relation between the two subpatterns themselves. It is the third component that is important and distinguishes structural descriptions from feature theories.

Consider how to translate the three components into unary relations for a feature theory. The "contains" relations between T and its parts are no problem. One simply defines two different unary relations by binding the two parts to the second argument of the "contains" relation. The features of T then become "contains-a-vertical-line" and "contains-a-horizontal-line," both of which are familiar features in existing feature theories. But the last relation is a problem for feature theory. It is not a problem for structural description, because both the horizontal and vertical lines are independent object-elements in their descriptions. Therefore, representing the relation between them is no different in principle from representing the relations between T and the subpatterns. In a feature theory, however, the horizontal and vertical lines do not have independent status as representational objects. They are inextricably bound within the two constructed unary relations. The usual solution is to add more unary relations that indirectly constrain how the horizontal and vertical lines can be arranged. For example, many possible arrangements of the two lines are ruled out when the following features are added to the definition of T: "has an intersection," "has two right angles," "is open," and "is symmetrical." Despite these complex, higher-order features, the indirect constraints are seldom tight enough to rule out all illegal patterns. The only sure-fire feature would be something like "has-a-horizontal-line-whose-middle-is-connected-to-the-top-of-a-vertical-line." At this level of complexity, one might just as well have a feature called "looks-like-a-T."

The sure-fire solution for feature theory has the unfortunate side effect of proliferating represented relations. Suppose that there are just 10 basic subpatterns for a given class of patterns and 10 possible relations that might hold between any pair. The structural description theory would have 20 primitive elements, one for each subpattern and one for each relation. They would be combined in appropriate ways to define the patterns. The corresponding feature theory would require, in principle, 1000 features to have the same power. Each complex feature would be pairing of each of the 100 possible ordered pairs of basic subpatterns with each of the 10 possible relations. Thus, it may well be the case that there is always a feature theory that is informationally equivalent to a given structural description theory, but the latter is preferable on grounds of simplicity.

Augmented Structural Descriptions. One potential drawback to simple structural descriptions is that, like templates, their representations ultimately rely on just locations and colors of points. Although these primitives are combined in powerful ways into higher-order parts and patterns, every bit of information must be derived from them. The problem is that when higher-order parts are formed by relationships among component parts, the larger patterns frequently have "emergent properties" not defined for the components. For example, a line can be defined as a particular relationship among a set of points, but the line has properties like length and orientation that are not properties of the component points. Similarly, when lines are combined into a square, the square has properties like area and closedness that are not properties of the component lines.

An obvious solution to this problem is to augment simple structural descriptions with features for the higher-order patterns. The result is a hybrid of feature theory and structural descriptions that we call *augmented structural descriptions.* The general assumptions are that any pattern is represented *both* as a set of unary dimensional values and as a set of relationships among component parts. This provides the power necessary to represent emergent properties like those mentioned previously. Examples include the models of Palmer (1975a) and Winston (1975).

By this point, we have reached a type of "theory" that is so powerful that it no longer is any theory at all. Notice that there are virtually no constraints on what information can be represented. There can be any number of dimensions that can hold among any number of objects. The dimensions can represent any kind of information with any resolution and any uniqueness properties. In their most general form, then, augmented structural descriptions are an untestable theory of perceptual representation as a general class. Particular examples of the class, however, can be tested. But one must do things like specify what dimensions are represented and how they are represented. Only then does an augmented structural description theory become more than an abstract framework in which to construct particular theories.

Prototypes

A great deal of interest has recently been generated about the possible role of prototypes in cognitive representation and processing. This development is due in large part to the seminal work of Eleanor Rosch on categorical prototypes (Rosch, 1973, 1977; Chapter 2 of this volume). She has demonstrated the existence of prototypes for natural categories like colors and animals as well as for artificial categories like dot patterns and schematic drawings. The evidence that prototypes of some sort play a critical role in human categorization is compelling. The question that concerns us here is the nature of the representational assumptions required by prototype theories.

The most common belief about prototypes is that they must be templates of some sort. This is partly because prototypes are frequently discussed as "images" and because they are associated with particular examples of the category. The association between prototypes and templates is further strengthened by the fact that templates are universally described as "prototypical" examples of their class. Because everyone who has read an introductory text in cognition has been informed that templates are *wrong*, however, prototypes are usually thought to be only "template-like." For example, in a recent book on pattern recognition (Reed, 1973), we find the following discussion of results demonstrating the importance of prototypes:

> Insofar as a prototype may be thought of as a type of template, these results also support a template theory. But a prototype is not an unanalyzed template in which the amount of overlap is used to judge its similarity to other patterns. Instead, a prototype consists of features and when it represents the central tendency, is determined by the mean value of each feature when the mean is calculated from all patterns in the category. [p. 32].

This passage illustrates the confusion about prototypes; they are template-like and yet they are not templates but features. In what sense are they like templates and in what sense like features? Are they necessarily related to these concepts at all?

Let us begin by considering how a prototype theory of perceptual classification operates. There are categorical representations stored in memory. These are assumed to be highly specific in the sense that they approximate the "most typical" or the "ideal" instance of the category. However these representations are constructed, the input pattern is represented along the same dimensions as the prototypes. A measure of similarity is computed between the input pattern and each categorical prototype. The similarity is assumed to be highly resolved or even continuous. A decision strategy is used to assign the pattern to a category on the basis of degree of similarity. The most common classification rule is of the best-fit variety such that each pattern is classified into one-and-only-one category.

The general form of this process is the same as before. The input pattern is represented and compared to stored representations for similarity. The similarity measures are then used to categorize the pattern. The major elaborations for prototype theories are: (1) the stored representations are highly specific; (2) the similarity dimension is highly resolved; and (3) a best-fit criterion is used for classification. Note that both (2) and (3) are pragmatically determined by (1). That is, if the categorical representation is highly specific, then using a similarity dimension with low resolution and/or using strict 100% threshold decision criteria would result in unacceptable categorization performance. Either too few instances would be classified at all, or some instances would be classified into many categories. Thus the basic assumptions of prototype process-models of classification all follow from the single assumption that categorical representations are highly specific.

Let us consider this assumption more carefully. In what sense is the categorical representation highly specific? The prototype approach is properly considered in opposition to the "invariant attribute" approach (e.g., E.J. Gibson, 1969). The essence of these theories is a very general representation of categories such that each instance is completely and equally consistent with it. For this to be true, invariant-attribute representations of categories cannot represent dimensions that vary within the category. They represent only dimensions that vary across categories. Now it becomes clear that the specificity of prototypes is with respect to within-category variation. A prototype representation is one that has relatively high resolution for dimensions of information that vary within the category.

The standard view seems to be that the prototype and invariant-attribute approaches are dichotomous. The present analysis leads to a different view — namely, that underlying the dichotomy is a broad range of possible theories, which differ in their representation of within-category variation. At one extreme is the usual prototype approach — the prototypical prototype approach, if you will — in which every aspect of within-category variation is represented. At the other extreme is the standard invariant-attributes approach, in which no aspect of within-category variation is represented. In between are numerous sensible compromises. A categorical representation need not be uniformly specific for all dimensions of variation, for example. Some might be quite specific, others less so, and still others not at all.

Nothing has yet been said about exactly what the dimensions are nor just how they are represented. This is because prototype theories as a general class do not require such assumptions except when they are particularized for a given category. Certainly, standard templates satisfy the specificity constraint, but they are not the only kind of theory that does so. Binary feature theories can also represent within-category variations, provided there are sufficiently many such features (e.g., Smith, Shoben, & Rips, 1974). In fact, any reasonable theory of perceptual representation in general will have to be consistent with the notion of prototypes, because it will have to have the capability of representing highly specific instances. If not, the theory would never be able to account for how people can distinguish their own house from other houses or their own dog from other dogs. In short, prototypes are a construct of categorical representations, not of representations in general. As a class, they are equally compatible with virtually any theory that can represent specific instances.

Shepard's Principles of Isomorphism

Roger Shepard has discussed the nature of possible forms of isomorphism that might hold between the real world and people's internal representations of that world (Shepard & Chipman, 1970; Shepard, 1975). In particular, he has distinguished between what he calls "first-order" and "second-order" isomorphism. These concepts have gained wide currency within cognitive psychology and are believed to have implications for the field. I discuss the nature and importance of Shepard's proposals because they seem to be frequently misunderstood. First, I formulate them within the new framework of representation to clarify them. Then I argue that second-order isomorphism, in its most general sense, is not a theory of representation but a definition. Finally, I argue that the distinction between first- and second-order isomorphism is irrelevant for cognitive psychology.

First-Order Isomorphism.   Simply stated, first-order isomorphism is a concept of mental representation in which the properties of real-world objects are retained in the internal representation of those objects. To use Shepard's original examples (Shepard & Chipman, 1970), in a first-order isomorphism, the representations of green things must be themselves green, and those of square things must be themselves square. Shepard rejects this notion of the correspondence between the real world and the mental world by arguing that it is physiologically absurd to suppose that the internal representations of green things are themselves green and that it is unnecessary and implausible to suppose that those of square things are themselves square. In a later paper, Shepard (1975) refers to this as concrete first-order isomorphism.

Translating this concept into the present framework is straightforward. A representation is concretely first-order isomorphic to its referent if the unary relations (properties) of the represented objects are preserved by the physically equivalent unary relations (properties) of the representing objects. Thus, greenness is reflected by greenness and squareness by squareness. The most sensible interpretation for the name of this concept is that "first-order" signifies that relations on individual objects (properties) constitute the information of interest and that "concrete" signifies that the corresponding relations must be physically the same.

Shepard distinguishes concrete from abstract first-order isomorphism in a later paper (Shepard, 1975). His example is that an abstract first-order isomorphism would hold if the internal representation of a square contained four parts, each of which correspondended to a corner of the square. Unfortunately, the example is ambiguous, and Shepard does not discuss it fully enough for the reader to know exactly what he intended.

The "abstract" version of our previous definition should be that a representation is abstractly first-order isomorphic if the unary relations of the represented objects are preserved by functionally (or operationally) equivalent unary relations of the representing objects. This example is then interpreted as follows. One of the properties of squares is that they have corners as parts, four of them in fact. This is reflected in the representing world by the square-representation having corner-representations as parts, four of them in fact. The isomorphism is not concrete, because "having-four-corners-as-parts" is not physically equivalent to "having-four-corner-representations-as-parts." In the special case where the corner-representations are themselves corners, concrete first-order isomorphism would hold.

In the other interpretation, we consider binary relations within each world rather than unary ones. The square has a relationship to each of its corners: Namely, the corners are "part of" the square. Similarly, the square-representation has a relationship to each of its corner-representations: Namely, the corner-representations are "part of" the square-representation. Now it seems that the represented binary relation is physically the same as the representing binary relation. In other words, the example might also be considered an instance of concrete second-order isomorphism by simple extension of our previous definition. I am not sure that Shepard actually meant to convey either of these concepts, but within the present framework, they are both possible.

Second-Order Isomorphism.   Shepard's alternative to first-order isomorphism is second-order isomorphism. His example is that the internal representation of a square need not be itself square, but — whatever it is — it must be functionally more similar to a rectangle than to a green flash or the taste of persimmon

(Shepard & Chipman, 1970). It is important to realize that more than one thing has changed from the initial example of concrete first-order isomorphism. As the name implies, one change is from talking about the correspondence between properties of single objects to talking about that between relationships among more than one object. One would think this is the important change, but it is not.

Consider the binary relation "greener than" in contrast to the unary relation "green." First-order isomorphism implies that if an external object is green, its internal representation is also green. If second-orderness is the essence of second-order isomorphism, then replacing "green" with "greener than" relationships should yield an example of second-order isomorphism. Thus, if object A is greener than object B, then the representation of A should be greener than the representation of B. The only constraint that has been lifted is that the properties of individual objects in the external and internal worlds need not be identical. That is, the representation of A need not be itself green (it might be blue-green or even blue), but it still must be greener than the representation of B.

Now we see that the other change is from physical sameness to functional sameness. This is the important one. Because of it, external greenness need not be like internal greenness in any physical sense but only in a functional sense. That is, when the greenness of an external object changes, there is *some* corresponding change in the internal object that may be nothing like changes in greenness. This functional correspondences is what effectively decouples the internal and external world in terms of resemblances. Shepard's terminology is unfortunate, because it emphasizes the wrong change. It would be better to call first-order isomorphism "physical isomorphism" and second-order isomorphism "functional isomorphism," where either can hold for properties or any higher-order relations.

Second-Order Isomorphism: Theory or Definition?   Regardless of what one chooses to call it, the basic concept referred to as second-order isomorphism can be defined as follows. A representation is second-order isomorphic to its referent world if the similarity of represented objects is functionally reflected by the similarity of the corresponding representing objects. What makes this difficult to pin down is the construct of similarity in both the external and internal worlds. Whether second-order isomorphism is a theory (or class of theories) of cognitive representation or just a definition depends on how broadly the concept of similarity is interpreted.

In its most general sense, similarity is a binary dimension containing at least two values. That is, the crudest sort of similarity is a one-bit classification into "same" or "different" relations. Inserting this into the previous definition we have: A representation is second-order isomorphic to its referent world if a binary dimension containing at least two values is functionally reflected by a binary dimension containing at least two values for the corresponding representing objects. This must be true even for purely nominal representations, because they preserve same/different binary relations. Thus, verbal labels for objects satisfy this broad interpretation of second-order isomorphism. (It is perhaps worth noting at this point that verbal descriptions constructed by selecting one label from each of n sets of possible descriptions are no different in principle from nominal feature sets of the kind discussed earlier. Both are purely nominal, unary dimensions in which only same/different relationships are meaningful.)

I suspect Shepard's intention was to convey a more restricted concept of similarity, however. The intuitive notion of similarity connotes a highly resolved or even continuous dimension to most psychologists. With this notion of similariry, second-order isomorphism becomes more specific. It rules out, for example, representations containing only a few nominal dimensions. If the concept of second-order isomorphism is further required to hold within a single dimension, then it rules out all representations with low resolution of their dimensions (e.g., standard binary features). In any case, the status of second-order isomorphism as a theory or a definition of representation is unclear as long as the construct of similarity is left undefined.

Distinguishing First- from Second-Order Isomorphism. As Shepard has pointed out, all first-order isomorphisms are necessarily second-order iso-morphisms, but the reverse is not true. The present question is whether cognitive psychology can hope to distinguish between them given the methods of experi-mental, behavioral psychology.

Suppose that there are two models of cognitive representation, one first-order and one second-order isomorph of the external world. The first-order model specifies that external greenness is modeled by internal greenness and external squareness by internal squareness. The second-order model specifies that external greenness is modeled by internal squareness and external squareness by internal greenness. There are two points to be made. First, a second-order isomorphism cannot be distinguished from a first-order one without "looking inside the head" at the actual representing world. Moreover, just looking inside the head will not be sufficient to determine whether the representation is first- or second-order isomorphic to the world, because both models are characterized by just internal-greenness and internal-squareness. In order to test the two models, one must have access to the mapping function from the outside world. Does internal greenness correspond to external greenness or external squareness? Both looking inside the head and determining the mapping function are tasks for physiological psychology, not cognitive psychology.

The second point is that a second-order isomorphism is not necessarily any more plausible than a first-order isomorphism in physiological terms. The present example illustrates this obvious fact, assuming that no part of the nervous system is actually green or that, if it is, this fact is irrelevant to how it represents in-formation. The only thing that matters is whether the postulated physical properties of the internal representation are consistent with the known physical properties of the nervous system. One can try to figure out what dimensions could possibly be represented as first-order isomorphisms, but this is armchair speculation for cognitive psychologists. More than anything else, the notion of second-order isomorphism (in its general interpretation) is simply a philosophical comfort to cognitive psychologists, because it provides a justification for not worrying about precisely those issues involved in first-order isomorphism.

The Propositional/Analog Controversy

One of the most hotly debated issues of cognition these days is whether representations are "propositional" or "analog" in nature (e.g., Pylyshyn, 1973, 1975; Kosslyn, 1975b; Kosslyn & Pomerantz, 1977; Palmer, 1975b). The arguments began with the appearance of Pylyshyn's (1973) influential paper attacking the "picture metaphor" of visual imagery. The arguments seem to have spread to perceptually related representations in general. The terms "propositional" and "analog" have become emotionally charged buzz words capable of provoking arguments almost instantaneously.

Naturally, the entire controversy rests on the presupposition that propositional and analog representations are fundamentally opposed in some way that is relevant to cognitive theories and/or experiments. Whether this is true or not depends on how the terms are defined and what one takes to be the domain of cognitive psychology. In the following subsection, I define propositional representations and discuss their implications. Then I discuss a few of the concepts of analog representation that seem to be in current use. I also suggest a new way of looking at the notions of propositional and analog representation based on the distinction between intrinsic and extrinsic representation. To anticipate the conclusion, it turns out that propositions and analogs are fundamentally opposed but in ways that are not relevant for cognitive psychology. Further, I suggest that the reason for the controversy lies in differences between the two camps in terms of theoretical goals and styles.

Propositional Representation.   The fundamental nature of propositional representation is quite simple. Recall the definition of representation: A world, X, is a representation of another world, Y, if at least some of the relations among objects of X are preserved by relations among objects of Y. This definition requires that any representation must have "object elements" to correspond to the represented objects. It might also have "relational elements" that model the relations (e.g., the arrows of World G in Fig. 9.1) or it might not (e.g., Worlds B—F in Fig. 9.1). Propositional representations are simply those in which there exist relational elements that model relations by virtue of themselves being related to object elements. The result is that relationships among n object elements cannot be determined simply by examining those n elements. One must determine them by examining their relationships to the additional relational elements.

Language is the paradigm case of propositional representation. Words referring to objects are related in syntactically ordered strings through relational words (verbs, prepositions, and the like). The sentence, "The ball is under the table," specifies a relationship between the ball and the table that can only be understood by virtue of their syntactic relationships to the relational construction "is under." Other kinds of propositional representations have the same basic properties. Lists of sentences in predicate calculus notation contain explicit relational elements and devices for specifying ordered-connectedness to them. Relational networks do also. Somewhat surprisingly, binary features are usually expressed propositionally. In a feature table, for example, the element representing the object is usually a row (or column) and the element representing the unary relation is usually a column (or row). The relational elements are "predicated" of the object elements by virtue of their being row—column connected by "+" or "1" rather than by a "−" or "0". In fact, there are many quite different-looking propositional representations in current use, including some with bizzarre notational devices (e.g., Schank, 1972; Leeuwenberg, 1971).

Analog Representations.   The problem in attempting to characterize analog representations is that they seem to be different things to different people. I briefly characterize three notions that seem to be used most frequently.

The clearest and most obvious interpretation is that "analog" representations are those in which dimensions are continuous rather than discrete. The intended contrast is between analog and digital computers. Analog computers represent information in a physical dimension that, for all functional purposes, varies continuously (voltage). Digital computers do so in discrete, quantized units (bits). Although the continuous/discrete distinction may be of theoretical interest, it is not a question that seems to be answerable given state-of-the-art behavioral techniques. The cruder question of high versus low resolution within a given dimension is answerable, but having high resolution is not the same thing as being continuous.

The other two meanings for "analog" are both related to the visual imagery controversy. The claim is that visual images are, in some sense, "spatial" (Kosslyn, 1975a; Chapter 8 of this volume). The weaker version of this claim is that visual images preserve spatial information about that which they represent. For example, if object *A* is above object *B* in the represented world, then the representing world − whatever it is − will have objects *A* and *B* in some relationship that functionally corresponds to aboveness in the external world. Thus the weak spatial claim is equivalent to proposing that the image represents spatial dimensions in some fashion. This is a very mild and sensible position, one that is not opposed to propositional representation in any way.

The stronger spatial claim is, I suspect, the more usual one. In this interpretation, spatial information is not only preserved, but it is preserved (1) in a spatial medium, and (2) in such a way that the image *resembles* that which it represents.

For example, if A is above B in the external world, the strong claim would be that the representation of A is physically above (or perhaps below, if the image is inverted) the representation of B in the image. Although this is not a physiologically absurd type of first-order isomorphism, it is a first-order isomorphism nevertheless. Like all proposals of first-order isomorphism, it is functionally indistinguishable from informationally equivalent representations that are not first-order isomorphic.

Intrinsic Versus Extrinsic Representation.   Although I have never heard anyone define "analog" in quite the way I now suggest, I suspect it is close to what most "analog" theorists have in mind. It is a weaker claim than physical isomorphism but a stronger one that functional isomorphism. Moreover, it does put analog and propositional representations in opposition to one another.

Recall that in discussing methods of preserving relational structure, we noted two different approaches. The intrinsic method was to model a represented relation or dimension by using a representing relation or dimension that has the same inherent structure as that which it represents. In such cases, the preservation of logical structure is a "natural" consequence of the representing relation or dimension chosen. The extrinsic method was to model the represented information using a relation or dimension that has no inherent structure, but to build the necessary structure into the system explicitly to conform to the represented world. The propositional/analog controversy makes sense if we associate analog representation with intrinsic methods and propositional representations with extrinsic methods. Let us see how this proposal ties in with what has been discussed so far.

The previous discussion of propositional representation was mainly concerned with surface manifestations. At a deeper level, the significance of using relational elements in representing relations is that propositions are extrinsic representations. The reason is that any object can, in principle, be connected to any relational element in any fashion. Hooking up object elements by relations to relational elements places no constraints whatsoever on the nature of the relations represented. Thus, *whatever structure there is in a propositional representation exists solely by virtue of the extrinsic constraints placed on it by the truth-preserving informational correspondence with the represented world.*

This fact is closely related to characterizations of propositional representations as "descriptive" and "interpreted" (Pylyshyn, 1973). The essence of a description is that it can be either true or false. There is nothing about descriptions that precludes contradiction with fact. One can *say,* for example, "*A* is above *B*," and "*B* is above *A*," although not both descriptions could be true of the relationship between *B* and *A* in the world. But if one is constrained to make only *true* statements, not both descriptions could be used. Thus, if descriptions are to serve as a representation, the constraints are external to the descriptive world. By definition, then, descriptions are extrinsic representations.

Analog representations are now seen to be those that contain no relational elements — i.e., nonpropositional representations. In such cases, the properties of individual represented objects are modeled by properties of individual representing objects, and relationships among sets of represented objects are modeled by relationships among sets of the corresponding representing objects. These representations are necessarily intrinsic, because the structure of the representing relations is inherent and therefore determines completely the kind of represented relations they can model. Thus, *whatever structure is present in an analog representation exists by virtue of the inherent constraints within the representing world itself, without reference to the represented world.*

Another way to view the nature of analog representation is in terms of a form of isomorphism somewhere between physical (first-order) and functional (second-order) isomorphisms. Recall that physical isomorphisms preserve information by virtue of the representing relations being themselves the same as their represented relations in a physical sense. Any physical isomorphism is analog (intrinsic), because the same relations must have the same inherent structure in both worlds, provided their operational definitions are constant across worlds. Now, suppose we relax the strict interpretation of physical sameness to allow representing relations to be physically the same in a more abstract sense. In the present framework, the sense in which representing and represented relations are the same is precisely that they have the same inherent structural constraints. We might call this concept "natural isomorphism" to emphasize that structure is preserved by the nature of corresponding relations themselves. Whatever one calls it, this concept is a stronger claim than functional (second-order) isomorphism, because the latter requires only a correspondence that preserves structure, regardless of whether it is done by intrinsic or extrinsic means. Thus propositional representations are functional isomorphisms but not natural isomorphisms. In general, any representation that is physically isomorphic is necessarily both naturally and functionally isomorphic to its represented world. Any representation that is naturally isomorphic is necessarily functionally isomorphic, but not physically isomorphic, to its represented world. Finally, any representation that is functionally isomorphic is not necessarily either naturally or physically isomorphic to its represented world. Thus there is a strict hierarchy of isomorphisms in which physical isomorphism is the most concrete and functional isomorphism the most abstract.

Relevance to Cognitive Psychology. If the distinction between intrinsic and extrinsic representation is actually the fundamental issue underlying the propositional/analog controversy, is it relevant to and resolvable by cognitive psychology? One can attempt to construct experiments to distinguish between the propositions and analogs on the basis of intuitive notions about the properties of "descriptive" versus "nondescriptive" or "interpreted" versus "noninterpreted" representations. It has been my experience that such experiments are never convincing. Usually they are based on a simplistic notion of how the alternative type of theory might operate (see Kosslyn & Pomerantz, 1977, for some examples). Although such experiments may succeed in showing that analog-theory-X predicts better than propositional-theory-Y, the results do not seem to generalize beyond the particular examples.

The most compelling reason to believe that analog and propositional representations are not distinguishably different requires no experiments at all. Assuming that the intrinsic/extrinsic distinction is the fundamental issue, the answer to the controversy rests on the inherent nature of the representing relations and their relationship to the inherent nature of the corresponding represented relations. I see no way this can be determined without "looking inside the head." The concept of the inherent nature of representing relations concerns the physical medium that caries information. It is an *abstract* question about their physical nature, but one that concerns the physical medium nevertheless. Therefore, resolving the controversy over whether mental representation is analog or propositional is a task beyond the scope of cognitive psychology. It should be relegated to physiological psychologists, whose job it is to figure out the physical nature of inside-the-head and to determine its correspondence to outside-the-head.[4]

Approaches to Cognitive Models.   There remains the interesting question of why the controversy arose in the first place. The answer provides some insights into different approaches to modeling in cognitive psychology.

There are two camps involved in the controversy. By and large, they divide cleanly in that proponents of the propositional view construct models by writing computer simulations, whereas proponents of the analog view do so by formulating analogies to known physical or formal systems. [Kosslyn is an exception, because he first worked by analogy (Kosslyn, 1973, 1975a; Kosslyn & Pomerantz, 1977) but has since simulated this analogy (Chapter 8 of this volume).] According to the analysis given here, this division is no accident.

---

[4]It should be emphasized that the argument is that analog representations are indistinguishable from propositional ones because they can be informationally equivalent as representations. It is possible that they differ in some nonrepresentational way that makes one preferable to the other. Perhaps testable differences exist in processing operations, for example. Whether this is true or not depends on the outcome of a rigorous analysis of the fundamental properties of processing operations. I suspect that such an analysis will yield a result parallel to the present one. That is, given that some operation has certain performance characteristics, it might be that these characteristics are a *necessary* consequence of the physical operation (i.e., intrinsic to the operation) or merely a *possible* consequence of the physical operation (i.e., extrinsic to the operation). If so, intrinsic and extrinsic methods of modeling performance characteristics are just as indistinguishable as intrinsic and extrinsic methods of preserving information. There are also other grounds for preferring one type of theory over another, such as parsimony, simplicity, and other pragmatic or esthetic considerations.

As Weizenbaum (1976) has pointed out, computers are systems in which the programmer is freed from the constraints of the physical world. He or she works in the domain of "possible worlds" that can be constructed within the computer. Therefore, when a program is intended to model something else, the programmer needs to know everything about those aspects of the modeled world that are of interest in order to simulate them. In the most general symbolic languages, virtually nothing can be hidden in implicit structure, because in the domain of possible computer-worlds, there is no structure in which it can be hidden. Thus, if a computer-modeled relation is transitive or connected, it is because either the programmer or something in the program makes it have these properties. Any unspecified aspect is "magic" until it can be spelled out precisely. Once the behavior of the simulated world is known to the required level of analysis, it can be simulated. Being able to predict new things not specifically built into the program is largely an accidental byproduct of constructing very complex programs. There is little or no intent to predict.

Modeling by analogy is quite different. The analogizer works in the domain of actual worlds that nearly always contain a great deal of structure. In some sense, the more structure that is hidden in the inherent constraints of the analogous system the better. This structure provides a rich base of possible future predictions from aspects of the system over which the modeler has no direct control. A good example of modeling by analogy is the notion of multidimensional spaces. If psychological concepts are conceived as points in a multidimensional space and similarity as distances between points, a great deal of structure is built into the model "accidentally." Of course, it is not really an accident at all but the mark of a clever theorist who has recognized at least some of the structural correspondences. In the spatial analogy, all of the dimensional features automatically have mutually exclusive values, because this is inherent in the axes of a space. In addition, similarity automatically has properties of symmetry, minimality, and the triangle inequality (see Tversky, 1977; Chapter 4 of this volume). That many of these structural properties are hidden is evidenced by the fact that the assumptions underlying the similarity-as-distance analogy have been tested only recently, more than a decade after the analogy gained popularity.

In short, computer modelers and systematic analogizers differ in the amount of structure they choose to have in their modeling medium. Computer modelers use an exceptionally flexible, unstructured medium. As a result, most structure must be built in explicitly to correspond to that of the modeled system. Analogizers work by choosing from among many rigid, highly structured media, each of which has constraints independent of its potential as a model of something else. It is not too surprising, then, that propositional models were developed by those who work with computers and that analog models were developed by those who work with more structured media. The amount of structure provided by the representing medium is precisely the difference between propositional (extrinsic) and analog (intrinsic) approaches to representation.

CONCLUSION

Representation is a complex and elusive concept, much more so than is generally supposed. Within psychology at least, it has been associated with an information-containing "thing" that is operated upon by processes. I used to believe that if I was looking at that "thing" in a diagram or illustration, then I knew the nature of that representation. The view presented in this chapter indicates this to be untrue. Our understanding of the current concepts in representation is based largely on superficial trappings that have little to do with their fundamental nature. If we are to make significant progress on the nature of cognitive representation, we need a deeper understanding of our theories.

One aspect of this deeper understanding is the realization that the representational nature of this "thing" cannot be dissociated from the operations that define the information it contains. Considering those operations may reveal that much of the information that *seems* to be there is not really there at all. Conversely, it may turn out that much information that does not seem to be there actually is. To determine what the representational nature of the "thing" is, one must first consider its functional information content as defined by those processes that use it. This is not to say that representation is indistinguishable from processing. There are many aspects of processing that are entirely independent of representational assumptions and other aspects that are only partly dependent on them. In general, however, operations are much more intricately woven into the fabric of representation than is usually acknowledged.

Once the information content has been discovered, it must be related back to the world it represents. In order for a "thing" to be a representation of any sort, it must preserve at least some information about its referent world. There is an important sense in which the nature of a representation is simply the view it presents of the represented world. Representations that provide the same view of the same world are at least informationally equivalent. Representations that provide views of the same world are not representationally equivalent, no matter how similar they may seem on the surface. The importance of the correspondence between represented and representing worlds should not be underestimated. More than anything else, it is what representation is all about.

For the purposes of cognitive psychology, there is yet another step in understanding our models of representation. Once the information has been discovered and related to the represented world, all other aspects of the representing world must be disregarded. In other words, the *only* thing that matters about the model of representation is what information it preserves about the representing world. Issues that pertain to any physical aspects of the representing world are simply beyond the scope of cognitive theories. The proper level of discourse for cognitive theory concerns information, not the medium used to carry it. It is this last step that allows us to see *through* the "thing" we find in illustrations to the representational assumptions that define the theory it embodies.

Perhaps the most general lesson to be learned from our discussions is that we cannot properly understand our theories and models of cognitive representation without some larger, metatheoretical framework in which to view them. The concepts currently used to talk about representation are seriously confused and inadequate. As a result, we lack the insight that allows us to separate relevant issues from irrelevant ones and to see the relationships among our models and theories in a clear and systematic way. I have attempted to provide the sort of framework I believe is necessary. It has helped me to notice things that were previously obscure and to clarify things that were previously confused. Once we understand the problems involved in cognitive representation properly, perhaps we can solve them more quickly.

ACKNOWLEDGMENTS

I would like to thank Amos Tversky, Donald Norman, Zenon Pylyshyn, and Elizabeth Bates for their helpful comments on earlier versions of this chapter. Most of all, I thank Eleanor Rosch for her constant encouragement; without it I would have given up on this project long ago.

REFERENCES

Cooper, L. A. Mental transformation of random two-dimensional shapes. *Cognitive Psychology*, 1975, 7, 20–43.

Cooper, L. A., & Shepard, R. N. Chronometric studies of the rotation of mental images. In W. G. Chase (Ed.), *Visual information processing*. New York: Academic Press, 1973.

Garner, W. R. *The processing of information and structure*. Potomac, Md.: Lawrence Erlbaum Associates, 1974.

Garner, W. R. Interaction of stimulus dimensions in concept and choice processes. *Cognitive Psychology*, 1976, 8, 98–123.

Gibson, E. J. *Principles of perceptual learning and development*. New York: Appleton-Century-Crofts, 1969.

Gibson, J. J. *The senses considered as perceptual systems*. Boston: Houghton-Mifflin, 1966.

Grice, H. P., & Strawson, P. F. In defense of dogma. *Philosophical Review*, 1956, 65, 141–158.

Jacobson, R., Fant, G. G. M., & Halle, M. *Preliminaries to speech analysis: The distinctive features and their correlates*. Cambridge, Mass.: M.I.T. Press, 1961.

Kosslyn, S. M. Scanning visual images: Some structural implications. *Perception and Psychophysics*, 1973, 14, 90–94.

Kosslyn, S. M. Information representation in visual images. *Cognitive Psychology*, 1975, 7, 341–370. (a)

Kosslyn, S. M. On retrieving information from visual images. In R. C. Schank & B. L. Schank & B. L. Nash-Webber (Eds.), *Theoretical issues in natural language processing*. Arlington, Va.: Tinlap Press, 1975. (b)

Kosslyn, S. M., & Pomerantz, J. R. Imagery, propositions, and the form of internal representations. *Cognitive Psychology,* 1977, *9,* 52–76.

Krantz, D. H., Luce, R. D., Suppes, P. H., & Tversky, A. *Foundations of measurement* (Vol. 1). New York: Academic Press, 1971.

Kuhn, T. S. *The structure of scientific revolutions.* Chicago: University of Chicago Press, 1962.

Leeuwenberg, E. L. J. A perceptual coding language for visual and auditory patterns. *American Journal of Psychology,* 1971, *84,* 307–350.

Lindsay, P. H., & Norman, D. A. *Human information processing.* New York: Academic Press, 1972.

Narasimhan, R. On the description, generation, and recognition of classes of pictures. In A. Grasselli (Ed.), *Automatic interpretation and classification of images.* New York: Academic Press, 1969.

Narasimhan, R., & Reddy, V. S. N. A generative model for handprinted English letters and its computer implementation. *ICC Bulletin,* 1967, *6,* 275–287.

Neisser, U. *Cognitive psychology.* New York: Appleton-Century-Crofts, 1967.

Palmer, S. E. Visual perception and world knowledge: Notes on a model of sensory–cognitive interaction. In D. A. Norman, D. E. Rumelhart, & LNR Research Group, *Explorations in cognition.* San Francisco: Freeman, 1975. (a)

Palmer, S. E. The nature of perceptual representation: An examination of the analog/propositional debate. In R. C. Schank & B. L. Nash-Webber (Eds.), *Theoretical issues in natural language processing.* Arlington, Va.: Tinlap Press, 1975. (b)

Pylyshyn, Z. W. What the mind's eye tells the mind's brain: A critique of mental imagery. *Psychological Bulletin,* 1973, *80,* 1–24.

Pylyshyn, Z. W. Do we need images and analogues? In R. C. Schank & B. L. Nash-Webber (Eds.), *Theoretical issues in natural language processing.* Arlington, Va.: Tinlap Press, 1975.

Quine, W. V. Two dogmas of empiricism. *Philosophical Review,* 1951, *60,* 20–43.

Reed, S. K. *Psychological processes in pattern recognition.* New York: Academic Press, 1973.

Rips, L. J., Shoben, E. J., & Smith, E. E. Semantic distance and the verification of semantic relations. *Journal of Verbal Learning and Verbal Behavior,* 1973, *12,* 1–20.

Rosch, E. H. On the internal structure of perceptual and semantic categories. In T. M. Moore (Ed.), *Cognitive development and the acquisition of language.* New York: Academic Press, 1973.

Rosch, E. H. Human categorization. In N. Warren (Ed.), *Advances in cross-cultural psychology* (Vol. 1). London: Academic Press, 1977.

Schank, R. C. Conceptual dependency: A theory of natural language understanding. *Cognitive Psychology,* 1972, *3,* 552–631.

Scott, D., & Suppes, P. H. Foundational aspects of theories of measurement. *Journal of Symbolic Logic,* 1958, *23,* 113–128.

Shepard, R. N. The analysis of proximities: Multidimensional scaling with an unknown distance function. I. *Psychometrika,* 1962, *27,* 125–140. (a)

Shepard, R. N. The analysis of proximities: Multidimensional scaling with an unknown distance function. II. *Psychometrika,* 1962, *27,* 219–246. (b)

Shepard, R. N. Form, formation, and transformation of internal representations. In R. L. Solso (Ed.), *Information processing and cognition: The Loyola Symposium.* Hillsdale, N.J.: Lawrence Erlbaum Associates, 1975.

Shepard, R. N., & Chipman, S. Second-order isomorphism of internal representations: Shapes of states. *Cognitive Psychology,* 1970, *1,* 1–17.

Shepard, R. N., & Metzler, J. Mental rotation of three-dimensional objects. *Science,* 1971, *171,* 801–703.

Shepard, R. N., Kilpatrick, D. W., & Cunningham, J. P. The internal representation of numbers. *Cognitive Psychology*, 1975, *7*, 82–138.

Smith, E. E., Shoben, E. J., & Rips, L. J. Structure and processing in semantic memory: A feature model for semantic decision. *Psychological Review*, 1974, *81*, 214–241.

Sperling, G. A. The information available in brief visual presentation. *Psychological Monographs*, 1960, *74*(Whole No. 498).

Suppes, P. H., & Zinnes, J. L. Basic measurement theory. In R. D. Luce, R. R. Bush, & E. Galanter (Eds.), *Handbook of mathematical psychology*, (Vol. 1). New York: Wiley, 1963.

Tarski, A. Contributions to the theory of models, I, II. *Indigationes Mathematicae*, 1954, *16*, 572–288.

Tversky, A. Features of similarity. *Psychological Review*, 1977, *84*, 327–352.

Weizenbaum, J. *Computer power and human reason.* San Francisco: Freeman, 1976.

Winston, P. H. Learning structural description from examples. In P. H. Winston (Ed.O, *The psychology of computer vision*. New York: McGraw-Hill, 1975.

10 Practical and Lexical Knowledge

George A. Miller
The Rockefeller University

This chapter addresses the question of what people know when they know categories that are named by nominal expressions in their language. Although the question may seem relatively straightforward, the range of opinions expressed about categorical knowledge by psychologists, linguists, philosophers, and others is too broad for any simple summary. In order to stay within reasonable bounds, therefore, the particular aspect to be discussed here concerns the possibility of making some reasonable division of that categorical knowledge into two parts, one part having to do with a person's general knowledge about the world and the things that happen in it, and another part having to do with entailments that follow from a claim that something is a member or instance of a category. In order to talk about this possible division, it is convenient to introduce the terms "practical knowledge" and "lexical knowledge," but that terminology should not be taken to represent a prejudgment about their distinguishability.

The main body of this chapter presents an argument relevant to this distinction in as simple a form as possible. At three points, however, the argument relates to psychological matters that the author feels deserve fuller discussion than a simple exposition would allow. Rather than interrupt the thought, therefore, these diversions are relegated to appendices.

THE KNOWLEDGE PROBLEM

Let us begin with an example. The sentence, *The Smiths saw the Rocky Mountains while they were flying to California,* is ambiguous, because it is not clear whether the Smiths, the Rocky Mountains, or both were flying to California when the sighting took place. Most people fail at first to notice the ambiguity, because the interpretation in which the Smiths are flying is far more salient than interpretations in which the Rocky Mountains are. The reason is obvious. Anyone who knows what mountains are knows that they do not fly.

This fact — that mountains do not fly — is practical knowledge. It is not a fact that can be discovered by consulting dictionaries and would not be included in any reasonable account of a person's lexical knowledge. Yet it affects the interpretation of the ambiguous sentence almost as directly and immediately as does any knowledge that would be conventionally regarded as lexical. Given that one's practical knowledge of mountains enters as directly as one's lexical knowledge of the word *mountain,* it is natural to ask how this is possible. Because practical knowledge must play an important role in most of the uses we make of language, we might even wonder whether any purpose is served by distinguishing two kinds of knowledge.

The advantage of distinguishing lexical from practical knowledge is that it helps to set manageable bounds on what phenomena a theory of linguistic communication can be expected to treat. There is more than enough to explain even if we limit our theorizing to the lexical meanings of words and phrases and their linguistic entailments. If we must also include a theory of knowledge in general, the theoretical task will become unmanageable. Moreover, the difference is readily illustrated. One feels that the relation of *John's children are asleep* to *John has children* is very different from its relation to *John is married.* In the latter case, an inference can be justified by practical knowledge, but it lacks the requiredness of the former relation, which can be justified in terms of the linguistic meaning of *John's children,* in terms of lexical and linguistic knowledge.

Students of language are, therefore, strongly motivated to draw the distinction. But if we place practical knowledge outside the basic machinery of linguistic comprehension, we create the problem of explaining when and how it is invoked for interpretive purposes. That is what "the knowledge problem" will be taken to mean in the present context.

The usual disposition of this problem consists of waving the hands vaguely toward a distant bridge that may someday need to be crossed. Perhaps the output of the linguistic component is passed on to some further cognitive component where practical knowledge is ready and waiting to add its contribution; how this interface could be achieved is left as a problem for future research. Its resolution is a matter of some psychological importance, however, because a language machine that does not interact smoothly with a person's practical knowledge will say little or nothing of importance about the central problems of cognitive psychology. The goal of this chapter is to propose one tentative hypothesis about this so-called knowledge problem, as much in hope of calling attention to it as of solving it.

A second example moves us a step closer to this goal. Imagine two people using a tree stump for a picnic lunch. One of them says, *This stump is a good table.* The problem here, of course, is that a stump is not a table. How are we to explain the fact that *This stump is a good table* can be true at the same time that *This stump is table,* literally interpreted, is false? Calling a stump a table doesn't make it one, but calling a stump a good table (or a poor table) is perfectly acceptable.

This example admits explanations either in terms of practical knowledge or in terms of lexical knowledge. We might say, for example, that in addition to knowing the lexical meaning of *table,* a person has practical knowledge of the function that tables serve, and that this practical knowledge is somehow invoked in order to interpret a metaphorical extension of the lexical meaning. Or, on the other hand, we might say that the mental lexicon includes two related but distinct meanings of *table,* the literal meaning and a more general meaning of *anything serving the function of a table.* Neither account has any explanatory force. The appeal to practical knowledge leaves unsettled how such knowledge is used to produce or evaluate metaphorical extensions. The appeal to lexical knowledge leaves unsettled how one recognizes that something can serve the function of a table. And the role of the evaluative adjective *good* in signaling the alleged metaphor or retrieving the alleged second meaning is left as a curious puzzle on either account.

We are now squarely facing the theoretical "knowledge problem" that I want to discuss. Before we can deal with it, however, we must introduce more of a framework in which to work.

IDENTIFYING INSTANCES

If we stay with the problem of the stump and the table, we might phrase it as follows. How are we to formulate a plausible procedure for recognizing instances of the category named by *table* that will accept both tables and stumps without destroying the conventional differences in meaning between *table* and *stump?* Before we can discuss possible answers, we need some way to talk about how we can identify instances of a category at all.

A common-sense view of the matter would be that, in order to determine whether some object is a table, you look at it to see whether it has the perceptual properties that you have learned are characteristic of tables. That is to say, you look to see whether it is a rigid, three-dimensional object with a flat horizontal surface supported by one or more vertical legs. It is possible to reduce these perceptual criteria to a set of judgments based on the visual input. It is even possible to formulate the judgments in such a way that a computer can recognize instances in a visual field that is presented to it in an appropriate manner. If the necessary perceptual predicates are satisfied, the sentence, *This is a table,* is accepted as true; if not, the sentence is rejected as indeterminate or false.

There are problems, however. For example, (1) people recognize that some tables are more typical than others, whereas the identification device just described would accept all instances as equivalent. Moreover, many category boundaries are (2) vague and (3) movable; an object that would be accepted as a table in one context may be identified as a bench on some other occasion. Or, again, (4) the identification device described previously would recognize tables only in their normal orientation, whereas people who encounter tables that are on end or upside down are still able to recognize them as tables. These difficulties — (1) equivalence of instances, (2) vagueness, (3) insensitivity to context, (4) dependence on normal orientation — can all be overcome but only at the cost of considerable complication in the identification process.

A major objection to a purely perceptual theory of how instances are recognized is that it takes no account of the function that instances are expected to serve. For example, the same object may, at different times of day, serve as a breakfast table, coffee table, lunch table, kitchen table, dinner table, poker table. Perceptual criteria are inadequate to distinguish among these various subcategories of *table*. A natural solution would be functional: used for eating breakfast, used to serve coffee, and so on. But an identification device based solely on testing a set of perceptual criteria is ill-suited to recognize what functions an object might serve.

Given that a functional characterization is a necessary part of an identification device, one might wonder whether perceptual aspects could be dispensed with entirely. After all, a functional characterization of a table (as something that can support various objects used in eating, working, or playing games) goes a long way toward determining the acceptable shapes of tables. In some cases — a word like *ornament,* for example — any appearance is satisfactory as long as it serves the function that instances are expected to serve. But to abandon perceptual criteria completely leaves us without a sensible distinction between tables and stumps; a large, low, tree stump can serve all the functions of a picnic table (getting your feet under it is not an essential condition) and so should be an unquestioned instance. Or, to turn the problem around, how would *stump* be defined in functional terms? To dispense with the perceptual aspect of identification is to go too far. The present claim is merely that it must be supplemented by functional information.

Adding function to form may reduce the other problems we noted, but it does not solve them all. Just as (1) there is a difference among instances in how much they look like tables are expected to look, so there are differences in how well they serve the function that tables are expected to serve. And just as (2) the boundaries of what looks like a table are vague, so the boundaries of what can function as a table are vague. Nonequivalence of instances and vagueness still need to be explained. But one might argue plausibly that (3) shifts in category boundaries are dependent on the function that an instance happens to be serving, and that (4) the existence of normal orientations is entailed by functional requirements.

Vagueness of category boundaries, whether based on perceptual or functional criteria, is an unavoidable consequence of the nature of human perception and judgment. If machines were built to do the task, they could be given precise measurements to use in distinguishing, say, a table from a bench, or a cup from a bowl. But people must rely on uncertain estimates and so must judge whether the object in question is more like one category or more like another; the fact that people are able to judge degrees of similarity in this manner is well documented by hundreds of psychological experiments. The implication for our present discussion, however, is that identifying category membership is a matter of more or less, not a matter of all or nothing.

One might conclude that such uncertainties would greatly reduce the usefulness of human language in just those boundary cases where precision is most needed. In fact, however, it is no great inconvenience, because we almost always identify an object relative to a set of alternative objects; the communicative purpose of identification is not to establish some absolute and timeless categorization but simply to establish agreement as to what things or events we are referring to in a particular situation at a particular time. Moreover, identifying features are usually redundant (an instance that fails to satisfy one or two criteria for a category will usually fail on several).

The identification process is relativistic, therefore, admitting both perceptual and functional tests and admitting degrees of typicality and vague boundaries. A psychologist must think both in terms of perceptual recognition and in terms of dispositions to respond to candidate instances in particular ways. The functional side of the picture has not been ignored by psychologists, particularly in studies of child language, but the formal theory of such criteria has lagged well behind the theory of perceptual recognition. This lag is particularly unfortunate for the knowledge problem, because it leaves us with all the same uncertainties about function that we noted about practical knowledge. Is expected function part of lexical knowledge or part of practical knowledge? Can we use functional criteria to build a bridge between lexical and practical knowledge? As long as the role of functional knowledge remains unclear, these important questions must remain unanswered.

FORM AND FUNCTION

We have argued that human categorization exploits relativistic judgments involving estimates of deviation from typical instances of the category. Will this fact explain how it is possible for people to call a stump a table without misunderstanding one another? Such an explanation would imply that a person makes a subjective judgment that a particular stump is sufficiently like a table to merit inclusion in that category. If a person does consider a stump to be a table on those grounds, however, it would surely be a poor instance. Yet in the example given previously, the picnicker did not say, *This stump is a poor table.* On the contrary, he said, *This stump is a good table,* where the adjective *good* plays an important role in marking the extended sense of *table.*

If the extension of the category *table* to include a tree stump is not to be explained in terms of category vagueness, perhaps we can explain it in terms of functional criteria. Such an explanation would imply that a person makes a subjective judgment that a particular stump serves the function of a table sufficiently well to merit inclusion in that category. Although this account is closer to what he probably means, it is still not precise. He does not mean that this tree stump is literally an instance of the category table. He means merely that the stump serves the functions of a table sufficiently well to justify calling it a table on this occasion. The adjective *good* signals that only functional criteria are involved.

If the identification device for *table* has both perceptual criteria P and functional criteria F, then presumably each candidate instance x is evaluated with respect to both. A conventional table should yield values for both $P(x)$ and $F(x)$ that are above the somewhat vague thresholds for inclusion in the category. Objects satisfying both kinds of criteria are literal tables. The meaning of *table* can be extended, however, by applying criteria of only one or the other kind. *Table* can be applied to a picture of a table, for example, even though a picture could not serve the function that tables are expected to serve; *table* can be applied to a packing crate, for example, even though the crate does not have the appearance that tables are expected to have. Objects satisfying only one kind of criterion are figurative tables.

Philosophers of language call evaluative adjectives like *good* syncategorematic, because their meaning seems to change according to the noun they modify. In *a good chair, good* means *comfortable;* in *a good clock,* it means *accurate;* in *a good view,* it means *unrestricted;* in *a good nurse,* it means *skillful;* and so on. It would be footless to define *good* by listing all these possible interpretations as alternative senses, and therefore it is necessary to define it in terms of features of the head noun it modifies. *Good* can select a salient feature of the meaning of its noun and assign a positive evaluation to that feature. For example, the salient feature of the meaning of *red* is color, and *a good red* is one that has that color in more than usual degree; the salient feature of the meaning of *knife* is that it is used for cutting, and *a good knife* is one that cuts well. Thus the salient feature that *good* evaluates may be either perceptual or functional. In some cases, there is no salient feature. *Good electricity,* for example, seems odd without an explanation of why this instance is superior; out of context, all electricity is equally good. *A good president,* on the other hand, leaves unresolved what particular feature of the meaning of *president* the speaker assigns his evaluation to: political skill, honesty, leadership, knowledge, personal appearance, etc. But many categories do have salient features that are known to provide the conventional basis for evaluating their instances.

Out of context, *a good table* is mildly ambiguous in much the same way that *a good president* is ambiguous. It is not clear whether the speaker is evaluating an instance on the basis of form or function: whether it looks to more than average degree the way he expects tables to look or whether it serves unusually well the functions that he expects tables to serve. As applied to a picture, however, *good table* can only express an evaluation on the basis of form; as applied to a tree stump, it can only express an evaluation on the basis of function.

In the case of tables, the functional criterion concerns what it is possible to do with a table. It may be important to distinguish this kind of functional information from information about what an instance is normally expected to do. *A good cook,* for example, is not a cook you can do something with but is somebody who does something well. It is not necessary to draw this distinction for the purposes of the present argument, but various psychological theories (see Appendix A) suggest that it should be drawn.

Our claim that both form and function enter into the identification of instances of the category *table* seems to fit well with this analysis of the syncategorematic adjective *good* and yields a natural and plausible interpretation of *This stump is a good table.* However, we are still unable to say whether this use of *table* should be explained in terms of practical or lexical knowledge. If we think of functional information as part of our practical knowledge of tables, it falls on one side of the dichotomy; if we think of it as part of our lexical knowledge of *table,* it falls on the other.

TRUE AND POSSIBLE

Let us consider the claim that functional information is part of lexical knowledge. That is to say, if P states the perceptual features of *table* and F states the functional features, the lexical entry for *table* would take this form:

Something x is a *table* if $P(x)$ is true or $F(x)$ is possible.   (1)

The candidate x is a literal table if both terms of the disjunction are satisfied, a figurative table if only one is. Because this general schema is imagined to fit many nouns other than *table,* we are not really concerned here with the particular formulations of P and F. The terms of special interest are *true* and *possible.*

The importance of truth for a theory of meaning has long been recognized. It is sometimes stated in the form: "To know what a sentence means is to know the circumstances under which it would be true." We have nothing to add to the vast literature on this topic, most of which is irrelevant to the substantive problems of psychology. In the present context, *true* is used to denote the outcome of a psychological process that involves attending to various perceptual aspects of a candidate instance x and judging whether they fall within the range of values specified by P.

The task, therefore, is to provide a comparable account of *possible.* The technical literature on the modal concepts *possible* and *necessary* is almost as vast as that on *true* and *false,* and just as irrelevant to psychological theory. The following approach is intended to provide a plausible account in terms of cognitive operations.[1]

We wish to define an operator M that can take $F(x)$ as its argument and yield another statement, M (F), to the effect that $F(x)$ is possible. We assume that a person will say F is possible if he can derive it by applying something he knows, k_i, to the current situation, or, failing that, if nothing that he knows yields not$F$. This formulation must be made more precise (see Appendix B), but the general idea is that some action is possible, relative to the circumstances, if you know how it is done (if you can reduce it to procedures that you already know are possible under the circumstances) or if you do not know any reason why it could not be done. It is easier to think about procedural formulations if we ask how plans might be derived for carrying them out, but the formulation should be more general – it should also apply to possible states of affairs, like *It may be raining in Chicago.* The relation "derived," therefore, must be thought of as a general cognitive operation that a person uses to go from his practical knowledge and his assessment of the prevailing circumstances to some description of a state or course of action.

If we let $D(F)$ represent the situation in which a person can derive F by applying something he knows, k_i, to the existing circumstances or to circumstances that he could cause to exist, then we can define the operator M as:

$$M(F): \ D(F) \text{ or notD(not}F\text{), but not both.} \tag{2}$$

It is assumed that a person searches through his store of knowledge for a relevant subsystem k_i that will support either D (F) or D(not$F$) under the circumstances, and the outcome of that search determines his judgment as to whether F is possible.

Given some such formulation of the psychological interpretation of *possible,* we can substitute it into lexical entries for words like *table.* An expanded entry for *table,* for example, would look something like this:

Something x is a table if $P(x)$ is true of if applying what you   (3)
know to the circumstances either yields $F(x)$ or, alternatively, does
not yield not$F(x)$.

We can think of picnickers walking through the woods looking for something to use as a (figurative) table. They see a rock, but it does not have a sufficiently horizontal surface; the circumstances require using containers, and the laws of

---

[1]This formulation is the result of collaboration with P.N. Johnson-Laird.

mechanics entail that their jars and glasses will not stand up on this rock. They do not derive $F(x)$ under these circumstances; the rock will not serve the functions of a table. They look further, find a large tree stump, derive $F(x)$ under the circumstances, and so proceed to set out their luncheon.

The knowledge that is invoked in order to determine whether F is possible can be as well formulated as the laws of mechanics or electricity, or even a moral code. Or it can represent nothing more than the systematized conclusions that a person has reached, perhaps unconsciously, on the basis of his previous experience with the function F under a variety of circumstances. But some such knowledge is required to determine whether F is possible, and it must be organized in such a way that, given F, practical knowledge can be searched rapidly for relevant subsystems k_i.

THE KNOWLEDGE PROBLEM AGAIN

The direction of our argument should now be obvious. If a person's knowledge is divided into two parts, practical and lexical, it is necessary to explain how practical knowledge can affect processes of linguistic comprehension. We first argued that the lexical knowledge associated with many nominal categories includes functional information. Next we argued that descriptions of expected functions must be stated modally, in terms of *possible.* Then we argued that judgments of possibility depend on systems of practical knowledge. The final step is to point out that this formulation provides a place in the lexical entry for the insertion of nonlexical, practical knowledge.

It is critically important to this conclusion to note that the expanded formulation given previously for *table* does not specify which body of knowledge must be invoked. It is left as a problem for the language user to determine whether there is a k_i that, under the circumstances, yields not$F$; how well he will be able to do that will depend on how much he knows, how what he knows is organized for search, what he happens to think of while he is searching, and so on. And even if he does remember some information that yields not$F$ under the circumstances, he may (if his need is great enough) go on to consider ways to change the circumstances. But all that is outside the system of lexical knowledge. The definition merely provides a place where such practical knowledge is to be consulted.

We have, therefore, proposed a way for those who wish to draw a division between practical and lexical knowledge to do so without isolating the linguistic machinery from everything else a person knows and does. The solution requires that lexical knowledge include both form and function for many entries — that a lexical entry be sufficiently rich to include both information about form that can be judged true or false and information about function that can be judged possible or impossible. Just as the formal description provides a locus of interaction between perceptual processes and lexical choice, so the functional description provides a locus of interaction between practical knowledge and lexical choice. There is nothing in this solution that requires a theorist to divide knowledge into the practical and lexical varieties, of course, and for some purposes, the division may be counterproductive. But when the division is advantageous, the knowledge problem cannot be used as an argument against adopting it.

In conclusion, a comment about potential implications of this general line of argument for the more general problem of linguistic comprehension is necessary. Consider once more the initial example, *The Smiths saw the Rocky Mountains while they were flying to California.* It is also necessary to bring practical knowledge to bear on the interpretation of this sentence. How would we introduce it? There does not seem to be a convenient lexical slot: It is implausible that *mountain* should include functional information of the kind discussed for *table*. Perhaps we should shift attention to the verb *fly*. Some linguists would say that *Mountains fly* violates the selectional restrictions of *fly*, and that is true enough. But why does it violate the selectional restrictions? Do we assume some special semantic category of flyable objects from which mountains are excluded? Or do we assume some inferential process that finds a contradiction between flying and being part of the earth's surface?

An inferential process seems more plausible than an ad hoc list of flyable objects. Indeed, there may be an inferential base for all selectional restrictions, although in more regular cases it is probably not necessary to repeat the inferential process; in some cases, the set of admissible subjects or objects of a verb seem to form a coherent class that can simply be remembered. But in other cases — and probably in most cases for young children — inferences based on practical knowledge and prevailing circumstances are the ultimate court of appeal.

But how should inferences about possibilities be introduced? In the case of *table*, we argued for a lexical locus, but that alternative seems unavailable for *Mountains fly*. It is necessary to assume that questions about both truth and possibility are raised in the course of thinking about sentences as well as in the course of identifying instances of categories. Possibility may be the only consideration for sentences that ask questions or request actions; truth may be the only consideration for sentences that assert logical relations. It would go far beyond the limits set for this chapter to develop the argument that practical knowledge is involved in understanding most sentences. Because the claim is hardly surprising even without development, however, it is sufficient for present purposes merely to point out that the analysis of lexical categories proposed here is but one aspect of the ubiquitous process of introducing practical knowledge into the comprehension of linguistic messages. The processes we have assumed for evaluating functions may even be related to the processes whereby practical knowledge is accumulated (see Appendix C).

APPENDIX A

The claim that the identification of instances of *table* depends, at least in part, on what you can do with tables should not be confused with a familiar behavioristic theory of meaning. For example, Osgood (1957) has proposed that "The essential characteristic of sign behavior is that the organism behaves towards the sign (be it linguistic or perceptual) in a way that is somehow 'appropriate to' something other than itself [p. 354]." In particular, "Whenever a neutral stimulus (sign-to-be) is paired with a significate and this pairing occurs sufficiently close in time to a reinforcing state of affairs, the neutral stimulus will acquire an increment of association with some distinctive portion of the total behavior elicited by the significate [p. 355]." This "distinctive portion of the total behavior elicited by the significate" is called a *representational mediation process,* which is taken to be the behavioristic term corresponding to "meaning" in mentalistic theories.

Rosch et al. (1976) have asked people to imagine and describe in detail the whole set of body and muscle movements that they make when they use or interact with certain objects. For example, when the superordinate term *furniture* was given as the stimulus, only one motor movement was common to all the responses; when "basic terms" like *table, lamp,* or *chair* were given, an average of 11.7 common movements were reported; when subordinate terms like *kitchen table, dining room table, floor lamp, desk lamp, kitchen chair,* or *living room chair* were given, the average was 12.3. In short, basic terms represent the most generic level in the hierarchy at which a significant number of common motor movements are elicited by all instances of the category. Basic terms are also the ones that children learn first.

At least for basic terms, therefore, people do seem to learn particular patterns of behavior that are characteristic of the category. There is no evidence, however, that a distinctive portion of this behavior can represent the whole pattern. Moreover, any assumption that what you tend to do with an instance of a given category is the meaning of that category implies that generic terms like *furniture* are either meaningless or hopelessly polysemous. (The one motor movement common to *furniture* was scanning it with the eyes, which could hardly serve as a distinctive representational mediation process for the category.) Miller and Johnson-Laird (1976) propose that the identification procedure associated with superordinate terms like *furniture* is a disjunction of the identification procedures for each of its hyponyms.

The theory that meaning is a behavioral response encounters other problems when applied to nouns like *cook.* There is probably no characteristic pattern of behavior toward cooks (other than scanning them with the eyes, perhaps), and therefore the theory must be defended in terms of the behavior one would evidence if one were performing the role that cooks normally perform. The meanings of generic role terms (e.g., *person*) are again unclear, and the theory seems to imply that someone who cannot perform the motor movements characteristic of a social role could not know what the term denoting that role meant. The point, however, is that such a theory must distinguish two types of meanings, because the movements characteristic of using an object must define one class of categories, and the movements characteristic of performing a role must define a different class of categories. Otherwise, the meanings of *pot* and *cook* might be difficult to distinguish.

Because this behavioristic approach leads to many puzzles, functional criteria for category membership are probably better formulated in cognitive terms. A person can know that any instance of a given category can serve or perform a particular function without knowing what behaviors, if any, are required. Because function is but one type of criterion for category membership, two objects performing or used for the same function need not be instances of the same category. Moreover, because function is not equated here to meaning, two terms denoting categories of objects performing or used for the same function need not be synonyms, and terms denoting objects having no function at all need not be meaningless. (For a discussion of the differences between procedures for identifying instances of a category and the meanings of terms denoting categories, see Miller and Johnson-Laird, 1976, sec. 4.4.)

Evaluation of the functions that a candidate instance can serve or perform must draw on practical knowledge, but, as this chapter argues, that practical knowledge need not be included as part of the lexical meaning of terms that refer to it; certainly, practical knowledge need not be represented solely in terms of implicit motor movements. The distinction between what a thing does and what can be done with it must be represented as part of lexical knowledge, but that distinction does not imply two different modes of functional evaluation.

APPENDIX B

The problem is to formulate an operator M such that $M(F)$ corresponds to what people mean when they say "F is possible." This will be done in terms of another operator, D, such that $D(F)$ means that the person can develop a plan for F.

Let us denote various circumstances that might obtain as $c_0, c_1, c_2, ..., c_j, ...$, where c_0 represents the circumstances that the person assumes to obtain. And let his system of practical knowledge be characterized by subsystems k_i, which describe facts that he has learned, including general rules and principles, and also procedures for carrying out various actions that he knows he or others are able to perform under appropriate circumstances — walking, reading, driving a car, and so on. To say that a person derives F is to say that when he searches through his practical knowledge, he finds a knowledge system k_i that can be applied to c_0 according to fixed rules to yield the statement or plan F. An enumeration of those fixed rules of derivation, of course, would be an information-processing theory of thinking. Although such theories have been explored (e.g., Newell & Simon, 1972), a complete account of human thinking in these terms is not presently available (even if it were, we could not summarize it here), but it would obviously include much more than the operations admitted in most systems of formal logic. Fortunately, our present needs are more modest and can be served by simply postulating a relation "$\rightarrow$" such that $k_i(c_0) \rightarrow F$ can be taken to mean that applying knowledge k_i to circumstances c_0 yields F.

Now we can define an operator D_0 as follows:

$$D_0(F): (Ek_i) \, [k_i(c_0) \rightarrow F]$$

This says that F is derived, relative to the circumstances c_0 that are assumed to obtain, if there is a system of knowledge k_i that can be applied to c_0 to yield F directly. It is obvious that D_0 must depend on what the person knows — a person with considerable experience should see more ways to derive F than would a novice. It is also obvious that D_0 is not a satisfactory definition of M, even though the two notions are related. One difficulty is that a person may say F is possible, even when it is not possible under the prevailing circumstances, if he can see some way to modify the circumstances in order to make F possible. A second difficulty arises from the fact that people tend to think something is possible, even when they cannot derive it, if they see no reason why it is impossible. Let us consider these difficulties in turn.

In order to accommodate the fact that a person can sometimes modify the circumstances in such a way as to make F possible, let us introduce F_j as follows:

$$F_j(c_0) = c_j$$

Then we can set up $D_0(F_j)$ as a subgoal. That is to say, we can define an operator D_j as follows:

$$D_j(F): (EF_j) \, [D_0(F_j)] \text{ and } (Ek_i) \, [k_i(c_j) \rightarrow F]$$

Of course, the derivation of F_j may also require modifications of c_0, in which case a further subgoal can be created. In this way, the person may develop a complex plan having several steps (Miller, Galanter, & Pribram, 1960). For our present purposes, however we can define D:

$$D(F): D_0(F) \text{ or } D_j(F)$$

$D(F)$ means that the person can derive F by applying what he knows either to the existing circumstances or to circumstances that he could cause to exist.

In order to include the fact that a person will also assume something is possible if he knows no reason why it is impossible, we must consider $\text{not}D(\text{not}F)$, which means that in his search for relevant knowledge, he does not succeed in finding knowledge needed to derive not$F$. The operator notD raises questions about the exhaustiveness of the search, but we need not assume that something is really not derivable just because a person has not derived it. For psychological purposes, if he has not derived something, the fact that he could have derived it with further thought is not important. We must leave room for the kinds of mistakes that we know people often make.

We can now define M in terms of D:

$M(F)$: $D(F)$ or notD(not$F$), but not both.

The exclusive "or" is required, because people do not normally say that something that is necessary is merely possible.[2] That is to say, if F is thought to be possible, then not$F$ is also thought to be possible. The definition of M respects this usage, because $M(F)$ and $M(not F)$ are equivalent:

$$
\begin{aligned}
M(F) &= [D(F) \text{ or } notD(notF)] \text{ and } not[D(F) \text{ and } notD(notF)] \\
&= not[notD(F) \text{ and } D(notF)] \text{ and } [notD(F) \text{ or } D(notF)] \\
&= [D(notF) \text{ or } notD(F)] \text{ and } not[D(notF) \text{ and } notD(F)] \\
&= M(notF)
\end{aligned}
$$

APPENDIX C

The present formulation of functional criteria in terms of modal psychological operators may have some relevance to the process of attribution, which has received considerable attention from social psychologists. For example, *John is aggressive* attributes aggressiveness to John. The basis for attribution theory is Heider's (1958) analysis of processes underlying such judgments, which has been developed further by subsequent workers (Jones & Davis, 1965; Kelley, 1973). One of Heider's assumptions is that the processes people use in perceiving other people are similar to those they use in perceiving physical objects. If we think of sentences like *That is a table* as attributing tableness to an object, therefore, the arguments developed here may be applicable to interpersonal categorizations as well.

Attribution theories assume that people like to explain what other people do by ascribing dispositions to them; those dispositions are thought of as causes for the observed or expected behavior. Although judgments of causality can be described in terms of judgments of the possibility of conjoined events (see Miller & Johnson-Laird, 1976, subsec. 6.3.5), a somewhat simpler account seems

---

[2]F is necessary, $N(F)$, would be defined as $D(F)$ and notD(not$F$), where both conjuncts must be true. If M is defined with inclusive "or," N implies M, which violates normal usage: It is odd to say that it is possible to obey the laws of gravity, for example. Then F is impossible would be defined as $N(notF)$.

sufficient for the present argument. In Appendix B, we proposed that the judgment that F is possible depends on finding a subsystem of knowledge k such that, when k is applied to the circumstances c, it yields F. However, if F is observed to occur under circumstances c, it is clearly possible, even though an observer might not know anything k that, applied to c, would yield F. If the observer is motivated to account for F, therefore, he might well add to his knowledge some information k — a dispositional statement, for example — such that $k(c) \rightarrow F$. If, for example, John has insulted you without apparent cause and this event is taken as F, then *John is aggressive* might be taken as k and added to your knowledge of John. Then k may be used in the future to yield predictions of other possible aggressive acts under appropriate circumstances. It is obvious that misattributions are possible and that the process can operate in accounting for one's own behavior as well as for the behavior of others.

In the categorization process, we assume that k is available and that F is to be derived; in the attribution process, we assume that F is given and that k is to be inferred and added to memory. This relation, if valid, adds nothing to attribution theory, of course, but it does suggest that a considerable body of psychological research may be relevant to the kind of cognitive processes involved in deciding whether some candidate instance can serve the function that all instances of a given category are expected to serve.

ACKNOWLEDGMENT

Preparation of this paper was supported in part by Grant No. GM21796 from the Public Health Services to The Rockefeller University.

REFERENCES

Heider, F. *The psychology of interpersonal relations.* New York: Wiley, 1958.

Jones, E. E., & Davis, K. E. From acts to dispositions: The attribution process in person perception. In L. Berkowitz (Ed.), *Advances in experimental social psychology.* New York: Academic Press, 1965.

Kelley, H. The process of causal attribution. *American Psychologist,* 1973, *28,* 107–128.

Miller, G. A., Galanter, E., & Pribram, K. *Plans and the structure of behavior.* New York: Holt, Rinehart & Winston, 1960.

Miller, G. A., Johnson-Laird, P. N. *Language and perception.* Cambridge: Harvard University Press, 1976.

Newell, A., & Simon, H. A. *Human problem solving.* Englewood Cliffs, N.J.: Prentice-Hall, 1972.

Osgood, C. E. Motivational dynamics of language behavior. In M. R. Jones (Ed.), *Nebraska symposium on motivation.* Lincoln: University of Nebraska Press, 1957.

Rosch, E., Mervis, C. B., Gray, W., Johnson, D., & Boyes-Braem, P. *Basic objects in natural categories.* Working Paper #40. Berkeley, California: Language Behavior Research Laboratory, University of California, 1976.

Author Index

Subject Index

A

American Sign Language (ASL), 5, 7, 35, 39, 49–70, 215
  compound lexical signs in, 7, 52, 55–64, 69, 70
  formational parameters in, 50, 53
  historical change in, 50
  iconicity in, 50–51, 53–54
  mimetic depiction in, 64, 67–68, 70
  simple lexical signs in, 7, 35, 52–54, 70
  temporal properties of, 56–57, 58, 63
Analog representational model
  (see Representational models, analog)
Analog
  (see Reasoning by analogy to stored instances)
Artificial categories, 37, 38, 39, 40, 76, 170–189, 200–206, 268
Artificial grammar experiments, 170–177
Aspects of a stimulus
  (see Stimulus aspects)
Association, 89
Attributes
  (see Stimulus attributes)
Attribution theory, 318–319

B

Basic-level categories, 6, 7, 27, 28, 30–35, 37, 49–50, 146
  in American Sign Language, 51–54
  and cognitive development, 35
  and concept learning, 191, 195
  in folk biological taxonomies
    (see Folk biological ranks, generic rank; Imagery) 34
  and language, 35, 315
  operational definitions of, 32–34
  and perception, 34–35
  relationship to perceived world structure, 30–31, 41–42

Basic-level categories *(contd)*
  role of context in, 42–43
  set-theoretic interpretation of, 30–31, 74
Basic plant categories, 14
Behaviorist theory of meaning, 315–316
Binary features, 278, 282–283, 290, 295
  (see also Distinctive features)
Blink transformations in imagery, 248–249
Blobs, 122
  (see also Simple wholes; Stimulus attributes)
Boundaries of categories, 36, 214, 308–309

C

Canonical forms, 123
Category development in children, 2, 13, 35, 38, 315
Category formation, 28–30, 36–37
Category learning, 2–3, 16, 35, 38, 40, 41, 46, 75–76, 99, 108–111, 130, 169–210, 213, 252, 253
Category resemblance
  (see Similarity relations)
Category structure
  (see Horizontal structure of categories; Vertical structure of categories)
Children's justifications of classifications, 160–162
Choice, 112–113
Class inclusion, 11, 30, 32
Clustering, 91–95, 96
Cognitive economy, 28–29, 35, 42, 193
Cognitive processing, 36, 38–41, 46, 75, 99, 105–108, 111–131, 164
  in children, 135–165
  (see also Category learning; Imagery; Judgments of similarity; Pattern recognition; Representation)
Cognitive psychology
  inference problem in, 217–220
  models vs. theories in, 275–277